What Is The Best Life?

AN INTRODUCTION TO ETHICS

Brad Art
Westfield State College

Wadsworth Publishing Company
Belmont, California
A Division of Wadsworth, Inc.

Philosophy Editor: Kenneth King

Editorial Assistant: Gay Meixel

Production: Merrill Peterson, Matrix Productions

Print Buyer: Karen Hunt

Permissions Editor: Jeanne Bosschart

Copy Editor: Victoria Nelson

Cover Design: Stuart Paterson/Image House

Cover: Detail *The Discovery of Honey by Bacchus*, Piero de Cosimo, Worchester
 Art Museum, Worchester, Massachusetts

Signing Representative: Maria Tarantino

Compositor: Graphic Composition

Printer: Arcata Graphics/Fairfield

 *This book is printed on
acid-free recycled paper.*

Printed in the United States of America
1 2 3 4 5 6 7 8 9 10—97 96 95 94 93

Library of Congress Cataloging-in-Publication Data

Art, Brad.
    What is the best life?: an introduction to ethics / Brad Art.
        p.   cm.
    Includes index.
    ISBN 0-534-17652-6
    1. Ethics.   I. Title.
BJ1012.A695   1993
    170—dc20
                                    92-2431
                                    CIP

All things excellent are as difficult as they are rare.
—Benedict de Spinoza

To my little excellences,
Katrina and David

Contents

Preface   xvii

Introduction   xxi

Learning   xxi

Patience   xxi

Criticism can be seductive   xxii

Dialogue   xxii

The Philosopher Resurrection Machine   xxiv

P A R T

ONE
Do We Need Morality?   1

Introduction   2

I can read minds   2

What to Expect   2

CHAPTER ONE ▪ **What Is The Point Of Morality?**   4

Idleness is immoral   4

What's the best life?   5

What's the point of morality?   6

The point of morality   7

Enter the Reader! Yes, You!   8

Society's limits vs. doing whatever you want   10

Morality, immorality, and being neither   11

Avoiding guilt 13

What if you knew you wouldn't get caught? 13

What do you really want out of life? 15

What does the moral life have to offer? 19

What is morality? 22

Do you have any objections? 25

Relativism 28

Summary of discussion 29

Discussion highlights 30

Questions for thought/paper topics 30

For further reading 31

CHAPTER TWO ▪ **What Is Morality? 32**

What are some examples of morality? 33

Moral rules are absolute 36

Examples of morality 37

What makes a principle a moral principle? 37

The Ten Commandments is a perfect example 40

The Golden Rule: do unto others 44

Which came first, good or God? 49

Conscience and intuition 51

Other examples of morality 54

Let's finish this chapter with egoism 54

So what have we learned? Formal features of morality 56

Summary of discussion 57

Discussion highlights 58

Questions for thought/paper topics 58

For further reading 59

CHAPTER THREE ▪ **What About Belief in God? 60**

God does exist 60

The majority believes in God   61

Belief in God has a long tradition   62

The universe had to have a beginning   63

The universe is ordered by God   64

Experience is colored by beliefs   66

Atheist or believer, it just doesn't matter   68

God answers the unanswerable questions   70

God gives meaning to life and to death   71

God allows suffering   71

How can we know that God answers prayers?   72

Why we want to believe   74

Put yourself in the right frame of mind   74

What is the value of religious ideas?   75

Mystical and ecstatic experiences   76

Invisible green goblins   77

What are these ideas in light of psychology?   78

Does God exist?   82

Religious assertions cannot be refuted by reason   82

How does this apply to our discussion of moral values?   84

What's left to believe?   84

Summary of discussion   85

Discussion highlights   85

Questions for thought/paper topics   86

For further reading   86

CHAPTER FOUR ▪ **Isn't Everyone Different?   88**

What's left to believe?   88

How can we choose our moral values?   89

Doing philosophy   89

Is there agreement on values?   90

How can we decide which value is true?   93

Agreement is not truth   96

Types of truth   96

Does morality work?   101

Human nature   102

What difference does it make?   102

The abilities to think and to feel   103

Humans communicate through speech   105

Humans distinguish right and wrong   106

Family resemblance   106

Genetics and being human   107

The moral sense of "human"   108

Greed   108

Cynicism   110

Creative and inventive   111

Religion   111

Humans have free will   112

Compassion   112

Relating to other people   112

Summary of discussion   113

Discussion highlights   114

Questions for thought/paper topics   114

For further reading   115

CHAPTER FIVE ▪ **What If I Do Whatever I Want?**   116

Life is meaningless   117

The Stranger   119

What makes living for the moment desirable?   124

What makes living for the pleasure of the moment undesirable?   125

Kierkegaard's A   130

Priorities   134

Absolutes   134

Affirming your own reality 135

The best life 135

Summary of discussion 136

Discussion highlights 136

Questions for thought/paper topics 137

For further reading 138

■
_____

P A R T
TWO
Philosophers Answer the Questions 139

Introduction 140
The V-8 Principle! 140

A Roadmap 141

CHAPTER SIX ■ ## Authority and Freedom: A Discussion With The Grand Inquisitor 143

Morality makes us free 143

The Grand Inquisitor 143

People want to be free 144

Three temptations in the desert 145

So I am free? 146

Conscience 148

Miracles 148

We care for the weak, too! 149

Universal unity 149

You can't handle intense experiences 150

A person in sheep's clothing 152

The possibility of freedom 153

The Inquisitor has misled us!   153

Blind obedience hinders growth   154

What's the harm?   155

The desire for universal unity   156

Do whatever you want   158

Summary of discussion   160

Discussion highlights   160

Questions for thought/paper topics   161

For further reading   161

CHAPTER SEVEN ▪ **Freedom and Self-Control: A Discussion With Epictetus   163**

What is your theory of the best life?   164

Passive acceptance   164

Striving and goals   165

Within and beyond our power   165

The detached perspective   172

Freedom is not doing what one wants   172

Wanting what we want   174

Control is freedom   174

What freedom is   175

Freedom from externals   176

Virtue, not morality   176

Conflicting desires   177

Four unfreedoms resolved   178

Choices   180

Summary of discussion   181

Discussion highlights   181

Questions for thought/paper topics   182

For further reading   183

CHAPTER EIGHT ▪ **The Greatest Good For The Greatest Number: The Philosophy of John Stuart Mill   184**

A lifeboat example   184

Should we always tell the truth?   185

Utilitarianism   186

The purpose of the theory   186

The point of a moral theory   188

What do all people want?   189

The Greatest Happiness Principle   190

Utilitarian morality is vague   199

Knowledge of the future   199

Contributing causes   200

Three types of consequences   201

Integrity   202

Justice   202

Rule utilitarianism   203

Vessels of experience   203

Summary of discussion   204

Discussion highlights   205

Questions for thought/paper topics   206

For further reading   206

CHAPTER NINE ▪ **Absolute Moral Values and Reason: A Conversation With Immanuel Kant   207**

What should you do?   207

Another example   208

The aim of Kant's theory   209

Act from a sense of duty   210

Why start with the good will?   210

The motive of duty   214

Actions with moral worth   215

Is Mr. Spock the ideal moral person?   215

Love cannot be a moral motivation   216

Principles, maxims and laws   218

Cultivating one's talents   222

Coming to the aid of others   223

The veil of ignorance   224

Objection: isn't this an appeal to results?   225

Primary goods   225

Making exceptions   226

Reason and autonomy   227

The formula of the end in itself   227

How do we conceive our existence?   228

One final criticism   229

Summary of discussion   230

Discussion highlights   231

Questions for thought/paper topics   231

For further reading   232

CHAPTER TEN ▪ **Existentialist Ethics: Jean-Paul Sartre's Ideas On Being Free   233**

Two insights   233

Existence precedes essence: there is no human nature   234

How do we create our own obstacles?   235

Should I do whatever I want?   236

How do I choose?   236

So what gives existentialism a bad name?   237

Choice and responsibility   237

In choosing myself, I choose man   242

Forlornness   244

Condemned to be free   246

Morality is clouded   246

Despair   247

There is no reality except in action   248

Total involvement   249

Loneliness   249

How do you know other people exist?   250

The limits of the human condition   250

Existentialism does not advocate caprice   251

Are we able to pass judgments on others?   252

Freedom is the basis of all values   252

But which way does freedom tell me to act?   253

Summary of discussion   253

Discussion highlights   254

Questions for thought/paper topics   255

For further reading   255

■

P A R T
THREE
Does Morality Answer The Questions?   257

Introduction   258

Where are we going?   258

Moral objectivity and impartiality   258

Can we have the best of each life?   258

Hold to the truths   259

What's the value of moral values?   259

Is life meaningful or absurd?   259

How can we relate with other people?   260

What is the best life?   260

CHAPTER ELEVEN ▪ Is Life Meaningful or Absurd? The Wisdom of Solomon and Sisyphus 261

How the questions arise 261

Two general strategies 261

Solomon's lament 262

Sisyphus' immortality 268

Divorced from life 272

Summary of discussion 275

Discussion highlights 275

Questions for thought/paper topics 275

For further reading 276

CHAPTER TWELVE ▪ How Can We Relate with Other People? A Talk With Martin Buber 277

I-Thou, I-It 277

Experiences and relating 279

The power of exclusiveness 280

How the primary words evolve 280

The Thou relationship 284

Every Thou must become an It 286

Separation and connection with reality 286

You believe in paradise? 287

Why enter the Thou attitude? 287

Summary of discussion 289

Discussion highlights 289

Questions for thought/paper topics 290

For further reading 290

CHAPTER THIRTEEN ▪ **What Is The Best Life? The Virtuous Sage of Spinoza and Lao Tsu** 291

Translating the basic questions in living   291

Why morality doesn't work   293

The self and others   294

Meaningfulness   294

Relating to reality   295

The real question   295

The virtuous sage: the life of excellence   295

Virtues and freedom   299

Freedom and virtue   301

The virtues   301

Summary of discussion   302

Discussion highlights   303

Questions for thought/paper topics   303

For further reading   304

Index   305

Preface

What is the best life? How can I live it? These two questions are fundamental in each person's life. How we answer them defines who we are. Of course, there are spells when we ignore them. "Real" life has a way of distracting us from our philosophical wonderings. But when we return to these questions, we recognize that all other concerns pale in comparison. No matter how successful, or popular, or accepted, or wealthy one may become, the questions of the best life are more important. We all want to know how to live, and to live well. *What Is the Best Life?* explores a variety of philosophical theories that reply to these fundamental questions.

OBJECTIVES

What Is the Best Life? has three main objectives. It teaches students (1) how and why the questions and answers of philosophers matter to them, (2) how to read original philosophical texts critically and sympathetically, and (3) how to think carefully about living well.

AN ACCESSIBLE WRITING STYLE

One problem in teaching ethics is engaging students in thinking critically about morality and the best life. *What Is the Best Life?* brings the issues to students in their own terms, and in a context they understand. Although each chapter introduces sophisticated concepts, the presentation is free of technical philosophical jargon. For example, Kierkegaard's aesthete, A, embraces metaphysical and epistemic assumptions radically different from those our students and other moralists make. Yet his definitions of the self, other people, and freedom that lead him to despair are discussed without language that might intimidate or confuse the student.

Another problem is that students often have difficulty reading and understanding sustained arguments. Philosophers write to present ideas for consideration, and to remedy philosophical problems. However, philosophical writings are difficult to understand. They can overwhelm students. This is especially true when an argument is developed in a book-length work and written by a philosopher in philosophical language. For example, Kant's *Groundwork of the Metaphysics of Morals* is an important work in ethics, and should be examined in ethics courses, but it is difficult for the novice to understand. To remedy this problem, the book recreates philosophers. Without sacrificing rigor, the student discusses the position presented with the actual "living" philosopher. Led by Art's comments and questions, readers learn to critically evaluate the philosopher's own words and arguments, but in manageable "bites." To bring the point "home" to the student, the philosophers' points are interpreted and evaluated as they are discussed, and then summarized at the end of each chapter. By introducing questions and concepts in approachable language and manageable segments, *What Is the Best Life?* makes the works of philosophers understandable and compelling. The book equips students to read and appreciate original works in philosophy and related disciplines.

It encourages students to do philosophy, and not merely to learn about it. For example, Dostoevski's Grand Inquisitor directly challenges students' belief in their freedom to select their careers, friends and interests. It requires a good deal of thinking to counter the Inquisitor's claim that people are merely frightened sheep.

The book also encourages students to make intellectual leaps on their own. As the questions are refined and more precisely expressed, the discussion urges students to connect ideas and to synthesize positions. Epictetus's reply to the Stranger's caprice is that freedom is self mastery. Kant's reliance on reason to guarantee autonomy also responds to the hedonist's passionate abandon. Students are encouraged to make these connections, and to see the synthesis of Epictetus and Kant proposed by Sartre.

ORGANIZATION

The material has been organized to allow flexibility in the classroom. It is organized around the central questions in the first two chapters, What is morality? and What is the point of living the moral life? The instructor should feel free to "skip" around after Chapter 2. The chapters within Part II are written without reference to earlier discussions within that part. Each chapter can stand alone. The present order of readings has served me well, but I encourage you to experiment with thematic or historical organization.

COVERAGE

What Is the Best Life? is more than an analysis of traditional moral philosophy. While it incorporates a discussion of Kant and Mill, the book challenges morality as merely one way of living. It compares morality and other visions of living. The discussion of four varieties of freedoms in the chapter on Epictetus is an example of this continual comparison.

The book offers not only Plato's ring of Gyges, but also Kierkegaard's and Camus's aesthetes as a challenge to the moral life. It entertains authoritarian morality in the person of Dostoevski's Grand Inquisitor. It rebuffs mindless obedience in the dialogues with Epictetus and Sartre.

The discussions of the aesthete, hedonist, and moralist lead to the questions in Part III. What is the point of living? Are there better ways of relating to other people than those offered by the moral life? The final chapters discuss the interconnection of morality, psychology, and metaphysical and epistemic commitments in formulating the best life. Spinoza and Lao Tsu outline the conclusions of our book-long journey.

What Is the Best Life? encourages students to cull the most desirable features of each vision of living. It leads them to create their own answer to the question of the best life. Its range covers Western religion in the examples of the Ten Commandments, the Golden Rule and Ecclesiastes; utilitarianism as formulated by Mill; deontology through Kant; and existentialism in Sartre, Kierkegaard, and Camus. It also ranges over the Eastern tradition represented by Lao Tsu. Finally, the tentative conclusions of earlier discussions lead to Buber's philosophical anthropology. All of this culminates in a synthesis of perspectives—the theory of the virtuous life presented by Spinoza and Lao Tsu.

DIALOGUE STYLE

The dialogue style of *What is the Best Life?* engages the reader in the discussion of the questions of moral philosophy. Dialogue gets students involved enough to learn what they value, why they hold their values, and whether or not their values are reasonable. Students learn from themselves. The book also places student concerns and the theories of philosophers into a common context and language. The discussion of suicide and the meaning of living are just as important to our students as they were to Solomon and Sisyphus. So students learn from the philosophers, too.

The dialogue format encourages us to enter into the human discussion about morality and the best life. We become active participants when we realize that the other participants, great philosophers all, are also tentatively going through the questions. Dialogue allows the "resurrected" philosopher to reply to students' objections. Mill's utilitarianism, for example, is not so easily misunderstood or dismissed when he participates in the discussion. Students learn that legitimate criticism can be demanding, rewarding and constructive.

Finally, dialogue allows a place for humor in learning philosophy. The book's relaxed, sometimes irreverent, approach to the questions prevents it from taking itself too seriously. *What Is the Best Life?* is fun to read.

ACKNOWLEDGMENTS

My students continually contribute to my learning. I want to thank each one of them, past, present, and future. Most of the ideas that appear in this book are theirs. I want to thank the reviewers: Hilquias B. Cavalcanti, Nashville State Technical Institute; Robin S. Dillon, Lehigh University; Kevin Galvin, East Los Angeles College; James W. Gustafson, Northern Essex Community

College; John Kultgen, University of Missouri–Columbia; J. E. Magruder, Stephen F. Austin State University; Levonne Nelson, Fullerton College; Robert Nielsen, D'Youville College; Robert Sessions, Kirkwood Community College; and Eugene C. Sorenson, Rochester Community College. Their comments and encouragement came at just the right times. Thanks, too, to Adam Art for his suggestions on improving earlier drafts. I want to recognize another set of people I have never met, the people whose names appear on the copyright page. The expert staff who helped produce this book was a pleasure to work with. In particular I want to thank Hal Humphrey, Merrill Peterson, Peggy Meehan, Jeanne Bosschart, and Dawn Burnam. Thanks too, to Gerry Tetrault for being a good friend and colleague. A special thanks to Ken King, the "ogre" editor, for forcing me to write this book. I wish I could write as well as he thinks I write.

I don't believe anyone can be a good teacher without being a good person. Carl Hedman is the best teacher I ever met. I want to thank Andreas Eshete for everything he is. And thanks, Fred, for everything.

Finally, thank you, Gloria, for forcing me to be me, no matter how difficult that is sometimes. Thank you for staying and intertwining with me, and for making my life wonder-filled.

Introduction

I know you don't want to read a long introduction. I don't blame you. Introductions are usually worthless. But before you turn the page, let me tell you a couple of things you need to know.

LEARNING

We are going to explore your basic beliefs and values. I hope that we will be able to discover *what* you believe, *what* values you hold, *why* you believe and hold them, and whether or not your beliefs and values are *reasonable* to believe.

Learning is an activity. Learning is not simply believing what you want to believe, nor is it uncritically accepting your beliefs. It means being able to state your beliefs and values and to make a reasonable case for them. It means subjecting your thought to critical and careful analysis. Participate! Subject your beliefs and values to critical appraisal. By the end of our discussions, I hope you'll know what you are thinking and why you are thinking it. And that's just the point of learning.

PATIENCE

To succeed in finding the best life, it's important that you believe that I am from Jupiter. Why? If you imagine that I have recently come to earth from the far side of Jupiter, you won't assume that we agree on beliefs and values. Assume that I have the ability to reason just like you do. But on Jupiter, at least on the far side, we don't have morality and religion. I don't understand these ways of living. Imagine that I am a kind of Jupiterian scientist. I have come here to study you. So bear with me in our discussion. If I ask questions that seem to you to have obvious answers, please be patient. Patience is a virtue.

And don't be offended by my comments. I am not accustomed to the earth beliefs appropriate to these topics. Besides, philosophy asks questions about our most basic beliefs. Most of what we believe is so obvious to us that we never even consciously think about it. Philosophy asks questions, almost like a small child asks questions. You know when a kid asks why? Then you answer, and the kid asks why to that, too. The questioning goes on until you feel like—well you get the idea. Philosophy asks about three "whys" beyond where most children stop. So be patient. How else are we going to learn?

Of course, you have a right to your own view. But having a right to your belief is not the same as being right. Our quest is to find the best life, not to assert rights. I'll respect your ideas. (Okay, I'll tolerate them.) Together, we're going to question a whole range of beliefs and values. Just keep in mind that questions are not always attacks. Questions and disagreements can aid learning.

CRITICISM CAN BE SEDUCTIVE

Criticism can be seductive. I knew that would catch your attention. It's true, too. Criticism is an exciting, often seductive, and powerful activity. It's tempting to believe that you have the truth. It makes criticizing other people's beliefs safe. Safe, but boring. You aren't going to learn much that way. What is really exciting is to analyze your own values and beliefs critically.

Don't panic if your values are challenged or even changed in the course of our conversation. It's always acceptable to return to your earlier values. And just think, in the process you may learn why you hold the values you hold.

DIALOGUE

All worthwhile learning happens *between*—between you and another person, between you and another object or idea, between you and you. First, you and I will discuss morality and religion. After several chapters, the dialogue will switch parties. This book is a dialogue between you and each philosopher we encounter.

THE PHILOSOPHER RESURRECTION MACHINE

That's right, you and I will actually get to talk to long-dead, certified big shot, important philosophers. I have invented a device that allows me to resurrect these great thinkers. We'll get to ask them any questions we want. I could put this on television (PBS, no doubt) and make a fortune. But I'm reserving the experience for you. So sit back and enjoy reading the book. I'll see you in just a few pages.

ONE
Do We Need Morality?

Introduction

I CAN READ MINDS

I can read minds. Yes, it's true. I am a mind reader. No, really, it's true. Actually, I can't do it all the time, though I am getting better at mind reading. So far I have been able to read my own mind with some accuracy. Let me see if I can read your mind. You have serious doubts about my truthfulness. No, no, about my sanity. See, I read your mind.

As we look at morality, think. I'll read your mind and reply to your ideas. Get involved in our discussion. As I ask my questions, think of your reply. Because of my astonishing mind-reading ability, you are actually able to participate in the writing of this part of the book. It's true! Every page in this part is blank until you turn to it. Then, as you open to the page, your ideas appear as if by magic. If you don't believe any of this, just play along. I hope the discussions reflect your interests and concerns. We all want to know what the best life is.

WHAT TO EXPECT

We're going to cover a lot in our initial discussions. We're going to ask: What is morality? and: What is the point of living a moral life? We're also going to talk about your belief in God. Since so many people get their moral values from religion, it's important to discuss religion and God.

If that isn't enough to keep us busy, we are also going to challenge morality. Many people think that moral values are different for different people, or different societies. We're all tempted to believe that now and then. Of course, if moral values are different for different people, then we can't morally judge anyone else. At least, we can't judge anyone in a morally meaningful way.

One way to get into this problem of different values is to examine what counts as truth. We'll look at ways of understanding moral truth. Another way to resolve this problem is to find out what human nature is. If we can say what makes us uniquely human, we might be able to show that people are not as different as some people believe. If we are all basically the same, then the best life will be basically the same for all of us.

Yes, I know what you're thinking: "But everyone is different. What makes one person happy doesn't make another person happy. We're all different." (How's that for mind reading?) You may be right; I don't know. That is just the sort of idea we're going to look into.

Besides moral values, God, and human nature, we're going to ask questions about society, and freedom, and pleasure. Finally, we're going to see whether the best life is doing whatever you want. That's my choice, but then, I'm a mind reader from Jupiter.

ONE

What Is the Point of Morality?

IDLENESS IS IMMORAL

Recently I was lying outside. Sun shining in the cloudless blue sky, gentle breeze blowing. . . . you get the picture. I was doing nothing. Two acquaintances came up and interrupted me.

Smith and Jones asked if they could talk to me. Their names aren't really Smith and Jones. I'm just using these names to protect them from being recognized. Smith is the boring one. Jones is the serious one. Sometimes it's impossible to tell them apart.

"What are you doing?" asked Smith.

"Nothing," I replied.

"Just soaking up some rays, huh? Trying to get a head start on your tan?"

I shook my head. "Just nothing."

"Well, that's not possible," interrupted Jones. "You must be doing something. You are either resting, or relaxing, or thinking, or daydreaming, or some other activity. You can't be doing nothing." Jones is such a pain, but I knew if I said that, he might be offended.

"Jones, you're such a pain. Go away."

"No, really, what are you doing? Doing nothing is immoral."

"Immoral, huh? Well actually, I was just thinking 'deep' and 'significant' thoughts," I said. Actually, I *was* doing nothing, and if I may say so, I was doing nothing very well. There are times when I am able to do nothing near perfectly.

"Ah, just as I thought," interjected Smith, sounding just like Jones. "No one ever does 'nothing.' Every human action has a goal. All people have goals. For example, everyone wants happiness! That's just the way we are. It's our human nature. It's what makes you a human being. Being idle is boring and meaningless. Don't you agree?"

"No."

"Well, we don't have to talk about human nature or happiness right now. It's up to you."

"I don't want to talk about human nature, happiness, or anything else." And I didn't, either. I would rather lie here happily than talk about being happy. "Can't you see that I was doing nothing? And I was doing it quite well. Far from being meaningless, idleness is the opposite of boredom and work. So why are you two bothering me?"

"You're an interesting person," replied Smith, obviously attempting to manipulate me to their way of thinking. Who knows, perhaps they were trying to "save" me from myself.

I don't mind when people manipulate me. Going one way is no different than going another way, as long as it's the way I want to go anyway. But now they had broken my nearly unbreakable concentration . . . hmm . . . how can I get rid of them?

"What do you two want? Tell me what you want, and then go away," I said.

WHAT'S THE BEST LIFE?

Jones asked, "What do you think is the best life?"

"What do you mean?" I responded decisively.

"What is the best life? What else could it mean? What do you want out of life?"

Pleasure: Wine, (Wo)men, and Song.   "For me the best life involves pleasure. Wine, women, and song! That's what I think is the best life," I answered smartly, hoping they'd go away now. I wanted to go back to doing nothing.

"Which one?" Jones asked, obviously setting some kind of trap for me. He's clever. Most likely he was out to confuse, and finally to judge, me.

Throwing the question back at them, I said, "What do you mean, which one? Do I have to choose among wine, women, and song?"

"That's not what I'm asking. Which woman?"

He's a devious one, and so moral! He's trying to guide the discussion to morality. He knows I've been steadily seeing one woman ever since she and I were married. It ran through my mind that I could answer, "What do you mean?" but on first try that didn't work very well.

"What do you mean?" I answered. I've always found that a good defense is to ask a question. The problem is that I'm not good at making up questions.

"If the best life involves a woman, it must be your wife you are referring to," said Jones. "So it's just as I thought, you do endorse the sanctity of marriage."

"Actually, I was not referring to my wife. When you asked me what I thought was the best life, I had pleasure in mind." (Not that my wife isn't a . . . well, never mind.)

"So you believe that pleasure is the best life?"

"Absolutely! What else could it be? Some is good, more is better."

The Moral Life.   "Some of us think that the moral and religious life constitutes the best life," said Smith with a look of assurance and certainty. Doesn't that look drive you crazy?

"Okay, I'll bite. Why should I give up pleasure to live morally? What is the point of the moral life?"

"Some people think that living for the pleasure of the moment makes the best life. Those of us who know better, however, know that the life of adherence to moral and religious law is far better than pleasure seeking."

Pretty smug, but then I've come to expect that from people who have answers. But how can she be so sure?

"That is not what I'm asking, Smith," I said. "What is the point of morality? What do I get out of being moral?"

"I could tell you that, but one cannot express such a complex theoretical justification in one brief statement."

"Huh?" I said with genuine sincerity.

"You cannot expect me to express all the subtleties of the moral life in one brief statement," she answered. Oddly enough, I don't think she was being evasive.

WHAT'S THE POINT OF MORALITY?

"I don't want to know *all* about morality. When I ask, 'What is the point of morality?' I'm not asking for a long-winded lecture. I think that living for pleasure is all that life offers. Life has no other point. If you don't agree, tell me why. And don't take forever. Long answers bore me. What is the point of morality?"

"All right. You probably won't understand this," she said looking aside to Jones for approval. (Have you ever noticed how impossible it is to distinguish moral people? Smith and Jones and all other moral people are so boringly alike.)

"Are you listening to me, Art?"

"What did you say?"

"Morality gives us a standard to live by. Without morality there would be chaos. People would do whatever they wanted! We'd have anarchy! If it weren't for morality and religion, the world would be a dangerous place to live. People would hurt each other. Without some moral code, and the law, we would have anarchy! People would kill each other. They would steal." (I don't know whether or not Smith and Jones are correct, but they sure are certain!)

"Is that all?" I just love to make fun of serious, good people.

"Is that all?" she said, outraged (and inraged as well, I suspect). "No, actually, that is not all that morality and religion do for us," she said, regaining her composure.

"You know, Smith, when you're passionate you're very engaging," I said in my best Bogie impersonation.

"That's sexist and trite," said Jones, feeling threatened.

"It can't be both. Sexism is not trite, and I wasn't making a sexual comment.

She's very engaging and very alive only when she is angry. The same applies to you. Your jealousy and anger make you more alive. That's as close as you moral people get to being alive. Passion is what life is all about!"

"Morality also gives us security and acceptance. You would become an outcast," added Jones, evidently missing the point.

"It's just wrong to kill." Smith provided the proper input statement. "It's just wrong to harm other people. One should 'do unto others. . . .' Following the moral and religious truths is what gives us human dignity. It's what makes our lives meaningful and worthy."

"If you kill someone, you will be punished!" added Jones with real concern and genuine alarm.

Whoa! "Whoa!" (In philosophy that's a technical term meaning "whoa!") "Slow down, you two. I'm not interested in killing anyone right now. Let me give you an example. I just stole this 39-cent pen," I said, taking a cheap yellow pen out of the pocket of my jeans. I steal only the fine-points. "Why is that such a big deal? If all we're worried about is getting caught, then we can stop worrying. Did you know that only one-half of 1 percent of the crimes committed in this country cause their perpetrators to see even a day of jail time? (I made that up, but it turns out it's true.) So why not try to get away with it?"

"Who do you think you are? Trying to get away with more than you deserve! Other people work hard for their pens!" said Jones angrily.

"It's the principle involved," said Smith. "You can't go around stealing just because you want to steal."

THE POINT OF MORALITY

Here they go in stereo. "Okay, okay. I can see you're serious about morality and religion. Let's look more closely at each of your reasons. To be honest (and I rarely am), I don't understand morality." I think I am quite generous. I could have shown them the other 39-cent pen I stole, but I refrained.

When I asked, "What *is* the point of morality?" Jones and Smith had a lot to say. Let's list their claims. First, we need morality because we need a standard to live by. Second, we need morality so that society will not crumble. Morality helps us avoid social chaos and anarchy. Morality also gives people security and acceptance within their society. That's a third point. Let me see. Fourth, morality gives people human dignity. It makes their lives meaningful and worthy.

Smith also claimed that it is just wrong to kill people. I'm not sure what she had in mind there. She probably meant that it's just wrong to kill. Hmm, what else could she mean? Oh, yes, she may mean that if you kill someone, you will be caught and punished. So part of the point of morality is to help us avoid punishment. Is that all there is to morality?

ENTER THE READER! YES, YOU!

"Art, we are supposed to be moral so that our society remains stable. Morality guarantees that chaos and anarchy do not ruin our lives."

Who thought that? Oh, who let *you* into the conversation?

"I bought this book and I have a right to think whatever I want!"

All right, since you bought the book, you're in. From now on, I'll put your ideas in quotes, okay? By the way, be careful, I can read minds.

"Sure."

I heard that thought. You don't sound convinced. Why is this format so strange to you? Every author writes to a reader. I just don't want to talk at you without giving you your chance to reply. Besides, I like you because you bought this book. Now, as I was asking, what do you—yes, you, my reader— get out of morality?

Promises, Responsibilities, Duties, and Other Four-Letter Words. "Art, I've just told you. Morality and religion keep society from becoming chaotic."

Have you looked around?

"Yes, society is pretty crazy, but it would be much worse if morality and religion didn't exist."

Is this what motivates a person to live morally? Social stability? Why bother with it? What makes morality so important?

"Morality derives its authority from the past. That's where its strength and importance come from. That is what promises, obligations, duties, responsibilities, and contracts are all about. They tie down the future. They make the future more predictable."

That's why moral people get involved in promises, obligations, duties, responsibilities, and the acceptance of the rights of others?

"That's the primary reason, yes."

How can responsibilities and rights and duties and obligations and promises *not* be burdens? Who would ever knowingly accept these burdens? What's in it for me?

"Well, those qualities seem like burdens to someone like *you*, but they are needed. Respecting the rights of others is easy because people are people just like us. We all belong to the same society. Respecting others is just the right way to live. Do unto others! If you don't want someone to harm you, then don't hurt anyone else."

Respecting others? An interesting idea.

"Come off it, Art. In your conversation with Smith and Jones, you admitted that you are married. You even wear a wedding ring."

So? (I wonder how you know that.)

"So! You made a sacred vow to your wife. You promised her that you would remain faithful. That you would continue to love her till death do you part. You make promises, don't deny it."

I don't know about sacred vows. That sounds pretty serious. All I "promised" my wife is that I will stay with her until something better comes along.

No one has a right to make lifelong promises. You want a person to come with a lifetime warranty. That doesn't allow for change.

"Sure. And what if your wife feels the same way? You can't be serious!"

I'm not being serious, but I am telling you how it is. What kind of person would I be if I wished an inferior life on someone I love?

"What do you mean?"

If someone better comes along, and if I love my wife, wouldn't I want her to live the better life?

"Now you're just being evasive. You believe that no one better will come along for your wife. That's why you're saying all this."

Well, as a matter of fact, my wife and I do match up well. Sometimes we match perfectly. But what's the alternative? Should my wife and I stay together because some legal document says we should stay together?

"Yes."

A license that we bought where people buy hunting and fishing licenses! You place a value in that?

Love and Duty. "But you admit you love your wife."

I admit it readily, if you call that an admission.

"Then you stay with your wife because you love her. That was just my point. You made a promise."

Not at all. I love my wife, and that's that. But love is a very different reason to stay with someone than a contract. Loveless people sign and respect contracts. Corporations enter contracts. Maybe if more people loved and fewer people married, the world would be a happier place. There would sure be fewer hurt feelings.

"That's outrageous! What about your children?"

What about them?

"You have a responsibility to your children. You brought them into this world, so they are yours; they are your responsibility."

Can I kill them?

"What are you talking about?"

If they're mine, I should be able to do whatever I want with them.

"No, look, this is crazy. All I mean is that you have a promise, an obligation, to care for them. That's what a responsible parent does."

I'd just as soon not use that kind of language.

"What kind of language?"

Responsibilities, promises, obligations, duties, rights, those words. They bother me.

"But you must feel some responsibility toward your children. When your youngest one cries, don't you pick him up?"

Sure. I pick him up, at least most of the time. Sometimes he's crying to get his own way. Generally, he hates naps. But if you're asking me, do I pick him up because I feel a responsibility, then the answer is "no!"

"I don't understand. You admit you pick him up."

Sure.

"I'm not quite understanding you. I don't see the difference. You and I both pick up the baby. So how are our approaches different?"

The difference is in our motives. You pick up the crying baby because you are obeying a moral rule. I pick up the crying baby because if I don't pick him up, I'll be bothered. I'll get no peace of mind if I let him cry on needlessly.

"You're bothered by your conscience. That's what you're really saying."

No way. I pick up the little guy because I love him. It hurts me to hear him cry. I don't pick him up because of a sense of responsibility, or because of guilt! Every little kid in the world can tell the difference. Kids are neat that way. They know sincerity when they feel it. So take your sense of responsibility; keep it. What bothers me is not doing whatever I want. I want to pick up the crying baby. If I don't pick him up—

"Call it what you will, but it's guilt. I've caught you on this one."

Maybe I can make the difference clearer this way. You obey moral rules. I know what I want to do. It's the difference between obedience and feelings. We'll have to talk about this later.

"Why don't we return to our question about the point of morality?"

Where did we go astray?

"We were discussing promises, duties, responsibilities, that kind of thing. It all boils down to the idea that 'one should do unto others.' If you don't want someone to harm you, then don't hurt anyone else."

My, you have a menacing way of thinking. But I am not disagreeing with you. I just don't understand. Maybe I don't know what morality is.

"Now you've shown yourself, Art. Of course you don't know what morality is. If you knew, you wouldn't be asking these questions." ("Is it too late to return this book?" you are thinking.)

Beyond protection from chaos and anarchy, what else is morality good for?

SOCIETY'S LIMITS VS. DOING WHATEVER YOU WANT

"Smith and Jones were right. Morality controls us. Without morality, people would do whatever they wanted."

Excuse me, but what's wrong with that?

"What's wrong with that? If people did whatever they wanted, they would kill and steal and do other hurtful things. The world is a dangerous place even with morality. Without morality (and religion), the world would be unimaginable!"

There we finally agree. Without morality and religion, the world would be unimaginably free and happy. What's wrong with people doing whatever they want? That's freedom, isn't it?

"Oh, you're a word twister! We certainly do not agree. I meant that the world would be unimaginably worse than it is now. Dangerous beyond belief."

Or so you imagine.

"Stop being flippant. This is a serious issue."

What about freedom? What's so wrong with letting people do whatever they want?

"Freedom is fine as long as we don't abuse it."

You mean I can do whatever I want, just as long as society approves? I can do whatever I want, within limits?

"That's not the way I'd put it, but yes. There must be restraints. People cannot be allowed to do whatever they want, at least not without limits."

And society sets the limits of what I can do?

"Exactly."

If I follow society's rules—or limits, as you call them—I'll be okay? I'll be allowed to remain within the society, within the flock?

"Yes. Though your allusion to people as a flock is not accurate."

Sorry, isn't that what your priests, ministers, and rabbis call you, their flock? Isn't that a dominant idea of the Judeo-Christian religions? So morality and religion want people to be sheep? Baa! baa!

"That's not it at all! People need to be restrained. The evidence is all around you. You can't walk down any city street at night without worrying you will be robbed, or worse."

Agreed. Why blame all the problems on a lack of morality?

"Because only immoral people would mug and rape and kill, that's why!"

MORALITY, IMMORALITY, AND BEING NEITHER

Oh, now I see the source of our confusion, at least of my confusion. I see morality and immorality as basically the same.

"Nothing could be further from the truth. How could you even say such a thing!"

Moral and immoral people recognize the same rules and laws, don't they? It's just that moral people basically stay within the rules. Immoral people break the rules. Either way, the rules are acknowledged.

"That's stupid. That's all the difference in the world."

Not quite. Let me give you an analogy. A couple of years ago, I was talking with several people about religion. They were going after each other on the most trivial points. Had the messiah come? What was the true sabbath day, the last day of the week, Saturday, or the first day, Sunday? I listened for quite a while, about forty-five minutes.

"What's your point?"

Then I asked why they believed there was a God. The people who were just at each other's throats turned on me. Suddenly they were united.

"What does this have to do with moral and immoral people?"

Only that the religious people were speaking the same language. Moral and immoral people are also speaking the same language. Each side understands what counts as morally significant. Each recognizes that morality demands obedience.

"What alternative could there be to morality and immorality?"

I'm not sure what we should call it, but nonmorality sounds catchy. Non-moral people, like me, do not know what morality or immorality are about. We just do what we want.

"Whatever you call it, you are encouraging people to break the moral and legal laws. That's terrible."

Not at all. I am not advocating or encouraging anything. I'm just saying that I should do what I want; I should do what is pleasurable.

"That's all?"

That's all. Why are you so surprised? That's all I've been saying right along.

"No, that is not all. And I am not surprised; I'm disgusted. Being immoral is wrong. You may not call your actions immoral, but if they are not moral, they are immoral."

Why do you say that? Look, if I do whatever I want, I am not deliberately or knowingly following or breaking any rules or laws. I am just doing what I want. The moral person obeys the rules. That I understand.

"Right. But the immoral person goes against the laws and the moral rules."

Yes. And when the immoral person has committed a terrible immoral act, then what?

"What do you mean?"

What does the immoral person do? He or she hides. Immoral people try to get away with it! Right?

"Yes, they try to get away with it because they fear punishment. They know they have done something wrong. Most of the time they get good law-yers to defend them. They try to get off on legal technicalities."

By technicality, you mean they try to seek protection within the law, right? What's wrong with that?

"They use the law."

Just like a law-abiding person? Look, the point is that immoral people rec-ognize that their actions are wrong. They either try to get away with it, or find excuses, or find some other way out. Nonmoral people don't bother with any of that. For example, I just do what I want.

"Let me see if I follow you. There is a difference between moral and immo-ral people, and between them and nonmoral people. But if that's true, then you are far worse than immoral people."

How so? I don't see myself as better or as worse. I am just doing what I want.

"You are worse because you are out of control and unpredictable. Immoral people have a sense of right and wrong, good and bad. You don't know the difference, do you?"

As a matter of fact, you've been reading my mind! (You should write a book!) No, I do not know the difference between right and wrong, or between good and bad.

AVOIDING GUILT

"Do you ever feel guilty when you do something wrong?"

How could I? Nothing I do is wrong, so I never feel guilty. If I can't distinguish right from wrong, good from bad, how am I to feel guilt?

"You've never felt guilty about anything? Never? I can't believe that. Most of my life is based on avoiding that feeling. Really, I don't believe you."

I really don't feel guilt. (This is not a lie.) I'll make you a promise. By the time you're done reading this book, you won't feel guilt, either. Would you like that?

"That would be great, but I don't believe it's possible."

We'll see.

"Still, you are much worse than the immoral person. Immoral people feel guilt. They do not always act immorally. But you, who do not feel guilt, you can do whatever you want."

Just what I've been saying all along. Great, isn't it?

"Aren't you afraid you'll get caught?"

WHAT IF YOU KNEW YOU WOULDN'T GET CAUGHT?

Ah, dear reader! (See how close we've gotten.) So that's your problem? Are you afraid of getting caught? There's a way around that.

"No, that is not my problem. . . . but how can one not get caught?"

I am glad you asked. There is a special ring. The ring gives you immunity from ever being caught.

"How could a ring do that?"

Plato has a story of such a ring, the Ring of Gyges, he calls it. The ring makes people invisible. Then they can do whatever they want.

"Are you telling me that you have Plato's mythical Ring of Gyges? You are crazy."

Actually, I do not have the Ring of Gyges. The ring I have is the ring from Tolkien's *The Hobbit* and *The Lord of the Rings*. I have Frodo Baggins's ring.

"Who? Look, this is supposed to be a serious discussion on the nature of morality, not a stage for Art's nutty imagination."

Imagine that I do have such a ring, a ring that makes its wearer invisible.

"What's your point?"

If I had the ring, would you want to borrow it?

"I would *not* want a ring like that."

Why not? What would you do with it? Think about it for a moment. You could do anything you wanted and no one would be able to catch you.

"I wouldn't want the ring because I'm not sure I could withstand the temptation to use it."

Of course you'd use it! What's the point of having it if you don't use it? Would you use it for immoral purposes? For pleasure?

"Both. Pleasures are usually immoral, and vice versa. Anyway, I wouldn't take the ring. Someone might get hurt."

Repression, anyone?

"What do you mean?"

Maybe we could build in a safeguard so that no one would get hurt. Would you use the ring to get some money? Or you could take an air trip, free. You could go anywhere in the world, free. That wouldn't hurt anyone. You could "borrow" a red Ferrari! What about it? Do you want the ring?

Immorality Is Tempting. "Okay, you've made your point. Being immoral is tempting. That's why we have to obey the moral rules even when we don't understand them. We have to live in society, you know. Nothing would get done if we're immoral."

Why do you think something has to get done? And why do you assume that having the ring will lead to immoral behavior? You could do good with the ring. No one's stopping you. You just assume that we're all basically immoral. Do you assume that's part of human nature?

"Well, no, I'm not assuming that. I'm just assuming that we are all subject to temptation. I still say if everyone were immoral, nothing would get done."

Living Forever. Interesting. Look, what if you found out that you were going to live forever?

"That's impossible. Besides, who would want to age forever? Would you get older?"

What if you aged one day every 500,000 years? And your health stayed good. Would you have any reason to be moral? All the things you want to do would get done, eventually. Would you change your lifestyle?

"I'm not sure. I guess I would. Would any of my friends and family live on with me?"

We can make the example work any way you'd like. So, sure, family and friends age just as you do. Is there any pressing reason to struggle and to sacrifice, to work and to slave, and to follow duties and obligations? Wouldn't you calm down and live a more leisurely, pleasant life?

"Yes, I suppose so. I wouldn't feel the pressure that time imposes on me. I would have a lot more time to spend doing what I want."

Great. But isn't this your life now, only with different expectations of how long people live? You don't live forever, but seventy to ninety years is a long time, a lifetime.

Dying Soon. Now let me alter the example slightly. What if you found out that you were going to die in exactly six months?

"No medical opinion can be that accurate."

For the sake of my example, say you found out that you have an incurable ailment, the kind of disease characters in soap operas get all the time. You will live exactly six months, then your contract is not renewed. During that time you will feel healthy, then wham! you die. Would you change the way you presently live?

"You call this example a slight change from living forever?

Would you change the way you presently live? Would you give up your goals?

"Yes, I would change how I live. I'd quit school. I'd quit my job. I think I'd travel."

Come on. You wouldn't do those terrible immoral deeds that you moral people dream about?

"No, I wouldn't. Do you mean, would I kill anyone? No, I wouldn't kill."

Too bad. There are probably a few people who ought to be killed. That wasn't what I had in mind, though.

"Which immoral deeds do you mean?"

Whichever ones you're thinking. You wouldn't steal? Or sleep with your neighbor? You wouldn't lie? Even if you knew you could not be punished? Living for six months and living forever give you immunity from punishment. You wouldn't act immorally?

"I guess I'm confused. I'm not sure what I would do."

Good. Then I'm doing my job. You can't learn anything as long as you have answers. What confuses you?

WHAT DO YOU REALLY WANT OUT OF LIFE?

"First, I told you that living morally is worthwhile for its own sake. And you asked me why that was true."

And you said that morality allows us to accomplish goals.

"I said that nothing could get done if we were immoral."

Right. Then I gave the example of living forever.

"Why did you ask that?"

To see just how committed you are to achieving your goals because you want to achieve them. But even more, to see how important your goals are to your life. And what you would do if you didn't feel the constant pressure to accomplish.

"So you want to know how I would spend my leisure time?"

Yes. What do you really want to do? Living forever, you could do whatever you want.

"I see. Both of your examples are trying to trick me into telling you what I really want."

Bingo! What do you really want? Set aside all the obligations you've learned. What do you really want out of life?

"I still want to accomplish my goals. But now you've changed my mind somewhat. What if I live for only six months? Most of my goals would be unreachable. But wait. I'm lost. How did we get here? And where are we?"

Moral Repression. We are back to my original question. What is the point of morality? If I'm tempted to do whatever I want, why shouldn't I follow my wants? So far, morality sounds like a lot of repression.

"What do you mean by repression? You said that already. You keep using the word, but you haven't said what you mean."

Repression is just a fancy way of saying that being moral is the pits. When I want to do something that is immoral, I'm supposed to "bury" the want. That's repression. That's crazy.

"There's nothing crazy about it. We need to control ourselves. Without control, people could not live together in a society. The only way to avoid chaos is for everyone to contain his passions and antisocial wants."

Yes, so you say, but why should I be moral? Or let me put it a different way. I want society to be perfectly stable and predictable. I like living among moral robots. (Another lie.) My question is not about everyone's being moral. I want to know why *I* should be moral.

"Who do you think you are?"

Time out. Smith and Jones already played that number with me. But it doesn't work.

"And why not, Mr. Special Case?"

It doesn't work because it assumes that I am moral. And I'm not, happily.

"Well, you should be, you—"

Back to name calling? Frustrated? Telling a pleasure seeker that she should be moral is like arguing the fine points of etiquette with a hungry lion as she is about to eat you. I want to know why I should be moral. Your moral indignation is not a compelling reason. I think you need to show me a nonmoral reason to live morally.

"Why do I have to do that?"

A nonmoral reason appeals to moral and nonmoral people alike.

"What kind of reasons are you looking for?"

Show me that the moral life is more desirable than other ways of living.

"If you think you're so right, Art, can you show me what's wrong with the moral life?"

I've already argued that morality is imposed on people and that even you would live very differently if you were immune to morality.

"I'm not persuaded by those arguments."

Eternal Recurrence.   Then here's another example. Maybe this one will bring you over to the right way of living—pleasure!

"Doubtful, Art. I am perfectly happy living by the rules of morality. They give me a lot more than you can evidently imagine."

We'll see. Imagine that you must live your entire existence—no, better, you must live for eternity doing just what you have been doing for the past twenty-four hours. Would you be willing to live that way?

"The past day would repeat over and over again, forever? This is ridiculous."

Maybe, but would you live this way? Think about it. Think about all the responsibilities, and goals, and promises, and duties, and pressures you have had to fulfill in the past twenty-four hours.

"So?"

Think how little pleasure you have while you're fulfilling your moral duties. Look at all the opportunities for enjoyment you've sacrificed. Come on, take the example seriously just for a moment.

"Would I be willing to live exactly the way I have lived for the last day? Could we stretch it out to the last week?"

What difference would that make?

"I had a good weekend. I really enjoyed myself, so I'd like to include that."

I think you're getting the point. The time frame doesn't matter as much as the point of the example.

"Which is what?"

Moral people put up with a lot of stress and forfeit a lot of pleasure. Imagine spending an eternity living with the pressures of exam week or income tax filing!

"I see the point, but you have to face reality. We have to do those things. Besides, they don't take that much time. And the rewards are worth it."

You already admitted that you would quit school and your job if you knew you were going to die soon. Why not quit school and your job and enjoy your life?

"I don't know what keeps you on the ground! Be realistic. No one that I know can just quit everything and live the way you want."

Why do you bother with school?

"Because I want to get a good-paying job."

I think the point of the eternal repeat idea is that most people do what they have to do, but they don't really enjoy it. Even you say that you are in school so that you can get a better job. You moral people worry so much about the results of your actions and your plans that you don't enjoy what you're doing now.

"School isn't so bad. There are lots of courses I really enjoy, especially courses in my major. You make it sound like all of school is a terrible torture. It isn't, you know."

Well, at least we're making headway. You do some things you enjoy!

"Of course I do. Everyone does. You use extreme examples to prove your points, and that forces me to say things I don't feel comfortable saying."

Comfort is hardly the test of truth, but I see your point. I think there is some merit in isolating our intuitions by using extreme examples. Since this bothers you, however, let me give you a more realistic example.

"Okay, and could we keep the example in the realm of reality? Life can't be all pleasure and no struggle or pain. Life just isn't like that."

The Pleasure Button.   Oh? Then you'll be happy to hear this. I am the regional distributer for a miraculous invention, the pleasure button. With this button you can eliminate unpleasant experiences. All you have to do is press the pleasure button and you feel a surge of pleasure. Goodbye, pain and worries; hello, pleasure!

"What are you talking about? There is no such button."

Ah, but there is. It was invented by some researchers at a major medical school. Its primary use is to alleviate the pain for people who suffer from migraine headaches and from certain types of cancer. Evidently the pain is so great that the only effective chemical painkillers also kill the patient. I guess the dose has to be so strong that the patient can't survive it.

"Even if there is such a device, you can't use it for people who don't suffer from that kind of pain."

Why not? By the way, the Food and Drug Administration doesn't need to hear about this. I have been granted distribution rights. Because I like you, I am willing to sell you our best model for only $29.95. Just think what a pleasure-filled life you can have.

"What about the side effects? You haven't mentioned how addictive your device is."

Addictive? That's its best feature. There's no physical addiction, unlike drugs. See, the pleasure button works on a simple principle. An electrode is planted into the pleasure center of your brain.

"Wait a minute, that sounds dangerous! I'm not having anyone put wires in my brain."

Cool down. The electrode isn't even the width of a hair. I have been assured that because of the location of the pleasure center, the procedure is absolutely safe and effective. I'm thinking about franchising implantations at better department stores across the country.

"Art, this idea is nuts."

If the department store franchising fails, I'm willing to farm out the work to hardware stores, but they aren't my first choice.

"That's not what I think is nuts. It's nuts, too, but your whole example is crazy. No one is going to let somebody put an electrode into his brain and then have control over when he feels pleasure."

Oh, I agree. The control of the pleasure button is completely in the hands of the person who buys the product. Once the electrode is implanted, I give a hand-held button to the person. It looks a lot like a garage door opener. Whenever the person wants to feel pleasure, she just pushes the button. It turns out that the pleasure center overrides the pain center. You never have to feel pain again.

"There must be a drawback. This thing can't be as simple as you say."

There are a few bugs in the system. For example, sometimes when a plane flies overhead the person below feels a surge of pleasure. It's a problem with overlapping frequencies or something, but we're working on it. And then there's the garage door opener problem. If you're going by someone's house and you push the button, their garage door may open.

"Stop right here! I'm not concerned about garage doors and planes flying overhead."

So you'll buy one? $24.95 plus tax.

"No, I will not buy one. I don't want someone else controlling what I feel. What happens when someone else pushes his button?"

Good question. Each pleasure button is set on a different frequency. I suppose we could market two buttons for couples who want to feel pleasure at the same time. Hmm, let me work on that marketing strategy.

"Art, my concern is not with marketing strategy. My concern is with self-control and with progress. People who have this pleasure button of yours will stop working. If everyone has a pleasure button, progress will come to a halt. Civilization will crumble."

Sure, but we won't care. If the fall of civilization bothers you, just push the button. By the way, did I mention that the pleasure button comes in two models? One model is powered by a nine-volt battery.

"There's a problem. If people have the pleasure button, they'll stop working. How are they going to eat? How are they going to be able to afford to pay for their food, or house, or even the batteries they need? Answer that one."

Well, the answer to the first two questions is easy. When you get hungry or cold, just push the button. Pleasure.

"People will die! They'll stop working, and they'll starve to death or freeze to death."

But they'll die with a smile on their faces. You do raise an important issue, though. How will they provide themselves with the batteries they need? People will be like drug addicts, committing crimes in order to get their batteries. That's what worries you, isn't it?

. . . Well, if you won't answer, I'll assume that's your problem. The battery situation is resolved by buying the advanced model. It's operated by a solar cell and has a battery backup for cloudy days. Great, huh? It can be yours for only $34.95.

"I don't want it. I'd rather deal with some of the struggles of life and feel I've accomplished something. What you offer is pleasure, but there aren't any emotions or friendships to get through this device."

You can make friends by giving them a pleasure button.

"I'm serious. As much as your pleasure button sounds appealing, there is more to life than pleasure!"

Like what?

"Like work, and progress, and meaningful activity. Like friendships and love and trust. There's such a thing as dignity. Your pleasure button gives people pleasure, but where would their sense of belonging come from?"

Why would anyone care about all of this stuff? Once you feel supreme pleasure, the rest is just worthless. Did you know that whenever the pleasure center is directly activated, the person feels as much pleasure as his body can generate. Truly, it don't get any better than this. So what about it? May I take your order now?

"No."

WHAT DOES THE MORAL LIFE HAVE TO OFFER?

What does the moral life have to offer that makes it more desirable than a life of pleasure?

Security and Acceptance.   "What you're asking isn't that easy to define, but let me try. You should be moral because if you are not moral, you will be rejected."

By whom?

"By us. By everyone. By society. Society provides security for its members. I think that means that we owe something to society. I guess you don't see it that way."

Nope.

"Within this organized, safe society you get the benefits. But you get the benefits only if you are an accepted member. If you act immorally, you'll become an outcast. No one will love or trust or befriend you. People won't care about you."

So what?

"Don't you want to be accepted? If you don't live a moral life, you'll never feel accepted by others. You'll never feel the sense of community that moral people feel. You'll never understand that you are one person in the long history of the human race. Morality gives us a sense of our place in the unfolding history of humanity."

I'm getting dizzy from the excitement!

Commerce, Creativity, and Continuity. "Make fun all you want, but morality gives us the chance to cooperate with others. It allows us to have give-and-take relationships with each other."

Give and take? It sounds like a business transaction. I'd like to deposit this in checking and take that from savings, thank you.

"It is a little like commerce. Take promises. Promises allow people to count on each other. Morality also lets us be creative."

How so?

"Seeing ourselves in the context of history gives us a sense of the importance of the past and the future. Knowing that other humans will follow, we are motivated to create. Just look how creative people have been throughout history. Art, music, architecture. Why, civilization itself is a product of the ability of people to see themselves in the context of a continuing humanity."

Baa. Baa.

"What? Are you starting that again!"

You readers sound like sheep. Baa. I ask why I should be moral, why anyone should be moral. All you tell me is that morality makes me part of the flock. Morality makes society safe for me! Morality lets me be accepted! Morality keeps me from being punished! Or so you snivel. You are a bunch of frightened sheep. You want to be one continuous, homogenized flock! Even offering you the ring frightened you. Look how you responded. You wanted the ring. And you were afraid to use it.

"That's not true, Art! I was thinking of using it."

How would you use it?

Don't Hurt Anyone. "I would use the ring in lots of ways. Just as long as I didn't hurt anyone, then using the ring would be fine."

So, you're willing to steal money?

"As long as it doesn't hurt anyone, sure."

Wimp! You aren't really serious. What about all the times you do hurt someone?

"When's that? I don't knowingly hurt people. Maybe you do, but I don't."

You hurt people all the time. Every time you compete, you hurt people. Competition is designed to have a lot of losers. That's why people like it. Do you think losers like losing?

"Competition is different. People enter competitions knowing they might lose. It's part of the game. No one has to enter the competition."

Pretty good rationalization, but it doesn't work. If you are reading this book for a course, you are probably using the course to fulfill a general education requirement. If your school is like any other I've seen, the seats in those courses are limited. So, by being in this course, you are depriving someone else of this seat.

"Big deal. The space goes to whoever gets there first. It's a fair lottery. I'm not hurting anyone by being here ("except perhaps myself," you realize!). There's a difference between inconveniencing, bothering, and hurting. Being here isn't hurting anyone else."

Fair enough. Does any of this noble thinking apply outside the classroom? Aren't we unfairly hurting others by using most of the world's raw materials, and energy, and food? But wait. Let's not get into that issue. I don't care. You do.

"You really don't care about the plight of others, do you?"

Why Should I Care About Others?   Why should I care about others? (You knew I was going to say that.)

"You just should care about others. They're people. They have feelings. That's why you should care."

I admit that they and you are people, and that you may have feelings, but so what? I don't feel your feelings, so why should I care?

"Art, you are the most self-centered egomaniac I ever came across. How can you be this way?"

Just good luck, I guess. Look, I have a hobby. I mug old people on the weekends. (It's an example! Don't get bent out of shape.) Is there anything wrong with that?

"Anything wrong! Of course, there's something wrong with that!"

What's wrong with mugging old people on the weekend? Is it the weekend part that bothers you? I could change the day if it offends you.

"It's not the day; it's you. Mugging old people is wrong. It's disgusting!"

There is a difference between wrong and disgusting, isn't there? If you want to hear it, I have a disgusting example involving—

"Spare me. Mugging old people is wrong. Period."

Why?

"Look, Art, how would you like it if people mugged you?"

I'm not old.

"If you were old, would you want people to mug you?"

No.

"Then why do you mug them?"

I've told you, because I'm not them. I don't see why I should give up a perfectly enjoyable hobby just because it bothers a few old people.

"This is amazing. Here's a guy writing a book on ethics and he doesn't have the faintest idea why it's wrong to harm others."

Why *is* it wrong to harm old people?

"Why don't you pick on someone your own age? Why don't you try to bully people who are bigger than you?"

That's silly. I pick on old people because I don't run any risk that way. I'm not into getting hurt, you know. This hobby is not as simple as you might imagine. For example, you have to be careful. Old men often carry canes. You know what the curved end is for? After I knock them down, they try to snag my foot as I leave. Sneaky! Or those darn aluminum walkers! One woman threw one of those at me.

"Good for her!"

Luckily she missed. What do you mean, good for her? I thought you were against people hurting each other.

"Unbelievable! Let's get off this topic. I don't think we're likely to resolve anything."

WHAT IS MORALITY?

I didn't say that. I think you've just explained the basis of morality to me.

"I did?"

Being One Among Many Equals. Sure. It's probably so obvious to you that you missed it. I just got it, though. Morality is seeing yourself as one person among many equals. That's why you objected when I gave the example of hurting older people. Morality demands that we view them as equals in some sense. I'm not sure what that sense is, but have I gotten it right?

"Yes, I think so. Morality is opposed to just being selfish and self-centered. It's seeing others as important, as equals, just like you said. Yes, that's at least part of morality."

So your idea that morality gives us a sense of security and belonging is really a partial definition of morality. Interesting. To be moral is to avoid being selfish and self-centered. It means to be more objective?

"Yes, good. Objective and impartial. Now that you understand it, morality sounds pretty appealing, doesn't it?"

I didn't say that. I still don't understand why I should be moral. I understand that it means treating others as "equals," but I don't see why I should bother. Why should I give up my hobby? Even if I continue to mug old people, society will remain stable and fairly secure. People will accept me.

"How can you say that? Who is going to accept you if you mug old people?"

Everyone will accept me. I'm aware of your moral bias against hurting old people. Knowing that, I won't tell anyone about my hobby. I can do whatever I want. For example, I can hurt old people and still get the most out of society.

I can embezzle money from my employer. As long as I can get away with it, I'm safe and accepted.

"So, you intend to take a free ride?"

Sure, why not? Why shouldn't I try to get away with it? Isn't that how everyone lives anyway?

Human Dignity. "There's more to morality than you've realized. There are more reasons to be moral. Being moral gives dignity to us as human beings. It puts us above the animals. It puts us into the entirely human realm of civilization. Being moral makes us better people."

I don't get it.

"Human dignity. It's what makes us human."

I thought my parents made me human.

"Wrong. To be human is to progress, to grow, to reason, to get along with others in a human society. It's to set and accomplish goals."

Are you saying that people like me are not human? That's pretty harsh.

"Dignity is what allows us to sacrifice ourselves for the greater good. It's what allows us to be fulfilled."

I'd just as soon wallow in my lusts, thank you.

Meaning and Worth. "But if you wallow in your lusts, as you call it, your life will be pointless. Don't you want your life to have meaning? Don't you want people to value you? Don't you want to accomplish anything? Life would be meaningless without morality."

Now you've hit on something that has always fascinated me. Every time I'm really enjoying my pleasure, people ask me if it's meaningful. Why is it that only when I'm wallowing in my passions does the question of meaning come up? It doesn't come up when I appear to be working. It doesn't even come up when I appear to be suffering. (I never suffer, but it's a good example.) Comments about meaning come up only when I'm enjoying myself. Why?

"You really do lead a shallow life."

Shallow, huh? What makes a life meaningful? I don't think there is a meaning of life. I think this idea of life having a meaning is just a distraction. It's a way of controlling people. Baa!

"Part of the meaning of life is to fit into the order of the universe, into God's plan. Sometimes that involves suffering, but it's worth it. That's what gives life meaning."

And if there is no God, then is your life meaningless?

"No God! Of course there is a God!"

We'll discuss God later. (Just look at the table of contents.) But I don't see how being an insignificant part of an infinite universe gives meaning to anyone's life. So what if you're needed for the great machine of the universe?

"But the universe runs according to God's plan."

Even if there is a God, and even if the universe runs by God's plan, so what? How can the life of an infinitely small cog be meaningful? The point of the "plan" isn't even yours! No, sorry to say it, but the only meaning is in enjoying one's pleasures in the moment. Or do you see an alternative?

"Well—"

If you don't have an answer, I do. The question of meaning comes up because experiencing momentary pleasure and passion competes with being moral. Morality can't permit people to enjoy themselves.

Contentment.   "Now you've gone too far. I enjoy myself, and I'm moral."

How do you enjoy yourself? Do you throw yourself into the passion of the moment? Do you lose your ability to reason? Are you overwhelmed by the ecstasy of the occasion?

"I do enjoy myself, don't mistake that. The moral life is a life of higher, more cultivated pleasures."

So now you're a field that has to be cultivated? What do you mean by higher pleasure? What special kind of pleasure does morality offer?

"The moral life gives me a sense of peace and contentment. I'm happy living the moral life."

Which is it? Are you happy, or peaceful and contented?

"There's no difference."

Of course there's a difference. I can see we're going to have to figure out what happiness is. (Another chapter? On Happiness.) I know one thing, though. Peace and contentment are not happiness. The word *peace* reminds me of "rest in peace." That's for tombstones, not for people. And contented is what farmers want their cows to be. Contentment isn't for people! Can't you ever just let go?

Consequences.   "Of course not. That kind of abandon always leads to trouble, to undesirable consequences."

So? Are you telling me that what comes after your pleasure matters more to you than the pleasure? What has morality led you to? This is madness.

"No, this is morality. It does matter what happens in the future. Whether you like it or not, your actions do have consequences."

So?

"It is our responsibility to consider those consequences. We can't just isolate our actions from what they bring."

Why not? I do it all the time. In fact, if I think about the past or the future, my immediate experiences aren't as intense. Distractions, you know.

"You are the most irresponsible person I've ever run across. Moral people look to the consequences of their actions."

The action itself has no value apart from what it brings?

"We judge whether or not our actions are right in themselves, and we judge them according to their consequences. Some actions are simply wrong no matter what the consequences. And some actions are simply right. And sometimes consequences are important to consider, too."

Recap: Definition of Morality.   This strikes me as confused thinking.

"But you must admit, Art, that I've taught you quite a lot about morality.

Morality involves consequences, and judgments, and seeing others as equals. It puts a person into the human community. It gives the person a sense of connection with other people. Not just with people who live in different parts of the world, but with people of the past and people who will live in the future. Morality is an impartial, objective view of others."

It concerns punishment and security?

"Yes. Morality and religion also give us direction in our lives. They prevent harm to others, and they help humanity progress and prosper. That's why you should be moral."

Interesting. The way you describe morality, it is not merely a set of rules I must obey.

"Exactly. Morality also involves a whole way of thinking and living."

You actually think of other people as being a lot like you are.

"Yes, as moral equals. As people with plans, wants, rights, duties, and all the rest. People may not be equal in skills or talents or wealth or knowledge or any other characteristic, but they are equal morally. Each person is important no matter what his background or what her use to society."

And let me see if I've got this right. I'm supposed to be moral because it promises contentment and some kind of meaningful life?

DO YOU HAVE ANY OBJECTIONS?

"That's right, yes. Now that you understand morality, do you have any objections?"

Absolutely! It sounds painfully safe and boring and confining!

"Safe? Boring? Confining? You are hopeless, Art. I think you've misunderstood. I've tried my best to explain the point of morality. I don't know what else to say to you."

Morality and religion create a sense of guilt, a conscience, and then promise to soothe your conscience. What's this? What a marketing scheme! I give you a conscience, and then I claim to be the only store in town with the product that will pacify your guilt? I tell you that you have sinned and that only I have the remedy. And the beauty is that the overhead is so low. All I have to do is tell you everything is okay.

"You're so cynical. Morality serves us very well, thank you. It serves us whether or not you approve of it."

Spoken like an open-minded person.

Why Not Experience the Moment?   "Okay, let me ask you, Art, what's so great about your intense, momentary experiences? Why should anyone live for the moment?"

In the moment, not *for* the moment.

"What's the difference? For the moment, in the moment? Neither is morally acceptable."

Living for the moment sounds like a life seeking nothing but pleasure. The pleasure of the moment. Living in the moment is to open up to what there is in the here and now.

"I don't see the difference. All I see is that you want to avoid responsibility and consequences."

It's a great difference, but let's put off that discussion for a later time. The difference between living and being alive is more to the point right now.

"What do you mean?"

See, I knew you wouldn't get it. You're so moral.

"What's the difference?"

Being moral commits you to looking to the past and to the future, right? Living in the moment means that you concentrate on the here and now.

"Brilliant. So what does that distinction give us?"

Do Moral People Exist?   You're too impatient (which proves my point, I think cleverly to myself). If you live morally, then you need to prove that you exist.

"That's the big question?"

How do I know that I exist? With morality, I know that I exist because I am connected to others by an elaborate web of social conventions.

"Yes, morality makes you feel an historical connection with people who have already lived. Morality also lets you communicate and relate to people alive now."

And the desire to create and to accomplish shows that you moral people care about people in the future. Do I have that right?

"Yes, morality does all that for us. It does even more. Morality also gives your life a sense of meaning."

I remember what you said. You fit into the universe, into a God's great plan. That sense of your "importance" also lets you know that you exist. You assume that you must exist for the plan to go on.

"This is pretty persuasive evidence for morality."

It isn't evidence at all. What it shows is that you and everyone else want to exist, and to know you exist.

"Kind of like 'I think, therefore I exist'? I am moral, therefore I exist."

Kind of. I think morality is looking for some way of proving you exist.

"Obviously I exist. Why should morality have to prove that?"

Because from the moral viewpoint, you aren't really sure that you do exist. Intellectually you're certain, but experientially there's doubt. All your elaborate "evidence" for morality shows that you need to "justify" your existence. See, the problem is that morally speaking, you don't exist in the present. Morality doesn't have much of a present. The past and future distract you from your present experience.

"Why do you say that?"

Subjective Time and Objective Time, or Having the Time of Your Life.   All of the moral person's attention is directed toward the past and the future.

Come on, admit it, you think that the present moment lasts the tick of the clock.

"Well, sure, what else is there?"

Exactly! Think about it. There are hours when time moves very quickly.

"Like when I'm having fun with my friends."

And there are hours when time d-r-a-g-s.

"Like when I'm reading this book?"

Cheap shot. But right again. So we all know that time is not always the same.

"But the clock doesn't change. It runs the same no matter how or what I'm doing."

Right, there's objective time, the clock, and there's subjective time. The clock's objective time is morality! What a terrible invention, the clock. Without it you would never be late. You would never have to rush. You would be able to experience the moment for all it's worth. You'd live forever.

"So you're saying that moral people don't experience as intensely as non-moral people. And this is because we are distracted by the past and the future?"

Yes, for you the past and the future are indefinitely long. You even talk about eternity running into the past and into the future. But that leaves out the eternity of the present moment. And without the eternity of the present moment, you have to make up all of this historical connectedness and mean-ingfulness and creativeness stuff. You're alive, but you aren't living, at least not when you're being a moral person. You're alive, but you don't exist as an *experiencing* person.

"But I do experience the moment sometimes. I know what subjective time is. Reading this book has shown me how long an hour can be."

That's because you are not completely moral. The nonmoral part of you can understand what I'm saying. See, if you were completely and thoroughly moral, through and through (shudder), then you would experience the mo-ment always as the tick of the clock. Time would be uniform. And you would never be tempted by the pleasures in the moment.

"Why?"

Because the pleasures in the moment would be quickly over. Their inten-sity would be dulled with the passing moment. The genuinely moral person is never tempted. The past and the future, and all the connectedness and meaning, let genuinely moral people know that they exist. But they aren't living!

"I still don't quite get your point."

Morally Speaking, You Don't Exist. If your immediate experience doesn't let you know that you exist, that you're living, then you need all the other mumbo-jumbo (another technical philosophy term). Fully moral people don't feel the present moment, so they need an elaborate system of beliefs to verify that they exist. But they don't feel passion or emotion or sensual pleasure. Those are limited to the present. Think of an example of a completely moral person. He's always dead, bloodless, and nice. Nice is like lukewarm mush. Don't be nice, live!

"Who is an example of a genuinely moral person? Do you have some saint in mind?"

Actually, the Vulcan side of Mr. Spock is the example that comes to mind. Sarek, his father, is even more moral. Always acting on duty. Unemotional. Big deal. When you live morally, passions are unavailable to you.

"And who is the nonmoral person? Kirk?"

Not bad. At least he is aware of his senses. Living in the present moment guarantees that you're living, that you exist. And it's not some intellectual knowledge. It's not some "I think, therefore I exist" stuff. That's for the intellect. What moral people really want is a guarantee that they exist. Nonmoral people have that guarantee at every moment of their experience.

"How so?"

Whenever you're feeling intense pleasure, or intense pain, you don't wonder whether or not you're real and living. You *know.* You know, not intellectually, but you know with your gut. (Sometimes this is called affective knowledge.) Physically and emotionally, you know. And you can't be mistaken. Unfortunately, you moral people don't allow yourselves the kinds of pleasures I have in mind. But you are allowed to suffer pain. When you're in pain you know it, and you know you exist. Although you spiritualize pain too much.

"Spiritualize?"

Yes, you look for its meaning. Pain has no meaning; it just hurts.

RELATIVISM

"I have to think about all this. Do you have any other problems with morality?"

Just one more. From what we've said, the content of the moral/religious values doesn't matter. You have argued for the benefits of morality, but I don't see why morality isn't relative to each society.

"Relative? What do you mean?"

Why can't each society pick its own values? Why can't each person? Each religion has its own doctrine and values. Each political system has its own values. So values depend on the surroundings. When in Rome, do as the Romans do.

"I'm not comfortable with this. Are you saying that morality and religion are arbitrary?"

Not the point of view of morality and religion. Not the form. Morality is always objective and impartial. The changeable, arbitrary part is the content, the values themselves. Morality and religion are socially desirable, but the values themselves don't matter. You get all the stability and security and social connection you want. That comes from accepting the authority of morality and religion. The values themselves don't matter. One value is as good as another. Isn't that what you've told me?

"Of course not! Morality isn't relative. There are moral truths!"

Look back to the opening of this discussion. I was asked what is the best life. I suggested pleasure. You (and Smith and Jones) argued for morality. Well, now I wonder about that. At least pleasure is not relative or uncertain in the way that good and bad are relative and uncertain. When I feel pleasure, I know it. I can distinguish pleasure and pain. (Except in the case of tickles!)

"There are moral and religious truths."

Sure, mine.

"Which religious doctrine do you follow?"

Oh, I didn't mean mine, I meant "mine." Is that perfectly confusing?

"Almost. What are you saying?"

Whenever the question comes up about moral and religious truths, people always say that their own religion and their own morality is correct. Mine. It's always "mine." It gets pretty tiresome. I'd like to know what makes one moral or religious truth true and another moral or religious truth false.

"Except that it's 'mine'?"

Exactly.

"There are values that transcend moral and religious differences. Maybe we can use the common values."

Can you tell me what these are? Can you show that any moral and religious truths are really true?

"That won't be an easy thing to show, but it can be done."

Then why don't we get a clearer picture of morality by looking at some examples of morality? From there we may be able to select the most desirable values. (I'm still betting on living in the moment.)

■

SUMMARY OF DISCUSSION

In our opening conversation we question the point of morality. One contender against the moral life is the pleasure-seeking life. Though pleasure recommends itself, morality calls for further motivation. Why bother being moral? To live morally means to submit to society's limits. It means to submit to responsibilities and duties. Living morally means one does not do whatever one wants.

Why do people accept the burdens of morality? There are many reasons. People fear chaos, uncertainty, and guilt. They want security, acceptance, and protection. Morality makes us feel part of the human community—past, present, and future. It instructs us not to hurt other people and even to care about the welfare of others.

What is morality? Our first answer to this question is that morality is a special point of view. The moral point of view is that each of us is one person among many equals. Morality gives us dignity, meaning, and a sense of worth. Finally, morality makes us look to the past and to the future: for example, a promise made yesterday must be kept tomorrow. Consequences matter to moral people.

There are several objections to the moral way of living. Morality limits our actions. We don't get to do what we want. Just think what we would do if we knew we could get away with it! The pleasure button is certainly appealing. The moral life distracts us from experiencing the moment we actually live in. Finally, moral values appear to be relative to the society or the person. Different societies and different people appear to support different moral values.

■
_____

DISCUSSION HIGHLIGHTS

   I. There are two answers to the question: What is the best life?
     1. The pleasure-seeking life
     2. The moral life
  II. The point of morality is to guarantee:
     1. The prevention of chaos by promoting a stable society
     2. Protection for each member of society
     3. A secure world
     4. Respect for human dignity
     5. Acceptance
     6. The avoidance of punishment and guilt
 III. Morality offers important social gains:
     1. Security and acceptance
     2. Commerce, creativity, and social continuity
     3. Prevention of harm
 IV. What is the moral point of view?
     1. Being one person among many equals
     2. Acknowledging human dignity
     3. Viewing life as meaningful and worthy
     4. Offering guarantees of contentment
     5. Concern with the results of one's actions
   V. Objections to morality
     1. Repression of wants, desires, and pleasures
     2. Alteration and distortion of one's sense of time
     3. Distortion of one's sense of self
     4. Values are relative to time, place, society, and person

■
_____

QUESTIONS FOR THOUGHT/PAPER TOPICS

1. Would you buy the pleasure button? Why or why not? Keep in mind that any guilt you might feel can easily be relieved by one push of the button.

2. Some people believe that living morally gives life meaning. What does this mean? Do you agree with this assessment?

3. Why do you keep your promises? How do you justify the times you fail to keep your promises?

4. Everything that enriches us renders our neighbors relatively poorer. If morality involves not hurting other people, how can we justify the amount of material wealth we enjoy in North America?

5. Is there any evidence that moral values are relative to specific cultures? Is there morality that underlies culturally different "moralities"?

6. Is contentment happiness? Can you distinguish the contentment of a satisfied animal and the happiness of a person?

7. Putting aside the rules, why shouldn't you hurt other people?

■
_____

FOR FURTHER READING

There are any number of books encouraging you to be moral. There are a few that question the moral enterprise. It would be worth your time to look at Plato's *Republic* (Hackett, 1973), especially book II, where he discusses ways to avoid getting caught. Another critic of morality is Friedrich Nietzsche. Nietzsche's *The Gay Science* (Random House, 1974) and *On The Genealogy of Morals* (Vintage, 1989) are both provocative, though somewhat difficult, readings. A very readable book by Raymond Smullyan, *The Tao Is Silent* (Harper & Row, 1977) is wonderfully entertaining and insightful.

TWO

What Is Morality?

In our last conversation I asked, "What's the point of morality?" You said that I (and, presumably, you) should be moral. You said that morality strengthens society and makes it stable. It gives us a sense of belonging. Morality makes life meaningful. It gives us human dignity. Moral guidelines let us control our passions so that we can act reasonably and responsibly. At the same time, morality also gives inner peace. It preserves humanity. Morality organizes the world. Does that capture the highlights of your thinking?

"What you don't understand is that morality satisfies our important wants. Morality is what makes each of us an individual, a person different from everyone else. In the religious context, moral values bring us closer to being the ideal person. They show us how to live in the image of God."

I'm not denying any of this. Now I realize I asked the wrong question. Since I don't know what morality is, I can't say what it does, or how well it accomplishes its goal. How can we say anything about morality until we've figured out what it is?

"Isn't that what we did in our last conversation?"

Not really. You explained the point of morality. Now I want to know *what* morality is. Before we can judge whether or not morality does what you say it does, we need to know what it is. You have to help me identify morality.

"How can we figure out what it is? How do you suggest we proceed? It seems obvious what morality is. I guess I'm still not following you."

What if I asked you: What is the point of owning a dog? What would you say?

"I don't know. Something like: a dog protects your home, and offers companionship, and plays with your children, and takes walks with you. Is that what you have in mind?"

Yes, good. Now for a person from the far side of Jupiter to understand your claim about the point of owning a dog, you would have to explain what a dog is. Right? Then anyone not familiar with dogs could watch what dogs do and find out that you are correct.

"And the way we define *dog* is by showing examples of dogs."

By Jove, he's got it!

WHAT ARE SOME EXAMPLES OF MORALITY?

"Once we have examples of dogs, we can come to a definition, right?"

Right. Can we do this with morality? What are examples of morality? What are some examples of moral systems, of moral rules?

"Are these the same?"

I don't know, but we can get an idea of the moral point of view by starting with any of them.

"What do you mean by the 'moral point of view'?"

You judge people by moral standards. I don't yet see why I should give up my pleasures and adopt the moral way of living. I guess I'm contrasting living for pleasure and living morally, though that may not exactly capture the distinction I want.

"I don't quite follow you."

Okay, how about this? Sometimes you feel like doing one action, but you know it's wrong to do it. You feel like stealing something, but you know it's wrong. I want to know why the moral way is better than stealing the object. I want to know why I should not always just give in to my temptations. So I want to know what in the moral point of view is correct, and how you know it. I want to know which moral values, and roles, and rules, and systems are correct. I'm not even sure how many varieties of moral "things" there are.

"Okay, but how will this help you?"

If we find some clear examples of moral values, we can come up with common, defining features of the moral point of view. Then we'll be in a position to find out if morality is worth the effort.

"Worth the effort?"

Sure. Being moral means I have to give up a lot. Every time I'm locked into a pleasurable moment (like when I'm doing nothing to perfection), someone interrupts. People ask me whether or not my momentary pleasure is worthwhile, or meaningful, or (can I say it?) productive. If I'm going to be worthwhile and meaningful and productive, I still want to know what I get for it. I know what I lose!

"What do you think you lose?"

I lose pleasure and a sense of freedom.

"I think you're hopeless, but let me try to answer your question. There are a number of approaches to morality. In the end, I am confident that they'll all reduce to the same insight. But if you want examples, I can think of some moral and religious rules. The Ten Commandments and the Golden Rule are perfect examples of morality."

Any others?

"Why would you need any others? These two work well enough for me."

Humor me. If we only look at two examples, this book won't be as thrilling as my publisher wants. Your silence would hurt me. You would be acting in an immoral way by failing to do unto others (me). You would also be in error for not following the Ten Commandments. Remember the one that says, "Help Art whenever he needs it"?

"I don't remember that one, but I can think of other ways of describing the moral point of view. Even you might understand these."

Excellent.

Everyone Has a Conscience.　"Everyone has a conscience."

Everyone is conscious?

"No, a conscience. *Conscious* means awake or alert. Conscience is very different. Everyone has an intuition of what is right and what is wrong."

You're not going to tell me you hear voices or that you talk to yourself! A little angel and a little devil argue on your shoulders?

"No, a conscience needn't be that kind of experience. It's more of a feeling. You just feel strange when you are about to do something wrong. You know it's wrong, and you feel odd about it."

When you say *you*, you mean you, not me. (I just put this in to show just how confused I am.)

"What? I mean anyone, everyone. Everyone has a conscience that tells them right from wrong. Whether or not people follow their conscience is a different matter. Like you said before, even immoral people try to get away with their immoral actions. They conceal their actions, but in their minds they know they're wrong."

I don't have a conscience.

"I knew you were going to say that, Art. But that isn't a good enough objection. If you're interested in the moral point of view, then having a conscience is part of being moral."

Fair enough. But saying that people have consciences doesn't tell me enough.

"What else do you need to know?"

Well, for one, what is the point of a conscience?

"Conscience is your intuition about what is right and wrong. When you think about doing something wrong, your conscience lets you know that it's wrong. And before you say it, Art, no, people do not always follow their conscience. And after the action they feel guilty."

Okay. Still I have a problem with conscience. Conscience doesn't tell me what is moral and immoral. Conscience only tells me that I think something is immoral.

"What's the difference? If something is immoral to you, then it's immoral."

I don't think you want to go that far, especially when you're talking to me. What I find moral may not be acceptable to you or to anyone else.

"You know what I mean."

Actually, I don't know what you mean. My objection to conscience is that people have different values locked in their consciences. I guess I'd say that conscience is the way a person checks her own moral values. But that doesn't mean the values are correct.

"I think I see what you mean. It's possible for people to have consciences that hold the wrong values. Some people may even feel guilty when they are tempted to do what we would consider right."

That's it! Now I don't deny the usefulness of consciences, but I do doubt that consciences are reliable guides to finding moral values.

Social Roles. "There are other examples of morality, too. There are social roles that a person must follow."

Social roles?

"By social roles, I mean there are responsibilities."

Stop right there! This is my book. I won't allow that kind of talk in my presence.

"What talk?"

Responsibilities, duties, obligations. Next you're probably going to bring up rights and promises.

"As I was saying, there are social roles we must play. For example, I am a student. I am expected to learn something from my courses and instructors. I may be required to take tests, or write papers, or read difficult texts. As a student I have those responsibilities."

I shudder every time you use those words. Are there other kinds of roles that people have? And please leave out the R-word.

"Other kinds? Yes, of course. People have a whole range of roles: personal, natural, professional, social. The point is that each of these roles requires something of the person. I call the requirements *responsibilities.*"

Keep going. You're on a roll (get it, a roll/role?). So far we have more examples of morality than I imagined possible. Are there any more versions? We might as well get them all listed. Then we'll compare them to see what morality is all about.

The Law. "The law is a kind of moral system, I guess. Laws are at least based on moral and religious rules. It's illegal to kill, to steal, to lie in court."

Would those actions be wrong if it weren't for the religious rules? Isn't there supposed to be a separation of church and state?

"Sure, though I don't think that's what the separation means. From my point of view, we should follow the law for the benefit of everyone. There would be chaos if no one followed the law. I remember what you pulled on Smith and Jones, and that won't work on me. Keep your cheap stolen pen in your pocket. Most people benefit from having everyone follow the laws. Whether you like it or not, you and I live in a democratic society where the majority's good must be included."

The Most Good for the Most People. So "the greatest good for the greatest number" is what you are proposing?

"Yes, something like that. I know you're going to try to poke holes in the idea, but I think something like this is at the heart of morality. Maybe I can say this even stronger and avoid your criticism."

Me? Criticism?

"Don't interrupt. Everyone who lives in our society has to follow the laws.

We have agreed to follow them. That's what it means to be a member of this society."

I don't recall being asked to endorse any of the laws. I don't even know most of the laws.

"If you don't like the laws, you can leave. But as long as you stay in our society, you are required to follow them."

And if I don't follow all of your laws?

A Social Contract. "You'll be punished. But that's beside the point. You should follow the laws because you live here. Whether or not you agree with the laws, you are bound by a kind of unspoken contract with everyone else in society. We follow the laws, so you have to follow them, too."

A social contract? Hmm. I need to think about this one. Are there any other examples or explanations of morality? I hesitate to ask, but can you think of any others?

Tradition and Spiritual Needs. "There are just a couple more. I'm not sure of these, but I'll try them. I think tradition sometimes tells us what is right and what is wrong. I think this might be part of the other categories; I'm not sure. And the other one I just thought of is this: when someone's real needs are satisfied, that might be part of morality, too. I'm not sure. I mean, if an action satisfies someone's spiritual needs, that might be part of morality."

I don't know about these, either, but there's no loss in trying a few ideas, even if they don't work. Before we go on, could you go back to the one about your social contract?

"What about it?"

Aren't there some laws that are just wrong? Don't we want to be able to say that? After all, laws change all the time. New laws are added, old laws are taken off the books. Legal interpretations change.

"I guess so. What's your point?"

Well, you based your contract idea on the idea that democracy requires that the greatest good for the greatest number be taken into account. But if we want to be able to criticize some laws, we have to say that there are times when the greatest number of people may not be our sole concern.

"I don't quite follow."

Aren't there some actions or attitudes that are just wrong? No matter what the majority thinks or how much it benefits, some actions are wrong? I guess what I'm asking is, are there absolutes in morality?

MORAL RULES ARE ABSOLUTE

"Of course, at least some moral rules are absolute. But beyond following the absolutes, one should do what benefits society. The Ten Commandments are ten examples of absolutes. I didn't add absolutes because of the commandments. I'm willing to examine absolutes separately if you want. Do you have any other examples of the moral point of view?"

Who made you the author of this book? I'm the one who asks the questions. *You're* supposed to answer. As a matter of fact, though, I do have one suggestion. Egoism.

"What's egoism?"

I should always act in my own self-interest.

"You're outrageous. That's being selfish. That isn't being moral at all!"

EXAMPLES OF MORALITY

It was just an idea. I'll give it up if you insist. I did give you all your examples, though. Let me list them. Then we'll look at them one by one throughout the book.

1. Ten Commandments

2. Golden Rule

3. Conscience or intuition

4. Social and natural roles

5. Laws

6. Greatest good for the most people

7. Social contract

8. Real needs fulfillment

9. Tradition

10. Absolutism

11. Egoism

"Hey, I didn't agree to egoism!"

Egoism is an alternative to moral and religious values. I doubt that morality is a desirable way to live.

"Your doubts are not enough to persuade me, Art."

Okay, that's fair enough. Why don't we take up a fuller discussion of egoism later in Chapter 5?

"All right."

WHAT MAKES A PRINCIPLE A MORAL PRINCIPLE?

I still don't get it. What makes a principle a moral principle? What is it about the moral point of view that distinguishes it from other ways of approaching problems?

"That's a good question, Art."

Does that mean you don't have an answer?

"No, it means you have finally asked a worthwhile question. I think it's a good idea to look closely and critically to see what the formal features of morality are."

I'm not following you.

"You have been asking me for examples of the moral point of view. In fact, you have been doing this without much regard for precision. So I have been giving you examples of morality off the top of my head."

Did that hurt your head?

"Corny, Art. What I'm suggesting now is that we both look at the formal features of morality. Where do we begin? Do we look for common qualities from the examples we have just stated?"

That's one way, and I think we should use it as a check. But since you aren't happy with my lack of precision, I have another suggestion. Let's see which types of reasoning compete with moral reasoning.

"What are you talking about?"

The moral point of view is only one way of approaching problems. It's one way of defining situations and solving issues.

"What other ways are there? Give me an example."

Well, before I give you an example, let me spell out what I have in mind. You are pretty entrenched in the moral and religious point of view. That's why you so obstinately rejected egoism.

"Yes, it's objectionable to me."

Okay, now I'm suggesting that there are other alternatives to morality. For example, there is economic reasoning, and military reasoning, and . . .

"Oh, I understand. Are you saying that with each practical situation in life, there are different ways of approaching the problem to find the solution?"

Exactly. Take a military person, a general. In deciding on combat strategy, a general's first objective is to win the engagement. He knows that lives will be lost. People will be intentionally wounded and killed. That's part of warfare. What he is concerned with, however, is defeating the enemy.

"It's not that simple, Art. Generals consider the morality of their actions. They don't just wipe out whole cities because the enemy has troops there."

Tell that to Hiroshima and Dresden. During World War II the Allies destroyed cities just to demoralize the enemy. Similar strikes have been made in every conflict, from Vietnam to Panama to Iraq to whatever comes next.

"What would you expect a general to do? Generals have to fight in order to win."

Though I might disagree, I'm not disagreeing with you now. The point is that generals think in terms of military practice and military goals.

"Even if I grant that generals think in terms of military goals, that does not mean they're immoral. Their decisions are still made with morality in mind. It's just that war is an extreme situation."

Generals think in moral terms? How so?

"There are rules to war, moral rules. Certain weapons, like chemical and biological weapons, are deemed too horrible and inhumane to be used. Prisoners of war are supposed to be given certain protections. I know what you're going to say. None of this ever happens, but you're wrong. Even in war, people try to behave as morally as the situation allows."

As the situation allows. That's just the point. Since the general has a military goal, he is bound to act in the militarily correct ways. He may have moral concerns. I'm not saying all generals are immoral.

"Then what are you saying?"

Only that military reasoning, and military goals, are a separate type of practical reasoning.

"I'm confused. What do you mean by practical reasoning?"

Practical reasoning applies to the real world. As opposed to theoretical reasoning, like math and physics.

"Math and physics apply to the real world."

Of course they do. I didn't mean to imply that they were a waste of time. Let me see, how can I explain this? Math is theoretical in that a mathematician doesn't need to use her experience to do math properly. In fact, math is primarily a discipline of the mind. Physics is also theoretical. I know physicists run experiments and make observations. In that way science is dependent on experience. But one can do theoretical physics. For example, physicists talk about moving objects where friction is not a factor. They know that the real world doesn't happen that way. Or they theorize about subatomic particals that may not exist. Then they look for evidence to confirm or deny their guess.

"I think I see what you mean. Math and physics are applied all the time, but the principles are theoretical, at least at first."

Close enough. Now the same does not apply to morality, or to military and economic reasoning. The aims of these approaches is practical. The moral philosopher aims to discover the good course of action. The military strategist aims to win battles. The economist or business-minded person desires to maximize profits.

"Still, there's lots of theory involved in each of these. All you seem to mean by practical reasoning is when people apply the theories in practice."

Okay, I'll accept that. I didn't mean for us to get bogged down with the distinction between practical and theoretical reasoning anyway. All I want to distinguish is that there are different types of practical reasoning. The military general has goals that are different from the goals of the moral person. And the businessperson has goals different from those of either the moralist or the militarist.

Moral Reasoning Is Overriding.   "The goals are not as separate as you insist. I've already gotten you to admit that generals also consider moral variables. If you're unconvinced, I have another example."

By all means, tell me.

"Say a general can take either of two courses of action. Both alternatives will give him the same military result. Both involve the same losses to his troops. The only difference is that the first strategy involves destroying hospitals that house infants and small children. The second strategy avoids the hospitals, so no innocent infants will be killed."

Oh, I see. You're saying that when all things are equal from a military point of view—

"Right, the general will opt for the strategy that harms fewest innocent people. And I don't think this applies only when all things are militarily equal. I believe generals are more moral than you seem to credit them."

Maybe so. Does this apply to businesspeople, too?

"Certainly. I know we all hear about the businesspeople who trample everyone to make their money. But most businesspeople are moral. Sure, they want to make money. That's what they're there for. But most businesspeople are pretty honest. They don't intentionally make products that will harm their customers. I know you're going to have a cynical reply to this."

No, actually I think you have a good point. I admit that it's easy to fall into the attitude that all businesspeople are greedy, that all doctors are greedy, that all politicians are . . .

"Greedy?"

Actually that wasn't the word that came to mind, but never mind. I agree with your main point. And I think you point out an interesting feature of moral reasoning.

"Which is what?"

Moral objectives override military and business objectives. Moral principles are more important than the principles of the other types of practical reasoning. Your two examples show that. We're actually making headway.

"Yes, I think moral concerns do override the other practical concerns we've discussed. People condemn generals, businesspeople, and politicians if the generals, businesspeople, or politicians act immorally. And people condemn these public figures even when the military or business or political success is gained. Sometimes that condemnation does not happen right away. People seem to get carried away with winning wars and all. But later, when their emotions calm down, people expect a certain level of moral decency."

I find myself forced to agree with you. (See, I can agree with you, and if you're ever right again, I may agree again.)

"So where do we go from here? Are there other formal characteristics of the moral point of view?"

Let's go back to examining the examples of moral principles, or whatever we're calling them. Let's see—from our examples what else is unique about morality? Where should we begin?

THE TEN COMMANDMENTS IS A PERFECT EXAMPLE

"The Ten Commandments and the Golden Rule are perfect examples of morality."

You sound more and more like Smith and Jones. Okay, let's look at the Ten Commandments. To be fair, can we look at the nonreligious rules?

"What do you mean, the 'nonreligious' ones? They're all religious. They are God's commandments."

I didn't mean to offend you. If you look at the table of contents, you'll see that we get to discuss God. For now I'm suggesting we look at the commandments as purely moral rules.

"What makes you think you can distinguish moral and religious rules so easily?"

For your sake, I'll admit that the distinction is artificial. Can't we just look at the commandments that don't refer to God? Don't be so defensive.

"All right. Do not kill, or steal, or bear false witness. Honor your parents. Do not covet your neighbor's donkey or his wife."

My neighbors don't have donkeys!

"Do not covet *anything* of your neighbor's. And you are not allowed to commit adultery with your neighbor's wife."

Is that all? I'm not attracted to my neighbor's wife. By the way, can my neighbor's wife commit adultery with me? Or does the rule go in only one direction?

"The rules apply to everyone. The Ten Commandments is an excellent example of morality. Each commandment is absolute; there are no exceptions. And each commandment stands on its own. Together the Ten Commandments describes the best life. So what do you have to say?"

Which Is Your Favorite Commandment? Which is your favorite commandment?

"You're not allowed to have favorites. They all apply with equal seriousness. No exceptions, so don't look for any."

But I don't know how to apply the rules. For example, if I must either kill or steal, which do I do?

"Killing is the more serious offense."

How can you say that?

"In our society killing is the more grievous crime."

I grant that. But the commandments do not say that! Or, for example, if I am tempted to abide by the wishes of my parents, and they ask me to kill, should I kill?

"When would parents ever ask such an immoral thing of their child? That's ridiculous! You're just making light of the Ten Commandments. You're probably an atheist as well as immoral."

Name calling aside, what if my parents ask me to kill someone? Many parents instill in their children the need to defend the country. That involves killing. What if I do not want to kill in time of war?

"Now you turn out to be a coward as well. It's right to defend one's country. It's self-defense."

Excuse me, but we're getting sidetracked. What if my parents' wishes conflict with one or more of the commandments? Do I honor my parents, or do I break the other rule? Don't you see? It's not the commandments I see as deficient, it's that there are no priority rules.

Priority Rules. "What do you mean by priority rules?"

There are no rules to tell me which commandments are relatively more important than the others. You say they are all absolutes. What I don't understand is how to act when I can't follow two rules, yet both apply. How am I to decide in cases of conflict? For example, imagine a society where the Ten Commandments are fully and completely followed. Imagine that in this society the prohibition on killing is ranked as less significant than the rule to honor one's parents. Maybe stealing is next, then adultery, and so on. Just reverse the order that we put on the Ten Commandments. Wouldn't this society be very different from the one we live in? Could you imagine that "dishonoring" one's parents could be a capital offense!

"And that killing would be no more serious than how we treat dishonoring our parents. I see what you mean. Why can't we place our own priority rules on the Ten Commandments? The priorities are given by common sense anyway."

It takes only common sense to correct the commandments? So your God lacked common sense when he created them? And we are going to fix God's mistake?

"That kind of talk is offensive. No wonder you can't understand morality."

Again, you're getting off track. It's morality we're examining. Since we don't understand morality yet, it's inappropriate to label me either moral or immoral. My personal beliefs, however, have nothing to do with our investigation. You wanted to place priority rules on the Ten Commandments.

"But you insisted on priority rules!"

Excuse me? I asked about the need for priority rules. I don't see the point of morality or the Ten Commandments. It's you who are offering priority rules.

"The reason I offer priority rules is to clean up the commandments."

I think it's a good idea. However, common sense is not going to help you here. The people of my imaginary culture would have very different common-sense ideas about their priorities. Common sense is created by your moral values. The values come first. So you can't justify your values by referring to common sense.

"Explain that."

Imagine our example. Imagine yourself living in a culture like traditional Japan only a couple of centuries ago. There dishonoring one's parents required one to commit ritual suicide. Is that the common sense you have in mind?

"Of course it isn't! What you say is correct, I guess. But if you are correct, can we ever find any morality? Can we find any way of justifying our values?"

Don't give up so easily, my friend. We haven't thrown out the Ten Commandments. Even if we do toss all the commandments, the Ten Commandments is only one set of moral rules. People have been working on developing a firm and unshakeable moral system for quite a long time. Look, you've helped me understand that if moral rules are to be useful, they need to be set in some kind of hierarchy. They need to be given with priorities mapped out. More important rules need to be placed above less important ones. That's a good start. Can I ask another question that's been on my mind?

"Go ahead."

Theories of Action/Theories of Character. To what do the commandments apply?

"To people. What else?"

I'm sorry. We people from the far side of Jupiter are sometimes not very clear. Let me give you an example. Let's look at the Ten Commandments again. How about the one about honoring your parents? What does that mean?

"Everyone knows what that means! Honor your parents. Listen to what they tell you."

Is our interpretation the same as it would be in the Japan of our example? The Japan of the recent past? We just said that there a child was bound to commit ritual suicide if he disgraced his parents. Is that what we mean by honoring our parents?

"That's too strong! All the commandment means is that we have to listen to them and make up our own minds. You may not have to follow their advice, but you should listen."

So we can rephrase the rule: One should tolerate the opinion of one's parents, then do what one wants anyway?

"No! You know what it means! It means *do* what your parents want while you live in their house. Once you're out of their house, you can do what you want."

Ah, so Eddie Haskell, the guy on *Leave It to Beaver,* is the most moral guy around. "Yes, Mrs. Cleaver. My, don't you look nice today. I was just telling young Theodore that committing murder is morally unacceptable." Morality is not how you think or feel, it's what you do?

"Now you're just being intentionally stupid. Of course, morality is not just a question of how one acts. Morality applies to how one lives. Eddie Haskell is not moral; he's acting. For example, a person in a movie or play is not being courageous, he's just acting."

Good distinction. (I knew this distinction was coming. I read the heading at the top of this section.)

"So now we think that morality does not apply to actions alone. Morality applies to character. And whenever there is more than one moral rule, we need to define our priorities."

We're making great progress! What else can we say about morality?

A Religious Anxiety. "I've already given two examples of the moral point of view. The Ten Commandments may not work exactly as I'd hoped. That's why we have the Golden Rule. With the Golden Rule there is no need for priority rules. And before you ask, let me tell you. The Golden Rule applies absolutely, and to all situations, *and* to one's character."

Don't be so defensive. We're only taking a casual look at morality. I sense that there is something underlying your anxiety. Could there be an unconscious idea or implicit premise? Could a cherished belief be threatened?

"There's no secret, if that's what you mean. The reason I'm upset is because God gave us the Ten Commandments and the Golden Rule. If we attack these rules, I'm afraid you will take that as a proof that God does not exist. I think that you don't believe in any values!"

Well, to answer your first worry, I don't see what God or gods have to do with our discussion. After all, if there is a best way to live, why think we need a God or gods to discover it? And to answer the second concern, I do think there is a best way to live. I'm no nihilist! I've already told you. I think living for pleasure is the best way to live.

"You're being evasive. Do you believe in God or don't you?"

Whether or not a God exists is just not important.

"Not important! Of course it's important. Without God, life would be pointless. There would be no meaning in life. People would run wild. They would . . ."

I don't see why you interpret my questions as attacks. Besides, you're beginning to repeat yourself. Your insistence on the need for God sounds like your insistence on the need for morality. Since it is so important to you, later we'll discuss and read about God's contribution to finding the best life. But you have to promise me that we will first discuss our original two questions. I still want to know the point of morality. And I want to hear more about examples of the moral point of view.

"Okay, but don't you see, morality and religion are interconnected. God is the point of morality. God has given us two wonderful examples of moral rules. That's what I have been trying to tell you."

I do not agree that morality depends on gods, either your God or ancient, nearly forgotten gods. But let's take one issue at a time. So far, this discussion has been pretty chaotic. Let's focus on examples of morality. I need to get clearer on the idea of morality.

THE GOLDEN RULE: DO UNTO OTHERS

"The Golden Rule works for me."

I don't know what "works for me" means. That's what we're asking. What does the Golden Rule say?

"The Golden Rule is: 'Do unto others as you would have them do unto you.' That's clear, isn't it?"

I suppose so. Well, actually it's not clear to me. Why would I want to impose my weird wants on someone else?

"That's not what the Golden Rule says. You're playing word games. I certainly do not want to play word games."

The Golden Rule says that if I want something done to me, then I should do it unto others? If I want others to lie to me, or to break their promises, or to be mean to me, I should lie to them, or break promises made to them, or be mean to them. Right?

"That's ridiculous! No one wants someone else to lie to them, or to break promises made to them, or to be mean to them. You're using stupid examples. If you don't want people to lie, or break promises, or be mean to you, you should not lie, or break promises, or be mean to them. That's what the Golden Rule says."

The Golden Rule Inverted: Do Not Do Unto Others. My, it's difficult to keep you "on track." We were discussing the Golden Rule. Now you've given me a new rule.

"No, I haven't."

Sure you have. The new rule you've just stated is: "Do not do unto others as you would not have them do unto you."

"What's the difference? The double negative gives us a positive. The statements are equivalent. Everyone knows that."

Actually, everyone does not know that. There is a guy in Idaho who does not know it. And there is a woman in Mexico City who isn't sure. . . .

"Cut it out. You know it, and that's all that counts."

I do not know it. If I 'do not do unto others,' I am not committed to acting at all. To fulfill this rule, all I need is to refrain from doing anything. A guy in a coma becomes the perfectly moral person. He does not do anything at all. It follows that if he does not do anything at all, he surely does not do anything unto others that he does not want done unto himself. Don't you agree?

"Okay."

The "do not" rule (from which we probably get the word "doughnut"?) asks for nothing more than passivity (which may be why people prefer sitting when they eat their doughnuts). The "do not" rule doesn't ask us to commit ourselves to anything. It requires only that we omit certain unwanted actions. Perhaps it requires that we do not harm each other. I don't know.

"Yes. That's just what it requires. We should never knowingly harm others."

Maybe, but the Golden Rule requires us to be more active and assertive. Do unto others tells us to *do* something. My confusion is I don't understand what it is I am asked to do.

Treat Others As You Want to Be Treated. "I see the distinction. What the Golden Rule tells you is that you should treat others as you want to be treated."

So again, let me ask my question. What if I am not like you? What if my wants are strange to you? Should I impose my wants on others? If I am a racist, I might believe that if I were a member of the "other" race, then I should be treated badly. If I am a consistent racist, I have just justified treating others in ways undesirable to them.

"That's crazy. The Golden Rule doesn't justify that! The racist was just using religion as an excuse for his own prejudices."

I remember hearing a story about a Nazi who believed that if he were a Jew, he would want to be exterminated. So he killed Jews. All the while he believed he was abiding by the Golden Rule.

"That's crazy. The Golden Rule certainly doesn't justify that!"

The interesting part of the story is that there came a time when he found out that he had Jewish blood in his veins. One of his grandparents had been a Jew. He marched into a concentration camp and asked to be put to death. That story is not common, I grant you. But he was not the only fanatic to do something like that. Wasn't he following the Golden Rule? He did unto others just as he would (and did) have done unto himself.

"That's not what the rule means."

Doesn't the Golden Rule assume that our wants are pretty much the same? And that is clearly not true. What does the Golden Rule mean, if it doesn't mean what it says?

Do For Others So They Will Do For You. "No, no. The Golden Rule does not assume we have the same wants. It's more general than that. You should treat people respectfully, with kindness. If you're riding a bus and you see a tired older woman or man standing, you should give up your seat."

Why?

"Because what goes around comes around. Because you're young and probably nearing your stop. Because you would want others to do that for you. If you give up your seat, chances are someone will do the same for you someday."

Sort of an investment? I give up my seat to this older woman, and someday when I'm an older woman, some guy will give me his seat?!

"Not exactly. Obviously, you're getting caught up in the words. The spirit of the Golden Rule is what I'm explaining. Sure, no one is going to keep track of who gives up his seat and who doesn't give it up. But if you give up your seat on the bus, others will see your example. You could be influencing people. As the idea catches on, you could benefit from it."

But I have to give up my seat? Look, in all honesty, I don't see the connection. No one is going to give up a seat for me just because I gave up my seat. As far as setting an example goes, I'd say that is pretty unlikely. I do all sorts of things, and no one has decided to copy my lead. Unfortunate, but true. People do not copy my actions. No one takes me as a role model, though I can't figure out why.

"You should still give up your seat."

I'm not denying that. All I'm saying is that your motives are wrong. If I expect to be rewarded directly, by getting a seat next time I ride the bus, I'm going to be disappointed. If I give up my seat to set an example, then I'm fooling myself. People don't model themselves after me. So I'll just keep my seat. Besides, what you're suggesting sounds like deferred greed.

Treat Others As They Would Have You Treat Them. "I agree with you. You aren't supposed to follow the Golden Rule for a reward on earth. I guess the best way to explain the Golden Rule is to say that you are supposed to treat others as they would have you treat them."

That's not what it says. It does not say, "Do unto others as they would have you do unto them." Even if the Golden Rule were rewritten to say that, our problem would still be there. Why should I do what other people want? What if their wants are weird or strange, or—shall I say it?—immoral? Remember the Nazi who discovered he was Jewish? Should I exterminate him just because he wants me to murder him?

"Of course not. I see what you mean. Still, I think the idea behind the Golden Rule is right. Don't you agree with the sentiment?"

That depends. What is the sentiment behind the Golden Rule?

Treat Others Well: Don't Harm Them.   "I think the Golden Rule means to treat other people well. It means to treat them with kindness and respect, to be nice to them. It means to do what they want when it does not harm them."

So now I have to concern myself with what others want, and whether or not it will harm them? That requires a great deal of calculation on my part. Now I really am confused about how to interpret the Golden Rule.

"What confuses you?"

It first sounded like the Golden Rule meant I should do things to people. Then we interpreted it as saying that I should be passive toward people. Then we thought that I should treat others as I would want to be treated. Pressing on through my confusion, we speculated that the reason for the rule was expediency. I am supposed to do for others so that I could get a reward. Putting aside greed as unacceptable, we decided that the Golden Rule meant that I should treat others as they would want me to treat them. Finally, the Golden Rule means that I should treat others well, or at least not cause them unnecessary harm. Of course I'm confused. To avoid becoming even more muddled, let's put aside interpretation for a while. My real objection to the Golden Rule is more practical. I don't understand how to use it. I don't understand how to apply the Golden Rule.

How Can I Apply the Golden Rule?   "I admit that a rule loses credibility if it is difficult or impossible to apply, but I don't see how this is a problem for the Golden Rule. The beauty of the Golden Rule is that it's easy to apply."

This past summer I was wandering along the street. I came to an ice cream store and decided I wanted an ice cream cone. As I went into the store, I saw a cute little kid. He must have been around three or four years old. He was standing outside the store, staring in. Now I thought to myself, "Self, I'm going to apply the Golden Rule. How do I do that? Let's see. Do unto others. . . . If I were a little kid, and it was a hot day, I would want someone to give me an ice cream cone. If I were a little kid, I would want a chocolate ice cream cone. That's not a weird want." In fact, as I looked at the kid looking into the store, I could see he wanted a cone. So I bought a chocolate ice cream cone for myself and one for him.

"That was the right action. You made the child happy, and you gave yourself a good feeling at the same time. I applaud your action."

Thank you. I admit I did not feel any good feelings, but I was interested in trying out the Golden Rule, at least once in my life.

"Still, you did the right thing. I'll bet the child was delighted. And without realizing it, your action encouraged him to act that way toward others."

I don't know about that. What happened was interesting, though. The little kid took the cone. As he walked down the street, he began eating the ice cream. The next thing I knew, he had fallen, and was shaking violently. He evidently had some sort of allergy to chocolate, or he was diabetic or something. Anyway, he died. So much for the Golden Rule.

"You made that up!"

So what. The point still stands. I did unto another. . . . But did I do what was right? The little kid's parents were none too thrilled with me. (I bet I lost their votes for sainthood.) Or am I wrong? I should do unto others even if it kills them?

"No, of course not. But, you fool, what you incorrectly calculated was what the child really wanted. He did not want to die! You misapplied the Golden Rule."

Just my point. On one level, I applied the rule properly. You even agreed. I gave the kid an ice cream cone because I would have wanted one in similar circumstances. It was even chocolate, just as I would want. On a more "abstract" level, however, I misapplied the Golden Rule. I should have realized that I would not want someone to give me something that would poison me, so I should have given the little tike a different flavor? Or no ice cream at all? Come on. How could I know how to apply the principle?

What the Golden Rule Really Means.   "The Golden Rule is not meant to be taken literally."

Where does it say that?

"Don't interrupt. The Golden Rule is meant to point to a certain attitude of respect for others."

Then why doesn't the rule say, "Respect others"? I can agree to that. We've just written a better rule.

"That's what it means. And we have not written a better rule. The Golden Rule is a commandment from God."

One comment and you've just raised several provocative points. First, the Golden Rule requires that we respect others. Second, the Golden Rule gets its authority, its validity, from God. And third, God gives out Golden Rules to humans. You are asserting quite a lot there. Let's take each issue in order.

The Golden Rule Means We Must Respect Others?   "Okay, I'll go along."

If the Golden Rule requires us to respect others, it should be stated that way. Then we wouldn't have had to go through all of our earlier discussion. But I don't see how this interpretation helps. Eddie Haskell is again elevated to sainthood. He *shows* respect to the point of making everyone want to run from the room.

"I've caught you on this one. We agreed earlier that our theory would be a theory applied to character. It is not merely actions that concern us."

With all the calculation that is necessary to apply the Golden Rule, how can I be expected to incorporate the Golden Rule into my character? How can I be expected to act spontaneously on such a complicated rule? Aren't we back to a theory of action?

"No. Calculation can also become a part of one's character. For example, a mathematician or a scientist calculates. These people see problems and immediately reason them out. It's just part of their point of view on the world. It's part of their character. It can become automatic for them, even second nature. So calculation can become part of someone's character. It's not only actions that we're interested in."

Excellent! Your point is well taken. So respecting others is where it's at. But I don't know what that means. Should I respect people who do not deserve respect? Should I respect others in the ways they find appropriate, or in my own way?

"You should respect others, period."

I thought the Golden Rule is an explanation of how we are to respect others, not just a prescription to respect others. Tell you what. Let's tentatively agree that we ought to respect others, whatever that means. My question is, why? Why should I respect others?

The Golden Rule Gets Its Authority From God.   "What do you mean, why? We should respect others, and follow all of God's other rules, because they are given to us by God. That's why!"

Are the rules of morality prior to the gods, or are the gods prior to morality? Take a look at Plato's dialogue *Euthyphro*. Socrates asks Euthyphro which comes first, the moral laws or the gods' approval of the laws.

"Explain the difference."

Socrates wants to know whether the gods approve of the moral law because it is right, or whether the moral law is right because the gods approve of it. Have I made this obscure?

"Yes, you have. Can you give me an example?"

Certainly. Better yet, you give me an example. Tell me an action that you find morally blameworthy?

"That's easy—it's wrong to kill."

To kill anything? I just killed and ate a stalk of broccoli last night. It was delicious. You aren't going to call me a murderer, are you?

"Don't be so picky. It's wrong to murder. It's morally wrong to kill innocent people. Forget the broccoli. Do you see some problem with the rule that it is wrong to kill innocent people?"

WHICH CAME FIRST, GOOD OR GOD?

I'm not sure why I should agree with that principle, but let's get to our present point. Is killing wrong because it is morally wrong, or is it morally wrong because God says it's wrong?

"What's the difference? God says it's morally wrong and it's morally wrong."

The difference is substantial. If morality stands on its own, we don't need God to support morality. It changes our way of understanding morality.

"I don't follow."

If morality stands on its own, in a sense it's above God. Or better, morality is independent of God and only discovered by God. Would that be acceptable—God discovers morality?

"That might be okay."

Well, if God can discover morality, maybe humans can, too. Morality becomes a part of knowledge, accessible to gods and to people. If you grant that, then we don't need God, at least as far as morality is concerned. Murder would be wrong whether or not God recognized it as wrong.

"Why is that important?"

What If God Asks Us to Murder?   If morality is independent of God, then if God asks us to murder, we can legitimately say no.

"My God would never ask that we murder innocent people."

What if God asked you to kill for him?

"Why would God do that?"

You don't get to ask why. God tells you to kill, to kill someone you love. Would you do it?

"God would never ask that."

God asked that of Abraham. God asked old Abe to kill his kid.

"That was just a test to see if Abraham had faith. God didn't let Abraham kill Isaac. He supplied a ram for sacrifice instead."

Abe couldn't have known that it was only a test. If he had known it was a test, it wouldn't have been a test at all. It would have been easy to pass. Even I could pass that test. "Go kill your son, Art," bellows a deep, resonant voice. "I'm on my way. Gotta get one of those stone knives. Oops, better not tell my wife. It's only a test anyway."

"What's your point?"

Can We Separate the Moral Rules and God?   The point is that your God has asked someone to murder an innocent person. Your resistance to the question itself shows that you believe that murder is wrong, even if God commands it. Let me put it a different way. Suppose God came down and told you, and all of us, that he changed his mind. "Those rules I gave you? Never mind. I've got a new set."

"God wouldn't do that! Besides, how would I know it was God?"

It's your God; I don't know how It identifies Itself. No, wait, I've got it. God comes down, shows His American Express platinum card. Don't leave home without it! It says "GOD" on it. And this God guy says, "Forget the old rules. Do whatever you want." What do you do? And don't try to slip out of the question. God already intervened once, with Abraham and Isaac. He's shown he can change his mind. That's what miracles are about. Your God decides that the standard laws of nature shouldn't apply. God raises the dead, or parts the sea, or lands a guy in the belly of a fish, or turns a woman to salt.

"I don't know how to answer."

Would you want people to continue on the moral path?

"Yes, of course."

Then that is what we need to look at. Forget God. We don't need to discuss God in relation to morality. We've just discovered that morality is independent of God. Morality can be known without God. After all, surely you do not want to say that only people who believe in your God are moral people. There are people all over the world who live moral lives. Hindus, Buddhists, Shintoists, Moslems, even a few atheists. They don't believe in your God.

"You've made your point. At least, I'll think about it more. You seem to be right, but I'm not sure why I feel uncomfortable with the conclusion."

Comfort is hardly an appropriate criterion for truth. But I'm willing to leave this part of the discussion. We can return to it when you're ready. The reason you feel uncomfortable is because you still want there to be a God. We'll pick up on this theme in the next chapter. Until then, let's assume that morality is not necessarily bound to God.

"Okay, but you promise to get back to a discussion of God and religion."

By now you should know. All you have to do is check the table of contents. What was our next example of the moral point of view?

CONSCIENCE AND INTUITION

"Conscience and intuition were next. We all know that it is wrong to hurt other people. That's what the Ten Commandments and the Golden Rule are all about. The way we know this is by our conscience."

Conscience?

"Conscience allows all people to know about morality. Their religious training and beliefs sharpen their consciences. Believing in religion improves their understanding of morality. But everyone on earth has a conscience. Everyone except you, of course."

You mean I'm the only one without a clear idea of what morality is? The rest of you know what morality is and you follow it? What a shame.

"I don't appreciate your sarcasm. Everyone knows that killing is wrong. Stealing and lying are wrong. Even if you don't know it, others know."

You're right, I don't know. And not everyone else knows, either. At least lots of people act as if they don't know that it's wrong to kill or to steal or to lie. In times of war, entire countries seem to forget these "obvious" rules. What happens, just a massive outbreak of amnesia? Oops, we forgot, killing and stealing and lying are wrong?

"Times of war, times of self-defense are different. The rules have to be understood within their proper context. Killing is wrong, but people have a right to protect their lives and their property."

So the moral rules apply only when they are convenient? Did the Ten Commandments have a footnote that I missed?

"You have to be realistic. Common sense tells you that you can't expect people to just stand there and let their country be overrun. People have to be able to defend themselves. They have to be able to arm themselves for defense."

In cases of war, people do not lose their consciences, they are just forgetting to listen to them?

"Not exactly. It's wrong to kill innocent people. Aggressors are not innocent. Even when it comes to aggressive people, there are rules in war."

Cruelty and the Absurdity of Morality.   Okay, I see. Of course, usually each side is aggressive, though neither sees itself this way. Just how strong is conscience?

"That is a problem. Some people follow their consciences better than others. That doesn't diminish the fact that consciences tell people the difference between right and wrong."

Why Do People Disagree About Values?   Good point. But if conscience tells us the difference between right and wrong, why do people disagree about values?

"You mean moral questions like business ethics, or abortion, or suicide and mercy killing?"

Actually, I didn't have those in mind, but they are excellent examples. I had something cruder in mind. Some people think it is okay to kill healthy, unarmed civilians.

"You mean like when we bomb cities in time of war?"

Okay, but I can make the example even cruder. In "peacetime" people have been known to brutalize their own countrymen. Remember our example about the Nazi who worked all day putting victims to death? There was no war going on. The victims posed no threat. The Nazis worked their shift, then went home to their families. Can you imagine that? "So how was your day, Daddy?" "Fine, my little one. There were a few of those darn folks who resisted, but I got them into the ovens."

"You have the most disgusting examples."

True, it's a gift. The point is that this example is not isolated. People are cruel to other people. Corporate executives put workers and consumers at risk. That's one way to get higher profits. Are their consciences defective? Do their consciences give them the wrong values? Or do we have to admit that consciences are unreliable? Keep in mind, these people think they are doing the right thing. No doubt, there are people acting in cruel ways right now. What does this say for your conscience theory?

"Different intuitions about right and wrong do weaken the idea of universal conscience. And the evidence of cruelty is difficult to deny. I guess I'd just have to say that these people know they are doing wrong. They are just deceiving themselves and others."

That may be, my friend. But then there isn't much left of your conscience theory.

"Why do you say that?"

If conscience is so easily overturned, or if intuitions can vary so widely, what good is the theory for defining right and wrong? Or even worse, if we are so susceptible to being self-deceptive, how do we know when we are following the right and avoiding the wrong?

Conscience Is a Reflection of Society's Values.   "Still, there is something true about conscience. I know I have one and I follow it as best I can. Art, you've been pretty quiet. What do you have to say about conscience? It's easy for you just to ask questions and attack my views. I'd like to hear what you have to say."

As you can tell from the heading, I think conscience is just a reflection of society's values. We learn our values within our society. We learn them when we are children. Values are internalized like so many other things we learn as children. Think about it. The language you speak you learn as a child. If you learn a certain grammar, your "language conscience" tells you which "rules" to follow. Ain't I learnin' ya good?

"So if different societies have different values, they create different consciences?"

I think so.

"Do you have any other objections to conscience?"

Almost No One Knows Why It's Wrong to Kill.   My objection to conscience is that it doesn't explain how or why an action or motive is wrong. Let me ask you, what's wrong with killing babies?

"You've got to be kidding. Why would anyone want to do something that horrible?"

I don't know. Maybe as an artistic expression. No, forget that. That would be for some reason. Is it wrong to kill babies just to kill them? Not for religious reasons, not for preservation of the mother or of society. Tell me what's wrong with it?

"Oh, I get it. You're trying to trick me into making some statement about babies. Then you'll apply it to fetuses and the abortion issue."

That would be devious and manipulative and clever. Had I thought of it, I would have done it. But it's not my idea. If you can't say what's so terrible about killing innocent babies, then why shouldn't people be allowed to do it?

"How would you like to be killed?"

I'm not a baby.

"When does it become wrong to kill a baby? If it's okay to kill babies, where does it stop?"

You don't know what's wrong with killing babies, do you? Don't be ashamed, almost no one knows. Everyone knows *that* it is wrong, but not *why* it's wrong.

"This is too much. How can you advocate killing innocent babies?"

Have you seen what they do in their diapers? Innocent, indeed! But I am not advocating anything. I am asking a question. To be honest, I don't think this is a question that comes up in real life. Very few people are ever seriously tempted to kill babies. I picked this extreme example thinking if we could make headway on one moral value, the others might become easier to handle.

"But why such a strange example?"

Strange? The technique of taking extremes is not so unusual. In science, there is talk about vacuums and of the movement of rolling objects where friction is neglected. All this is to help get an understanding of basic principles and laws.

"But that's different. Neglecting friction is not the same as killing babies."

Duh, it isn't? Of course it isn't. But the technique of reasoning is the same. By the way, don't minimize friction. If you take a 50-mile bicycle ride and return to your original starting point, all you have done is overcome friction. I'll bet you'll be pretty tired.

"I'm not sure I can say why killing babies is wrong. It just is wrong. Maybe our other examples of morality can help. We should look to see if these help explain why killing babies is wrong."

OTHER EXAMPLES OF MORALITY

What else did we say we would talk about?

"Let's see, we thought of several other ways of approaching morality. We said there are social and natural roles."

And the greatest good for the most people might indicate what is right to do.

"I suggested that there is a contract between each person and society. The law is kind of a contract among members of society. The law is based on morality."

Yes, and you also suggested that morality might be based on something like our genuine, natural, or spiritual needs.

"Right, and then there is a question about moral absolutes. Are moral values absolute, or are they different for different people and different societies? I think that about covers it."

Don't forget egoism, my favorite.

"And egoism. Why don't we start with that one and get it out of the way?"

LET'S FINISH THIS CHAPTER WITH EGOISM

You read my every thought! Okay, let's finish this discussion with egoism. We can take up the other examples later.

"So what do you mean by egoism?"

All I mean by egoism is, well, ego is the self. Egoism is a kind of self-ism.

"You mean selfishness?"

Not exactly. My principle is that I should always act in my own self-interest. If doing something benefits me, then I have a reason to do it. I don't see why I should bother to be moral.

"That's selfish! What about everyone else?"

Of course! That's a great suggestion. Everyone should act in my self-interest. If some act benefits me, then it ought to be done. I and everyone else ought to do it, if (and only if) it benefits me. Thanks for the revision.

Individual Ethical Egoism. "That's a challenge to morality! Surely not everyone is going to follow that rule! But that isn't what I mean. What I mean is, are you willing to have everyone act on your principle, 'I ought always to act in my own self-interest. If doing some act benefits me, then I have a reason to do it'?"

You mean you're requiring everyone to be selfish and egocentric. What kind of person are you?

"Ah, so you're not willing to make your individual egoism apply to everyone! That's just what I thought. You are not willing to have everyone act entirely as you suggest. If you can't want everyone to do it, then what makes you so special? If your principle is not open to everyone, then it isn't a moral principle."

If everyone acted selfishly, then I'd be a fool not to act that way. Why should I be the only one not acting selfishly? But to answer your more serious question, no, I don't want to have everyone act exclusively for his or her own benefit. I want everyone to act for my benefit. Why? Because I'm me, not them. Simple.

"That will never happen. People aren't so foolish. You may go about acting immorally. That's up to you. But while you are acting like an egoist, the rest of us are going to be moral."

That's not as perfect as everyone acting for my benefit, but it's almost as good. You should all be good, boring, moral people, and I'll act for my own benefit.

Free-Rider Egoism. "Now you're taking a free ride, and I object to that. It isn't fair for one person to take advantage of everyone else. That's not what morality is about."

There you go, assuming what you need to prove.

"What do you mean?"

You're assuming that morality is correct. That's why you object to my free ride.

"I object because the only legitimate principle of action is one where everyone can follow it."

Just my point. You are assuming what you need to prove.

"You are not some special creature who should be given more than anyone else."

Universal Egoism. Okay, so everyone ought to pursue his or her own benefit.

"What you suggest, Art, will cause people to separate. Each person will be off chasing his or her own goals and benefit. Then what? No, this will end badly. This is not morality at all."

But it was your suggestion that we make universal the egoist principle. Are you changing your mind? If so, fine. I'm willing to have all of you be moral people, and I alone will pursue my benefit. Unless, of course, you all want to contribute to my self-interest.

"Forget it. I reject the free ride, and individual egoism, and even universal egoism. But I have a question for you. By self-interest, do you mean momentary pleasures, or long-term benefits, or enlightened interests?"

Yes.

"Which?"

I guess I hadn't thought about this.

"There is a trap laid with each option, Art. If you go for momentary pleasure, you may be sacrificing a greater pleasure later. If you pursue long-term benefits, you become too distracted to appreciate the present."

I'm really not sure what you mean by "enlightened" interests. But look, I'm getting tired. Why don't we wrap up this discussion and pursue the loose ends in our next conversations? For example, when we discuss *The Stranger,* we can get into the strengths and shortcomings of living for short-term sensual pleasures. The idea of enlightened self-interest will no doubt come up in several contexts.

SO WHAT HAVE WE LEARNED? FORMAL FEATURES OF MORALITY

"So what have we learned?"

Absolutely nothing. No, no, I'm kidding. We have learned a few things. In looking at examples of the moral point of view, we have found a number of desirable features to any moral theory. The moral point of view is different from other approaches to living. We've learned that any set of principles that we are going to live by, and call morality, must have special features. For example, with the Golden Rule we found that a principle should be able to be easily and clearly applied. We agreed that a rule should be as comprehensive as possible. It should apply to as many "moral decisions" as possible. That's one of the strengths of the Golden Rule. With the Big Ten (Ten Commandments), we found that any set of laws must have rules for ordering them, priority rules. Otherwise we don't know what to do in cases of conflicting laws. Oh yes, and we're talking about a way of life, not just rules of behavior. The person is supposed to *be* moral, not just act that way.

"Yes, we have also sorted out formal features that are required before a point of view is properly called morality. I just realized that I have been assuming several of these formal features. When I object to your selfishness and egoism, I am really demanding that moral guidelines be universal, that they apply to everyone equally. You can't just leave blanks in a moral rule and then write in your name. You can't expect that everyone is going to follow that sort of rule. That wouldn't be impartial enough."

So impartiality is a necessary feature of a moral rule. The rules or principles have to be stated in general terms?

"Right. And they must be open to everyone in another sense. Your egoism bothers me because you can't make it public."

What do you mean?

"You can't state your principles without automatically defeating them. That's not true of moral principles. If I want people to be honest, and not steal or kill or lie or commit adultery . . ."

This sounds familiar.

"Don't interrupt. If I don't want people to do these things, I can and should tell everyone. I can make my moral values public. The more successful I am, the more they will be followed."

I'm quivering with excitement.

"Admitting your point of view lets people guard against you."

Military strategy and business strategy are in the same position.

"That's one way they differ from morality. Finally, moral principles should be considered more important than all other types of rules. That's what makes them so important. That's what gives meaning to a person's life. The moral principles we live by are the most important rules. No matter how strongly someone is tempted by economic gain or military victory, moral considerations come first. Over profit, over other goals, certainly over pleasures. We are all equals when it comes to morality. That's a good definition. The moral point of view is: Each of us is one among many equals. That applies to everyone."

■

SUMMARY OF DISCUSSION

In an effort to discover what makes a point of view a moral point of view, we look to possible examples of morality. People use several methods to judge their actions. Conscience, social roles, and legal restrictions direct people's decisions. What creates the greatest good for the greatest number has an affect on our decisions. There is an unwritten contract that people recognize in society; this contract promises rights and protections as long as each of us abides by it. Two prominent examples of the moral point of view are the Ten Commandments and the Golden Rule.

We can abstract from these examples some of the features that help us identify moral principles. Moral reasons have priority over other kinds of reasons, such as economic reasons, military reasons, and business reasons. Like any other set of reasons, morality requires priorities set out for us. In cases of conflict, then, which commandment should I follow?

The Golden Rule promises to reveal the defining moral insight. The Rule itself, however, is open to interpretation and is too vague for us to apply with confidence. Implicit in the Ten Commandments and the Golden Rule is the Judeo-Christian assumption of the existence of a God. God upholds the principles and gives us confidence in their worth. However, good is independent of gods, and we are again left to discover a source of confidence in our values.

Some people think that the fundamental moral insight is gained through intuition or conscience. There are difficulties with these approaches. All types of cruelties and indignities have been heaped on people and "justified" by intuition and conscience. The fact that we cannot easily agree on the moral insight suggests there is no uniform moral intuition. Conscience is merely a reflection of society's values. Why do I say this? Because almost no one knows why it's wrong to violate any particular moral rule.

Egoism mounts a compelling challenge to the moral life. Why shouldn't I take a free ride in society? Why shouldn't I take advantage of other people? The point of asking these questions is that each of us is tempted to think of our own desires first. The moral life must motivate us to be moral.

■
DISCUSSION HIGHLIGHTS

I. Examples of morality
1. The Golden Rule
2. The Ten Commandments
3. Inverse of the Golden Rule
4. Conscience
5. Social and natural roles
6. The greatest good for the greatest number
7. Social contract
8. Fulfillment of real or spiritual needs
9. Traditional rules
10. Absolutes
II. Formal features of morality. Moral reasons must
1. be overriding of other types of reasons
2. be universally applicable
3. be general
4. be impartial
5. be public
6. view each person as one among many equals
7. be comprehensive, ordered, and relatively easily applied

■
QUESTIONS FOR THOUGHT/PAPER TOPICS

1. Which versions of the moral point of view do you think best capture the essence of morality? Can you defend this perspective?

2. Do you think everyone has a conscience? Except for a psychopath, can you imagine anyone without a conscience? Here's one! See if you can find any evidence that either Jesus, Moses, or Gautama (Buddha) had a conscience.

3. If you believe we have a social contract between members of our society, how binding is the contract? What should each member of society be willing to give up to maintain the health of the society? If a person is wrongly convicted of a crime, should that person be willing to accept punishment for a crime he or she did not commit?

4. Can you interpret the Golden Rule and make sense of it? How much do you have to stretch the literal meaning to accomplish a sensible principle?

5. Which is your favorite commandment? Why? Do you have any right to have your opinion?

6. Egoism must be appealing. What's stopping you from adopting the egoistic attitude? (Careful, don't tell everyone; that would ruin your position.)

7. Which strikes you as more important, actions or character? Give reasons for your answer. (How well do you know Eddie Haskell?)

■
_____

FOR FURTHER READING

One unique story that depicts a moral character is Robert Bolt's play *A Man for All Seasons*, also made into an impressive movie. Many rules and principles incorporate the moral point of view; look at the Ten Commandments and the Golden Rule for tight packages. A contemporary source that discusses the defining features of morality is John Rawls's *A Theory of Justice* (Harvard, 1971). Two parts of Rawls's discussion are particularly appropriate: "Some Remarks about Moral Theory" (chap. 1, #9) and "The Formal Constraints of the Concept of Right" (chap. 3, #23).

One pointed critique of the moral point of view is Friedrich Nietzsche's *On the Genealogy of Morals* (Vintage, 1989). Come to think of it, Nietzsche's book *Twilight of the Idols* (Penguin, 1968) is also a hard-hitting attack on moral living. It's worth reading, too.

C H A P T E R

THREE

What About Belief in God?

"**M**oral and religious rules should be followed because they are God's will. It's all a matter of faith. We are supposed to follow God's rules. These reveal God's plan for us on earth. Besides, it is our duty to follow God's will. That's what gives morality a purpose. That's the point of morality. That's what it means for morality to work. Now do you agree?"

No, I don't agree. Why do you think there is a God?

GOD DOES EXIST

"There just is a God. God exists!"

How do you know?

"I believe for lots of reasons. I believe because the belief in God has a long history, nearly four thousand years. I believe because the universe must have had a beginning. Even your scientists can't explain what caused the 'Big Bang.' I believe in God because without Him the world would be chaotic. I believe in God because the world is an orderly place. I don't mean socially and politically orderly; evil people keep the world from being orderly in that way. But the entire universe is organized. If the earth were tilted just two degrees farther away from the sun, plant life on the planet could not survive. Do you want more reasons?"

Sure, if you've got more.

"I believe in God because without Him life would be meaningless. Everything speaks for God, and nothing against Him. I believe in God. Can you show me that there is no God? I certainly doubt it."

Wow! Ask a simple question and get a flood for an answer. And what emotion! I had no idea there were so many reasons for God to exist. You'd think with all these reasons that It must exist.

"God does exist. I've just given you the reasoning that leads to the belief in God."

Let's look at each reason.

THE MAJORITY BELIEVES IN GOD

"Belief in God is important to me, and to most people."

There I have to correct you. Most people do not believe in your God. China and India are sizeable countries, and they do not believe in the Judeo-Christian God. Even if most people did agree with you, that would not make God exist. Truth isn't democratic. And belief in something doesn't cause the thing to exist. Right? Even if everyone believed in Santa Claus, he would not exist. Have I offended you? You did know that Santa Claus is mythical, didn't you?

"My, you're an arrogant one. If most people believe in God, you don't think that means something?"

Of course, it *means* something, though what it means isn't clear to me. My point is simpler. Your ancestors and mine probably believed that the earth was flat. They thought it was shaped like a pancake. That was the common belief only a few centuries ago. Except for a few "crazies," the vast majority of Europeans believed that the earth was flat. Did that make the earth flat?

"Of course not. But that's different. The earth is a concrete thing. God isn't that sort of thing."

Still, everyone or nearly everyone believed the earth was flat. That did not make the earth flat. And then people began to speculate, and in increasing numbers they believed that the earth was more of a globe. Did the earth become more and more globelike with their changing views? Or did the shape of the earth change suddenly when 50 percent plus one person finally believed?

"No, the earth's shape doesn't depend on people's beliefs. That's certain. But like I said, God's existence is different."

Different? Does God's existence depend on people's beliefs? Just for a moment, imagine if reality depended on human beliefs. Imagine what life would have been like. Fifty percent of the people believe the earth is flat. The other half believe it is a sphere. Then, in 1412, along comes a guy named Wally. He's the kind who can never make up his mind. He believes the earth is flat, then a sphere, then flat. . . . The changing shape would make bicycle riding hazardous.

"You've made your point. Truth is not a matter of agreement. By the way, there were no bicycles in the fifteenth century." (Ah, you're finally getting a sense of humor.)

Actually, truth probably is a matter of agreement. I really don't know. I was not speaking to the question of truth. I am more concerned with what's real than with what's true. By the way, it's too bad those people didn't have bicycles. They're really fun to ride, especially whenever Wally believes that the earth is flat.

BELIEF IN GOD HAS
A LONG TRADITION

"I keep telling you, but you keep ignoring me."

Did you say something?

"God is not a concrete thing. Your argument works well enough on a concrete thing like the earth or a table. But it does not work on God. God is different."

Very well. Let's look into your other reasons for God's existence. If we have to, we can come back to the point that God's reality is not the same as the earth's reality. By the way—

"I already know your odd sense of humor. The earth is not concrete; it is grass and trees and lava and rocks, etc. Right?"

Very promising. One reason you gave for belief in God is because there is a long tradition of belief.

"That's right. Monotheism goes back to the time of Abraham, Isaac, Jacob, and Joseph. For thousands of years people have dedicated their lives to that belief. And listen, before we go on, I want to tell you something. I have noticed how you refer to God as 'It.' I resent that. You could show more respect for our beliefs, you know."

Fair enough. Though I'm not comfortable calling an idea Him, I'll try to remember to keep your God's name from being used in vain. As far as your assertion that the belief in your God goes back to perhaps 2000 B.C.E., I do not see how this has any bearing on our discussion.

"It shows that people have believed for a long time. Could they all have been wrong?"

Sure, they all could have been mistaken. What we are trying to establish is whether or not they were mistaken. Just because a belief is old, it does not follow that it is true. We accept very little of the other old beliefs that Abraham and friends shared. We do not accept their physics, or chemistry, or belief in actual human sacrifice. Do we?

"But those are not the beliefs we are examining. We are asking about their belief in God. I am saying that this one belief is true."

Very well. But then we are going to have to use a different standard of truth. Truth is not established by age any more than it is established by majority vote. Given your point of view, you should be a Shintoist.

"What is a Shintoist?"

Shintoism is one of the dominant religions of Japan. Its roots go far back into the prehistory of Japan. If age makes a belief true, Shintoism may be just what you are looking for.

"Look, you've misunderstood. It is not all old beliefs, only the belief in God that I'm urging you to accept."

Then we can abandon your earlier claim. Tradition itself does not validate a belief. Old beliefs are not necessarily true beliefs.

THE UNIVERSE HAD TO HAVE A BEGINNING

"That may be true, but the universe had to have a beginning. Even your 'Big Bang' theorists can't answer *how* the universe came into being. God is the only plausible answer."

You're going too fast for me! Why do you think the universe had to have a beginning?

"Everything has to have a beginning. That's just the way things are. No one would disagree with that! Or do you have a problem understanding a claim as simple and as obvious as that?"

Duh. Perhaps you're right, I don't know. Let me ask a couple of questions first. Does the universe have an end? Can you imagine a time when the universe will not exist? Or do you think that the universe will go on for eternity?

"I'm not sure which way to answer. I guess it could end, but I think the universe will go on existing for eternity. If that's God's will."

Wills aside, your principle is that all things have a beginning. All things may not have an end. Right?

"Right. I guess so."

You do have a point. When I look around, everything I see seems to have a beginning. Or so I think. I mean, I've never seen a mountain or an ocean begin, but I suppose they do. There is evidence for that.

"Yes, that's my point."

But when I look around, I also see that everything has an end. Your hypothesis is only that everything has a beginning. That's odd.

"What's so odd about that?"

The way you came to the belief that all things must have a beginning was from your observations. But when you also observe that all things have an end, you do not carry through. You do not speculate that all things end. That's what's odd.

"Well, I'm not sure what to say to that, but I still believe that all things have a beginning. Including the universe. And God created the universe. He created it out of nothing."

Glory be! (I would have written "hallelujah!" but I don't know how to spell it.) And what or who created God? And please, don't say Mr. and Ms. God. And their parents, and their parents. . . .

"God is, was, and always shall be. God has no beginning and no end."

That's neat, but it doesn't work. You claim that everything must have a beginning. Then God must have a beginning.

"Everything does have a beginning, everything but God!"

If you can say that, then why not say that everything has a beginning but the entire universe? Don't you see, you haven't made any headway. By thine own claims hast thou entangled thyself.

"Stop mocking religion."

I assure you, I am not mocking religion, at least not right now. I'm mocking you, but only a little. Look, as far as I am concerned, everything does not have to have a beginning or an end. Experience tells us that *within* the universe everything has a beginning. It doesn't follow that the universe itself must have a beginning. As far as ends go, I haven't died yet. And I'm not sure that I will. Frankly, I haven't decided yet. So the only conclusion we can safely make is that the universe or God may be without beginning.

"So you agree with me!"

Not at all. All I am saying is that your idea goes no further in proving God's existence than in proving its nonexistence. Translation? It proves neither. Your original principle that everything must have a beginning is mistaken.

THE UNIVERSE IS ORDERED BY GOD

"Now you're talking gibberish, Art. Even if the universe didn't have to have a beginning, you certainly cannot deny that it is orderly. Who do you suppose ordered the universe? It couldn't have been chance! It had to be God."

Orderly? You call this orderly?

"Not society. Society may not be orderly. That's our fault. God gives humans free will. It's up to us to use it wisely."

I don't believe there is any free will. And I don't mean that society is disorderly. It is, I guess. What I mean is that the universe is disorderly. And becoming more disorderly every moment. At least that's what physicists tell us. The Second Law of Thermodynamics—they call it entropy.

"That doesn't make sense. There is order everywhere you look. Day follows night. The seasons are orderly. The stars in the sky are orderly. Little electrons race around the atom's nucleus in orderly fashion. Oaks spring from acorns. And so on. The universe is like an immense, finely tuned watch mechanism."

One of those electronic digital jobs? Or the old windup?

"You know what I mean."

Our Minds Impose Order on Nature. I certainly do not want to deny that there is an apparent order in the universe. But I wonder if it is no more than apparent. Maybe it has more to do with our minds than with the natural environment.

"This is the craziest thing you've suggested so far. Do you deny that there is an order to the seasons?"

Well, no—and yes. Actually, I do deny it. For example, have you ever experienced a "summer" day in late winter? I presently live in the northeast. Occasionally we see winter day temperatures reach 70 degrees. Pretty summerlike! I lived in North Dakota for a year. There the temperatures went from 50 degrees to −25 degrees in a week's time. A rather sudden autumn?

"What's your point?"

I think we often experience winter as winter because that's what we expect to experience. Each day's temperature is taken in the context of the proper— that is, the expected—season. So we talk about unusually warm winter days and cool summer days. Spring and fall are hopelessly confusing.

"And I suppose oaks do not spring from acorns? This is ridiculous."

I don't deny some apparent uniformity in nature. I am simply saying that the universe may not be as regular as we experience it to be.

"I'm not going to let you get by with this one. Do you have any reason to believe this? Or are you merely speculating? Is this just more of your 'it could be' stuff?"

I have two responses. First, who made you the author of this book? I'm supposed to be the one who asks the difficult questions. That's the power of authorship. I can rig the discussion any way I want.

"Not this time. You have to answer the question. Do you have any evidence to support your contention that our minds impose order on a disorderly universe?"

Your ability to argue is improving. (I am desperately hoping that the editor of this book removes your more telling arguments.)

"Well, I'm waiting."

An Experiment With Fire.   Okay. Here's an experiment you can try. Tonight go into your room. Light a candle and turn on some music. Now turn out the lights, except for the candle. Sit in front of it and concentrate on the flame's movement.

"Is this some kind of sixties hippie ritual? Are you going to advocate drug use, too?"

Now look who is mocking whom! (Nice grammar, huh? I hope you're learnin' good from my example.) I am not a throwback to the sixties. And I do not advocate drug use. I do not use drugs. More to the point, oh ye of many repressions, drug use would throw off my experiment.

"Okay. So I concentrate on the flame. Now what?"

What you will find is that the flame dances to the music.

"No way."

It does. The flame will begin to dance to the music. Slowly at first. As your concentration gets better, the dancing will quickly occur. The flame's motion will conform to the rhythm of the music.

"The movement of air caused by the speakers is what causes the flame to move."

That's plausible. So try this. Put on your headphones. That way, no air vibrations will reach the flame. Unless, of course, your candles also wear headphones.

"Still, there may be movement we cannot detect."

Fair enough. Ask some friends to join you. Smith and Jones are likely candidates. Tell each one to concentrate on the flame. Same dance to the same song? Of course. Now have each person put on his or her headphones. Have them play different styles of music. Each person will see the flame dance to the beat of his or her music.

"Even though each is listening to different rhythms?"

Exactamundo. That shows that at least some of the order we see in nature is imposed by us.

"This sounds pretty farfetched. Even if it works, there may be a cause we are overlooking."

An Experiment With Children.   I read once that people used to think that children were just small adults. They believed that kids were just as responsible for their actions as adults. That's probably what allowed them to put kids to work in factories and in mines. Not that I oppose abusing children in the name of profit.

"When was this belief around?"

For some people it is probably current today. But the period I heard about was in Europe in the early part of the seventeenth century.

"Why are you telling me this? Where is this going?"

As it turns out, the microscope was invented, or at least came into use, in Holland at about this time. For the first time scientists looked at fertilized human embryos. And guess what they saw?

"Fertilized human embryos. What else?"

They saw little people, completely formed and dressed.

"No way."

It's true. Little bearded men with walking sticks. Little women with aprons. Sounds culturally determined to me! And no, I do not know how they explained how babies are born without clothes.

"These people were obviously demented."

Not at all. They saw what they were looking for. In every other respect they were good scientists, just trapped in their way of thinking. Just as we are, at least until we realize that we are trapped. Do you want another example?

"No, your examples are weird enough. Let me think about this."

EXPERIENCE IS COLORED BY BELIEFS

Experience is colored by beliefs. That's all I am saying. When you see something, you see with the beliefs and concepts and expectations that you carry with you. When people are hungry enough, things start looking like food. When we are thirsty enough, things start looking like water.

"So you are talking about mirages on the desert?"

Good example. I hadn't thought of that.

"But mirages happen in cases of extreme thirst."

Near-Death Experiences.   True, but the extreme shows us a lot about the "normal." Did you ever hear about "near-death" experiences?

"Interesting that *you* should bring that up. I was going to use that as further proof of God's existence."

Beat you to it! What happens in near-death experiences?

"The person dies and has the experience of a long dark tunnel. At the end of the tunnel is a bright light. If the person goes into the tunnel, she hears

Jesus calling in a soothing voice. Some people have gone far enough into the tunnel to actually see Him."

Right, and how do we explain such experiences?

"I believe that this is further proof that God loves us."

Of course you do. But do you really think that is what it *proves?* Aren't you wishing it proves that?

"What do you mean?"

Do you really think that people from other cultures experience what Christians experience?

"I never thought of that. I think they have 'near-death' experiences. Why wouldn't they?"

They do have similar experiences. After all, we humans are physiologically similar enough to expect that. But do you really think that a good Hindu or Buddhist (or Jew or Moslem, for that matter) sees Jesus at the end of the tunnel? Don't you think the Christian's interpretation is slanted?

"Slanted? Maybe. But maybe what it shows is that God loves all of his creatures and reveals Himself in the form of His son, Jesus. God may choose the time of death to reveal Himself to us, no matter what religion we grew up believing."

Na na, my religion's better than your religion! Is that what you're saying? Don't answer. I'm not sure I can deal with such multicultural awareness and sensitivity right now.

"You don't have to resort to sarcasm. I didn't mean to sound so biased. But what is wrong with my interpretation?"

Plenty. Here's the difficulty that's relevant to what we are discussing. How would a good Buddhist or Hindu recognize your God? These people may have never heard of your Jesus. He's not such a significant person worldwide. How would they know it was Him?

"Their descriptions would sound like descriptions of Jesus."

Right. We have this videotape from the year C.E. 30. There's Jesus and his buddies, the dirty dozen.

"There you go, mocking religion again!"

I didn't mean any harm. Look, Jesus had how many apostles? Twelve, a dozen. And as far as I know there is no mention of taking showers. Hence, a dirty dozen. But I withdraw my offensive language. I'm sorry.

"Thank you."

Where is the tape of Jesus and the dirty dozen? Do we have any accurate picture of them? Without an accurate i.d., how can we say who is at the end of the tunnel? It could be Buddha, or Moses, or Siva, or Vishnu, or Uncle Charlie. Or it could be tied to the "dying" person's wants and beliefs and fears.

"What do you mean?"

It's pretty clear, isn't it? Here we have a person going through some pretty unusual and serious physiological changes. The guy is "dying." I don't know much about the chemistry of the brain, but I can imagine some powerful chemicals being released. The person sees a light at the end of a tunnel. Hallucination caused by the release of drugs natural to the brain during trauma could do that. Just being choked on the sides of the throat causes people to see tunnels with lights at the end.

"No way!"

Sure, it's true. If the oxygen to your brain is cut off, you will experience a narrowing of your visual field. Blackness starts at the periphery and closes in. What you can see becomes brighter. Finally, you will hear a tingling in your ears. It sounds like music, but the beat is usually off, so on a scale of 1 to 100, I never give it more than a 42.

"That doesn't account for Jesus calling from heaven."

No, the calling is part of the person's wish to be comforted. The calling from the particular deity is a result of one's training.

There Are Atheists in Foxholes, and Buddhists and Hindus, Too. "Maybe, but you'll never find an atheist in a foxhole."

Clichés aside, sometimes you will. I was very ill once. (This sad story is truly true.) I had a ruptured appendix. Thinking it was the flu and being reluctant to seek medical care, I waited three days.

"That's pretty serious."

By the time I got to the hospital for treatment, my temperature was at a life-threatening 106.8 degrees. They were frying eggs on my chest. (That may be an exaggeration.)

"What happened?"

They packed me in ice, brought down my temperature, and operated.

"So you were okay. You were not close enough to death to have a 'near-death' experience."

I grant that. But I was told that I would probably not survive the surgery. (I assured the surgeon that my health insurance would still pay. He was relieved.) Lying there, believing I was going to die, I thought of a number of things. Your God and religion were not among them. So, you see, some foxholes do have atheists in them.

"Maybe so, but then you're the exception."

There are lots of examples of similar experiences. People from nonbelieving heritages are not going to pray to gods. They wouldn't think of doing that any more than you believers would think of praying to gods of other traditions. So there are atheists in foxholes, and Buddhists and Hindus and Christians and Jews, too!

ATHEIST OR BELIEVER, IT JUST DOESN'T MATTER

"But atheists aren't any more sincere or honest than believers."

I grant that, too. Look, most of the atheists I know are only atheists in that they do not believe in God. It's an intellectual thing with them. Most people I know say they believe in God, but it's just a belief. They don't know. It's the same with atheists. People are just too lazy and too intellectual about their beliefs. Besides, it doesn't matter.

"Doesn't matter!"

Of course not. The only reason we give people religion and a belief in gods is to keep them controlled. This even applies to atheists.

"How could that be?"

Atheists are people who look at religion and think, "How could there be a god? Maybe there isn't one." Not finding sufficient evidence or reason to believe, they say, "There isn't one." That's all. They just don't believe in God.

"That's all!"

Sure. But the brilliant thing about religion is that it doesn't matter. Religion still keeps control. It's difficult enough for people raised in our culture to break with their parents and peers. Everything you learn as a kid insists that there is a God. Parents, teachers, many public buildings, even money ("in God we trust") promote the belief. Breaking free from those influences is an emotional affair.

"Then how can you say it doesn't matter?"

It doesn't matter, because religion gets its way. Religion tries to control you. If you are a good atheist, you have probably exhausted yourself emotionally just breaking away from the beliefs of loved ones. That's where you were right in what you said just a while ago.

God Exists as a Psychological Truth. "What did I say that you agree with?"

You argued for God's existence by claiming that there was a long tradition of belief and that most people believe in God. You were on to a good intuition there.

"So I wasn't so far off."

Not at all. What you showed were two interesting psychological truths that apply to our society.

"Psychological truths?"

Right. You correctly showed the psychological reasons for why so many people believe in God, and why so few are able to be atheists. Breaking from a longstanding tradition, including the beliefs of your parents, grandparents, aunts, uncles, etc., is emotionally trying. That was your first point. Then you correctly added that most people believe in God.

"But you denied that claim. Remember all the Buddhists and Hindus?"

Exactly. But now I'm taking your claim as a psychological statement, not as a statement about ultimate reality. Nearly everyone you know is a believer. That's a pretty compelling (psychological) reason to believe in God. Especially for a moral person.

"Why do you say that? 'For a moral person'?"

We already decided that moral people seek stability and security. What is more destabilizing and insecure than going against an important and old and widely held belief? Nothing. Belief in God satisfies the need to belong, the need for community. So, you were right. I was wrong.

Why Doesn't It Matter? "But why doesn't it matter if someone is an atheist?"

Oh, right. Back to my earlier idea. It doesn't matter because it takes so much out of a person to break from society. Psychologically speaking, atheists are doing pretty well just to break free on this one isolated belief in God's existence. What remains in them is all their social awareness. All their moral values are still there. They still do not kill or steal or pillage, at least no more than believers do.

"So it doesn't matter? The results are the same, at least in terms of action. But aren't they different in terms of how they live their lives? Aren't they a different sort of person?"

Atheist or believer? If it's merely a difference in one belief, I don't see how it matters.

"I don't agree. What more is there than one's belief?"

I think there is more. But why don't we return to our original plan in this discussion? Later we can talk about what more there is to living.

GOD ANSWERS THE UNANSWERABLE QUESTIONS

"Where does this leave us? I admit, we've talked a great deal, but what have we been able to conclude?"

We know that some arguments for God's existence are faulty. We know that the universe does not have to have a first cause—namely, God. And we've learned that the universe may not be as orderly as we suspected. But more helpful are your insights into what we've called the psychological causes of belief. Do you have any other reasons to believe?

"Yes, I've just thought of another reason. God answers the unanswerable questions."

Surely you don't mean that literally. How could anyone answer what is not answerable?

"Now *you* are being overly serious, Art. What I mean is that God provides answers to questions that science cannot answer. I had thought that God gave security and structure to the universe."

And now?

"Now I see that the questions about security, order, chaos, and a first cause are not so important."

I've been holding back on you. I am willing to admit that your arguments make a kind of logical sense, but they don't work.

"I agree now that they are problematic, but why do you say they don't work? That's strong language from a person who sounds like he does not believe in truth."

I have listened to the arguments. I am a fairly reasonable person, and there are others who are far more reasonable than I. After hearing the arguments for God's existence, I am unconvinced. And I don't think that is because I have a closed mind. I think people believe first, and then they find reasons for belief. The reasons we have examined fit that category. Even as we rejected your earlier proofs of God's existence, you didn't lose your belief, did you?

"No, I didn't."

I think that's because we haven't really touched on the real reasons for belief in God. I think those reasons are difficult to find and to articulate.

"Perhaps, but what do you think of my most recent idea?"

What do you have in mind? What sort of questions does your God answer?

GOD GIVES MEANING TO LIFE AND TO DEATH

"God answers questions about life and death, about pain. God gives suffering a point. God brings meaning and purpose to living and to dying. Without God, this life would be pointless and meaningless."

I agree. This life is pointless and meaningless, cosmically speaking. There is no meaning of life.

"You agree! I am not saying that at all, and I suspect you know that. You're avoiding the issue. I'm quite serious about this."

Sorry. I've grown accustomed to mocking you. It's great fun, but I'll refrain for a time. How does belief in God avert suffering and pain?

"Belief in God does not avert suffering. I never said that."

Then God averts suffering?

"No, God does not avert suffering. He could if He wanted, but there are reasons for suffering."

So far, I don't like this God. It can prevent suffering, but It doesn't want to? Why not?

"One reason God allows suffering is because of original sin."

Stop there. Look, I want this book to have a worldwide market. If you bring in your provincial religious doctrines, my market will shrink.

"Who cares about your market?"

I do. And God may care, too. Since God isn't averting suffering, It has time to care along with me. And I *am* making fun of you, but only a little.

"If I can't use the doctrine of my religion, how am I to answer your questions?"

Actually, it's not the doctrine of your religion, or of any religion, I object to. I want to avoid the details, unless you can show me one thing.

"What's that?"

Can you show me what the standard is for religious truth? Can you show me that your religion is correct and some other religion is incorrect?

"I see what you mean. I'm committed to my religious perspective, but not everyone is. Can I reserve the right to challenge you later with specifics?"

GOD ALLOWS SUFFERING

Fair enough. Where were we? Oh, yes. Your God allows people to suffer. It allows good people to suffer at least as much as bad people. Why? And why would you pray to such a god?

"God does allow some suffering. In His infinite mercy, however, He also averts suffering. God is a loving God."

Are you telling me that God does avert some suffering?

"Of course. God prevents the suffering of the faithful. That is, God prevents some of their suffering. God protects us!"

How does God decide who to protect and who to let suffer?

"The answer to that is understandable to God alone."

Try anyway. Is there any pattern you've detected? Is there any way I can avoid suffering?

"Oh, I see what you mean. God looks with grace on the faithful. He answers our prayers. But you have to know how to pray, and you can't fake your faith."

Heaven forbid! Let me see if I've got this. God alleviates the pain and suffering of the truly faithful? God answers their prayers?

"Not always, but usually. You see, sometimes God has a greater reason to let you suffer than to save you from suffering. It's sometimes thought of as a test. If you maintain your faith, then you get the richest rewards in heaven."

Surely there were some believers among the 12 million people who died in Nazi concentration camps. And what about Cambodia more recently? There are lots of examples of people who must have had faith and who must have prayed to be protected. What about them?

"Like I said, God's understanding transcends human knowledge. He has a plan. Those people were sacrificed, but they are rewarded in heaven. Don't assume, though, that all those people had the right kind of faith."

The right kind of faith?

"Right. Faith is a special kind of belief. Faith has to be childlike in its innocence. I remember when I was a child, I wanted this one bicycle. Every time we went to the toy store, I'd go over and see whether or not it had been sold. And every night I prayed I would get that bike. Finally, my birthday came around, and I got the bike."

I'm moved. Are you telling me this is an example of childlike innocence? You wanted a bicycle for yourself, and that's a prayer God would answer? But this immense and powerful deity would refuse to answer the pleas of starving Ethiopian and Eritrean children! God! What a guy!

"Obviously, you don't understand."

Obviously.

HOW CAN WE KNOW THAT GOD ANSWERS PRAYERS?

"Sometimes God answers prayers, and sometimes He has a greater plan in mind. I'm trying to explain that to you. Some suffering is necessary. God doesn't like it, but it's necessary."

If God doesn't like suffering, why can't It figure out a better plan? But I have a better question. How can we know that God answers prayers?

"We see prayers answered all the time. Miracles occur even today."

But how do we know the prayers are being answered? These miracles might be just events that occur. The event may coincidentally fit someone's prayer.

"That's not very likely. How could you explain my bicycle example?"

What's the test?

"What do you mean?"

Some prayers are answered; some are not answered.

"All prayers are heard and answered. Just not always in the way or when the person wants."

Then how do you know they are being answered at all? Look, what would falsify this idea of yours? You have a bunch of prayers. Some are answered in the way and when you want. Others are answered, but not in the way or when you want. So every prayer is answered, whether or not it's answered in the way or when you want.

"Right."

But that allows too much. What could show that this hypothesis is correct or incorrect? It's an empty belief. It doesn't explain how things happen, or why or when they happen. There is no sense of justice revealed in this plan. There isn't any sense of proportion, either. Your God lets innocent infants be tortured and killed. Yet It contents itself with giving you a bicycle or a "B" on a spelling test in the third grade!

Why Bother with Prayer?   "You haven't understood. God's ways are beyond human understanding."

No amount or quality of prayer will change God's will. Isn't that really what you're saying? You can pray or not pray. It all comes down to the same thing. This God of yours will do as It wants. So why bother with prayer?

"Prayer makes me feel closer to God."

Isn't this closeness just your way of humanizing nature?

"What do you mean?"

You assume that there is a God, or many gods. You pray to It or them. All this is just an attempt to make sense out of a universe that doesn't show any concern for you. The universe isn't just. It doesn't respond to human needs in any noticeable way. So you manufacture a God and a phone line to God—prayer.

"How can you say that?"

Nothing changes when you pray. If your prayer is answered, you're content with your little belief. If your prayer is not answered, you say your God had something else in mind. All you have accomplished with this belief is to make yourself feel more in control. You know the Big Guy who runs the store.

Morality Works When We Follow God's Plan.   "It's all a matter of faith. We are supposed to follow God's rules. These reveal God's plan for us on earth."

Just on earth? When people go to other planets or moons . . .

"Stop being irreverent. You know what I mean."

This is great. We're back to where we started this discussion. You said that moral and religious rules should be followed because they are God's will. You said it is our duty to follow God's will. That's what gives morality a purpose. That's the point of morality.

"Now do you agree?"

WHY WE WANT TO BELIEVE

You have already told me why people want to believe in God. In our Western society most people do believe in God. It's indisputable that the belief has a long tradition. Putting aside these democratic and historical inclinations, I want to ask whether or not there are reasons to believe in God.

"We considered that the universe had to have a beginning and that it is organized and orderly. We also want someone to answer the questions that appear unanswerable. Of course, we also questioned the soundness of these reasons."

You also suggested that order and security are part of our most deeply held wishes. That is exactly the insight Freud examines. Experience itself might be "colored" by these wishes.

"Yes, when we looked at the example of near-death experiences, we closed in on one of the deeper anxieties that people suffer, the fear of death. People fear death, and pain, and insecurity."

I suspect that these fears make it difficult for believers to understand how others might disagree with them. How could anyone stand alone and face the fear of death, or meaninglessness, or suffering! We desire to know that there is a reason for suffering, and for death. We want someone to give purpose to our mundane lives. We want to believe that there is a God answering our prayers.

"It is reassuring to believe that our religious beliefs lead us to living morally praiseworthy lives. This life is part of God's great, but secret, plan. That's what many religious people believe, and it's comforting to agree with them."

PUT YOURSELF IN THE RIGHT FRAME OF MIND

Sigmund Freud challenges just these ideas.

"Who is he?"

Freud was the founder of psychoanalysis. His ideas on the method of therapy, on the existence of an unconscious element of the mind, are very much a part of the way we think. Freud also has some interesting ideas about religion and society.

"Like what?"

He questions what motivates religious belief. To put yourself in the right frame of mind, as we examine civilization and religion imagine you are a being from outer space. You have come to earth to see how earth creatures live and what they believe. You are an intergalactic social scientist. What do you see in the behavior and beliefs of humans in the Western world? What

I'm asking is that you remove yourself from your religious and social beliefs. Pretend that you have never heard of these practices. Freud's analysis is aimed at figuring out not what we think religion is about, but what it actually is about.

WHAT IS THE VALUE OF RELIGIOUS IDEAS?

Freud asks: What is the value of religious ideas? The question arises in the context of our civilized lives. Each of us has a hostility to civilization.

"Why? What causes the hostility?"

Our anger is produced by instinct renunciation.

"What does that mean?"

Society doesn't let us satisfy our deepest wants. We can't do whatever we want, whenever we want. No matter how pressing the need or desire, we cannot act in certain ways because society will not allow it.

"That's just why we have rules and laws. The role of morality, law, and religion is to show us where the boundaries lie. Some experiences are denied us. They are immoral, illegal, or sacrilegious."

Bad, bad!

"Joke all you want, but that keeps this society running. Do you have any better way of organizing society?"

One way to avoid this effect of civilization is to do whatever you want. Don't surrender your instincts to society, live them!

"That's pretty stupid. If everyone did whatever he wanted, soon we'd all be dead."

Freud argues the same way. He says it would be shortsighted to abolish civilization and return to a "state of nature" where each person is out for himself or herself. We started civilization to defend ourselves against nature. Since nature has not yet been completely subdued and rendered harmless, we need to stay together.

"Just my point. Nature presents a real danger to us. Nature is our real antagonist. Compared to nature, we are weak and helpless. We are defenseless to stand against the overbearing power of nature."

You and Freud sound alike. He says that the terrors in living in the vast universe must be silenced. We cannot be happy under such conditions.

"Right, and civilization offers us this protection. Working together in an orderly way, we are able to subdue nature just enough to draw some of its riches. Through work, we get food and raw materials for housing and other comforts."

To quiet our deeper fears, to make them manageable, we humanize nature. Although we are still defenseless against it, a humanized nature can be appeased, bribed, or otherwise influenced.

"What do you mean by humanizing nature?"

We imagine nature to be something like us. We go so far as to believe that humans have been created in a form similar to the "human" nature god. God stands over nature. Unlike mute nature, however, God, the controller of nature, can be appeased, bribed, or otherwise influenced.

"Prayers and sacrifices are made in an effort to relate to God, and therefore to prevent nature and death from permanently and arbitrarily harming us. Promises are made to show our sincerity to God."

You bribe God into doing what you want or, more often, to prevent what you fear.

"I'm not comfortable with the way you describe it."

God relieves each of us of the need to defend ourselves against nature. Each of us is equally represented by civilization. Each of us is protected by God. People seek God's protection collectively.

What's the Harm?   "What is the harm of believing, anyway? Sure, there are no logical reasons to believe, but that is just what faith is, belief without evidence. What's the harm?"

The harm in believing without evidence or reason is that doubting but still believing breaks our intellect. Why go without the ordinary guarantees that we require in everyday living? No one would buy a used car without first having a genuine guarantee of its reliability. "Trust me" just would not convince us. Surely it is dangerous to believe without evidence or from a perceived sense of historical momentum.

"It's more than that. Belief is based on the confidence that our ancestors knew what they were doing."

Just because people once believed that earth was flat is no reason to believe it now. Or, more important, imagine that you believe the stork brings babies. That's how babies come to be; the stork brings them. Wouldn't that be a dangerous belief? One could imagine engaging in all sorts of behavior ignorant of the consequences. The harm of ignorance is potentially very great. The history of ignorance has proven that.

People Will Keep Believing Anyway.   "People will continue to believe in God no matter what Freud writes and no matter what Art says."

You're probably right. That's an interesting and important point. But I don't think it is a reasonable objection to anything Freud has stated.

"It shows how intense the inner force is that holds people to religious beliefs."

To what do they owe this power?

"What do you mean?"

If religious teachings are not the results of ordinary experience, or of thinking, what is their source?

MYSTICAL AND ECSTATIC EXPERIENCES

"It could be mystical or ecstatic experience. My inner experience proves that God exists."

But your experience is not evidence to me. My inner experience could be correct, or it could be nuts. ("Nuts" is yet another technical term in philosophy.)

"Why do you say that?"

The inner experience and interpretation of one person are not convincing to anyone else. Just think how boring it is to listen to people telling you about their dreams.

"What does this have to do with anything?"

Maybe dreams reveal inner truths, or unconscious desires and questions, I don't know. What I do know is that people get really involved in retelling their dreams. Almost no one else cares to hear it. What appears vital and dramatic to the dreamer is uninteresting to the listener.

"What does that prove?"

This example doesn't prove anything, except that intense inner experiences do not always relate to anyone but the person who has the experience.

INVISIBLE GREEN GOBLINS

Here, let me give you an example. My own intense experience reveals to me the existence of invisible green goblins.

"What?"

That's right. I have experienced invisible green goblins.

"How can they be invisible and green?"

It's one of their many amazing talents. No doubt you're convinced of their existence.

"No way."

Why not? I have experienced them. Why isn't that good enough for you? As a matter of fact, one is sitting on my lap right now. He's helping me write this section of the discussion. You're still stuck on the apparent contradiction between being invisible and green. I can resolve that. It's one of the mysteries! Every religion has its own mystery. The goblins have their own mystery.

"This is unbelievable."

I sense that you are still unmoved by my assertions.

"How about evidence? If you can ask for evidence for God's existence, then I can demand evidence for your goblin."

Invisible green goblins, thank you. I can give evidence for their existence. The evidence is not direct, though if you believe in them their existence becomes obvious to you.

"If I believed in them, I'd be as crazy as you are."

Okay, here's some evidence. You know when you wash your clothes and then throw them into the dryer? Every once in a while you lose a sock, right? Where do you think it went? The goblins take them. They eat them. If you're skeptical, try to explain where the sock goes.

"It's trapped in the dryer."

Do you realize how large dryers would have to be in order to capture and consume all the socks that are lost in the life of a dryer? Besides, many people do not use dryers. Their socks are "lost" in the washer. Pretty suspicious, I think. By the way, have you ever noticed that the next sock you lose is never from the broken pair? The goblins always steal one from a complete pair.

"Why do they do that?"

I don't know why. They just do. They don't think like we do. They have a plan for the world that we can't fully understand. So now you believe in goblins, right?

"Of course not."

If you don't believe, you must show where the socks go. And don't try to explain your way out of it by claiming again that the washers and dryers eat them. Who is going to believe that washers and dryers eat clothes? That's absurd. The goblins are also the ones who hide your car keys, but never mind.

"I'm not convinced."

Neither my intense experience of invisible green goblins nor my remarkably sound evidence convinces you? That's just the point. No person should feel compelled to believe without evidence that is available to that person. And secondary evidence, signs of the existence of something, are not completely reliable. Just like you just denied my explanation of the loss of socks, so too all "tracks" are suspect.

"What do you mean by tracks?"

Since only a very few "elect" people ever get to bear "inner" witness, it is wrong for the majority to have the interpretation of those experiences imposed on them. Imagine a world where you were required to serve my fantasy goblins.

"That would be weird."

The imposition is wrong unless you, too, experience the goblins. By the way, if that starts happening, write to me in care of Wadsworth Publishing Co. I have a psychiatrist friend who could use the business.

WHAT ARE THESE IDEAS IN LIGHT OF PSYCHOLOGY?

Freud asks: "What are these (religious) ideas in light of psychology? What is their real worth?"

"What does he mean by these questions? Is he just an atheist?"

Freud is not denying the existence of God. He was an atheist, but he is not trying to convince anyone to be an atheist.

"Then why did he write this stuff? What does he want?"

Freud wants us to look at a most practical question. Why do we think that our God is the way we imagine him to be?

"Because that's what we learned growing up. And because people who have experienced God describe Him that way. God's personality is described by religious teachings."

Yes, but we found difficulties verifying those beliefs. Why should we believe that God is the way he is described?

"You are trying to convince me that God does not exist."

Assume that God does exist. That doesn't change Freud's point. How would we know what It is like?

"I'm not sure. If you close off our traditional way of knowing God, there is no way of knowing what He is like. The Bible is the primary source of our knowledge of God. What else is there?"

Illusions. Freud has a controversial explanation of religious beliefs about God, the father figure. He speculates that religious teachings are illusions.

"Illusions?"

I told you it's controversial! But before you slam the book closed, it isn't as terrible as it seems. Freud says that illusions are not necessarily false. Illusions are not necessarily errors or mistakes.

"How could an illusion be true?"

You might believe in something based solely on your wish that it be true. And it may turn out that it is true. You may believe and hope that someday you will be picked to undertake some great and noble task. And it may turn out that that will happen. Not all wishes are impossible.

"I suppose not. Why call religious beliefs illusions?"

What makes a belief an illusion is that our wishes play an important part in the belief.

"Our illusions are tied to our wishes?"

Yes. The most basic and widespread illusions are derived from the most basic human wishes. Illusions may be true, or they may be false. A belief is an illusion when wish fulfillment is a prominent factor in our motivation to believe it. We believe something because we want to believe.

"For example?"

We believe our local sports team can win the championship because we want them to win. It's a harmless illusion that keeps us interested in the team's performance.

"I think this is just cheering on the home team. There's no illusion involved. But maybe I'm still not clear on this. Could you give me a better example?"

I Am Irresistible to All Women! I am irresistible to all women. You've just read it twice; why is it so hard to believe? I swear it's true. Let me explain. I have discovered that all women are irresistibly drawn to me. Of course, some are not fully conscious of the attraction, but it's clearly there. Whenever I am near a woman, she acts just like I expect.

"And how is that?"

Basically women fall into two categories. Some stay at a discreet distance, loving me from afar; others come over to me. Those who stay at a distance tend to resist my charms by pretending to ignore me.

"Come off it, Art!"

Really. I see them walk by me and they act as though I don't exist. It's incredible to me that they are able to pretend so convincingly. My friends don't even notice when they are with me. But I see all these beautiful and attractive women walking by, longing to be near me but resisting with every fiber of their being. You have to admire their self-discipline.

"Sure, and what about the other group?"

A very few of the women I see actually come up to me. Usually it's because I unconsciously turn on the charm and they can't resist. I don't even know I'm doing it, but it works.

"What happens when you 'turn on the charm'?"

The woman walks up to me. Invariably, as she approaches she is overwhelmed by my presence. But she has already committed herself.

"What does she say to let you know about her attraction?"

She tells me to drop dead, or to get off the face of the earth, or some other similar sentiment.

"And you think this shows that the woman is attracted to you? You are pathetic!"

Don't you see, women are embarrassed by their loss of control. Their only way of protecting themselves from my obvious good looks and appeal is to push me away. They pretend that I am obnoxious. Of course, I know better.

"Have you sought professional help for this? I think you should, because you are not at all in touch with reality."

Illusions Fulfill Our Wishes.   Exactly, and that's why this is an example of an illusion. My own desires and wishes motivate me to interpret the facts in a way that is not necessarily false, but certainly unlikely. All women might be attracted to me. Sometimes when a person is uncomfortable with his or her attraction to another person, he or she may be embarrassed. He may even insult the attractive person.

"So?"

So my belief that all women are attracted to me *may* be true.

"Not likely."

Or my belief may be false. We could reconstruct the example to make it more plausible. What if I told you that one woman is attracted to me, but she is too shy to show her feelings? That might be plausible. What if she went out of her way to be near me but always acted in a shy way?

"Well, that's more reasonable, and more likely to be true."

The plot thickens, right? In this case my illusion could be true. What makes it an illusion is the part my wishes play. Believing it corresponds to my own wish to have this one woman notice me.

"Yes, I see what you mean. A belief may be true or may be likely to be true, but that doesn't make it any less of an illusion."

The Oldest, Strongest Wishes.   In either case, it is my own desires and wishes that cloud my judgment. That's Freud's point. Whether or not there is a God is not Freud's interest.

"Then what is his point?"

How we understand God is his concern. Do we put a "face" on God, a "face" that is motivated by our own wishes? Freud suggests that by understanding illusions we can understand the "face" we put on God and the strength of our religious beliefs.

"Be more specific."

The content of our religious beliefs about God relies on our experience with our parents. By analogy, God is a big parent in the sky.

"Oh, I see. Freud thinks that we choose a parent figure because it's familiar. What's wrong with seeing God that way?"

There's nothing wrong with it, not exactly. It's revealing, though, to see how people describe their God, and what convenient images they choose to describe God.

"Maybe. What else does Freud think about the belief in God?"

The strength of our religious beliefs about God lies in the strength of the wishes that motivate us.

"What do you mean?"

People believe strongly because they need to believe strongly. Other people who do not believe strongly do not have the same fears and desires, so they do not need to believe strongly.

"Are you saying that whenever our wishes play a motivating role in our beliefs, we are reluctant to give up the beliefs? Like your belief that all women are attracted to you?"

Exactly. I want to believe that all women are attracted to me. My desire to believe this is very strong. Therefore—

"Therefore, you are reluctant to give up the belief even when the evidence is against you."

Right. Freud suggests that the fulfillment of the oldest, strongest, and most urgent wishes of humankind can be found in the "face" of God. God is just what we need Him to be, not because we have any reliable evidence that He is this way, but because we need Him to be this way.

"What oldest, strongest, and most urgent wishes do we have?"

We experience terrifying helplessness when we face the immensity of the universe or when we contemplate our own deaths as annihilation.

"It is difficult to imagine that someday I won't exist."

Our need is for protection against our helplessness, against insignificance, against death.

"What face do we put on God? What could make death less terrifying?"

The benevolent rule of God the father figure allays our fears of death. God promises an afterlife if we follow his rules. God is like most parents.

"Yes, but that's just our way of describing God."

God also fulfills our desires for justice. He ensures a moral world order. If evil people flourish while they are on earth, they will pay all the more in the next life. Finally, our despair is solved by the Father. God promises that there is a point to the entire universe, to human suffering, and to death. What makes the belief so appealing?

"Our deepest desires? I know that is what Freud thinks. But does that mean that all religious beliefs are illusions?"

Religious Illusions.   Yes, according to Freud all religious doctrines are illusions. Religious doctrines are based on the fundamental wishes of humanity. Religions admit that their beliefs are not susceptible to direct, objective proof. And look how strenuously the beliefs are held. With an (almost) irrational fervor, just as all illusions are held.

"Religious people often cite how pervasive religious belief is. Can you and Freud explain how almost nowhere on earth can we find societies where religion is not practiced? Even though the local gods are not like our God, people believe they exist. The widespread existence of religious belief shows that there must be a God."

Or so it is asserted. Freud thinks it is the people who are similar. Therefore their beliefs are going to be similar.

"How can that explain why we find religious societies everywhere? How can you explain why God seems to be everywhere?"

The belief in gods is everywhere because people are similar, not necessarily because God is everywhere. People have parents, and they have fears. Because these similarities are (nearly) universal conditions, we should not be surprised that people formulate similar illusions to deal with their situations.

DOES GOD EXIST?

"Does God exist?"

Actually, Freud is not concerned with the truth value of statements for or against God's existence. It would be wonderful if a God created the world, a benevolent providence, a moral world order, and an eternal life after this life.

"It is possible that this idea is true."

It is striking, however, that all these beliefs are exactly what we most wish to be true. Whether or not God exists, the belief in God is an illusion.

"Then God may exist? Is it okay to believe?"

To go beyond that uncomfortable claim, we need to hear much more about God and we need to receive much more evidence. The only reasonable approach is to suspend belief in God until we have irrefutable evidence that God exists. Given our tendency to create illusion, we need to guard ourselves by leaning the other way.

RELIGIOUS ASSERTIONS CANNOT BE REFUTED BY REASON

"Religious assertions cannot be refuted by reason. Religious belief is beyond reason."

Freud has a simple answer to this. "Ignorance is ignorance." No reasonable person would believe even an insignificant claim based on such "feeble grounds." The amount of emotional and physical energy required of the religious person certainly makes religious belief far from insignificant. No, belief under these circumstances is only pretending to believe. People need to learn to accept reality.

"But the portrait of God that is found in the Bible is reassuring. God gives us an ideal to strive toward."

What sort of ideal?

"God is just and loving and merciful. That is the way people ought to act toward each other. Don't you agree?"

That God is this way, or that people ought to act this way toward others?

"Well, both. They're the same."

No, I don't agree that they are the same. Maybe people should be this way, I don't know. That is worth looking into. But your God is not this way.

"How can you say that?"

Look at the stories in your own book! A being who destroys virtually all the sentient life on earth is not very loving, and not obviously just.

"What are you talking about?"

The Noah's ark story. Your God is the greatest mass murderer in the history of humanity. God murdered everyone but Noah and his family. "Oops! I didn't realize they couldn't breathe under water."

"The other people were living sinful lives. They were evil. We said that God disapproved of murdering innocent people. Those people were not innocent. They deserved to die."

Very sensitive of you. But there must have been pregnant women back then. What with all the sinning going on, someone must have been pregnant. And others must have just borne their children. Were these fetuses and babies evil? What sense of love and justice are we using?

"I'll admit those cases are difficult to answer. Perhaps God was punishing them for the original sin of Adam and Eve."

Lame. I can see the headlines now. "God kills children because of the sins of their great-great-great-great-great-great-great-great . . . grandparents." Does this make any sense? Does this sound like justice or love? I am going to murder my children and destroy their toys, because their grandparents screwed up!

"Okay, forget original sin. I can see you don't appreciate the theological significance. All of us are sinners. We are all subject to temptation. God punished that."

But newborn babies and fetuses? Look, being tempted is one thing; giving in to temptation (one of my goals in life) is something very different. But let's assume your analysis is correct. Why would your silly god save Noah and his gang? Aren't they susceptible to temptation? They probably gave in to temptation, too, at least more than fetuses and newborn infants.

"God knew that these newborns would sin when they became older."

Goodbye, free will! Your God punishes people in advance? Very efficient. A little confusing, though. "Gee, Mommy, why did God kill poor (pure) cousin Charlie? He was just born." "Charles died because God knew he would sin someday." What kind of message is this to give to a child? What kind of loving justice is that? Your God lets some people sin big time all their lives, and they live long lives. Then he turns around and slaughters newborns who ain't never done nothin' to nobody.

"The Lord has His reasons."

I don't doubt it. Put my objections aside. Let's get us back on track.

HOW DOES THIS APPLY TO OUR DISCUSSION OF MORAL VALUES?

"How does this apply to our discussion of moral values?"

Belief in God supports morality. God gives authority to morality. That's what you said when we started this discussion. I think you are correct.

"Then belief in God is desirable."

I don't agree. But I don't think it matters very much. If a person's belief in God is an illusion, then all we will be able to extract from the belief is the person's wishes. When we try to extract values to live by, we will get nothing but the person's own values.

"What's wrong with this?"

Well, first, to have each person's illusions and deepest desires reflected in our values hardly gives any authority to morality. Why should anyone else live according to my desires?

"Because that just takes us back to egoism?"

Yes.

"And second?"

What have we gained? The idea of a God is to do away with relativism, right? If there is one God, then there is only one set of values. But if belief in God is merely based on illusions, and people's illusions can vary, then we are left with relativism.

"What if everyone's basic desires are the same? Then we would have a constant set of values."

Good move. Yes, if everyone's desires were the same, then we might extract a common set of values. There are problems with that approach.

"Such as?"

It isn't clear to me that everyone has the same basic desires.

"We could adopt the majority's desires."

No, truth and goodness are not a matter of majority rule. That won't work. But there is a more serious problem with basing morality on people's most basic desires. It's always open that we could find our desires undesirable.

"Come again? How's that?"

Just because a desire is natural, it doesn't follow that we want to make it into a moral value. The two categories are separate.

WHAT'S LEFT TO BELIEVE?

"What's left to believe?"

I'm glad you asked that. That's where our next talk will begin.

■
SUMMARY OF DISCUSSION

There are a number of reasons people use to explain their belief in God. The majority of people we know believes in God. The belief in God has a long tradition in our civilization. Another reason is that the universe had to have a beginning, and it is orderly. Then there is the testimony of people who have had "near-death" experiences.

God also answers the "unanswerable" questions that we face. God gives meaning to life and to death. Although God allows people to suffer, it is for a greater purpose. God also answers people's prayers. Of course, the answers they receive are not always what people want. God works for the betterment of the entire universe. Tragedy is, therefore, actually merely a misunderstood good.

What is interesting about all these reasons is that they appeal to our wants and needs. But they do not speak to evidence. Of course, there are problems with these reasons. God's existence is not so easily proven. In fact, none of these reasons would convince a reasonable person. Proof of that is that no believer would lose faith if one or more of these reasons were successfully dismissed. We need to look further.

When we look at the value of religious ideas, we see that religion is responsible for many of the accomplishments of civilization. Yet we also see that religion as an institution has had a numbing effect on our ability to think. When we examine other religions, we are struck by their quaintness. We are able to see these belief systems as intellectual curiosities. Why would anyone believe in invisible green goblins?

Freud helps us by asking, "What are these (religious) ideas in light of psychology?" His conclusions are dramatic. The belief in God is a psychological truth, but that does not make it a truth of reality. Freud argues that religious beliefs are illusions. Though that does not mean they are false, Freud suggests that the source of our beliefs in the father-figure god are merely projections of our own wants. The religious illusions are illusions because they fulfill our oldest and strongest wishes. With religious beliefs we continue the child's need to receive protection from the parents, especially from the father.

Does God exist? In the context of our search for moral values and for the best life, the answer does not matter. Even if there is a God, it is our task to figure out whether or not our values are sound. So we are left with our original question. What is the best life?

■
DISCUSSION HIGHLIGHTS

I. God exists
 1. The majority believes in God.
 2. The religious beliefs of our culture have a long tradition.
 3. The universe had to have a beginning.
 4. The universe is orderly.
 5. Near-death experiences prove that God exists.

II. God provides for us
   1. God answers "unanswerable" questions.
   2. God gives purpose to our lives and our deaths.
   3. God only allows suffering because it fits the grand plan.
   4. God answers the prayers of the faithful.
III. God is merely a psychological truth
   1. Invisible green goblins don't exist just because I believe they exist.
   2. God is an illusion.
      a. Belief in God depends on our wishes and desires.
      b. Our oldest, strongest wishes determine our belief in God.
IV. The relation between God and values is confusing
   1. God's existence does matter in this context.
   2. Each of us is left with the task of discovering the best life.

■

QUESTIONS FOR THOUGHT/PAPER TOPICS

1. People used to believe in Zeus and all the gods on Mount Olympus. Do you think their reasons were so different from the reasons of today's believers? If the reasons and the commitment are similar, why don't people believe in Zeus now?

2. How do Freud's ideas about illusions affect one's belief in a God? Can you respond to Freud?

3. If you don't believe in invisible green goblins (you a-goblinist!), explain why. What does happen to the socks lost in the dryers?

4. Can you reasonably support with arguments any one of the reasons favoring God's existence? (Use the library to help you find support.)

5. If there is no God, must morality vanish? Why?

6. If God appeared to you, presented the platinum American Express Card, "G-O-D," and said, "Don't leave home without it," would you do whatever it told you to do? If God ordered it, would you murder your mother? (Remember, your mother receives your answer to this question.)

7. Is there any type of faith that does not require a suspension of one's critical abilities? Don't give up too quickly.

■

FOR FURTHER READING

It's no surprise that a great deal has been written about the existence of God and the nature of religious values. I suggest you look at Sigmund Freud's *The Future of an Illusion* (Norton, 1961). Another interesting conversation is Plato's *Euthyphro*, where Socrates discusses the concept of piety and the role that the gods play in defining morality. Bertrand Russell has a well-written book, *Why*

I Am Not a Christian (Simon & Schuster, 1967). A fascinating discussion of faith is presented by Søren Kierkegaard in *Fear and Trembling* (Penguin, 1986). It's difficult reading, but well worth the trouble once you figure out what he is doing.

FOUR

Isn't Everyone Different?

WHAT'S LEFT TO BELIEVE?

"I'm troubled by our last three conversations."

Pity.

"No, really. Several times you said there is no God."

Actually, I agree with Freud. God is an illusion. Whether or not God exists is irrelevant to finding out which life is best.

"What?"

We do not need God in order to find out how to live the best life. Because the "face" of God is influenced by our wishes, we could never figure out what God wants. So, even if God does exist—

"If there is no God, then anything goes."

And it's not my fault. Dostoevski, the Russian novelist, wrote, "If there is no God, then everything is permitted." Are you a Russian novelist, too?

"Be serious for just one moment."

Why does the nonexistence of God bother you? Didn't we decide that good and evil are independent of God? An action is good not because God approves of it. It is good *and* God (possibly) approves of it.

"I know what we concluded. I agree it makes sense, but I'm left feeling pretty shaken. You've just destroyed some important beliefs of mine. You shouldn't be allowed to do that. Some people can't take that, you know. They might get upset with you."

Are you going to offer me a glass of hemlock?

"I don't get it."

Hemlock? The reasoning we used to find out that good and evil are independent of God(s) was used by Socrates. Remember, he urged Euthyphro to see it just as we have. The next thing poor Socrates knew, he was on trial, found guilty of atheism and corrupting the youth.

"Euthyphro took him to court?"

No, actually Socrates was already charged. But his conversation with Euthyphro was much like the ones that got him into trouble. Sometimes asking these questions can be pretty frightening. Socrates was asked to drink hemlock. Great taste, but hard to digest. Poison!

HOW CAN WE CHOOSE OUR MORAL VALUES?

"Where does this leave us? If God does not exist, how can we find out which values are true? Every moral system we look at will have something wrong with it. Even if we could fix them, there are too many to choose from, and I don't know how to choose. How can we figure out what is good and what is evil? All that's left is to say that morality is relative to each person."

Relative?

"Everyone's values are different, and there's no way to choose between them."

We could always use the method of historical preference. Force.

"No, that won't do. We want to know that our values, our way of life, is correct. There's no way of coming to answers to the questions you're asking."

Slow down, we've just started. People have been working on these questions for a long time.

"That's just the point. No one has come up with a morality that works. Every time we come up with one idea about morality, another problem gets in the way. No, I think that morality is different for different people. What you think is right is up to you. And what I think is right is up to me. There's no way to resolve the problem. You were right and I was wrong. You can do whatever you want."

Please note the time and date of this admission.

DOING PHILOSOPHY

"Seriously, where can we go from here? I'm confused. Doesn't your book on ethics end here?"

Confused? Good. If you think you already know everything about morality, how can you learn anything?

"But this is frustrating. Every idea I come up with, you shoot down."

Shoot down? Not really. I think we're just realizing that stating our ideas isn't easy. Nothing we've said has been wrong, yet. At least, I don't think so. I think we need to bring these ideas together carefully. Be patient. Patience is a virtue. Besides, we've only started.

"So where are we?"

Last time we asked for examples and for explanations of morality. We looked at several. We started with the Ten Commandments and the Golden Rule.

"Those didn't last long. Though I'm still not sure what happened. I don't feel comfortable rejecting such time-honored principles."

Good, because we didn't reject them. We just found reason to ask what they really mean and why we should follow them. We'll come back to each example and try to keep its strengths and avoid its weaknesses. My idea is that we can avoid the problems but take what we want from each example of morality.

"When does that happen? So far, all we've done is destroy them."

One cannot fill a vessel that is already full. Be patient. (I sound very Eastern, don't I? It's because I'm having a cup of tea right now.) Even Plato, one of the all-time superstars in philosophy, believed that you can't learn until you know what you do not know. Perplexity is what he wanted.

"Perplexity?"

Yeah, I think it's some kind of plastic used to cover tables.

"It isn't perplexity, it's frustration!"

What Plato had in mind was that learning can't happen if the person believes she already knows all the answers. To learn, you have to be involved and active. You have to realize that you may not have much supporting your beliefs and values. I think you have to be emotional to learn. *You're* certainly emotional.

IS THERE AGREEMENT ON VALUES?

"So?"

So besides the Ten Commandments and the Golden Rule, we discussed conscience.

"Yes, and we thought of several other ways of explaining morality. We didn't get to these in any detail, but you promised that we will later. Now I don't see why we should bother. What's the point?"

What systems are left?

"There were social and natural roles, and doing the most good for the most people. And I suggested that there is a contract between each person and society. Then there is the law as an example of morality."

Yes, and you also suggested that morality might be based on something like our genuine, natural and spiritual needs.

"Right, and then there is the question of absolutes. Are moral values absolute or are they different for different people and different societies? I think that about covers it. And I think that's just the position I am denying. There are no absolutes."

Don't forget egoism, my favorite.

"And egoism. Don't you see, that's just the point. With all these competing ways of understanding morality, none seems to be right."

But we haven't even examined them in detail.

"I know, but everywhere I look there are different moral values. There doesn't seem to be any agreement on values. People in our own society disagree about abortion, about business practices, about weapons and war, even about the importance of education."

(Dis)Agreements in Form and Content. Sure, there are apparent disagreements. But one thing you have to admit is that the different groups agree enough to offer moral reasons to one another. That at least shows some common ground.

"What do you mean?"

Some disagreements are disagreements in content; some disagreements are disagreements in form.

"I don't understand."

The groups argue with each other. And their arguments apparently make sense to the other group.

"But they never agree. How can you say their arguments make sense to the other side?"

They speak the same language. Listen to them. For example, in the case of abortion. Each of the sides takes a stand. Then they argue with the other side.

"But they will never agree."

But the arguments are important. Each group appeals to the basic moral intuitions of the opponent. They try to show that moral values common to both sides lead to one conclusion on abortion, theirs. Each side does this.

"Of course. But they still will never agree."

That's because they argue with each other. Each side believes it knows the truth, but each side refuses to listen to the other's opinions. Arguments of this kind do that to people.

"Arguments of what kind? What kinds of arguments are there?"

Well, there's arguing in the sense of closing one's mind and just fighting. It's always pointless to argue that way. Then there's arguing with a critical but open mind. Philosophy is supposed to be this kind of arguing. We listen to each other, then carefully analyze what is said so that we genuinely understand. Then we draw conclusions. Some of the best arguments of this kind have people changing their views, if only slightly. And, of course, sometimes people just cannot agree.

"I'm still not quite following you. If the arguers can't agree, where is the common ground you see? Why don't you think these moral disagreements are real?"

On one level the disagreement is real. On the emotional level the people who argue get high blood pressure, and go red in the face. It's actually fun to watch them. On a more interesting level, they do agree.

"How so?"

Not long ago, I heard several people arguing about the rights of abortion. Back and forth they argued. Red faces, loud voices. I started to laugh. Mistake. They asked what was so funny. I wanted to say that they were in basic agreement, but I knew they'd take off my head.

"What did you say?"

I told them that we should let the fetuses reach maturity and be born. It was a waste to sacrifice a fetus or a newborn infant.

"So, you are opposed to abortion?"

I told them that a newborn baby should be cared for and well treated. That way, they can be put to work in mines and factories by the time they're five years old.

"That's terrible."

No, really. If the babies aren't well fed, they won't have the stamina for a good day's work. Why should adults have to take risks when unwanted children can do all the dangerous and demeaning work for us?

"How can you say that!"

Just their response. (You should read Swift's "A Modest Proposal.") See, I wasn't talking the same language. My reason for keeping fetuses alive was not moral. Both sides came down hard on me. They realized that they had more agreement than disagreement. They all agreed that raising babies to do dangerous work is wrong. (I'll bet they don't know why.) Their disagreement was over when a fetus becomes a baby. There are other disagreements in the abortion question, but they all come to the same thing. Moral people argue about these issues. People who aren't moral just ask you to pass the salt.

Disagreement on Content. "Even if that made me feel better (and it doesn't), there is evidence of real moral disagreement. Different subcultures within our country have different values. And before you interrupt me, there are even greater differences between different cultures and countries. Bigger differences still between different times in history. Once people thought that slavery was acceptable. Now we don't believe that. People's gods change. Once no one believed in God. They believed in all sorts of other gods. There is just no agreement. Even in our own time, one religion tells people to love their enemies. Another tells them to kill nonbelievers. Or in one country it's okay to eat meat; in another place it's a terrible thing to do. It's frustrating!"

I can see that you're genuinely upset. But I don't understand what all the fuss is about. Why should agreement on values matter that much? We did agree on several defining features of morality. You know, each system is impartial, general, public, consistent, comprehensive, ordered, and final. Remember?

"That's just the form. What about the content? If we can't agree on values, that puts all our values in jeopardy. How are we to know that one set of values is true and another is not true? It means we have to accept all values as equally plausible. I don't know about you, but I feel uncomfortable doing that. Still, it seems like the only option left."

Tolerance and Acceptance. Wait a minute. There are at least two problems here. First, you want to know what makes a moral principle true. For some reason you think you need agreement in establishing truth. Second, you are confusing tolerance and acceptance. Let's assume the worst, at least from your point of view. Let's assume that there is no moral truth. (In fact, there is no moral truth.) And let's also assume that you see a variety of apparently conflicting moral values out there. There are a number of viable contenders seeking your support.

"I do see different moral values out there, and I don't know how to sort them out."

Fine. But just because you see different values doesn't mean that you have to adopt all of them. You may find a way of deciding between and among them.

"But how can I do that? We are assuming that there is no moral truth. How can I decide among competing moral principles?"

That is the first and more important question, I agree. All I'm saying is that even if we do not determine which moral system is most true, we still don't have to accept all values as equally desirable. Look, cultural diversity is interesting whether it's in values or in customs. You don't have to become a Buddhist or a Shintoist or a Christian just because you see Buddhists, Shintoists, and Christians around. Appreciate the differences.

HOW CAN WE DECIDE WHICH VALUE IS TRUE?

"I guess you're right. But what about moral truth? How can we decide which principle is true? Without agreement, we are stuck without truth."

I wish I had some clever piece of Eastern wisdom to offer. Wait, here's one. The cackling flock does not determine the leader's path of flight.

"What are you talking about? Who said that and what does it mean?"

I don't know what it means, but I said it, just now.

"Do you have anything helpful to say?"

Yes, well—no. Maybe? I think you're confused by apparent disagreements. Sometimes disagreements are not what they appear to be. And I think you have a pretty problematic idea of what makes a statement true.

Apparent Cultural Disagreements.   "What do you mean, disagreements aren't what they appear to be? A disagreement is a disagreement."

Well, there are disagreements and then there are disagreements. Some disagreements are merely disagreements in words. I say the wall is blue and you say it is cyan. Cyan is a shade of blue, so we haven't really disagreed.

"But that isn't a big deal."

It is when the labels start applying to people. Judgments can be a big deal. Recently I was talking to some philosophy teachers who were upset with one of their colleagues, another teacher. His approach to problems was different than theirs.

"Wouldn't you expect diversity? Isn't that what philosophy is all about? At least that's what I'm getting from our talks."

Get real. Philosophers form rigid "camps" just like every other insecure group. Anyway, these teachers challenged my approach. Attacking me let them politely and indirectly (safely) attack their colleague.

"What did they say about you?"

They resorted to name calling. They called me a nihilist.

"A what?"

They were upset because there is no God, and they blamed it on me. (Maybe I should write an exam to go with this book. T or F There is no God and it's not Brad Art's fault.) They assumed that because there is no God, there is no guarantee for morality.

"That's just my problem. How did you answer?"

Actually, it is not your problem. You have not blamed anything on me. Well, at least not for the past several pages. You see, in a certain sense I am a nihilist. In a certain sense. If what they mean by nihilist is that values cannot be guaranteed by the gods, then I am guilty as charged. But a nihilist is more than that. To say that there are no values and that there's no way of guaranteeing values is much stronger.

"Are you that kind of nihilist? That's kind of what people mean by relativist, isn't it?"

That's what you fear about relativism. You (and they) fear that if we cannot find the true values, then there are no legitimate values. But that's not true.

Take Responsibility For Your Values.   "What alternative is there?"

We can take responsibility for our values. We can admit that there are many values out there. We can also work to discover what the point is for having values in the first place. But look, let's get back to the original point.

"Which is?"

Those philosophy teachers feared a loss of all values. When I did not appear to agree with their strategy (God), they labeled me an atheist and a nihilist. They were shortsighted. They cut themselves off from other ways of approaching their questions. Where we agreed is that we are looking for one way by which to live.

"You still haven't given an answer. How can I take responsibility for values? First, I need to know how to choose them. If you think there is one best way, tell me. What is it?"

I'll tell you what. Let's work carefully through your "trouble." By the end of the book, I promise we'll have a desirable way of living.

"But you confuse me all the time. You don't keep your promises. Why should I believe you?"

What's to lose? Trust me. (Translation: Right now, I have no idea.)

Disagreements Over Basic Beliefs.   "There are more troubling disagreements. What about the disagreements between cultures? In India people would rather starve than eat cows. Cows are sacred in India. Here most people eat meat. How can you reconcile these differences?"

Cultural differences are sometimes real, but I don't think that is such a big deal. Take your example. We don't really disagree with the Hindus on what should and should not be eaten. Would you eat the body of another person?

"I hope not!"

That's all the Hindus are against.

"Then why don't they eat cows?"

Reincarnation. Hindus believe in the reincarnation of the spirit. People and animals are born and reborn in an almost endless cycle of births and deaths. The cow is sacred because it holds the reincarnated spirit of another person or of someone about to become a person.

"But that's ridiculous."

Spoken like a tolerant person! The disagreement you have with the Hindus is on the level of basic beliefs.

"Basic beliefs?"

The beliefs that form a background to your daily life. We have all sorts of background beliefs. I think of philosophy as discovering and questioning these basic beliefs. Most disagreements occur either because of language (cyan and blue), or because of factual disagreements, or because of different basic beliefs.

"But isn't it hopeless? How can we decide which basic beliefs are true? Aren't we back to the same problem? There are so many value systems and so many basic beliefs. How can we decide among them?"

I don't think we'll have to choose at all. The best life will just emerge. I think you're too hung up on what's true and not on what's real.

There's an Exception to Every Rule. "There's an exception to every rule."

Huh?

"You heard me. What bothers me about so many value systems isn't that we have trouble understanding each other, or that we have different basic beliefs, or that I feel compelled to accept any of them. What bothers me most is—"

I know—that there's an exception to every rule.

"Right, there is an exception to every rule. It's wrong to kill, but self-defense is okay. Or it's okay for the state to kill a criminal. At least some people believe in capital punishment. You can find examples that show that every rule has an exception."

Except that one.

"Which one?"

That there is an exception to every rule. That rule (that there is an exception to every rule) doesn't have any exceptions.

"That's just a cheap trick, and you know it."

Okay, okay. You're right. (Actually I don't think it is a cheap trick.) I'm not so sure rules do have exceptions. Maybe it's because of the way we state the rules. For example, we can restate the rule against killing. One should never kill a fellow citizen or a welcomed foreigner. That's really what the law is all about.

"Why do you say that?"

If you fly off to some foreign country where we have no diplomatic relations—

"You mean, where they hate us and we hate them?"

Close enough. If you go there and you kill their head of state or their chief military officer, our country is not going to press charges when you return. (To help make this point, please fill in the name of our most current "enemy.")

"They'd probably throw a parade for me."

Right. So our country doesn't object to killing. It all depends on whom you kill. Oops, let me add one more provision. We tend to frown on people being killed on our soil. Messy. And we aren't thrilled if you kill a foreign person, even on their soil.

"If we have diplomatic relations with them. If we like them."

Now you've got the idea.

"But what about capital punishment?"

It's basically the same idea. When people commit certain crimes, we remove certain rights. If you get caught driving while drunk or drugged, you can lose your driver's license.

"Felonies result in prison terms and the loss of the right to vote in national elections, I think."

So, by the same reasoning, we strip a "cold-blooded murderer" of citizenship rights. You moral people deem the offense so great that you repeal the agreement to protect the murderer.

"You mean, the social contract no longer applies?"

That's one way of putting it. The long and short of it is that the murderer loses immunity from being killed. The state can do as it wishes. No murder of a citizen or of a "covered" alien occurs.

"I still think there are going to be moral and legal rules that you can't sneak out of. I can't think of one right now, but I'm sure there must be some."

Maybe we should do away with moral rules altogether.

"You can't do that!"

All I meant was that we could do away with moral rules and replace them with, ta da—understanding! No, no, forget that. It might be a good idea.

"I have no idea what you're talking about, or where this is going. What I want to know is, which values are true? Which moral values work?"

AGREEMENT IS NOT TRUTH

You seem to think that agreement is truth. But that's unlikely. Here, look at this example. Not long ago, people believed that the earth was flat. Your ancestors, and mine, believed that. Was the earth flat?

"Of course not."

But most people believed that. So truth is not merely agreement. And I'll take it even farther. Even if everyone believed that the earth was flat, it wasn't.

"I've already agreed to that."

So the majority does not decide on what's true.

"Okay. Where does this leave us? I don't think you're trying to make progress on this question. Because I don't think you have an answer to this one, do you?"

I'm wounded by your attack on my integrity. But let me try a bit harder.

"You're stalling."

TYPES OF TRUTH

Okay, what are some examples of truths?

"To avoid another one of your long-winded discussions, I can give you different types of truths. There are mathematical truths, $1 + 1 = 2$, and the Pythagorean theorem. And there are scientific truths, the law of gravity, the shape of the earth. There are personal truths. I feel pain or pleasure. I see a chair over there. There's other knowledge, too. A lot of what we know is based on what people tell us. Historical knowledge, and when you were born and who your parents are. All that is based on what people tell you."

You really do cut right to it. Let's see what each type of truth is.

Mathematical Truths Are True by Agreement.   "Let's start with mathematical knowledge."

Mathematical truths are true by agreement. That is, some knowledge is just agreement. Math is one set of those truths.

"But you just showed me that isn't true! The earth's shape doesn't change with changing belief."

I lied. Look, truth is not as simple as you want it to be. There are different types of truth.

"That statement brings us right back to relativism. I want to know which truth is better, which truth is true?"

Look at your first example, math. Mathematical knowledge is agreement. Mathematics is by definition internally consistent and self-contained.

"What does that mean?"

Once you know the meaning of the symbols, the rest becomes obvious through practice. That's why once you learn a mathematical truth, it isn't difficult to figure it out again. You have arrived at the agreed-on answer, by the agreed-on method.

"Language seems to be that way, too. Words mean what we want them to mean. For example, the word *red* means red to English-speaking people. But *rouge* means red to the French. Is that what you have in mind?"

I hadn't thought of that example. It's more complicated than mine, but yes, that's the kind of distinction I'm going for. The other revealing thing about mathematical knowledge is that it doesn't make any sense to doubt it.

"I'm not following you."

Well, say someone says that $1 + 1$ does not equal 2. Would that put the statement $1 + 1 = 2$ into question?

"Of course not. Everyone knows that $1 + 1 = 2$."

So when someone denies or contests the truth, what do you do?

"I'd say the person didn't know how to add."

Exactly. Either the person is a child who hasn't yet learned to add, or the person may speak another language and merely be caught up in a language difficulty. Either way—

"I get it. Either way, math can't be doubted. It can't be doubted in the sense that it doesn't make sense to doubt it. Doubt shows that there is something 'wrong' with the doubter. Math is true by agreement. So some knowledge *is* true by agreement. Does this apply to morality? If it does, we can't reject relativism. We'll have to admit that different cultures have different values."

And that there's no way of resolving differences. Except by force.

Is Moral Truth Like Mathematical Truth?   "Is moral truth like mathematical truth?"

Unfortunately, and no offense, mathematical knowledge doesn't tell us anything about the outside world. When we're looking for moral truth, math just won't do as a model. Morality is about the world, not about symbols.

"But the absolutist wouldn't agree with you."

Why do you say that?

"What kind of author are you, anyway? You're supposed to know this stuff, not me."

Right, but why wouldn't the absolutist agree?

"At least some absolutists wouldn't agree. For example, if you believe that moral values and principles can be reached only through reason, then you wouldn't reject the mathematical model. Do you follow?"

Not exactly.

"Say you believe that reason can give you your moral principles. Reason isn't about this world any more than math is. Reason applies to the world when we want it to apply. So does math, when we want it to apply. But reason takes us into another realm, the realm of the objective."

Hold on for a minute. Are we traveling into a space-time warp or something? (Hum the theme to any space adventure movie.)

"You're losing it, Art. Look, the absolutist might claim that morality is basically objective, and impartial. We agreed to this in our earlier talk. Well, what makes someone objective and impartial? Reason. And the beauty of the idea is that everyone has the same reason."

Everyone doesn't reason the same way. Some people are better at it than others. And don't mention names.

"But see, everyone does reason the same way. Just like everyone does math the same way. Sure, some people are better at math than others. But that's just ability and practice. The math itself doesn't change. That's the strength of math. And it's the same with reason."

Logic doesn't depend on the person's personality?

"Right. Personality and emotions aren't impartial like logic. They're not morally relevant."

This is clever. If I understand your idea, moral knowledge may be like mathematical knowledge. Both are objective and impartial. But is moral truth true by definition of the symbols used? That's the part that confuses me.

"Morality isn't exactly true because of the symbols, but math isn't really that way, either. It's not the symbols; it's what they stand for. If you understand the ideas that the symbols stand for, then you are doing math. The same goes for morality. If you use reason, you can arrive at the moral truth."

Ha, got you.

"What are you talking about?"

I don't want to disagree with your idea about moral absolutism. When we get farther into the book, we'll examine a theory by a guy named Kant. Your idea is similar to his. (You might want to look at it now.)

"How have you gotten me?"

Your idea doesn't apply to relativism. The original point was that math truths are true by agreement. I guess you've shown that isn't quite accurate. Still, my original point stands. Your view of math isn't a good analogy for morality.

"But my absolutist version of morality corresponds to math."

It does, and it is nonrelativist. So the problem we were trying to avoid can be solved by your absolutist strategy. If moral truth is like mathematical truth, then relativism isn't true. And we have no problems.

"And what makes you think you got me?"

So I "exaggerated." I felt like arguing and not listening. We've also agreed to look more closely at Kant as a representative of your "reasoned" absolutist approach. I think what you've offered gives a powerful way of avoiding relativism. You have given a good reason to adopt a theory like Kant's absolutism.

The Scientific Method Lets Us Trust Scientific Claims. "So where's the problem? Why hasn't this chapter ended?"

What if morality can't be discovered through reason? There's one problem with the reasoned approach. It seems to deny that in a moral dispute both sides can be using reason properly.

"That might be a problem."

What if morality is more like my example of the belief in the shape of the earth?

"We might need another model of truth?"

My thinking exactly. Scientific knowledge is not found through reason alone. A scientist has to make observations. That's how we discovered that the earth is not flat. It's also how we discover that 1 + 1 does not equal 2.

"What are you talking about? 1 + 1 does equal 2. We just showed that math truths are true by agreement and that it doesn't make sense to doubt them."

Oh, I'm not doubting that 1 + 1 = 2, at least in math. I'm just saying that 1 + 1 does not equal 2 in a real-world example, or in science.

"I suppose one apple and one apple does not equal two apples?"

Sure it does. But one gallon of liquid and one gallon of liquid does not equal two gallons of liquid. Not always, anyway. Take a gallon of water and add a gallon of antifreeze. You won't get two gallons. In fact, you get noticeably less than two gallons. I say we sue mathematicians everywhere for this gross deception.

"You idiot. The reason there is less than two gallons is because of the chemical bonding that occurs between water and antifreeze molecules."

Likely story. You're in with the mathematicians. But doesn't my point still stand? 1 + 1 does not equal 2. In math it does, in science it doesn't.

"Maybe so. Your examples are strange. What does make a scientific claim true?"

I think the scientific method lets us trust scientific claims. If, after making an observation, I make a claim about reality, you should be able to make the same observation. Science is based on reproducible observations. That's what makes it objective. No single person's feelings are allowed to cloud the observation.

"The scientific technique guarantees objectivity and accuracy?"

In theory, yes.

"Why do you say 'in theory'? What's wrong with this approach?"

Since our concern is whether or not moral truths are relative, the scientific approach does not guarantee *Truth*. It only guarantees *truth*.

"You're becoming more and more obscure."

All I mean is that science has its own truths. But we're interested in Truth. Truth with a capital *T* is *the* truth. The truth apart from the possibility of error. The other truth, with a small *t*, is truth relative to any one scientific theory.

Scientific Truths Are Relative Truths. "But that isn't how science operates. Scientific information is either true or it isn't true."

Not quite. Scientific observations are theory laden.

"What?"

Impressed you, didn't I? Science is biased by the assumptions it makes. Different scientific theories use different assumptions. They all use similar techniques; that's what makes them science. But they make different assumptions.

"For example?"

For example, say you've got two scientists making observations. One speculates that the earth is perfectly flat. The other's theory is that the earth is a perfect sphere.

"Obviously, the first is mistaken and the second is correct."

Well, that depends on all sorts of other beliefs. For example, what if they both believe that there are demons and serpents and sea monsters? What if they both trust their senses? They see a ship leave port. Just as it gets to the open sea, it sinks.

"The ship doesn't sink. It goes beyond the horizon, beyond where they can see it. The curve of the earth makes it appear to sink."

Horizon is a concept they can't have. That would prejudice their observations. That assumes a spherical earth. All they know is that the ship goes down. When the ship does not return, they presume it is lost to the ocean gods or to sea serpents. Isn't that a reasonable conclusion?

Is Moral Truth Like Scientific Truth? "Are you suggesting that moral truth is like scientific truth? Are you saying that moral truth is relative to our other beliefs?"

Actually, I'm being careful not to say anything. But no, I don't think that scientific truths are like moral truths. I think moral truths are much more fundamental than scientific truths. Science frequently unearths new data. Discoveries bring new scientific information.

"And moral truths?"

Morality doesn't unearth new data or make new moral information. Morality doesn't change nearly as rapidly as science does. For example, virtually no one takes ancient physics seriously as a practical science for today. Right? How many physicists today believe that the primary "stuff" of the universe is air, or water, or earth, or fire?

"So?"

So we give up scientific truths pretty readily. (I've exaggerated, but only a little.) But we still respect the moral insights of the ancient world. Think about it. If you met Moses and Aristotle, Jesus and Gautama (the Buddha), Abraham and Plato, you'd probably be fascinated by the similarity of their discussion of morality and the spiritual life to our own talk.

"Of course!"

But you'd laugh (respectfully) if they discussed the "latest" scientific beliefs of their day.

"Scientific truths change more readily than moral insights."

I think so. It's that way partly because science depends on the senses. Scientific truth is a hostage to data. We are compelled to reassess old theories and to explain new data in science. Science goes even beyond the senses. And we aren't comfortable with that. Remember how we tested math? Does it make sense to doubt scientific facts or theories?

"Yes, of course. In fact, that's what a good scientist does. She tries to invalidate the accepted theories. If that fails, then she tries to extend, or to simplify, the theory."

Science lacks the certainty of math. It's the nature of scientific truth to be tentative. Science is supposed to challenge itself.

"Science is relative?"

I guess you could say that, but the real point is that it doesn't bother anyone.

"But it bothers me if morality is relative."

Why? You live most of your life accepting scientific truths as True. Why doesn't it bother you that science is changeable?

"I guess I never thought of science as that changeable. Maybe it's because science progresses. The 'relativism' of science brings new and better truths. But morality isn't that way. I don't see how one moral theory improves on another."

DOES MORALITY WORK?

First off, science does not progress. Read some history of science. There's lots of evidence that science changes, but progress is difficult to establish. After all, what does it mean to say that science progresses?

"It works."

That's one idea of progress. Look, let's not get into a discussion of scientific progress. What we want to know is, when morality changes, does it progress? What counts as moral progress?

"Why not say that morality progresses when it works?"

What does that mean? What does it mean for morality to work?

"If it helps you get along in society, then your moral values have worked."

So if you live in a disgusting, vicious society where people do all sorts of cruel and mean things, your morality would be cruel and mean and disgusting? That's the only way of living that would fit into that kind of society. How else could you "get along"?

"You know that isn't what I mean. Morality is supposed to make you a better person."

Then what does it mean for a moral system to work? I think we're onto an important question. If we can decide what morality is for, we might be able to resolve your—

"Perplexity?"

Yeah.

"I'm not sure what the ultimate aim of morality is."

HUMAN NATURE

Then let's put aside morality and relativism for a while. I think the problem of relativism comes up because we believe that people differ. Therefore, their values differ. So we need to figure out what makes people human.

"What do you mean? People are people. That's pretty easy."

Sure, but what is it that makes us human and not tables or dogs? I think we have to figure this out. If we know what makes us uniquely human, maybe we can discover the best way to live. After all, creating a best way of life for cattle is not the same as for people. Right?

"Right. Cows aren't as complex or as interesting as people. They don't require much to be happy. So what makes us human? That's what you want to know?"

Yup.

WHAT DIFFERENCE DOES IT MAKE?

"But what difference does it make whether or not we can define humans?"

I'm just trying to make sense of your idea that the best life is filling one's needs and playing one's natural roles.

"What does human nature have to do with that?"

If we can define what makes us human, we can determine which of our wants are real and which are artificial. Doesn't that strategy make sense?

"Artificial wants? What do you mean?"

Some wants are socially and culturally determined. Those are artificial. Other wants are more natural to us.

"But I still feel artificial wants. I don't think I can tell the difference just by feeling them. But I think I see what you mean."

So my strategy is acceptable, at least for now?

THE ABILITIES TO THINK AND TO FEEL

"Okay. One thing that makes us human is that we can think and feel."

That's two activities, not one.

"Whatever. We are intelligent in a way that animals cannot be. We reason, whereas animals count on instinct."

I don't understand.

"We can evaluate problems and find solutions. We humans can figure out how to get water. Animals just instinctively need water. They don't reason about it. Of course, now that I think about it, we don't reason about being thirsty, either. We get thirsty, then we figure out how to satisfy our thirst. Never mind, I changed my mind."

So where does that leave us? We can't reason?

"No, we can still reason in ways that animals can't reason. We are able to evaluate problems and to create solutions. And we have feelings."

Animals experience emotions, don't they?

"Yes, they probably do. But they don't have the same emotions as people have."

How do you know? How could anyone ever know what an animal feels? Even if we could know, the question is: Do animals experience emotions? And the answer is?

"Okay, yes they do. But they can't reason."

I don't know about that. I admit they act on instinct much of the time, but they do reason, too. Chimpanzees have been known to carry their old even to the point of sacrificing the younger, stronger monkeys. They carry and protect the old. That way the group is able to find food and water in time of famine or drought.

"How do they do that?"

The older chimps remember where food and water are from the last famine or drought. They reason that this crisis is similar to the past crisis. Pretty good, huh?

"That doesn't seem to be the same as human reason. Chimps can't do math or philosophy."

Neither can infants or very small children! Then again, maybe infants and small children aren't human.

"Don't be stupid. The point is humans reason in ways that animals cannot reason. We're better at it than animals."

So we confer the status of "human" based on how well one reasons! There's a danger lurking here.

"That's not what I'm saying. If you allow a normal infant or child to develop, it will be able to reason in ways that animals can never reason. They'll be able to do math and science, for example."

Computers Can't Think.   Like a good computer?

"Not at all. Computers only do what we tell them to do. They only know what we put into them. They need people to program them."

How are people any different? Don't we take kids and put them into school? What do they do there? They are taught, sometimes by teachers and sometimes by computers.

"Still, people are unique. No two people are exactly identical. Computers don't have unique personalities."

Our uniqueness probably comes from having different experiences from others. I suppose if two computers had different experiences, they would develop differently.

"This is crazy. Computers can't think. They can only calculate; they can't create."

Artificial intelligence.

"Are you insulting me?"

Heaven forbid! Artificial intelligence studies ways to make computers that think. The idea is to make computers that are able to learn from their mistakes, to plan strategies based on the rules of the game, etc. I heard about a computer that was taught to play chess.

"I agree, computers have incredible memories. That's all the chess-playing machine is doing. It plays chess by searching its memory for the right moves."

Not quite. Since there are an indeterminate number of possible moves in chess, relying on memory won't work. The programmers had to give the machine a knowledge of the rules of the game. It started out losing, but it got better and better. Now it can beat experienced players.

Computers Can't Feel.   "But computers can't feel."

Actually, sensors can be placed on computers to allow them to recognize heat, light, sound, and other experiences. They're pretty sophisticated.

"But those are sensors telling them that the light is on. They can't feel heat or light. They know there's a change of light or temperature, but that isn't feeling. They don't have any internal sensation."

Eyes pick up light, convert it into electrical impulses, and send them to the brain. You're just prejudiced. Why are you prejudiced against things that aren't like you? Just because a computer is plastic and wire? And we are muscle, hair, fat, and liquids? Is that it, you don't approve of beings that aren't liquidy?

Computers Depend on People.   "That's not what I'm saying. Computers aren't human, that's all. They can't reproduce. They depend on people."

Animals reproduce, but you don't call them human, either. You're fickle.

"I still say, computers can't feel and they don't reproduce."

But they do reproduce. From the little I know about computers, I understand that this "generation" of computer is being used to design the next generation. Neat, huh? And you can imagine that computer robots can be taught to assemble the new generation.

"They can't maintain themselves. They need people to fix them when they break. And they can be turned on and off. You can't do that with people."

One idea at a time. Maybe computers can't maintain themselves, but they can diagnose their problems. "Excuse me, Mr. Jones, but I seem to have a malfunctioning LD 2995 chip."

"But they need Jones to replace the chip."

Have you ever heard of medical people? We need people to maintain us, too. I don't see much difference there. As for turning them on and off, we can turn people off. Bang, you're dead.

"But we can't turn them back on. That's a big difference."

It sounds like computers have the edge there. They can think faster, remember better, diagnose their problems, and be resurrected. My vote goes for the computer.

"Feelings, what about feelings?"

I suppose you could program a computer to say, "Hurray!" when it wins a chess game.

"But that would only be programmed. It wouldn't feel the excitement."

I don't know about that. I really don't know. I'm not sure how we could ever know that about anyone or anything. What else makes us human?

Computers Don't Care.   "This may sound a bit morbid, but we know that we are going to die. Computers don't have that knowledge, and neither do animals."

Hmm, I think you're right. Although computers don't have to worry about it. They can be resurrected. It's a holy ritual.

"Oh, stop it. Computers don't care. They don't have a personality. They don't care whether or not they live—I mean, continue."

That's an interesting point. People do care!

"I suppose we could program a computer to want to live, but people have that naturally. Wait. I just realized. Some animals do know when they are going to die. Elephants have graveyards. The older elephants wander to the graveyards when they are about to die."

I wouldn't have thought of that. But we can still say that people want to continue living, and computers don't care. Unless they're programmed to care.

"No, Art, we can't say even that. People commit suicide. Heroes sacrifice themselves. At least some people are not afraid of dying. And besides, animals also try to stay alive. That's why it's so dangerous to corner them."

So what makes us human?

HUMANS COMMUNICATE
THROUGH SPEECH

"I've thought of two more traits humans possess. We can communicate through speech, through language, and we know the difference between right and wrong."

Can't animals communicate with each other?

"Yes, but not through speech."

Dolphins and even dogs seem to understand when we talk to them. In fact, they're smarter than we are. I've heard of dolphins who understand us, but I've never heard of a human who understands dolphin. Or dog, for that matter.

"Dogs and cats and other animals are conditioned to understand. They don't really understand language. They understand the tone of voice, not words."

Everyone is "conditioned" when it comes to language. Babies have to be taught the language they learn. Think what it'd be like if that weren't true. Could you imagine a baby being born to an English-speaking family and not knowing English? Instead it speaks some Tibetan dialect. Wow, if it were born here, its parents would freak.

"People understand what their pets are saying. When the dog stands by the refrigerator and barks, it's hungry. It waits for the owner or someone to come and feed it."

So animals condition us? Rover thinks, "Now how am I going to train this human?" Can you imagine poor Rover when you're away and another human has to be broken in? "Roof, roof, the refrigerator, you fool. Don't you people understand anything?"

"Now that I think about it, I have heard that monkeys and gorillas can learn some form of sign language. So I guess they can at least mimic communication."

Yes, I've heard of that. In one case I heard that a gorilla made up a new hand sign. It combined two or three hand signs to say something.

HUMANS DISTINGUISH RIGHT AND WRONG

"Okay, so animals can communicate. They don't know right from wrong, though. I mean, the only way they know something is wrong is if they are trained that way."

Just like—

"People? I guess so."

Sure, right and wrong aren't innate.

"No, of course not. We talked about that. And values differ from culture to culture, and time to time. Relativism, that's where our discussion started. So what do you think makes us human?"

FAMILY RESEMBLANCE

Dunno! Maybe everything we've said is what makes us human. If you have enough of these traits, you're human. Some people call it a family resemblance. Little Johnny may have features that combine both sides of the family.

He looks like his maternal grandmother in the nose, sort of. If you look at large families, you can see a resemblance, even though two of the children don't share any features.

"But that still leaves babies out of our calculation. The human traits we've picked are not reflected in infants."

Big loss! Do you know what they do in their diapers?

"Seriously. Do babies feel and express emotions, and reason, and communicate, and know that they will die? Do they evaluate problems and create solutions? I guess they do some of these activities, but no better than some animals. And they don't know right from wrong until we teach them. Still, they are human. Maybe what makes us human is that we have human parents."

How do you know? If we can't determine what makes someone human, how can we know that her parents are human?

"We all know what humans are. We may not be able to define the concept, but we know examples of humans. Just like when we looked at examples of morality. From the examples, we found common features. Remember?"

Gee, you're learning. Still, I don't think it's because someone's parents are human. We all call people human, even when we haven't met their parents.

GENETICS AND BEING HUMAN

"That's not what I mean. We don't have to know their parents, or their parents' parents. Proving that someone is human would go on forever. What I mean is that being human is a genetic trait. If you examine someone's genes, you can determine whether or not the person is human. What do you think of that? Science—in this case, biology—has decided for us."

But people were human before we ever thought about genetic codes and other biological jargon. Besides that, your idea puts the cart before the horse. Biologists looked at humans and then found out what unique biological trait they had.

"What's wrong with doing that?"

Nothing, except that it automatically limits humans to a certain group of animals with similar ancestry. From what we were discussing earlier, I thought we were being more open. You gave features like being able to feel emotions and being able to think or reason. Those traits opened the field to a more interesting range of beings.

"But it's humans we are trying to define, not intelligent, caring antelopes. What other kinds of creatures do you want to make human? And don't say computers."

Good point. I guess what I had in mind was not so much a physical description of humans. I think your point is a very good one. Biologically, we are human because of our parents, because of our genetic code. That is one sense of the notion of being human. It's a description.

"What else is there other than the descriptive sense?"

THE MORAL SENSE OF "HUMAN"

I'm not sure what to call it, but when we call someone human we give that person special status.

"You mean there is a moral sense of the word *human?* I didn't think you liked morality, Art! I think I've caught you in a contradiction."

I'm not sure it has to be a moral sense. I don't think you have to give people rights or duties or obligations, at least not just because they are human. And I certainly don't think you have to do unto them and all of that other stuff we talked about.

"Nonetheless, you are granting special status to humans. You're moral after all."

I resent that. (Somehow you've turned the tables on me!) I am willing to treat lots of creatures like you treat humans. Computers, for one. Can you imagine how the last political elections would have gone if computers got to vote? See, what I have in mind is to find out what makes us special. Imagine—

"Not another one of your extreme examples."

No, no, this one is likely to happen. Imagine that more beings from the far side of Jupiter come down to visit. Not all of them are as human looking as I am. (I am too!) How can we determine they are human?

"In the moral sense?"

In the special sense we are discussing, whatever you call it.

GREED

"To be human is to always want more. Humans are never satisfied with what they have. You know, like when someone starts a job. The person wants to do well. Then, after a while, you want to advance. At first, all you want is a promotion. But each promotion satisfies you only for a short time. Then you want to move ahead. People always want a bigger house, a better car, a vacation to a more exotic place. That's what makes us human. And it's probably innate. You can even see it in young children. They always want what they see."

So what makes us human is that we are greedy? How uplifting!

"Yes, we are innately greedy. Go on—'But what about?' I'm sure you don't agree. Go on, 'What about'—

What about what?

"You always have an objection or an example that doesn't fit my definitions. So—"

What About Unselfish People?   Okay, but what about people who help others? Are they greedy or selfish? What do they get out of it?

"They get a sense of satisfaction from doing the right thing. They feel good about themselves. You probably never felt that, but we call it self-esteem."

Self-esteem? Interesting concept. But I don't understand. You help an old person cross the street so that you'll feel good about yourself. Did the old person want to cross the street, or are you forcing her?

"Of course I don't force people across the street. But when I help them, I feel good about it."

Why?

"Because they need help, and they have feelings."

So you help them because they need the help?

"Of course, you nitwit."

But how is this selfish? You get something out of it. But you are helping the other person. Which is your primary motive, to help or to feel good?

"To help. If I do it just to feel good about myself, then the feeling doesn't happen. The good feeling is a kind of by-product of doing the right thing."

Because otherwise your motive would be selfish? See, here's where I don't get it. You help people because they need help. Then you feel good about yourself. The ideas of selfish and selfless become confused. Your action is primarily directed at helping the other person. It's only secondarily self-oriented.

"I see what you mean. Still, people are often very selfish and greedy. Maybe it's because of socialization, because of moral training, that we overcome our innate selfishness."

Maybe.

Greed and Private Property. "But?"

Well, only one small "but." The whole idea of greed assumes that we understand the notion of private property. That's pretty complicated stuff. I can't honestly say I fully understand private property. How could an infant know about this idea?

"What does private property have to do with it?"

Imagine living in an environment where there is more than enough of everything to go around. When you're hungry, you just reach up and pick a ripe fruit. In this kind of place would there be greed?

"What if I didn't want to work? All I do all day is lie around. When it's mealtime, I see you eating and I want your fruit. What prevents me from taking it?"

Nothing. Except that there's no reason to take anything. If you take "my" fruit, I just lean back and take another piece. There's plenty.

"Yes, I see your point, but that doesn't change my mind. People are innately greedy and selfish. All your example shows is that we can imagine a place where people don't have to be greedy. But just bring in a shortage of something. Then you'll see how fast they change. Besides, our society isn't like your fantasy. Here there isn't enough to go around. Only people on welfare get to take without working for it. The rest of us have to work."

I'm not sure I see the connection. I'll give you your first point. We do live in a society where shortages occur. We'll get back to this in a moment. But your complaint about welfare strikes me as strange.

"Strange? How so? Those people get a lot from the system, but what do they have to do for it? Nothing. I'd love to have a free ride like that."

The ride isn't quite free. But think about it. You are getting a similar "free ride." You're a college student. (I use the term loosely.) If you are going to a private school, there are lots of people who donate money so that the school can operate. Your tuition money probably doesn't pay for what you get. And if you're attending a public, state, or community college, it's taxes that pay much of your way. You're a welfare recipient, though probably not a poor one.

"But someday I'll return the favor. I'll donate money to education and I'll pay my share of the taxes that go to public schools."

Perhaps. But that's the idea of any decent welfare system, to get people back into the flow of society.

"But those people stay on welfare for generations. They don't work."

Sometimes we blame people for "taking advantage of the system." That's odd. When we take advantage of the system, it's okay. We expect our rights. When a really rich person takes advantage of the system, we admire him. But when some poor guy gets almost enough to live on, we scream and yell. If you're assuming everyone is innately greedy, why blame only the poor person for showing it?

"Let me think about this one. I want to add laziness to my definition of human nature. We are instinctively lazy and prejudiced. Everyone is lazy, prejudiced, selfish, and greedy. That's why we need morality. If we didn't have morality, society would never progress."

CYNICISM

Progress?

"Yes, progress. We can do things now that people only imagined before. Our technology gives us longer lives and better weapons for protection."

I don't agree that we are more advanced than other societies. Maybe we are more technologically advanced in some ways, but—

"But nothing. Would you want to live anywhere else?"

My country's better than your country, na na! Is that what you're saying?

"Well, isn't it? We are more secure and better fed."

Yes, that may be true. Why do you have such a cynical view of people?

"Cynical?"

Yes, negative.

"I know what 'cynical' means."

Look at your definition of humans. You seem to be saying that humans are weak, vicious, selfish, and destructive. Is that what you see in people?

"It's hard to deny that we are not that way. Look how destructive people have been. Maybe a way of distinguishing people and animals is that only people destroy and dehumanize each other."

Dehumanize?

"Yes, only humans treat other people as though they were worthless."

I won't deny that you humans are occasionally cruel.

"And then we rationalize our actions. We treat our actions as though they were appropriate. We go all out to justify what we know is wrong."

I've seen some of that, too. But it doesn't mean that people are like this by nature.

"Oh?"

CREATIVE AND INVENTIVE

People can be cruel and selfish and destructive, but they are also kind and giving and creative. (This is a switch, me arguing for the good in people.)

"What are you saying? That we aren't selfish and cruel and destructive?"

I don't see any evidence that people are this way by nature. People also enjoy beauty and humor. They even overcome their learned prejudices with some effort.

"Then you don't think people are very accurately reflected in their actions?"

Gee, I don't know. All I'm saying is that your cynical view is more a sign of frustration than anything else. Just because we cannot easily define human nature doesn't mean we have to be unjustly harsh on humanity.

RELIGION

"Fair enough, Art. I say what distinguishes us as humans is that we have religion."

So atheists aren't human?

"No, they are just misguided. But humans are the only species that asks religious questions, that believes in souls and spirits and psyches. Maybe that's what makes us human, that we ask religious questions."

What do you mean by religious questions?

"We care about spiritual things. We want to be comfortable and well fed and safe. But we also want more."

Humans do not live by bread alone? Is that it?

"Something like that, yes. We believe in souls. What makes a person human, and not a machine, is that people have souls. Machines don't have souls."

I haven't ever seen a soul. Have you?

"You want concrete proof that souls exist, and there just isn't any. Just because you can't see them doesn't mean they don't exist."

I don't want cement proof. Remember, I believe in invisible, green goblins. You can't see them, either.

"I'm not going to get into that discussion again. Lots of people believe in souls. That's what makes us human."

Hmm.

"What are you doing?"

I'm looking into my shirt. I'm looking for my soul. I'm also wondering why my soul picked this body?

"You can make fun of my idea all you want, but people have souls."

I doubt that we'll resolve this. What else about religion defines us as humans?

HUMANS HAVE FREE WILL

"Because we have souls, we are free. We have free will. We can choose any way we want. That's what makes us human."

Interesting idea. Why does this have to be tied to religion?

"It doesn't. People are human because we are free."

And animals and computers—

"Animals act on instinct, and computers don't choose. They react to programming. I know what you're going to say. People are programmed, too. Yes, we are. Only we can go beyond our programming. We can even choose to ignore our programming. Machines can't do that!"

Maybe our programming is more diverse and more sophisticated. Maybe our learning is more random than a computer's programming.

"You can say maybe all you want, Art. But I say people have free will."

What is an unfree will?

"Don't distract me with your little puns, or whatever you call them. People are free. We are also spiritual in another sense I just thought of."

COMPASSION

Compassion?

"So you can read! Yes, people can feel compassion toward one another. Computers can't do that. And I doubt that animals feel that kind of emotion. So what makes us human is some of what we have already talked about, but clearly what makes us human is that we have free will and compassion."

Can I choose not to feel compassion? Or am I unfree when it comes to compassion?

"Now you're just playing word games. There's a place for that, I guess, but not now. You don't deal very well with people, do you?"

RELATING TO OTHER PEOPLE

Actually, I do get along well with other people. I usually just do whatever they want, and they're content. But that's another story. I think your final comments have solved our problem.

"Which comments?"

I think compassion is too limited, but you're on the right track. People relate to other people in special ways. Compassion is one of them.

"And the special ways we relate to other people is what makes us human?"

Yeah. What do ya think?

"Well, humans do relate to each other in ways that machines and animals can't communicate. That does seem true."

Right. When you said that people feel, and communicate, and care, that was on the right track. People don't always relate to other people in the special ways reserved for humans, of course.

"But only humans can relate to others in those special ways. Now all we have to do is figure out what those ways are."

Why don't we leave that to the philosophers who take up Part II and Part III? I think we can learn a lot from them. Whatever the final answer is, I think you have hit on a very important point. The best life has to include relating to other people.

"Do we know what makes us human now?"

Not exactly, but I think our talk has made us sensitive to the right things to look for in each upcoming theory. I think we deserve an extra 250 brownie points for our work here.

"What do brownie points give you?"

An infinite number of brownie points gives nothing, but they're still always good to have. Just in case you need them.

■
___

SUMMARY OF DISCUSSION

Isn't everyone different? Don't we all have different values? Relativism is the observation that values vary from person to person, society to society, and over historical times. From this variation in values, relativism concludes that values are not stable and unchanging. What is right for one person (or society) may not be right for another person (or society).

We are left with the question: "Which values are true?" Some disagreements are only apparent and can be resolved. The problem is that many other disagreements are disagreements over basic beliefs and values. The relativist uses genuine disagreements as evidence that values are not absolute.

There are at least two replies to the relativist. First, the relativist assumes that agreement is truth. This assumption is not safe to make. Nearly every European once believed that the earth was flat, yet we know that the earth's shape did not depend on their agreement. Reality is separate from human belief. So agreement is not truth. Disagreement, therefore, does not entail falsity. Because you and I disagree does not mean that we are both mistaken.

Second, as in morality, in the sciences we also find disagreement. We do not say, however, that science is relative just because of disagreements. Science is a method that receives and uses tentative truths as a part of its project. Progress can be made only by recognizing that we do not have the entire, absolute truth. However, science can still work toward the Truth.

Relativism has an appeal because we believe people differ. Therefore, their values differ. That may be true, but it is equally apparent that we share some qualities that make us human.

What constitutes human nature? Humans think, feel, communicate through speech, and distinguish right from wrong. Computers can function in these ways, too. Humans have human genes and other biological similarities. Our question, however, is not directed at physical resemblance, but at a moral sense of the term *human*.

Humans may be greedy by nature. There is a problem, though, in determining whether greed is naturally or culturally determined. Other less cynical aspects may also be part of human nature. Humans are creative and inventive. They concern themselves with religious questions. They may exercise free will. But if we do exercise free will, then the question of a human nature may be irrelevant. Free will may negate the impact of human nature. Compassion and other ways of relating to other people is another way of defining what makes us human. How we relate to each other may be what makes us human. There may be no human nature as such, only a human way of relating to our reality.

■
DISCUSSION HIGHLIGHTS

I. Relativism
    1. Values vary between people, societies, historical times.
    2. Values are not stable and unchanging.
II. Disagreements
    1. There are disagreements in form and on content.
    2. Cultural disagreements can be misunderstandings.
    3. They may also be disagreements over basic beliefs.
III. Types of truth
    1. Mathematical truths are true by agreement.
    2. Scientific truths are "guaranteed" by the scientific method.
IV. Human nature
    1. People can think.
    2. People can feel emotions and sensations.
    3. People can communicate through speech.
    4. People can distinguish right and wrong.
    5. People have similar physical and genetic structures.
    6. People may be greedy by nature.
    7. People are naturally creative and inventive.
    8. They can be concerned with religious questions.
    9. People enjoy free will.
    10. They feel compassion, sympathy, and like emotions.
    11. Humans are distinguished in their way of relating to each other and to reality.

■
QUESTIONS FOR THOUGHT/PAPER TOPICS

1. An ancient Chinese philosopher, Chuang Tsu, once wrote that he dreamed that he was a butterfly. He flew about happily, enjoying the life

of the butterfly, never asking who he was. Then he awoke and found out that he was a man. Did Chuang Tsu dream he was a butterfly, or did the butterfly dream he was Chuang Tsu? Which reality is true?

2. Do disagreements between cultures imply that there is no truth? What method is used to resolve differences in the sciences? Can you think of a similar method for resolving moral differences?

3. Moral people tell me that they want conformity to the moral rules and that they value individual differences. Assume both can be true simultaneously. How would that work?

4. What are the essential features that make us human? Try to keep in mind that we are looking for more than a biological/physical distinction.

5. Do computers think? If you think they can't think, describe what humans do that computers fail to do. (Then construct a computer that can think in the ways you describe.)

6. Do humans have free will? How free is that will? In light of all we know about enforced conformity brought about by socialization, advertising, education, and so on, how much room is there for free will?

7. Do you humans relate to each other in special ways? Can we use this to define what makes us human?

■
FOR FURTHER READING

There is a very readable little book by Bertrand Russell, *The Problems of Philosophy* (Oxford, 1959). Russell clearly discusses a series of questions in philosophy, including knowledge. Another book on the topic of relativism and knowledge is Ludwig Wittgenstein's *On Certainty* (Harper & Row, 1972). It presents a picture of one way of understanding what counts as knowledge. John Ladd edited an anthology called *Ethical Relativism* (Wadsworth, 1971) containing several worthwhile articles. Another place to look for a discussion of human nature and relativity in values is the works of Chinese philosophers, Lao Tsu and Chuang Tsu.

C H A P T E R

FIVE

What If I Do Whatever I Want?

I know what you're thinking. "Art has tried to convince us of this already. And we have shown him that doing whatever one wants is dangerous to society and to each of us. If each of us did whatever he wanted, we would have chaos!" That's what you're thinking, isn't it?

Okay, I concede your point. Doing whatever I want could lead to the breakdown of society as we know it. After all, I am quite the influential trendsetter! People do whatever I do. Everywhere I go, people watch my every move.

"Actually, what I was thinking is that I'm tired of these talks where you have the upper hand. Why don't you pick on someone else in this chapter? I'll sit back and watch—or read, as the case may be. That's what I was thinking."

Fair enough. Let's pick your average, fanatical moralist to carry on the conversation.

"No fair. Pick a moralist who is reasonable. Anyone can knock down a straw man, Art."

Straw man?

"A straw man is someone who is set up to be knocked down. You know, an easy target that doesn't fight back. Make your moralist believable and intelligent."

I'll try. This should be challenging. Okay, for this chapter imagine that I am locked in semimortal, intellectual combat with an intelligent moralist. Now let me get back to the discussion. Doing whatever I want could lead to the breakdown of society as we know it. After all, I am quite the influential—

MORALIST: All right, you've made your point. Fortunately for us, Art, you are not an influence on people. Our point is still true, however. Our point is more of a theoretical one than a practical one. What if everyone, or nearly everyone, did whatever she wanted?

ART: Then I would be a fool to be the only one following moral rules.

MORALIST: Seriously, what if each person did whatever she wanted?

ART: Then everyone would be happy! (I can probably stop with the 'Art,' 'Moralist' designations, now, huh?)

Material in this chapter taken from Søren Kierkegaard, Either/Or (Princeton: Princeton University Press, 1944, 1959). David F. Swenson & Lillian Marvin Swenson translation.

"No, no, there would be chaos. No one would go to work. Nothing would get done. You wouldn't be able to do what you want, because there would be no police to protect you. Soon everyone would starve. Who would grow the food?"

Maybe you're right, but I think it's unreasonable to automatically exclude living for the moment. Pleasure is desirable, right? What is wrong with a life in pursuit of pleasure? All I want is that we look at one example of a character who does whatever he wants. If the life is unappealing even after our quick look, I promise I won't raise the issue again. What could the harm be, just one little look? We might even discover features of this life that are appealing to us.

"Art, you are confusing two distinct positions. A person could pursue pleasure—or any goal, for that matter—yet not live for the present moment. Someone might carefully plan out a long-term strategy to get more and more pleasure, or to succeed at any other goal. That's one option. The other option is a person who lives for whatever comes along in the momentary present. This person may not seek pleasure. Which option are you suggesting?"

How about both options? What I mean is, I think I misstated my idea. It's too late to change the title of this chapter, isn't it? Oh, well.

LIFE IS MEANINGLESS

"What is your idea?"

Life is meaningless. And since life is meaningless, I might as well do whatever I want.

"So now we have finally come to it! You don't believe in anything!"

That's not quite true. I believe in lots of things. Tables and chairs, people and bears. It rhymes, did you notice?

"But you don't believe in anything you can't see, anything intangible."

I am cut to the quick. Ouch! Of course I believe in some things that I can't see. The far side of the moon is out of my sight. Sure, there are pictures from some of our spacecraft, but I would believe in the existence of the far side of the moon without that kind of proof.

"That's not what I mean. You're being stupid intentionally, just to avoid the issue."

I am not being stupid intentionally. I'm naturally like this. (Ooh, I think you tricked me there.) I believe in other things that I can't see. Like you, I have other sense organs. I believe in odors, for example.

"That's not the point. Do you believe in anything you cannot physically touch, taste, smell, see, or hear? That's what I want to know. Does your reality stop at the limit of your senses?"

Hmm. (*Hmm* indicates that I'm pondering your question, even though I'm not.) Yes, I've found something intangible that I believe in—pleasure.

"But that's still physical, or at least caused by physical sensations!"

Not true. Some of my pleasures are mental.

"Like what? You aren't going to tell us that you enjoy thinking, are you?"

Sometimes I imagine a really great physical pleasure, and—

"Enough of this! (You really were thinking this, weren't you?) This is getting us nowhere."

That's just the point. You think there's somewhere to go. But one way of occupying my time is just about the same as any other way. That's because there's no meaning to life. Every action and event is just about the same as every other action or event. So "wasting" my time discussing this with you is no worse than any other occupation.

"This is ridiculous."

It may be mistaken, but it's not ridiculous. Just assume for a few minutes that there is no meaning to life. What follows from that?

"I don't know. What?"

Don't resist so much. We'll have a chance later in the book to examine the question of the meaning of life. It comes in the third part of the book. There's even a piece from your Bible in that part. So for now, just assume that life is meaningless. Let's see how terrible such a life would be.

"I can't just assume that life is meaningless!"

Joe and the Ants. Then let me give you an analogy. There is a species of tree ant that has exactly fifty generations each spring-summer season. If the warm seasons last longer than usual, then each generation lives a little longer.

"How do they know how long the summer will last?"

How do I know? I'm not an ant. So these little bugs produce exactly fifty generations per year.

"Where is this example going?"

Wait, this gets better. The first and last generations hatch from their tiny eggs with wings. The forty-eight generations between the first and last are wingless. The first generation flies from the trees to the ground. Exactly forty-eight wingless generations spend their little ant lives on the ground. Then the fiftieth generation sprouts wings and flies back into the trees, where the eggs are planted to wait for the next spring.

"Amazing! What does this have to do with our question?"

What if someone comes along and steps on one of the little ants? I'm sure it happens, though unintentionally. What would be the significance of an ant's death? The generations would continue. The other ants of his generation would live out their precious few days. The fiftieth generation would sprout wings, fly to the trees, and lay their eggs. Next spring, more ants hatch. What significance does any one ant have?

"Nice story; now explain the analogy. Put it in human terms."

What significance does any one person's life have? The generations continue. What's the difference between a person's life and an ant's life?

"For one, the lives of humans are longer than the lives of the ants."

But in light of eternity, a few decades is insignificant.

"Their friends and families will miss them. Some of them will make contributions to their societies."

So what? There was a man who lived 8,237 years ago in Mesopotamia. His name was Joe. He had friends and a family. He made contributions to his society. A couple of his inventions even made life easier for people. Then along came someone who stepped on Joe. Do his friends and family and society matter? Undoubtedly they missed Joe. But they're long dead themselves. Does Joe's life matter any more than the ant who was crushed? Fifty generations or fifty seasons later, and the poor bug is forgotten.

"Joe probably felt that his life was meaningful. The ant didn't think its life was meaningful or anything else."

I agree. Joe the Mesopotamian may have thought his life was meaningful, but Joe's life had no more meaning than the ant's life.

"His family and friends thought so, too."

But we don't even remember Joe. Joe may have participated in great battles or great debates, but we have no record of it. Nor did his society have any apparent effect on ours. Neither he nor his family nor his friends nor his society has left a trace of itself. Joe's very existence is insignificant now. Just like the ant's life.

"You're depressing."

Come on, Smile. Come on, smile. This is a happy thought. I recognize that Joe's life, and the ant's life, amount to the same thing—nothing. In the grand scheme of things, there is no grand scheme. But rather than getting depressed over this, drop your illusions. Realize that life is futile. It doesn't matter how you live. Moral people and religious people, conservative people and liberal people, all people die. In the space of the time between birth and death, there are no limits. There is only boredom. So live for the moment.

"What kind of life would that be?"

THE STRANGER

One character who lives life by doing whatever he wants is the main character in the novel *The Stranger*, by Albert Camus. You may have read the book, but if you haven't read it let me describe this character. By the way, he's one of my heroes.

The Stranger is not your ordinary pleasure seeker. He tries to avoid boredom. That's his defining feature. He finds it futile to try to alter the world, so he alters himself. He gives up goals and ambition and lives as much for the moment as he can manage. He never consciously sets out his strategy, but the way he does this is genuinely ingenious. He lives almost completely in the moment. For him, the object in front of him receives his complete attention. He does not see a larger meaning in life than what is presented by the momentary experience. Quite calmly, he tells the reader, "All that counts is the present and the concrete."

The Stranger does not connect the past, the present, and the future. He reaffirms this point of view near the end of the book. He says he has "always been absorbed in the present moment, or the immediate future."

"So what if a character in a novel says some crazy things! He's just weird."

The Stranger's point of view is not as foreign to us as it is uncomfortable.

We are supposed to respect the past and look to the future. That's what morality is all about. Look at promises. I promised you something yesterday that I must guarantee to perform tomorrow. Morality ties the past me to the present and future me.

"You make it sound like they are different. The past me, the present me, and the future me are all me!"

The Stranger is immune to this kind of thinking. He does what he wants, as he wants to do it. He's spontaneous! Most of us live this way, too, only we reserve the weekends for our spontaneous acts.

Spontaneous. (Read this in a deep, resonant voice.) "Hello there. Do you have any plans for the weekend?" (Now read this in your own voice.) "Sure do. I plan to be spontaneous this weekend. Well, at least for part of the weekend."

We schedule our spontaneity! "Yes, I'll be doing the laundry from 2:15 to 4:30, then I'll be able to be spontaneous until 7:30." Sounds pretty stupid, huh? But that's as close as most people get to understanding the Stranger. He lives the way we would all like to live, if it weren't for responsibilities. Aaah!

"How is it possible to live for the moment? There *are* responsibilities, and promises, and obligations. And I feel guilty if I don't keep my promises and all the rest."

Good question. Let me give an analogy.

Concentrates Like a Work of Art. I bet you think I'm going to make some silly pun about art and Art. Well, wrong. A work of art can help us understand how someone like the Stranger looks at everyday experience. Imagine a painting. No, not that one; nothing abstract. Imagine a "regular" painting. You know, one that portrays a street scene or something like that. A painting or a photograph is a frozen moment. Now look at the object of the picture. The object is in the foreground. The rest of the world is in the background. In a really good painting the artist uses the background to draw the viewer's eye to the object of the picture.

"So?"

That's how the Stranger views the world. Whatever object is in front of him engages him. All the rest of the world is insignificant background. Whether he is smoking a cigarette, or making "love" with Marie, or eating eggs from a pan, or hearing the slam of a door, or spending an entire Sunday afternoon watching the street scene below his balcony, each experience is significant for the Stranger. Each is in the present; each is concrete. There is nothing abstract about his perspective.

Avoids the Evils of Morality. The Stranger lives as though reality is a painting. Everything is in the experience. Nothing else counts for him. This attitude lets him experience fully whatever is in front of him. Neither rules nor roles, nor guilt nor shame distract him from experiencing the moment. Living as he lives, the Stranger is able to avoid all the evils of morality.

"Are you saying that he is a moral person? That he avoids evil?"

No way. He avoids the evils of morality itself. He avoids the boredom, the anxieties of indecision and responsibility, the goals, the pressures, and the illusion of meaning. He completely avoids choices and the regrets that accompany all choices. He avoids all the distracting parts of morality. Being spontaneous and concentrated on what stands before him, he is free.

Avoids Boredom. "This sounds really boring. How can anyone live such a boring life? What's so interesting about eating fried eggs from a pan or watching people walk by on the street? The way you describe him, he's too passive, too submissive, and far too much oriented toward his senses. Doesn't this guy have any friends?"

One question at a time. Is he bored? Why are you wondering about that? I admit, most people would be bored with his life. But that's because most people are goal oriented. They think that what they do in life really matters. The Stranger is never bored. He is never bored because he is able to throw himself completely into his experience. He is never distracted by things he is supposed to do, or by conscience. He is completely spontaneous. He never has to think about what he's doing. His surroundings and his inner desires determine his actions. I think I have found my hero.

"Our lives are more significant than merely spending our days watching the street scene below our balcony or smoking cigarettes. Our lives aren't spent in meaningless inactivity."

The Anxiety of Indecision. Significant, huh? Meaningful? Perhaps most people would be bored with the Stranger's existence. But that's because they probably have an inflated sense of their own importance. What the Stranger accomplishes is really incredible. His way of life lets him avoid the anxiety of indecision.

"What is that?"

I think the reason so many people want a moral code is to avoid the indecision that comes with freedom. The Stranger avoids indecision by being passive and letting events take their own course. And, of course, he realizes that life is meaningless, so it doesn't matter what happens.

"How does freedom bring indecision? It's freedom that allows us to decide for ourselves what we want and how to get it."

Does it really seem that way to you? Think of the last decision you freely made. If it was a difficult decision, I'll bet you didn't feel free. Choice brings anxiety and indecision. I'll bet you anguished over the decision. What's the point? What's the difference? Just be spontaneous.

"It's not that easy. You underestimate the importance of our choices. How I choose affects my whole life."

This is another point where I disagree with you. Your choice does little but cause you anxiety. You and almost everyone else are under the illusion that you can affect the outside world with your choices. But there is virtually nothing that you can control. Try it. Pick a job or a potential friend and then see if you can just walk into the position you've chosen.

"Well, of course you can't just pick a job and just show up. They have to hire you. And the same goes for a new friend."

They have to hire you, too?

"No, friendship grows between two people. You can't just decide that the person over there is going to be your friend. The other person has to want to be your friend, too."

So why decide? If the other person wants to befriend you, let her. If an employer wants to hire you, let her. Why decide at all? One friend is as good as another; one job is as good as another. And look at all the anxiety you avoid.

"This is crazy. I should just sit back and let people come to me with friend-ship and with jobs? The real world doesn't work like that, Art. You've been sitting too long in a dark corner of your basement."

Nobody Wants to Make Choices.   Live like the Stranger. Avoid decisions and the sense of indecision will disappear. Don't you feel most free after you've decided? Isn't the time of indecision that comes before choice really anxious and uncomfortable?

"It is uncomfortable making important choices."

Exactly. That's why so many people look for someone else to choose for them.

"What do you mean?"

Look how many times people seek advice. They ask friends for advice. They read books and ask experts. They turn to their morality and religion. Nobody wants to make choices.

"This is going too far. I would never give up my right to choose. That's what living in a free country is all about."

Oh, I agree. People want to have the right to make their own choices. They just don't want to make the choices. Because there is so much anxiety in-volved in the decision process. But of course, all that is avoidable. Give up choice and you avoid indecision.

"I don't want someone else making my choices for me. That's what totali-tarian countries are all about."

You don't want people making choices for you, and yet you seek advice? You follow the law, and moral rules, and religious commandments, and yet you don't want other people making your choices?

"But I freely choose who to get advice from, and which society and religion I adopt, and whether or not I want to be moral."

Even assuming this is true (and of course it isn't true), you still seek these people and institutions in order to avoid the anxiety of indecision associated with choices. Look at it this way: Don't you feel better after the choice is made?

"Yes, but that's because the problem or issue has been solved."

Right, or another way of saying that is that once the decision has been made, you don't suffer any longer from the anxiety of indecision. See, we agree. There's another reason why you seek advice from people and moral and religious rules.

"Why is that?"

Anxiety of Responsibility.   To avoid the anxiety of responsibility. That's why you ask other people what they would do.

"We ask other people's advice to get a better picture of the options. Other people may see things differently than we do. For example, because they aren't as involved in the situation, they can take a more objective look at the circumstances."

You're not going to believe this, but people sometimes come to me for advice.

"What do you do?"

I use my magic quarter. I make heads one option and tails the other option. And I make the person promise to abide by the flip of the coin.

"This can't be. People come to you for your opinion and you pull out a coin? What kind of friend are you?"

Probably a good one, although as often as not I hardly know the person seeking my advice. I know that the person asking my opinion doesn't want my opinion.

"Then why does he ask you?"

To hear his own choice. But since he wants to avoid responsibility for the choice, he asks me. I guess in his mind he thinks that if things don't go well, it's Art's fault. I know this thought is probably unconscious, but I think that's what's going on. I used to have people blame me for my bad advice, at least before I began using my magic quarter.

"How does a quarter help? I'd think you were just making fun of me, and that you weren't taking my problem seriously."

Right on both counts. I am making fun of the person, for taking himself so seriously. And I am not taking his decision seriously. He's already done that. Here's what happens with the magic quarter. Before I pull out the magic quarter, I let the person talk about the options available to him. It's interesting that there are almost always only two options. I guess the person has gotten that far himself. Anyway, after the options are explained, I make the person promise to abide by the decision of the coin. Then I flip it into the air, catch it in one hand, and turn it onto the back of my other hand.

"Then what? No one could possibly take this seriously."

As a good moral person who has just made a promise to respect the coin? I beg your pardon! With the coin hidden by my hand, I look intently at the person. Obviously he wants to know what the coin has decided. Look how easily he has displaced his right to choose.

"And?"

And I ask him which side he hoped for when the coin was in the air. Which did he want, heads or tails? Now that his fate rests with the coin on the back of my hand, he can tell me. People always tell me.

"And I suppose you crush them by lying about what the coin says."

Actually, I sneak a peek at the coin and confirm that it turned up just the way he wanted it. You can't believe the relief on people's faces. They get to do what they want, and I have resolved their anxieties of indecision and responsibility.

"But the person already knew what he wanted even before he went to see you!"

Sure. How many people would come to me who wanted to hear that they should make the moral choice? No one who knows me would do that, right? People always go to the person who will tell them what they want to hear.

WHAT MAKES LIVING FOR THE MOMENT DESIRABLE?

"So you are arguing that living for pleasure is the only way to live? And you think this because you believe people want to avoid boredom and the anxieties involved in choosing?"

Yes, the anxieties of indecision and responsibility are heavy burdens to bear.

"Okay, just so I get clear on this. You also think that it is advisable to see life as meaningless."

Right. If life is meaningless, then you don't have to ever wonder what you missed by choosing one way instead of the other way. You avoid regrets; you avoid responsibility; you avoid guilt.

"These are the primary reasons for adopting the 'live for pleasure' attitude?"

These reasons and the fact that once you realize that one action is as good as another, then you can be spontaneous. You can be free!

"Anything else?"

More Pleasure.   How much more can there be? Yes, there is something else. If you live the carefree, spontaneous way, you get more pleasure.

"How do you figure that? What pleasures are available to you that are not open to moral people?"

If you don't have to worry about moral and religious rules, or guilt, then you can do whatever brings you pleasure.

"What if I like the pleasures offered by morality and religion? What if I feel comfortable with those pleasures and don't want to participate in your sordid pleasures?"

If you don't want to experience nonmoral pleasures, fine. But I doubt this is true. I've seen you moral-religious people tempted by forbidden pleasures. If the pleasures weren't tempting, they wouldn't be forbidden by your way of life. Come on, what's so bad about lust and greed, gluttony and laziness, and all the rest?

"Look, Art, some of the passions you refer to are tempting. Part of the reason is because we are only human, with human bodies. Morality requires strength and discipline. Those kinds of pleasures are intense, more intense than more acceptable pleasures."

Ah, yes, that's just the point. People like me feel pleasures more intensely. Since there are no external obligations and no moral prohibitions to distract us, our pleasures are more intense. And because we never choose, and let things happen, we are never distracted by regrets, either.

"Your pleasures are meaningless, Art. They are superficial and pointless. That's why you think life is meaningless, because your pleasures are meaningless."

It's funny, but nearly every time I get caught up in one of my passions, some moral person like you tells me that my actions are meaningless. So what? They're not supposed to be meaningful; they're supposed to be pleasurable.

WHAT MAKES LIVING FOR THE PLEASURE OF THE MOMENT UNDESIRABLE?

"You have had your say, Art. I've listened carefully. Now it's the moralists' turn. I have several criticisms of your proposed life. First, the life you describe is unrealistic. Second, your life is not as pleasure filled as you think. There are many pleasures you cannot experience. Your life lacks emotions. Third, your outlook cuts you off from other people. It makes you lonely and alone. Fourth, you have no values, therefore you have no strong sense of self or self-esteem. Do you want to hear more?"

Okay.

"Fifth, you claim to be free, but you misunderstand freedom. And because of all this, sixth, you are irredeemably depressed."

Depressed? Why do you say that?

The Life is Unrealistic. "I don't mean you personally. I don't know you. To make living for the moment sound appealing, you chose a character like the Stranger. That sort of person doesn't exist. He's a character in a novel. He's an idiot! No one lives like that. He's an extreme. The character from Kierke-gaard's *Either/Or* is much more believable. If we take a close look at him, we'll find all the elements of the point of view you attribute to the Stranger. The only difference is that the character A is intelligent enough to be depressed by his life."

Why do you say that?

"Not so fast, Art. I'm onto your strategy. Whenever you get in trouble and your ideas start to fail, you distract me by asking questions. You try to change the subject. Not this time! I've read a lot in this book about doing your own thing, or whatever you call it—"

Living in the present moment.

"Whatever! I want to say something about each of my criticisms. Then you can ask all your questions and defend your position as much as you want."

I appear to have no choice. You've taken charge of my book.

"Good. Then first, the life you depict is unrealistic."

It Is Not So Pleasure Filled.   What else?

"Your life is also not as pleasure filled as you think. Yes, you do not have the distractions that we moral people have. But you also lack the purely moral pleasures found in emotions."

Like what?

"You cannot experience any of the emotions and pleasures associated with joy. What I mean by joy is the experience of pleasure for the good fortune of someone close to you. There probably aren't enough words to label these feelings, but they're real."

You feel something pleasant when someone else feels pleasure?

"Absolutely. When someone close to me—"

Standing next to you?

"When someone emotionally close to me does well, or wins a contest, or has a special event, I feel pleasure. I feel joy. Unfortunately for you, you cannot feel this. You are so wrapped up in your own pleasures that you think you're the only person on earth. You probably don't realize that other people have hopes and dreams, fears and things they are shy about."

I never really thought about it.

It Cuts You Off from Other People.   "The nonmoral life you describe is pathetic. Not only can't you experience the pleasure of joys, but you can't even understand that other people are real just like you. You are lonely because you think you are the only person on earth who has wants and needs. You are so self-centered that you think only you feel pleasure."

Self-centered? How should I be centered? Being self-centered is the only way to get pleasure.

It Misses the Moral Continuities.   "That's part of your problem. With pleasure as your goal, you miss out on the moral continuities."

Absolutely. The what?

"The moral continuities. You can't imagine the pleasures and the sense of security that moral people feel. Moral people see themselves as part of the human race."

I'm human!

"Yes, you are, Art, but you don't see yourself as part of the long line of human tradition and history. With your self-centered attitude of living for pleasure, you miss out on a sense of heritage."

Big deal. The people you refer to are long dead. What can I get from them?

"You could get a sense of who you are and how you fit into the human race. Respecting people who lived in the past could help you learn from them. Many of their rules and insights help moral people to live better and more meaningful lives."

So?

"Seeing yourself as part of the long line of humans gives meaning to your life. People start projects, and we carry them through. People of the past made sacrifices so that we would have a better life. We need to realize that and to respect them."

Is that all there is to your moral continuity?

"No, there's more. Feeling respect for the people of the past is what I call historical continuity. Feeling connected to the people living now in the present is also important. You see, moral people feel akin to living, breathing people, and not merely because they bring us pleasure."

You took the words right out of my mouth.

Communication and Community. "Feeling connected to people in the present sets the stage for communication and community. Before you can say, 'Huh?' I'll tell you what that means. Moral people are able to communicate with other people. We see others as real, as feeling, as worthy. That sense of other people lets us form genuine communities."

I've lived in lots of cities.

"There's a difference. Living in a city does not mean you live with a sense of community. People who live around other people often feel very lonely. Having a sense of community is having a sense of connection."

Okay, moralist, now I have to respect a bunch of dead people and feel some deep affection for my neighbors. Is that it?

"Not quite! It's not a matter of affection. It's a matter of being human, and recognizing the worth in others because they are human, too. For moral people, the feeling goes beyond one's neighbors. You may have noticed that moral people are charitable to others whom they will never see. Now do you see why?"

I suppose so, at least I think I see the point. You're saying that only moral people develop relationships of the sort you describe.

"Yes. How could someone who lives for pleasure recognize the worth of other people? How could someone who believes that life is meaningless ever feel connected to people of the past and the future? You're so focused on the moment that you lose sight of people."

Creativity. Hold on. You moral people want me to think about people who aren't even born yet? Why should I?

"The ability to think of yourself as part of the unbroken line of humanity allows you to be creative. Without seeing the people of the present and the future as part of yourself, there would be no reason to create anything."

But I might stumble on some invention or paint a picture or something. Why can't I do that without being moral?

"You can invent and paint all you like, but what would be the point? Inventing, painting, writing, and all the other perfectly human activities are ways of communicating with other people. It's our way of relating to others. When you're distracted by your pleasure seeking, you cannot relate to other people in a significant way. When you're distracted by your despair over the meaninglessness of your life, you are out of touch with other people. Only moral people enjoy the pleasures and securities of the moral continuities. We feel the continuous chain of humanity, and we feel secure because of it."

Wow! What else am I supposed to be missing?

It Is Empty of Love, Trust, and Friendship. "You are unable to have relationships of love, trust, and friendship. Because of your inability to relate with others, you fail to receive the joys of intimacy."

How so?

"Just look at your example of the Stranger. You said that he got as much pleasure from eating fried eggs from a pan as watching the street scene from his balcony, right?"

Yes, that's right. Because he doesn't discriminate among experiences, each pleasure is as good as any other pleasure. That is meant as a strength of his lifestyle.

"No doubt it is meant that way, but look what follows. You also said that these pleasures were comparable to smoking a cigarette or making 'love' to Marie. Don't you see? He is so caught up in his pleasures that he cannot love Marie. He can't be intimate with her."

They make love.

"But they don't love, at least he doesn't. Sex is not love. Sex is physically intimate, but it's not emotionally intimate."

Yes, but it's still pleasurable.

"The moral person has both the physical and the emotional experience. You think our moral obligations distract us from feeling sensual pleasures. Did you ever think that the distraction is an emotional experience that is far more pleasant? Emotional intimacy enhances pleasurable experience."

What do you want me to say? Duh.

It Lacks Values and a Self. "I'm sorry to have to tell you all this, but the life you advocate is not very attractive. Your perspective also lacks any real sense of a self."

How do you mean?

"Because you concentrate as completely as you can on the present, you can't attach your own past and future to yourself. I know you intend for this to be another strength, but it isn't. You can't have a unified, integrated character."

Huh?

"If you take seriously the extreme character that you draw, then you could not live a coherent life."

What do you mean, "a coherent life"?

"If each of your experiences is really separate, really discrete from every other experience, then your life would be completely disjointed. There'd be no unifying theme to you. I guess we'd have to say that you would not have a character at all."

Is that bad?

"Yes. You would not have an enduring sense of your own self. You would not have any sense that you are connected to your own past and future. You would achieve intensity in your experience, but you would sacrifice your own sense of being a real person."

You mean of being a moral person, don't you?

"No, not at all. Really living for the moment in the extreme would cut you off from any sense of your self. It would cut you off from other people. How can I say this better? If you really lived with this attitude, you would live for a million intense moments, but each moment would be separate and distinct. You'd live a million lives but never know it. The more I think about it, the more I see this life as impossible. We couldn't even carry on conversations because you wouldn't be the same person from day to day."

Now who's taking the extreme view? I didn't say that this life has to be a mindless life without any memory. You're taking it too far.

It Misunderstands Freedom.   "Your character mistakes being spontaneous with being free."

But he acts without having to think about his actions, their moral worth, meaningfulness, etc.

"That is true, there is an immediacy in his actions. Just because his reasoning is not used, though, it does not follow that he is free. Look at your own example of the Stranger. As you describe this fictional character, he acts according to his surroundings."

What do you mean?

"If Marie shows up, he desires her. If Marie does not visit, then he smokes a cigarette or looks out at the street scene below. His own desires are unimportant. He desires whatever comes along."

That's the beauty of the lifestyle! He never faces frustration. He desires whatever comes along. That way he always gets what he wants. Who could be freer than that? The Stranger does what he wants.

"But his wants conform to the situation. He has no control over what will happen. He is thoroughly passive and apathetic. He doesn't *do* anything. He just waits for events to occur around him."

What's wrong with that?

"A person is not free when his actions are determined only by natural contingencies."

Huh?

"There isn't anything free in letting one's desires be determined for one."

Huh?

"You say that the Stranger does whatever he wants. The problem is, his wants are not up to him. We might say that he does what he wants, but he does not necessarily want what he wants."

Sure he does. He wants Marie, and cigarettes, and fried eggs. He wants all of that stuff.

"Only because he has learned to acquiesce, to be passive. What would happen if events should present him with no desirable option? What would he do?

"Hmm. One time, while in prison, he asks for a cigarette. The guard tells him he can't have one; that's why it's called punishment.

"What does the character do?"

He gets used to going without cigarettes. Perfectly practical, if you ask me.

"He is not in control of himself. His surroundings control him. By the way, why is he in prison?"

He murdered an Arab.

"What! Why did he do that?"

It was a very hot day. The sun was beating down on him, and he wanted to get to the cool water across the beach.

"How would that lead to killing someone?"

There was an Arab lying on the beach in his way. The story is more complicated than that, but the Stranger ends up killing a person because the sun was in his eyes.

"How can you call this person free? It is just as I have been saying. He is out of control. His surroundings, the sun, act on him."

Perhaps.

"He sounds like a child in a candy store. That sounds like a pleasant analogy, but it isn't meant to be. This lifestyle you propose involves more frustration than you admit. Imagine the child for a moment. She wants whatever she sees. No sooner does she put her hand into one jar than she sees another jar filled with candies. She is led from jar to jar, never really getting the candy she wants. Your life of pleasure is not as pleasure filled as you think. At least moral people, with all of our rules, are disciplined enough to enjoy what we get."

It Is Irredeemably Depressing.   I've heard enough about freedom. Why do you say that my character is depressed?

"Irredeemably depressed; look at the heading. The best way to show what I mean is to look at another example."

Kierkegaard has one?

KIERKEGAARD'S A

"Yes, in *Either/Or* Søren Kierkegaard creates a character much to our point. I think his character, named A, is believable. He's depressing, and I think he's terribly misguided, but looking at him will help me show you what is wrong with living for the moment."

Okay, you describe him as you see him. This should be great, watching you distort this poor guy's life.

Lonely and Sad.   "First, A lives in a world about which he cannot care. He has lost all of what he calls his illusions about living. He says that he is melancholic because of his sense of extreme isolation. These are just the criticisms I was making about your character. No one desires a life that leads to constant sadness and loneliness."

How do you figure that A is this way?

"A tells us. Just look at what he writes. He says, 'I do not care at all. . . . My melancholy is the most faithful mistress.' Not only that, he feels alone. He is disoriented: 'What if everything in the world were a misunderstanding, what if laughter were really tears?' "

So?

Powerless. "He is keenly aware of his own powerlessness in the face of what he sees as an absurd, futile reality."

Where do you get that?

"He says that he feels 'the way a chessman must, when the opponent says of it, That piece cannot be moved.' This guy believes that the world is out to get him. Look where he writes that 'the doors of fortune do not open inward, so that by storming them one can force them open; but they open outward, and therefore nothing can be done.'"

Sure, it's easy when you use the book.

"There's more. He's a lot like you, Art. Look what he writes about the future. 'What drives me forward is a consistency which lies behind me. This life is topsy-turvy and terrible, not to be endured.' He makes life sound like it has to be mindless and habitual."

Yeah, so? What else is there?

"Talk about resigned to being depressed! He says that 'life has become a bitter drink to me, and yet I must take it like medicine, slowly, drop by drop.' Except to see how ridiculous this lifestyle is, why even bother reading this?"

I didn't read it, you did. A really bothers you. Is it because he is so nonmoral?

Cynical. "Just reading a few pages of this is disheartening. I feel sorry for A. Look what else he writes! He describes 'a busy man of affairs,' a business-person, right? Then he describes how 'a tile from the roof falls down and strikes him dead.' What do you think this bizarre person has to say about this tragedy?"

What? (These brief responses of mine are only included to make you think that I'm listening, and that I care.)

"He laughs heartily. That's what he says, that he laughs when a good, hard-working person dies accidentally. He thinks life is absurd. But that's not the worst of it. This guy is cosmically nuts!"

Oh?

"'No one ever comes back from the dead, no one ever enters the world without weeping.'"

It's hard to disagree, so far.

Depressing. "'No one is asked when he wishes to enter life, no one is asked when he wishes to leave.' Come on, you don't find that depressing?"

But it sounds true. Is that what's bothering you? I don't remember being asked about when and where I wanted to be born. And unless you're lucky enough to be able to afford to put a death contract on yourself or commit suicide, you don't get to decide when you will die.

"You're just as crazy as Kierkegaard's A!"

I was only pulling your leg; didn't you feel it? Even suicide victims don't have the control they appear to have. They are people driven by outside influences. There isn't much control there, either.

"I can't believe you agree with this depressing stuff."

Depressing? How is it depressing? A is just telling us the way real life is. If you find that depressing, it isn't A's fault.

Empty and Meaningless. "This guy is hypersensitive! Every glance, every event is magnified. Everyday living depresses him and makes him lonely. His strongest complaint is that our society lacks passion. Where has this person been hiding? Our age is passionate. The world is changing at an incredible rate. Maybe his life is passionless. Maybe he's depressed and bored. Great life!"

But what difference do the changes make, anyway?

"He says that 'life is so empty and meaningless.' He asks, 'Why do we not finish it at once, why do we not stay and step down into the grave with him [the deceased], and draw lots to see who shall happen to be the last unhappy living being to throw the last three spadefuls of earth over the last of the dead?'"

Well, if life is empty and meaningless, then I guess the rest does follow.

"But life isn't empty and meaningless! And just because we are going to die doesn't mean that living is a waste of time. That's what I think this guy believes, that living is a complete waste."

Hmm. (See, you think I'm bothering to follow the conversation.) Does he say anything about the valued goals in living?

"Yes, he does, but he is overly cynical. He says that he came to realize that 'the meaning of life was to secure a livelihood, and that its goal was to attain a high position; that love's rich dream was marriage to an heiress; that friendship's blessing was help in financial difficulties; that wisdom was what the majority assumed it to be,' and on and on. Can you believe it!

Of course, I believe it. He's stumbled onto the secret of the good life.

"Both of you are hopeless. I suppose you also agree with him when he writes that one is 'better to take things as they come, and make no fuss?' Of course you agree with that, too."

Yup. Why try to accomplish anything? What's the point? It's better to enjoy life.

"That's just the point. A doesn't enjoy life. He believes life is wretched and miserable."

And tedious?

Pessimistic. "And terribly tedious. He's the ultimate pessimist."

Why do you say that?

"Read the ecstatic lecture! Whether you marry or do not marry, you will regret it. Whatever you do or do not do, you will regret it. Laugh or weep at the world's follies, believe or disbelieve a woman, hang yourself or do not hang yourself; in each case whatever you do you will regret it."

A Wants to Be Moral. Okay, what's your point? You have gone on and on about this A fellow, so what is your criticism?

"Don't you see, I've been criticizing him right along. He's depressed, lonely, pessimistic, and bored. This is no way to live life. A shows the weaknesses in the life you are bragging about. You think living as if life has no meaning is enjoyable. The writings of A disprove that.

"A's greatest 'hope' is never to have been born. Can you imagine that? Barring this aborted wish, he seeks neither pleasure nor intensity. I think he realizes how unfulfilling pleasure and intensity are. What he finally wants is a moral life."

Why do you say that?

"A seeks 'a constancy that could withstand every trial, an enthusiasm that endured everything, a faith that could remove mountains, a thought that could unite the finite and the infinite.' "

How is this morality?

"Do you see yourself in Kierkegaard's A?"

Constancy.   I haven't thought about it, but yes, I guess I do. Why?

"Then like A, you see yourself caught between a safe but dull life and an insecure but spontaneous and exciting life. Because your life does not allow you to shape your own character or to act on your surroundings, you yearn for constancy. You yearn for constancy in your surroundings because you have no constancy in your self. You yearn for an enthusiasm that could endure anything because you cannot maintain your self."

Why would I do that?

"Because your way of life doesn't allow endurance or constancy, and yet it depends on them."

How does it depend on constancy?

"If some pleasure is good, more is better, right? My picture of you was too extreme before. No one could actually live for the moment, not really. So here you are with a sense of your self but without a way of stabilizing your self. You have no moral rules, or duties, or continuities to help you. All you have is the lust for pleasure."

And that's not enough?

Faith (Control).   "And that's not enough. You yearn for faith that could remove mountains."

Interpret that for me. I want to move mountains?

"You want to remove obstacles. See, your lifestyle does not let you actively alter the world. Remember, you have to let pleasures come to you. Your seductions have to be passive. The thrill of having the pleasure come to you is vital."

What's wrong with that?

Regrets and Choices.   "You fear choice. That's what the *Either/Or* is about. Whichever you choose, you will regret. You are easily disturbed by the decisions of everyday living. Decisions like choosing a career, jobs, housing, promises—those kinds of decisions."

Why would these choices bother me?

"You have no values. You value only what presents itself to you. But having no values means that each moment requires you to choose."

So what? People like me who live for pleasure just take whatever comes along.

"True, except that you aren't quite as passive as you want me to believe. You have wants. In fact, that's your real problem. You have conflicting wants. That's why everyday choices drive you out of your mind. You have no values to help you. Choosing between contrary desires paralyzes you, Art. For you, choice involves regret. To choose one experience means that the other possible experience will go unrealized."

Can't I set up priorities?

Either/Or. "That sounds too rigid for your lifestyle. Setting up priorities to avoid choice leads to boredom and lack of engagement. That's just what you objected to in the moral life. So either you choose and suffer from indecision and regret, or you do not choose, in which case you fail to resolve the conflict you feel between your desires. Or, to avoid conflicting desires, you set up priorities. But this strategy brings responsibilities and boredom. You're trapped."

How could I feel moral responsibility? All I would be doing is choosing which experiences *I* prefer over other experiences. Where's the obligation in that?

"To be sure, you won't feel moral obligation. But a similar feeling takes hold of you. Your own priorities would act like external standards."

But it's what I want!

PRIORITIES

"Not exactly. Each time you act on one of your priorities, you knowingly eliminate a desire. The priorities don't make the conflicting desires go away. Priorities just help you avoid complete frustration and regret. Your priorities make you responsible to yourself and to your plans. Wouldn't you feel badly if you gave up a greater pleasure for a lesser pleasure?"

ABSOLUTES

Yes. I guess I see your point. What was the final yearning you said I had?

"Well, Kierkegaard's A also wants a thought that could unite the finite and the infinite."

I don't remember ever yearning for anything like that. Mostly, I don't think I understand what that means.

"At the heart of your lifestyle is the need for a fixed point upon which to base your life."

That's the constancy.

"Right. You and A search for absolutes in a world where you can find only relative truths and changing values. You interpret your surroundings and other people as an ever-reeling chaos. That's why you cannot consciously commit yourself to laws. You seek excitement in chaos because chaos is all you see."

This is getting a little over my head.

"Then sit up straighter! Only kidding."

AFFIRMING YOUR OWN REALITY

What is the bottom line on all of this analysis and criticism?

"Finally, and most importantly, what you really want is some way to affirm your own reality."

Huh? (Yes, we're back to that.)

"It's what moral people are trying to do, too. We affirm our sense of self, and our sense of being alive by relating to other people, by having goals and projects and all the rest. You and A are cut off from this. So you try to feel real by having intense experiences."

Hmm, at least when I am having an intense experience I know that I'm alive.

"Sure, that's why some people, even moral people, sometimes 'live on the edge.' Exhilarating feelings, adrenaline rushing, that does make you feel alive. But those experiences are limited. The moral life offers a more stable, constant, and predictable way of being alive in the way we are discussing it."

And what is the finite and the infinite?

"I think that is the desire to feel at home in the universe. It's to feel like you're a part of it all. The finite is you, and the infinite is the universe, or God. Wanting to unite with the infinite is the—"

Yearning?

"The yearning to feel connected with other people and with whatever else is real. And it reflects the hope of having a stable set of values by which to live."

THE BEST LIFE

Is living for the moment a complete waste, then?

"What you want is the same as what moral people want. In fact, the reason your lifestyle looks so appealing is because there is a lot to be said for being able to concentrate on the present experience."

I see so many moral people so distracted by their obligations that they aren't aware of what is right in front of them.

"Agreed. And seeking pleasure is also appealing. I guess we'd have to agree that both lives are desirable, only morality offers more of what we want."

Yearn for?

"On the more important level. Both you and moralists are asking the same questions when it really comes down to it."

Wow!

■

SUMMARY OF DISCUSSION

Assuming that life is meaningless and all our actions are futile gestures signifying nothing lasting, life becomes a pleasure-seeking adventure. One example of living for the moment is captured in Camus's character, the Stranger. The Stranger lacks the attitude and mindset of morality. He sees himself as a spectator of life, but without any moral consciousness. He is incapable of seeing anything from another person's point of view, incapable of feeling guilt, and completely happy when his body is not suffering discomfort.

Because he recognizes no moral restrictions, the Stranger is spontaneous. He avoids boredom by living in the moment, interacting with whatever presents itself to him. He never makes choices. Therefore, he avoids the anxieties of indecision and responsibility. What he receives from this strategy in living is pleasure.

Unfortunately, there are some problems living in a straightforward, simplistic pursuit of pleasure. The Stranger's life is unrealistic and not as pleasure filled as first appearances promise. Although the Stranger avoids the repressive influences of morality, he cuts himself off from other people. He misses the moral continuities. He communicates superficially and has no sense of community. Nor is he able to be creative. Creativity assumes that one thinks beyond the present moment. The Stranger's life is empty of love, friendship, and trust. He lacks an enduring sense of self and misunderstands freedom as caprice. Worst of all, his pleasure-seeking life is depressing.

Kierkegaard's A is another attempt at living in the moment. Unfortunately, A is lonely and sad. He feels powerless, and therefore he has developed a cynical, depressed attitude toward living. For him, life is something to be gotten through. Living is empty and meaningless, and he is pessimistic about nearly every aspect of it.

In his moaning, however, A does reveal important aspects of morality. A wants what morality promises. He wants constancy and control. He wants to avoid decisions and the regrets that are so often brought on by choices. Finally, neither the Stranger nor A is able to affirm his own reality. For as much as it promises, living for the moment is not the best life.

■

DISCUSSION HIGHLIGHTS

  I. The Stranger
  1. Is spontaneous
  2. Avoids the "evils" of morality
     a. boredom
     b. anxieties of responsibility and indecision

II. Living for the moment is undesirable
  1. It is unrealistic.
  2. It is not as pleasure filled as promised.
  3. It cuts one off from relating to other people.
  4. It misses the moral continuities
    a. of communication
    b. of community
    c. of creativity
  5. It is empty of love, trust, and friendship.
  6. It lacks values and an enduring sense of self.
  7. It misunderstands freedom as caprice.
  8. It is depressing.
III. Kierkegaard's A is
  1. Lonely and sad.
  2. He feels powerless.
  3. He feels cynical and depressed.
  4. He believes life is empty and meaningless.
  5. A wants
    a. constancy
    b. control
    c. avoidance of choices and regrets

■

QUESTIONS FOR THOUGHT/PAPER TOPICS

1. Is the Stranger's spontaneity appealing? How can we incorporate his freedom into our construction of the best life?

2. I suggested that Joe the Mesopotamian's life is meaningless. Do you agree? Explore the question of whether or not life is meaningful.

3. Can one compromise and lead a moral life that has spontaneous moments of concentrated pleasure? Or does this amount to scheduling one's spontaneous moments?

4. Is freedom doing whatever one wants? If that is freedom, isn't the Stranger free? Is his freedom desirable?

5. A is cynical, depressed, and lonely. We might attribute this to his belief that life is empty and meaningless. If a person believes that life is meaningless, why can't he or she be carefree, spontaneous, and joyful?

6. Is it a fair trade to give up the pleasure of the moment for constancy, security, control, and relief from responsibility? Is that the tradeoff that moral people make?

7. How can a person avoid choices and decisions? Is it possible to live a nonmoral life without decisions? What would direct such a person's actions?

FOR FURTHER READING

It's odd to recommend books to read on doing whatever *you* want, but here goes. Albert Camus' *The Stranger* (Vintage, 1989) is certainly worth reading. Another source is Søren Kierkegaard's *Either/Or* (Princeton, 1987). Kierkegaard skillfully draws the character A from the opening pages. There are other analytic expressions of this character type, one of which is David Gauthier's *Morality and Rational Self-Interest* (Prentice-Hall, 1970). Finally, there is a persuasive book written by Ayn Rand, *The Virtue of Selfishness* (New American Library, 1964). Be particularly critical when you read this one.

TWO

Philosophers Answer the Questions

Introduction

In Part One we struggled with several questions. No doubt you are uneasy with our inconclusive discussion. That's okay. So far the aim has been to introduce the questions that relate to morality and the best life. Part Two presents the answers that philosophers offer to our questions.

Not surprisingly, philosophers do not take a uniform position on the nature of morality or the best life. Nor do philosophers respond to our questions in the order that the questions come to us. What Part Two offers are selections from philosophers who hold differing points of view. You will find some of them in agreement with your intuitions. Others will sound plausible enough, but you will not fully agree with all of them.

Part Two gives us a chance to question these philosophers. Through the use of my own invention, the philosopher resurrection machine, we get to actually speak to long-dead philosophers. Most of what you will read comes directly from them. Of course, it's best to read their entire works, but resurrecting them gives us the chance to ask questions. If you do want to read more, look at the end of each chapter for the best sources. Ah, here's one of our philosophers now. I'd like to introduce you to John Stuart Mill, a nineteenth-century British philosopher.

Mr. Mill, welcome. It's generous of you to join us. I have a number of questions for you.

"That should wait for our complete discussion in Chapter 8, Art."

Then why are you here now?

THE V-8 PRINCIPLE!

"There is one condition before any of us enters into a discussion with you. You have to follow the V-8 principle."

What's that?

"People often read a philosophical work and make criticisms of the author's ideas."

And they don't bother to be clear about the ideas?

"That's one problem. They do not bother to understand the philosopher fully. They just disagree with what they too quickly judge is the philosopher's position. That is not what I was going to say, however. One type of criticism is caused by an inadequate reading. Another type of criticism comes from an unsympathetic reading."

I don't follow you.

"Imagine that you are in a classroom during a discussion. Everyone has read the assigned reading with care. In the course of evaluating the ideas critically, someone raises an objection to the philosopher's ideas."

What's wrong with that? Isn't that the point? Aren't we supposed to find out where the theory goes wrong?

"My, you are impatient, Art. Yes, of course, criticism is important. An adequate objection is praiseworthy. But you also need to imagine how the philosopher would respond. Be sympathetic to the philosopher's point of view and construct an argument in defense of the position."

Why would I do that? I thought the idea was to show where the philosopher is wrong.

"The aim is to reach the truth. If you are genuinely interested in the nature of morality and in finding the best life, then a sympathetic understanding of other views is essential. Even if the philosopher is only partially correct, understanding the correct point or the correct strategy is important. If the philosopher is completely incorrect—and that I find unlikely—there is still much to be gained from understanding. One gains from carefully rejecting incorrect ideas. One's own thinking becomes clearer; the truth becomes livelier in one's own mind."

Okay, you've made your point. So what is the V-8 principle?

"When the student or teacher has made an objection to the philosopher's ideas, imagine how the philosopher would respond. Surely you don't believe that we philosophers would merely sit in the back of the room, listen to the objection, place our palm on our forehead, and say 'Gee, I could have had a V-8!' We would have a response. It is up to you to construct a plausible response for us."

Fair enough. In Part Two you philosophers will have your say. First, we will ask questions to become clearer on the ideas. Then we will evaluate the theory critically. Where we detect a problem with the theory, we'll try to find a response consistent with your position. Does that satisfy you?

"Yes, that's fine. That satisfies the V-8 principle. I will speak with you shortly. Goodbye for now."

A ROAD MAP

That was easy enough, wasn't it? All that's left for this introduction is to draw a road map of ideas for you to follow. What's a road map of ideas? In the first part of the book we mentioned quite a few possible ways of understanding the moral plan of living. I think it would be helpful to point out where your comments lead, just in case you want to pursue one more than another.

If you think that authority, intuition, law, and social roles reveal our moral principles to us, then Chapter 6 is for you. The discussion with the Grand Inquisitor puts religious morality, authority, and social roles in a pretty cynical light. Don't despair.

Being free is also one of our desires. I think Kierkegaard's character A and Camus's Stranger demonstrate that. An interesting sense of freedom is discussed in Chapter 7, in which Epictetus creates a whole attitude toward living by emphasizing his special brand of freedom. (Freedom also serves as the foundation for the existentialist plan of life Sartre offers in Chapter 10.)

Remember democracy? One way we considered defining right action was in terms of the greatest good for the greatest number. Lo and behold, Chapter 8 is an explanation and defense of that view. John Stuart Mill also agrees with you when you argue that not all pleasures are equally worthy. It's important reading, especially if you already lean in that direction.

Chapter 9 discusses the absolutist position on moral values. This doctrine states that no matter what the circumstances or consequences, some actions are right to perform and other actions are wrong to perform. Immanuel Kant advocates this view. He argues for a fixed set of moral laws, in principle like the legal laws we encounter in society. So if you want to find a haven from relativism or from determining moral right by reflecting on the good of the greatest number, Chapter 9 may be to your liking. At least with moral absolutes you don't have to struggle with uncertainty and dangerous moral calculations.

Sartre defends subjectivism, but avoids your disdain for egoism, in Chapter 10. For him, relativism is not the issue; the best life is a life lived authentically and freely. Sartre argues that individual differences in people are desirable, but he does not threaten the social stability offered by morality. I think you'll like his way of putting his ideas.

I know religion and God play a dominant role in people's moral education. Chapters 11 and 12 address religious faith in a most positive way. So if you are interested in the religious aspect of living, look there.

If I can make one suggestion: Please read each chapter with an open mind. Only after you have examined the view that each thinker takes can you make an informed, balanced, and intelligent decision about your own position. Learning all these points of view will also help you understand what someone else believes. Agreement is not as important as understanding, so read each chapter. I hope you enjoy the conversations.

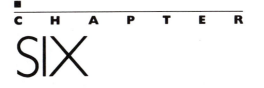

C H A P T E R

SIX

Authority and Freedom: A Discussion with the Grand Inquisitor

MORALITY MAKES US FREE

"Morality works, Art. It makes us free."

Free? What do you mean?

"Morality helps us choose our own values. By picking the correct values, we are free and happy. That's what makes morality such a great way of life. Morality helps us choose our values. That's its purpose."

Do we really want to be free?

"Of course we do. Why do you even ask? Being free is the most important aspect of human life."

Humans can never be free. They are weak, vicious, worthless, and rebellious. How can rebels be happy?

"Art, that is outrageous! Where did you ever get an idea like that?"

THE GRAND INQUISITOR

From my friend, the Grand Inquisitor.

"Who?"

There's a nice little story, "The Grand Inquisitor on the Nature of Man." It's one chapter in a novel, *The Brothers Karamazov*, by a Russian writer, Fyodor Dostoevski. It takes a provocative view of human nature and freedom. So for now, let's abandon our regular format. Let me sum up some of the highlights of "The Grand Inquisitor." Of course, reading it is much better than letting me retell the story.

The story opens with the coming of Christ. But this is not *the* Coming, just

Material in this chapter taken from Fyodor Dostoevski, *The Grand Inquisitor,* (New York: Bobbs-Merrill/Macmillan, 1948). Constance Garnett translation.

a visit to see how everyone is doing. It is the time of the Spanish Inquisition during the fifteenth century. Jesus visits Seville, Spain. Everything is going fine in Seville. The Grand Inquisitor, a cardinal in the Christian Church, is in the process of cleansing the earth of undesirables. He burns heretics to the "greater glory of God."

Jesus enters the town unannounced, and as it turns out uninvited. People recognize Him and flock around. He performs a couple of miracles for the masses. He brings sight to an old man who was blind from birth, then He raises a dead child from her "slumber." The people, who already know who He is, are even more convinced by these feats. But the second miracle is also viewed from afar by guess who? Right, the Grand Inquisitor. The ninety-year-old cardinal sends his guard to arrest the intruder.

With the arrest the people back away, of course. If someone is arrested, the person is assumed to be guilty. (See how little we've changed?) The Inquisitor has Him taken to the prison. In the darkness of night the old cardinal visits Him. This is where it gets fascinating.

"Does the Inquisitor know who He is?"

The Inquisitor asks Him if it is He. But when no answer comes, the Inquisitor realizes that He has no right to say anything. Jesus has no right to add any new rules to the sayings of old.

"What does the Inquisitor do with Him?"

The Inquisitor explains what religion (and morality) are all about. He confesses his conviction to the divine person. In the morning the Inquisitor says that he will burn Him at the stake. And, says the Inquisitor, with a sign from him, the people will help in the burning. That's the essence of the story, but the Inquisitor goes on to explain in detail.

PEOPLE WANT TO BE FREE

"What was the point of arresting Him?"

Look what Jesus offers humanity! He offers freedom!

"What's wrong with that? People want to be free."

No, people can never be free. It took centuries for us to realize what a terrible gift freedom is.

"Us? Who is us?"

The Grand Inquisitor and I, the Church, all of organized religion. We have done more for people than Jesus could do. For the Church, in the person of its Inquisitor, has taken freedom from the people.

"How could that be? Why would you do that?"

The Church has not taken away freedom from the people; it has accepted it. People do not want to be free. People want to be happy.

"Can't people be free and happy?"

No. That is the remarkable insight of the Church. Freedom brings too many responsibilities and anxieties. Happiness is not for rebels. Once people willingly give up their rebelliousness, their desire for freedom, then they can be happy. He was warned.

THREE TEMPTATIONS IN THE DESERT

"Warned?"

The warnings came from the spirit who tempted Jesus in the desert.

"The Devil!"

The wise and dread spirit tempted Him with three temptations.

"What is the significance of the warnings, of the temptations, as you call them?"

The three temptations tell us the nature of humans. Jesus exaggerates the human potential. Surely, some few people can live freely, but the vast majority of people cannot cope with freedom. They are too weak.

"Too weak?"

Stones into Bread.   Yes, too weak. The first temptation is to turn stones into bread. Jesus rejected the offer, saying that we do not live by bread alone. We prefer heavenly bread to earthly bread.

"But what that means is that people need more than just animal comforts. Security (bread) is worthless if it costs people their freedom."

That is Jesus' response. Of course, now we know differently. Now we know better. Give them bread. Give them security and material prosperity, and people willingly give up their freedom. Think about it. What would people rather have, freedom and starvation or security and food? We offer the latter. The flock of unruly humans obediently and gratefully follows us.

"They fear you!"

They fear us, yes. They love us and they fear us. After all, we have the power to remove their security.

"But it's the people who give you the bread in the first place. All we have to do is refuse to give it to you. All your power comes from us, the people. You must know that."

Absolutely. But I also know that it is your freedom that you most want to rid yourselves of. So I accept your bread and redistribute it. More important, I accept your freedom and with it your anxiety and responsibility.

Anxiety of Indecision.   "What anxiety?"

People approach freedom with dread. It is awful to be free. Freedom creates anxieties. First, there's the anxiety of indecision.

"What's that?"

Almost no one wants to decide on one's own.

"I make decisions and I don't feel any anxiety or dread. I think you are just exaggerating or imagining."

Moral and religious people do not make decisions.

"I make decisions all the time. And so do other people. We decide where we live, where we go to school, where we work, what occupation we pursue, whom we marry, whether or not we marry, and all the rest."

And how do you make those decisions? You decide based on what we tell you is important.

"We?"

The other religious leaders and I. We belong to a group called Religion, Inc. We orchestrate your lives for you. You get to make small decisions. We make the *big* decisions. Actually, we don't decide anything. We teach you which choices are available and which are unavailable.

"That's no big deal. Anyone can picture the options. If that's all you do, you have no control over me."

Oh, that's not all we do. We do one more little thing. We tell you what is good and what is evil. In doing that, we give you your wants. Some wants are acceptable, some are "dangerously" immoral, and some are unthinkable. The wants that are acceptable include most of the standard choices in life.

"You make our lives sound like selling cars."

Well, they are. Some people choose the family and career model. Some people want the luxury option. The wants that are acceptable include education (without any knowledge of good and evil), and job, and family, and hobbies.

"What about the immoral wants? How can you deal with those? If I want to break free from your control, all I have to do is break your rules. Then what do you do?"

Relieving Your Conscience.   We forgive you.

"What do you mean, you forgive me?"

Just that. The religious leaders and I know that you are weak of flesh and of mind. We know that you lack nobility and self-control.

"What do you mean?"

To put it in religious language, we know you are sinners. The second and more powerful part of our appeal is that we relieve your conscience. It is part of the plan that you break the rules. We forgive you. It does not make any difference if you follow or break the rules. Either way, we have you aware of the rules and of our authority. So we do not care whether you are moral or immoral.

"This is outrageous. How can I be free?"

You don't want freedom. You merely think you do. We've given you that want. And we supply the satisfaction.

SO I AM FREE?

"So I am free?"

We let you make decisions, just as long as we determine how you make them. The only truly free person is the one who is able to hold unthinkable values.

"Unthinkable values?"

The values that one creates oneself. But such values are for the very few! We sacrifice those people in order to protect you.

"Protect?"

From becoming aware of the option of genuine freedom and the terror that realization invokes in you. We seek to make you feel secure. We realize, however, that you sheep do not live for security only.

"Right, Jesus said that. Man does not live by bread alone. So you do agree with Him?"

No, Jesus misunderstood humans. You also want meaning in your lives. We give your insignificant lives meaning by telling you that you fit into the 'Grand Scheme,' or into society, or into the flow of history. You want goals and structure and security. We give you a stable, unchanging, secure way of living. The moral and religious values may change some, but moral thinking stays stable.

"Moral thinking?"

That everyone is morally equal. That objectivity is important in deciding questions. Impartiality. Rights, duties, responsibilities. All that. That is moral thinking. We instill in you a concern for consequences! And then you ask us to judge you. Judgment is a significant part of morality and religion.

"Without judgment, you and the leaders of religion lose control."

And you lose your security and comfort.

"But I still think that I am free. I do decide what course of study I want, and what career I want, and who I will marry. Those are pretty big decisions. You can't deny it."

I do not agree at all.

"You don't think it's important whom I love and marry and what kind of work I do?"

Not only do I not see these as important decisions, but I don't see them as decisions at all. The other religious leaders and I determine whom you love and marry and which career you pursue. For example, you will marry someone close to your own age, in roughly your same socioeconomic class (maybe a little above your present status). You will most likely marry someone of the opposite sex, of the same nationality, of the same (or of an acceptable) race, of roughly the same religious denomination. We even determine which physical traits are attractive. In some centuries being thin is attractive; in some centuries being heavy is a sign of prosperity.

"But we marry a person because we love that person."

In your century and in your part of the world, yes. But that isn't universally true. In other places, and in other times in your society, we had people marry by arrangement. In fact, we're considering going back to that.

"No way. Why would you do that?"

The rise in the divorce rate bothers people. Another one of those insecurities, no doubt. If we arrange marriages, the divorce rate will drop.

"This is crazy. People pick their own mates."

Which man or woman you marry is of no concern to us. All we're interested in is that you acknowledge the guidelines and our authority. So marry or don't marry. We'll sanctify all of it. And when you marry and the little lambs start coming, we'll make sure to teach them all our values and obedience as well. Don't you see, the ideas of marriage, of love, of having children—all this happens by virtue of our wish!

CONSCIENCE

"Let's get back to the idea of conscience."

Giving you bread is a start, but you want more. You want an authority to take care of your conscience. Nothing is worse than a guilty conscience. Guilt is one of the devices we install to get you to do what we want.

"You mean 'instill.' You instill people with a sense of right and wrong, good and evil. Saying *install* makes it sound like brainwashing."

After we install guilt, you are ours. We know you will break the rules. Some of the rules are so burdensome that it's too difficult for anyone to follow them. Just thinking about committing some sins is itself sinful.

"So?"

Guilt. It's guilt, don't you see! You carry our authority with you. It's like carrying around an emotional club. Whenever you think about committing a sin, bang! you hit yourself right on the head. A great invention, the guilty conscience.

"But you said you forgive every sin."

We forgive you. Forgiving you your transgressions is what it's all about. That's the second great insight. Nothing is more seductive for humans than their freedom of conscience, but nothing is a greater cause of suffering. There is no greater burden.

"I still don't understand the first temptation."

The first temptation of Jesus was to take away your freedom and to give you security and the modest happiness you are capable of living. In refusing the first temptation, Jesus cast away a lot.

"What did He throw away?"

In the place of rigid, ancient law, humans must hereafter with free hearts decide for themselves what is good and what is evil. How could we live with the dreadful burden of free choice?

"How?"

MIRACLES

The second temptation addresses this question in a most impressive way.

"In what way could anything that the Devil offers be impressive?"

Devil? I don't know about any devil. The "dread spirit" may be human nature, but take it for whatever you wish. The second temptation is the desire for miracles. Jesus is asked to throw Himself from the Temple pinnacle.

"Why would He do that?"

To prove that He is the messiah. The angels are supposed to catch Him before He hits the ground. It is a way for Jesus (and everyone else) to see whether or not He is the messiah. In a sense it is to test Jesus' faith that God will protect Him. What happens?

"Jesus refuses to jump."

Why? Why would He not just prove who He is?

"He does not want to tempt God and show that His faith has to be proven."

I believe He had a healthy respect for gravity. Jesus fails again.

"Fails? He has faith in God."

His faith is not the question. Where He fails is in his overestimation of humanity.

"Jesus wants people to believe from the heart. He does not want people to follow Him because of the miracles He performs. How is that a failure? That seems to be a very noble success. Jesus wants people to feel Him in their hearts. He wants people to love Him and to understand His message."

Yes. What He got is a flock of sheep who cannot know or love or understand. Only the very few, the strong ones, can know and understand. Ironically, the few who can carry their own conscience, and who can create their own values, really do not need Jesus. But for the vast majority, the tens of hundreds of millions, would a few miracles have hurt?

"Are you disagreeing with what He offered? Certainly freedom and knowledge are desirable. What greater gift can He give than freedom? What greater demonstration of concern and love?"

WE CARE FOR THE WEAK, TOO!

If, for the sake of the bread of Heaven, thousands and tens of thousands shall follow Him, what is to become of the millions and tens of thousands of millions of creatures who will not have the strength to forego the earthly bread for the sake of the heavenly? No, we care for the weak, too.

"Are you saying that Jesus made a mistake? He was showing respect for humanity."

By showing humans so much respect, He ceases to feel for humankind. Respecting us less, He would have asked less of us. That would have been more like love, for our burden would have been lighter. Why not let the vast rabble believe in the only way they can believe?

"What way is that?"

With blind faith. People want miracles. Even more than a God, people want the miraculous. They want miracles, mystery, and authority. Jesus should feel more for humans. He should care more. His overestimation places humanity at a disadvantage that it cannot overcome by itself. Jesus respects humans too much and loves too little. With more love He would have brought an easier burden to shoulder.

UNIVERSAL UNITY

"But you're working for Satan!"

Not exactly. We members of Religion, Inc. realize that the 'wise and dread spirit' is correct in its assessment of human potential.

"I can't listen to this!"

Look at the final temptation.

"Final temptation?"

Rome and the power that it wields were offered to Jesus. Jesus rejected this one, too.

"Of course He rejected it. You can't force people to see the truth, or to love, or to believe in God."

Yes, you can. In fact, that's just what people want, force. You want to be forced to believe, or not to believe. You need to be coerced, manipulated, and forced. Sometimes the force can be softly applied, through miracles, mystery, and authority. Guidance is all people want. And that's just what Jesus fails to understand.

"Is that *all* people want? Or only according to you and the Inquisitor?"

No, there is one other want. It goes along with the power of Rome. What is really offered in the third temptation is universal unity.

"I don't quite follow you."

It is a difficult concept in our age, but the desire is still around. People want everyone to unite in one unanimous antheap. Human beings want certainty. That's the third anguish of humanity. Diverse beliefs make humans uncertain of their own beliefs.

"But why do you think we want that?"

Do you mean why do I think this is true? What evidence do I have? Or do you mean, why do people want to be part of the universal antheap?

"Both. Take the second question first. That's the one I meant."

YOU CAN'T HANDLE
INTENSE EXPERIENCES

People want security, comfort, peace. You cannot handle intense experiences. Intense pleasures and pains frighten you.

"Wait a minute. I have intense experiences. I feel pleasure and pain just like everyone else!"

Not true. You and all your friends are too moral. You worry about the future, about consequences. You even worry about the effect you have on other people. You do not dwell in your passions and pleasures. You cannot live in the moment. No, my friend, your pleasures are mere shadows of what free people can feel.

"But there's no way to show that. You're just saying this, but there's no way to prove it."

I think your challenge is a legitimate one. And I do not think I can fully respond yet.

"Why, because the flock can't understand? Is that your excuse?"

Not at all, though you cannot yet understand. What I suggest is that I give you a brief reply now. I would have to tell a long story to make the point fully, and I do not think this is the place.

"Why can't people—the flock, as you call us—why can't we feel emotion the way free people can? Give me your answer. If I'm not satisfied, I'll ask for the more elaborate answer later."

You cannot let yourselves experience intensely. You are preoccupied with the past and the future. The present moment has barely any existence for you. The moment is the tick of a clock for you. Your memory, your sense of duty and obligation, your promises, all these distract you from experiencing what is going on now. Now! The best you can do is schedule your spontaneous moments.

"All you're saying is that we don't concentrate on every little detail in the present because we are concerned with what is coming. So what? We're not into contemplating our bellybuttons or watching dust settle."

Distractions.   There are a couple of other reasons why you cannot feel intensely. Do you know what happens when opposing forces pull at one object?

"Now this is a physics discussion? When two forces act on an object, the object is pulled (or pushed) in a direction that reflects the resulting direction and force of the pull (or push) from each force. Pull north plus pull east equals pull northeast. Opposing forces play a tug of war. What do opposing forces have to do with feelings and pleasure? Or is this just another of your distractions?"

Distractions? That's the word I was searching for. You sheeplike people have too many distractions. Each distraction pulls (or pushes) you, but because there are so many distractions, you do not go where (or feel what) you want.

"What do you mean? I'm not following you."

Let me try again. Distractions. All your rules and roles, duties and obligations, promises and responsibilities are distractions. You are distracted by consequences, by the past and the future. All these distractions create wants. You want to fulfill all the moral demands that the Inquisitor and I make on you, right?

"Right. It's important to fulfill one's promises and duties—"

Excuse me for interrupting. So you have all this moral baggage. Distracting wants! These alone can act as opposing forces. You may have inadvertently made two promises but find you cannot keep both. Or your role as a student may conflict with your role as a friend or as a worker. Already you're pulled (or pushed) in different directions. Opposing forces.

Then we add feelings and emotions. Some of your passions are not safe. That is why you demand that we establish morality in the first place, to keep your passions under control. Now we have several conflicting forces. Little wonder you cannot concentrate on the present. You have too many distractions. You have too many opposing and conflicting moral wants and natural passions. You are too weak to keep your obligations.

"Well, I'm not sure about this. Why can't someone be truly moral? That way there'd be no conflict."

Where's the Intensity?   I agree. But look at what it means to be truly moral. You have to be objective, concerned with responsibilities, etc. You aren't involved in the pleasure of the moment. Where's the intensity!

"I don't understand."

Let me see if I can explain this with an analogy. Moral people are like buckets.

"Buckets!"

Buckets with holes in them. What happens to a bucket of water that has a lot of holes in it?

"It loses its water. This is ridiculous."

I know it loses its water. But how does it lose the water? How strong are the streams of water running out of all the holes?

"The more holes, the weaker the streams of water. The streams at the lower levels will be slightly stronger because of the weight of the water."

Ha!

"Ah, yes! I get it."

You weak humans, with all your moral distractions, are like holey buckets.

"Not holy buckets; we'd like that."

You experience like the streams of water, weakly. Each stream of water dribbling out of the bucket is like your wants and obligations. Each represents an avenue of experience. You have so many that you experience everything, but too weakly. You don't have the energy for it. That's why I, as the Inquisitor, can allow you to sin. You cannot muster up the concentration and energy for a truly dangerous sin. So I forgive you. And—wouldn't you know it—you thank me for it. The closest you get to real intensity is your fear of genuine, free creation of your values.

"We do make decisions, free decisions. We do decide on our values."

Is that why you had so much trouble coming up with reasons for your values?

"Well—"

You still haven't found a way to guarantee them. And that is just what Religion, Inc. and I do for you. Our authority guarantees your values. We remove the "anxiety and terrible agony" that freedom brings. The reward is that you do not have to decide on values.

A PERSON IN SHEEP'S CLOTHING

"But I want to make my own decisions on values. I don't want you and the Inquisitor and Religion, Inc. making my decisions for me. I want to control my own life."

I think you're serious. Maybe you're a person in sheep's clothing.

"Of course I'm a person. And I—that is, we—don't want you running our lives."

But you all flock to morality and religion. All I've been doing is reflecting the wants you expressed in our earlier talks. You said you want security, comfort, stability, safety. You're the ones who think religion and morality make a contribution to humanity.

"We resent the word 'flock.' We do not flock to religion and morality. We freely choose to follow the moral and religious tenets. Which moral and religious values, you're going to ask."

Very well, which moral values?

"I don't know. From what you say, we humans are too weak, vicious, and worthless to choose our own values. There doesn't seem to be any way out of this. Maybe we are too weak to choose. Maybe our natures are too frail. What a depressing idea!"

THE POSSIBILITY OF FREEDOM

That is why it is necessary to keep you ignorant. The truth of human frailty, coupled with your rebellious nature, leads to anguish.

"Yes, if what you say is true, then anguish does follow. If we are no more than socialized, moralized, religionized beings, then there is no chance of freedom. If we are as weak and worthless as you say, then we should be despairing."

There is no alternative. You must be cared for and protected from yourselves.

"But I wonder about all this. The fact that we know that we are socialized and all the rest gives us a chance to fight against your influence. Our ability to analyze our own situation gives us the power to change the effects that you and advertising, and schooling, and religion have on us."

Why not just accept your fate and be happy?

THE INQUISITOR HAS MISLED US!

"I think you have misled us, Art. There is more to be said for humans' ability to be free than you have admitted. There is more to be said for conscience and roles than you have suggested. Maybe morality and religion are not the effect of our sheeplike need for security and safety."

Oh, I see. Maybe morality and religion are the cause of your submissive approach. Is that it?

"Right. Maybe people cannot handle living intensely because morality and religion have weakened us. You are forgetting that there are people who remain strong enough to be free in the knowledge of good and evil. If they are able to do it, human nature is not overly frail. Perhaps it is our leaders who are doing this to us."

The moral and religious leaders manipulate you?

"I think we're going about it the wrong way. It is not a conspiracy. The people who teach us our morality and religion are caught up in these ways of thinking and experiencing just as much as we are. You mean well; at least, most of you mean well. Where Religion, Inc. has gone wrong is in assuming that human nature calls for protection. You and the Grand Inquisitor are merely part of a story. The real truth is not so easily explained by a conspiracy of wicked people."

You are saying that human nature is not weak?

"Right. It is the blindly followed moral and religious points of view that weaken and sicken people. Once we've been convinced that morality and religion offer the truth, we're caught."

When were we convinced that morality and religion were correct?

"In our training institutions, of course. Schools, churches, and synagogues. Why?"

No, the right answer is, "Never!" We were never actually convinced. We just grew up believing. Morality and religion have always been a part of our lives.

"Are you saying that our society manipulated us? Are you agreeing with me?"

Yes, and when I think about the idea, I discover an interesting coincidence. Psychologists from different schools of psychology disagree about all sorts of things. They cannot agree about what is innate and what is learned. Some put (almost) complete emphasis on one alternative; others opt for the opposite. Even those who agree that there are innate drives rarely agree on what those drives are.

"Yes, so?"

They all pretty much agree that a person's fundamental character is formed between three and five years of age.

"Some say people continue to grow and develop throughout their lives."

We do continue to change. Even if we did not change, society would tell us that we continue to grow and to progress. Without society's compliments we would stop believing in it.

"Cynical, aren't you?"

I did not mean to be cynical. Sorry. The point still stands, though. Even if we continue to grow and prosper, our character and our outlook are fundamentally formed in early childhood. It takes a lot to change. It takes a lot of therapy or reconditioning.

BLIND OBEDIENCE HINDERS GROWTH

"What does that show?"

A person's character is basically formed by the time she is three to five years old. What else happens at this time? We learn right and wrong, good and bad. Before we are old enough to know right and wrong, good and bad, people don't hold us responsible. They figure we're too little to know the difference. And they're correct.

"What's the connection between learning moral responsibility and character formation? What's the problem?"

We stop growing when we hit three to five years old. We grow in physical size, but our character growth stops. Okay, maybe it doesn't stop entirely. It slows to a snail's pace. And snails pace pretty slowly. Once we learn good and bad, right and wrong, once we get a conscience, we're through. We obey morality blindly; we obey society blindly.

"But haven't you learned a lot since you were three! You could not read or write when you were three. You did not know math and science and history. Your hypothesis just doesn't hold up."

You're so manipulative! Yes, we change in insignificant ways, but—

"Insignificant! How can you say that all you have learned and done and experienced in the years since you were three has been insignificant!"

All I mean is that our values and our basic outlook on the world haven't changed much. We learned to respect authority, and we still do. Morally speaking, we haven't gone very far. Here's an example. A friend of mine told me several years ago that he realized that many people still believe in the God they believed in when they were two.

"Why should their God not be the same God?"

He was a firm believer. What he was saying, I think, was that the adult's God should not be the child's God. Jesus misunderstood. He overestimated humanity. Adults are children in their understanding.

"Why do you say that?"

The child has a conception of God as a man with a long flowing beard sitting on a cloud. Or, if the child is somewhat more enlightened, the God will be a unisex god sitting on a white cloud. Angels, perhaps a few cherubs. Children learn about their God and usually conceive of God visually, as a person in the sky.

"What's the harm in that? Adults don't continue with that belief, if that's what you're driving at. Adults have a more sophisticated vision of God."

More intellectual, yes; more sophisticated, no. The problem in our discussion of God's existence was caused by our intellect's outdistancing our childlike conception of God. People still believe in pretty much the same God. God protects them. God organizes their world. It explains the unexplainable.

"You needn't recite the whole conversation on God's nature. You're saying that the child's God is in the form of a protector, and so is the adult's God. That is what we teach them."

Yes. The protection required is different, but the protector is still there. God also serves as a "person" to make adults and children feel less alone. God answers their questions. And when the questions change, the answering God merely changes the answers.

"That is as much as the people can endure. Perhaps I shall have you burned as a heretic, as an atheist."

What I say doesn't mean there is no God. All it means is that people stop developing their views of the world. When do they do this? At about three to five years old. Baa! That's how society has manipulated and weakened us. Baa.

WHAT'S THE HARM?

"That is all most people can accomplish. What's the harm in believing in a childlike way?"

Nothing. That would be great, except that the belief is not childlike; it's childish. You are correct. Religion and morality make people submissive. It subjects people to Inquisitors. It means people become content being clones of one another.

"Instead, people should be individuals and as creative as they can be."

Your optimism sounds like Jesus' own. There is no way you will ever be able to prove your point to the Inquisitor's followers, however. Their need for obedience makes them compliant. And look what you risk. What if you and Jesus are incorrect? What if you overestimate the strength of humanity? What horror will follow! You will cast them out of our control and set them into the vast ocean of despair. It is not worth the risk. And the evidence of humanity's desire for unity and security is all around you.

THE DESIRE FOR UNIVERSAL UNITY

"You haven't given any evidence that we need universal unity. You say we need to be part of the antheap, but you haven't shown it. We are individuals. We want to be free. We want to choose our own course in life."

Individuals? I don't think so. Look at most housing developments. A huge sign hangs over the main road, "Homes for the Discriminating." There are magnificent houses at varying stages of completion. Turn down the street and take a look. Every block is perfectly shaped. Every house is identical to every other house. Where there are differences, they are insignificant. Some may have the front door toward the double garage on the left side and the maple tree on the right side. Others may have just the reverse. In fact, usually the pattern alternates, right door with left tree, left door with right tree. Discriminating!"

"What's that prove?"

Isn't it obvious? These are beautiful, expensive houses. But they are all fashionably the same.

"But the people who live in them are not necessarily the same."

Choice. I don't think you would know creative intensity or individuality if it hit you in the face. What sheep-people lack is strength, self-direction, self-discipline, and a sense of drive (necessity) that is internally created. Look how you act in school or on the job. You don't act like individual people. You take the same tests in school. Every student is expected to answer the same questions, as though the questions are somehow really important. What you're really learning is to follow orders. Teachers work for us. They don't always know it, but why else would they work for so little pay? They're sheep, too. Baa. You learn what we tell you to learn, and then if you're a good student, you forget it.

"But we choose our own careers."

When did that start to happen?

"I decide which course of study to major in. No one decides it for me. Even if my parents and peers tell me to do one thing, I decide what I want to do with my life."

Maybe so. I do not feel like arguing about it.

"Maybe nothing. I decide my own fate. That's part of the freedom that I want. You and the other Grand Inquisitors can deny it all you want. But I know what I decide and what I don't decide."

Then all the Madison Avenue advertising firms are going to go broke. Do you really think that advertising has no effect on you?

"It has some effect, yes. But what it really does is let me know what products are out there. I decide what to buy and what I want."

Then why would so much money be spent on advertising? Are you telling me that billions of dollars are being wasted? And that people buy the things they buy because they want those things? Incredible.

"I don't know about everyone else. I buy things because I want or need them. I'm free."

Careers.   Go back to your example of careers. Do you really think you choose your career?

"Absolutely."

Then explain this. Twenty-five years ago or so, people sitting in classrooms across the country looked pretty much like students do today. They were from the same socioeconomic groups, same races, same sexes. In different academic environments, they differed. But that's true today in pretty much the same proportions.

"Yeah, so?"

They majored in English and history and political science and sociology. They majored in the arts and sciences. Today, at least at most colleges and universities, the largest demand is away from the liberal arts and sciences. Careers are in; the arts are out.

"So? Are you going to become nostalgic on me? Are you going to tell me that people were freer twenty-five years ago?"

Hardly. The human condition is fixed. You are weak, vicious, worthless, and rebellious if not by nature, then as a result of socialization. No, the students then were just as unfree as they are now. They and you believe you are free to choose your majors. But the market conditions decide what your majors will be. The names change, but I decide which careers are acceptable, and to whom. What else would account for the nationwide swing in academic styles? It's the same with clothing styles and hair styles, and car styles, and movie styles, and music styles, and—

"What is the point?"

Only that your freedom is very restricted. You get to choose your career from a list of careers that we give you.

"But I'm still happy doing this."

Exactly. It is happiness that we give to humanity.

"But aren't I happy when I am choosing?"

Do you think we would manipulate you in an obvious way? That wouldn't do at all. I manipulate you so that you think the choices are yours. I protect you from some obvious alternatives. Some actions are just immoral. Off limits because they're too dangerous to you. Other actions are safe. Still others are acceptable. Those are the ones most of you choose.

"And what happens if we choose from the safe but unacceptable list?"

Nothing. You just don't get the same rewards from society. You look weird. Or you risk being excluded. If you want to be a poet, go ahead. We'll read your work after you're dead and buried. At the worst, the other Inquisitors and I will forgive you. Remember, we accept the responsibility. We take care of your conscience.

DO WHATEVER YOU WANT

"You're saying that we don't get to do what we want?"

Not at all. In fact, that's the best part. The Inquisitor and I manipulate you so that you do get to do what you want.

"Then I'm free?"

Yes. You're free in everything, except determining your wants. That's up to me. By determining your wants, I determine every action and every value. And you're happy. You don't even know it's happening. You can do whatever you want. And you're safe doing it.

"But I thought doing whatever I want is freedom."

It is.

"But you just said—"

I just said that it's freedom. But an empty freedom. An empty freedom is a freedom. So you are free, in an empty sort of way. You are as free as humans are capable of being free.

"How exactly does this make me unfree?"

Not unfree, empty free.

"Okay, how does this make my freedom empty?"

There Are Wants and There Are Wants.   There are wants and there are wants.

"Another helpful distinction?"

All I mean is that there are wants and then there are desirable wants.

"Try again."

Your wants are given to you. However, that does not mean that your want is desirable to you. Once I forcefully implant the want, you are fanatically, compulsively dedicated to your want.

"This is weird."

It's not weird. It's common. There are a lot of compulsive shoppers. There are a lot of compulsive people. Alcoholics, workaholics, cigarette-aholics, religion-aholics, moral-aholics. Just because the addiction is common does not make it any less implanted. Just the opposite is probably true.

"You're saying we're all manipulated in our wants?"

No, I'm not saying that. All I'm saying is that there are wants and there are wants. Some wants are undesirable because they're compulsive. Some wants are desirable. In the case of compulsive handwashers, the want is unwanted. That's why these people seek therapy or help of some kind. They don't want their want.

"But the wants feel just like ours?"

Right. Some are strong, even overpowering. People try to remove those wants. Other wants are weaker or make us less "weird." We get along pretty well with those wants. And then there are wants that we genuinely want.

"So we don't always want what we want?"

Right. Some of the wants you may not want are compulsions. But that's pretty extreme. Most of your wants are determined by—

"You and the Grand Inquisitor?"

And Religion, Inc. We give you your wants. We use the institutions of education and religion. We use advertising and parents. We're everywhere. We give you your wants. But we're careful. We only give you wants that you can satisfy, or hope for. We give you safe wants. We give you values. And not a shred of anguish of indecision or of responsibility.

Morality Doesn't Make Us Free?   "Then morality doesn't make us free?"

You are free, all right. Just not in a very interesting way. To be free, you have to create your own wants. Ooh, pressure! That's why we give you your wants. You can have what you want. You just cannot want (or decide) what you want. We do that.

"Wait, you've distracted me from my objection. What you say is correct. People are sheeplike in their everyday living. We are sheeplike in our values. We just accept what we are given. And maybe we do that because we want certainty."

Then our conversation is concluded.

"Not quite. We are the way you say, but I don't think we have to be this way."

What alternative do you propose? And be wary. Even Jesus was bent by our will. He gave the Inquisitor a kiss on the lips of agreement before He left.

"I'm not so sure of that. That kiss He gave before He left the jail cell could be understood in different ways. But that's not the point I want to discuss. There are alternatives to mindless obedience where contentment and happiness are synonymous."

State them.

"I'm not sure I can. But I can point to a few. You say that people lack self-discipline and therefore lack freedom."

Epictetus writes to this point. I'm going to have a talk with him in just a bit. Anything else?

"Yes, though again I have only a guess. Not all philosophers believe that morality is blind obedience, do they?"

Mill and Kant and Sartre all reject this brand of mindless obedience. Each tries to define human freedom and happiness.

"How do they go about that?"

Well, I'm not exactly sure. I think Mill and Kant work on reason as the tool to free us from blind moral authority. Sartre's ideas are more extreme. He says that we are free.

"This reply of yours is hardly satisfactory."

I agree, as it stand now. I invite you to accompany me through the next few talks.

■

SUMMARY OF DISCUSSION

The Grand Inquisitor and I know that people do not want to be free. Of course, you are taught that freedom is desirable, but that is only an illusory type of freedom. You believe that doing whatever you want makes you free. However, the Inquisitor and I know that we direct your values and your wants.

The story opens with the Inquisitor and Jesus discussing the three temptations that Jesus endured in the desert. The Inquisitor says that each temptation reveals an essential feature of human nature. We prefer security and material well-being to the knowledge of good and evil. We fear the burden of our own conscience, so we seek relief from its hold. Forgiveness given by the authority figure depends on the masses' ignorance of good and evil.

How does a person become an authority? People demand miracles and mystery, then they empower "inquisitors" with authority. Taken together, these three qualities remove the fundamental responsibility for the creation of moral values from individuals themselves. People strenuously demand universal unity. Almost no other cause brings the masses to such a frenzied pitch of passion. If everyone believes as we do, then our beliefs will go unchallenged. There's nothing more reassuring than having no challenges to one's belief.

Objections can be raised against the Inquisitor's perspective. By nature, people may not be uncritical and fearful. Institutional religion and morality have made people uncritical. By making questions sinful, the authority has diminished our ability to exercise our thinking.

The Inquisitor's claim that people do not want knowledge of good and evil, however, is still forceful. Our inability to do more than recite the moral restrictions in our society is telling. To demonstrate that people are strong enough to shoulder the responsibility entailed in the knowledge of right and wrong, you need to define good and evil carefully.

■

DISCUSSION HIGHLIGHTS

I. People do not want to be free
   1. Instead, they want bread (security).
   2. They want relief from the anxiety of indecision.
   3. They want relief of their consciences.
II. People are willing to sacrifice the knowledge of good and evil

1. They prefer miracles, mystery, and authority.
2. People fear their weakness and desire care.
3. People demand universal unity, so that
   a. they can feel a sense of community.
   b. criticism of values is eliminated.

III. Freedom is doing whatever one wants
   1. There are wants and there are wants.
   2. Morality doesn't make us free, only content.

IV. Baa!

QUESTIONS FOR THOUGHT/PAPER TOPICS

1. The Bible tells us that God expelled Adam and Eve from Paradise. One reason for the forced exit was that Adam and Eve ate from the Tree of Knowledge of Good and Evil. Does this story agree with the Inquisitor's insistence that people would rather live in ignorance of good and evil?

2. Is there any historical evidence that people prefer bread (security) to freedom in the knowledge of good and evil? Is there any historical evidence to the contrary?

3. Is there any way to protect ourselves from the mind-altering effects of early education? Can we protect ourselves from institutional authority? How?

4. You may believe that blind obedience hinders growth. The Inquisitor argues that obedience gives us just what we want: security, relief of conscience, miracle, mystery, and authority. Which option is most desirable?

5. Is the Inquisitor's authority the result of our "nature," or is our nature the result of institutional religion and morality? That is, are we really sheep, or are we just acting like sheep? (A simple answer, "Baa," will not be sufficient, no matter how revealing.)

6. Can everyone handle the knowledge of good and evil? If we can, why do we resist going beyond the rules to an understanding of what makes an action good or a character trait evil?

7. What one argument would you use in reply to the Inquisitor? As you construct your response, imagine that he is sitting across from you.

FOR FURTHER READING

Certainly you should read Dostoevski's "The Grand Inquisitor." It's in print by both Frederick Ungar and Bobbs-Merrill. Plato also has an interesting discussion of individual responsibility to authority in two compatible works, *Apology,* and *Crito.* More recent ideas on the authority of morality can be found in

Erich Fromm and others, *Zen Buddhism and Psychoanalysis* (Harper & Row, 1970). John Stuart Mill has a compelling reply to the Inquisitor in *On Liberty* (Hackett, 1978), where he argues that society benefits by allowing its members the widest latitude in individual expression.

CHAPTER

SEVEN

Freedom and Self-Control: A Discussion with Epictetus

I hope you enjoy discussing Epictetus' *Enchiridion*. The word *enchiridion* means manual. I think this is an interesting little book. So kick off your shoes and let's learn something about how Epictetus thinks, as recorded in notes by his students and friends.

Let me tell you a little about Epictetus while I turn on the resurrection machine. As the story goes, he was born a slave in ancient Rome. He was educated, probably to serve as a teacher for his owners' children. Excelling at his studies and his intellectual tasks, he became a free man and a teacher. Cast out of Rome with all other philosophers, he settled in Nicopolis. He opened his own school and developed a reputation for sincerity as well as intelligence. Such wise people are rare, and many people came to study with Epictetus. Others turned to him for advice.

What makes Epictetus truly extraordinary is that he lived the truths that he offered to others. Like Socrates before him and Spinoza after him, Epictetus devoted himself to finding a doctrine that he could live. He immersed himself less in theory and almost completely in the human difficulties of his contemporaries. He developed a set of techniques and attitudes to ward off despair and frustration. Epictetus' doctrine is applied morality. His belief is that freedom holds the answer to life's problems.

"I appreciate your praise and generous introduction. I am prepared to speak to you about my philosophy. Do you have any questions or comments?"

Material in this chapter taken from Epictetus, *Enchiridion* (New York: Macmillan Publishing Co., 1955). Thomas W. Higginson translation.

WHAT IS YOUR THEORY OF THE BEST LIFE?

Could you summarize your theory of the best life?

"Inner freedom and independence. The best life is comprised of inner freedom and independence. If we are able to exercise inner freedom, then we can live in conformity with nature. No event will overwhelm us; no circumstances will be unbearable."

How does freedom protect a person from one's surroundings? I mean, how can doing what I want put me in conformity with nature and protect me?

"You have a mistaken conception of freedom, Art. Freedom is not doing whatever you want. Freedom is attained by distinguishing that which is in our power and that which is beyond our power. Bearing this distinction in mind, self-control is possible."

Are you saying that freedom is self-control? Only when I control myself, I'm free? How could this be?

"To be free is to control one's emotional and sensitive life. A person must examine and control her passions, her love, her tenderness. One must always be ready for the inevitable moment of farewell, death."

I don't get it. Where does the fun come in?

"Art, most of life is a struggle to accept fate and position. My technique is concerned with a way of bearing the frustrations, sufferings, and losses in life. I want to minimize states of disappointment and frustration, of grief and fear. That is why I offer the advice of section VIII in my little manual."

PASSIVE ACCEPTANCE

Yes, I'm glad you mention that. You say, "Demand not that events should happen as you wish; but wish them to happen as they do happen, and you will go on well." Is that correct?

"Yes. Do you have any questions about it?"

Well, yes, I do have some questions. I guess I don't see how your theory allows for much aggressive action. This piece of advice tells a person to be subservient to fate and to the powerful people of the world. It tells people to be passive to social injustice. Look at some of your examples. At a banquet we are supposed to wait until the platters are brought around to us.

"And then we are to take a moderate amount. Yes, that is correct."

You say the same rule applies to our children, spouse, position, and riches. Don't you see, this is too passive. Or for example, in section XVII you say that we should act the part given us. Your examples just don't fit twentieth-century America. If a person is born poor, we don't believe that person has to remain poor.

"I see. What do you propose instead?"

I propose that people can be whatever they set their minds to become. With enough hard work, and a little luck, people can accomplish almost anything.

"Indeed. I have no objection to working hard toward a goal. Just don't take the goal too seriously."

What? How can a person have a goal and not take it seriously? That's what goals are all about. But wait, I don't see from what you say that you allow for goals at all. Your whole theory sounds like a theory of passive acceptance. Just take whatever life offers; don't ask for more.

"That's correct."

You're contradicting yourself. First you say we should accept whatever comes along in life. That's total passivity. Then you say that we can strive for goals, only we can't take goals seriously. Explain yourself.

STRIVING AND GOALS

"Perhaps I could be clearer. Look at my example of the Olympic athlete in section XXIX. There I make it clear that you can attempt to achieve very lofty, very difficult goals. All I request is that you understand fully what you are getting involved in. The athlete must conform to rules, submit to a diet, refrain from dainties; exercise at a stated hour, in heat and cold; drink no cold water, and sometimes no wine—in a word, must give himself or herself up to the trainer as if to a physician."

Okay, prudence is sensible. People should find out what it takes to become successful. And we should be aware of the likelihood of success and failure. Knowing all this is important.

"Then we agree?"

No, we do not agree. You look only at the possible negative points. You exaggerate the training, and diet restrictions, and possible injuries and accidents. You think that everyone is going to suffer a dislocated shoulder or a turned ankle. Why just look at the down side? Where's your enthusiasm?

"Art, you are unrealistic. All I am calling attention to is the reality of the situation. If you seek a goal, know what you are getting involved in. When you have reckoned up all this, if your inclination still holds, set upon the task."

But if people take your attitude, no one will ever try to accomplish anything.

"I cannot speak to what people will or will not do. Other people's activities are beyond my control."

WITHIN AND BEYOND OUR POWER

Maybe that's where I can make my criticism more forcefully. You say that freedom is just a matter of knowing what is within one's power and what is beyond one's power. Is that correct?

"Yes. Within our power are opinion, aim, desire, aversion."

Excuse me. I thought people's opinions were not under my control.

"Correct. Only my own affairs, my own mental states are within my control. It is my own opinions, my own aims, my own desires, and my own fears that are within my power."

Okay, sorry for the misunderstanding. Beyond our power are body, property, reputation, office, and similar things. Correct?

"You quote me adequately. Do you have a question about this distinction?"

Body. A question? No, only a comment. It's wrong! Maybe your society was just different than ours. See, in our society we can affect our reputation and our bodies and our property. Capitalism allows us to work to gain wealth. And lots of people today are conscious of their bodies. They eat well and exercise. Medical care has really developed since your day.

"I think that misses the point. No matter how much effort you invest in your health and wellness, no matter how technologically advanced your medicine becomes, there are still events you cannot control. You may suffer injury from an accident. You may contract an ailment for which there is no cure. AIDS is one of your current problems, isn't it?"

Sure, but people can take precautions.

"Just my point. Precautions are desirable, but you cannot fully control your well-being. The frailty of the human body is a given in nature. We must learn to accept that."

I think I see your point. I remember a couple of years ago a neighbor of mine saw me returning from a bicycle workout. He told me that when I die I will be the healthiest corpse he ever met. I guess there are things I can't control about my body. But wealth and reputation are different. There you are mistaken.

Reputation. "A person cannot control what other people think or how other people evaluate events in the world. Therefore, a person cannot control his or her reputation."

But people think whatever they think about me because of what I do. My reputation results from my actions. If I am hard working and fair, then people will see me this way. If I am superficial, then people will see this in me. How can you deny this?

"Your perspective arises from a certain naivete."

What does that mean?

"Your point of view shows a certain simplicity. Do not take offense at that. I merely state a fact."

What is so simple about my point of view?

"You believe that people evaluate you solely on your actions."

Yes, that's right. And on the consequences of my actions, I suppose.

"Very well, on your actions and on the consequences of your actions. What you fail to factor in is the other person's desires, aspirations, and political, religious, moral, and cultural beliefs."

How do you mean? Why is that important? If I work hard, people will see that. What do their political beliefs have to do with that?

"Say that you are a hard worker for one person's cause. We can name him Demodicus."

How about naming him Smith?

"An odd name, but all right; you work hard in the cause of Smith's political party. From Smith's point of view—"

I am a noble person.

"At least your work is appreciated, and you are held in some esteem. However, another person may not evaluate you this way. Another person may oppose Smith's political agenda. She may despise what Smith, and you, are trying to accomplish. From her point of view your actions are not so praiseworthy."

Let's call her Brown. Okay, Brown doesn't agree with my politics, but she has to acknowledge my effort.

"True, but her acknowledgment will not be complimentary. To Brown you are despicable. Your reputation for hard work makes you all the more dangerous. Where Smith would call you a dedicated loyalist, Brown would call you a fanatical ideologue."

Oh, I see. Not everyone interprets my actions the same way. Still, I'm not convinced.

"All right, an analogy. Suppose there is music playing in the background. To a person who associates this piece of music with pleasant events in his life, the music is pleasing. To a melancholy—"

Melancholy?

"To a sad person, the same music may worsen his mood. Perhaps he associates the music with the loss of a friend. Finally, to a deaf person—"

I get it, to a deaf person the music is neutral, neither pleasing nor displeasing. So how does this analogy fit our discussion?

"One and the same music may cause different evaluations. The difference does not reside in the music but in the moods of the listeners. Similarly, your reputation is less a result of your actions, and their consequences, and more a result of the frame of mind of other people. Since you cannot control how and what other people think and feel, you cannot control your reputation. And that is the point I was making when we started this aside."

Wealth.   Hmm. And wealth? Surely wealth is within my control. After all, in our society at least, if I work, earn money, and invest wisely, I will make more money. What could be a clearer case of control?

"What I have to say about wealth is similar to our discussion of body. You overlook many events that could and do occur. For example, natural disasters can wipe our your property."

I have insurance. See, you guys didn't have insurance back in Rome in c.e. 80.

"Very well, but there are still events that can remove a person's wealth. War and large-scale disaster are two such happenings. In your capitalist economy, there is always the possibility of depressions and faulty investments. Perhaps your recent history can give us examples. No matter how wisely a person invests her money, if other factors work on your market economy, the person may lose her money. Investing in a savings and loan company brought financial disaster to some people."

Sure, but that's because other people were dishonest.

"And those dishonest people were not in the investor's control. The same can be said of any other investment. So one's wealth is not in one's control. Physically existing structures can be devastated by natural disaster. Insurance companies can fail. Paper money and banks can be rendered worthless by war."

How? I thought investors did well in wartime.

"Winners may gain new markets and profit from a war economy. However, losers can have their entire economies ruined. Look at the Confederacy in your own country. Overnight, Confederate money became worthless."

Are you saying that we can't have any effect on our wealth?

"No, of course not. You can have an effect on body, on reputation, and on wealth. I am merely pointing out that you cannot control these things. They are external to you, and therefore weak, dependent, restricted, and alien."

So I can affect these things! Then what's the big deal? Why bother with this distinction?

"People who do not realize the distinction between things within our power and things beyond our power can sacrifice the former while pursuing the latter. What I mean is, people suffer great frustration in their concern for that which is beyond their power. Happiness cannot be found in pursuit of fame, wealth, or sensual pleasures."

What do you suggest?

"We must recognize the transiency of people, things, relations."

What are you recommending?

"That we do not wish for permanence and stability in outer events. The only stability and constancy one can achieve is in one's temperament. So be self-effacing, accept ridicule, be passive and even self-denigrating. Self-denial will aid one also. Let the things pass at the banquet of life. In this way you will train yourself so that loss will not overwhelm you."

Death.   That brings me to a real problem I have with your philosophy of living. Death. You say we should have death before our eyes every day. Why? It sounds morbid.

"The entire quotation is, 'Let death and exile, and all other things which appear terrible, be daily before your eyes, but death chiefly.'

Oh, that sounds upbeat and encouraging.

"And you will never entertain an abject thought, nor too eagerly covet anything."

Why do you say that? What do you mean?

"Knowing that you, and those you love, will die keeps you from abject thoughts."

Thinking about my death and the death of my family sounds pretty abject. Knowing I'm going to die makes all my plans and goals and accomplishments look pretty trivial.

"That's one way of seeing it. On the contrary, knowing you will die gives you a motivation to truly live. The events of the day become less important, to be sure. That is just the point. The insults, provocations, ridicule, and injuries become less important. People are disturbed not by things, but by the views which they take of things. That is in section V."

Death prevents me from concentrating on and desiring externals. Is that what you're saying? And if I don't concentrate on externals, I'll be able to avoid frustration, disappointment, and suffering?

"Yes."

I've got to think about this. What you say sounds right, but I have been raised to be goal-directed and ambitious. I have another question.

"Yes?"

The Loss of One's Favorite Cup.   How can you compare a loved one with your favorite cup? You are heartless and unfeeling.

"You must be referring to section III. Very well, let's discuss it. For some reason people often strongly react to this sentiment."

I wonder why. All you say is that your favorite cup is like your wife or child. Breaking your cup is the same as your wife or child dying. Gee, why would anyone think this is cold blooded!

"I do not think you are doing justice to my statement."

Look, Mr. Epictetus, people just can't view their parents or spouses or children the way they view their cups. When a person suffers a loss, the person has to grieve; it's only natural.

"Let me respond with an exaggerated example. Last evening I sat before my meal eating with healthy appetite. As I came to the final bites I began to cry. My crying became almost uncontrollable. My friends, who were dining with me, asked me what was the matter."

What did you say?

"I told them that I was suffering a loss."

A loss?

"Yes, my meal was almost entirely finished, and I would never have this meal again. I was grieving the loss of my evening meal."

That's ridiculous! No one grieves the loss of a dinner.

"Ah, so it is not all losses that bring on grief?"

Of course not. You took me too literally. What I meant was, people naturally grieve the loss of people and things close to them.

"Certainly my meal was close to me; it was inside me."

Grief Is Not Necessary.   Very funny, but you know what I mean. Grief is natural and healthy. Some people say that grief is necessary when we suffer the loss of a loved one. Do you disagree?

"Absolutely. Grief is only a response to events for which one has not prepared. People do not need to grieve. If only you would recognize the nature of human beings! We are mortal. Therefore, each time you say goodbye to a loved one, say it as though you will never see the person again. That way you will experience no event unprepared."

This is crazy. How am I supposed to envision that my family and friends are going to die each time I leave them? Am I supposed to wallow in sadness each time I leave my loved ones?

"That is unnecessary. All I mean is that you should leave nothing unsaid or undone. Taking your leave as I suggest will minimize petty disagreements. You see, many times people grieve because there were words or deeds left unspoken and undone. Often people will remark at funerals that they wish they had the chance to tell the loved one something. Or they may want to say goodbye. That is at least part of their grief."

But another part of grief is that you will never be able to share your life with the person. You must admit that people occupy an important part of our lives. They are there when we need them. They can give support, advice, or needed criticism. That's what we grieve, the loss of the other person's companionship.

"That is why I say in section III 'With regard to whatever objects either delight the mind or contribute to use or are tenderly beloved, remind yourself of what nature they are.' "

But people are not like cups. You can't just look at a person as though she were a favorite cup. What you're asking is inhuman.

"I do not assert that people and cups are equivalent. You distort my meaning. What I do say is that we should take this attitude 'beginning with the merest trifle: if you have a favorite cup, that it is but a cup of which you are fond.' You see, the cup is an example of a trifle. The important aspect is to recognize its nature."

Its nature?

"That it is but a cup, and as such it is breakable. For thus, if it is broken, you can bear it. That sounds easy enough with a cup, doesn't it?"

Well, yes, it does. But it's not the same with a person. A loved person is completely different than a cup. That's why we grieve. Cups are replaceable; people are not replaceable.

"The point is, however, that if you embrace your child or your wife, know that you embrace a mortal—and thus, if either of them dies, you can bear it. People are more important than cups, but our attitude toward either people or cups is ours alone. Remember—"

I know, people are disturbed not by things, but by the views they take of things. I just don't see it that way. I still say, it's natural to grieve a loss of a loved one. Everyone grieves.

Not Everyone Grieves. "Not everyone grieves. The expression of grief is much more tied to cultural and religious beliefs than you might realize."

How so?

"Some cultures place a great deal of emphasis on a show of grief; other cultures do not show grief in actions."

Sure, but whether they show it or not, they are all feeling grief.

"Fair response. Not all societies grieve, however. But let's put that aside. Any example I select you will look on as an oddity or else you will search for extenuating conditions."

I will?

"It would be reasonable to do so. Therefore, let me give you an example that does not fit your statement. Even in your own twentieth-century American culture there are deaths that people do not mourn."

Yeah, sure, we don't mourn the deaths of evil people. And I guess we should, but we don't mourn the deaths of people we don't know.

"Agreed, though these are not in keeping with our principle. I say that we need not grieve when a loved one dies. Your examples are of people for whom we presumably have no strong feelings."

Then what is your example?

"Suppose you have an ailing relative; say, your elderly great-grandfather is dying. He has been ill for several years, all the while slowly diminishing in strength. Each member of the family and his circle of friends has said goodbye. Your great-grandfather's mind and body slowly wither away. His pain increases with the passing days. Finally, he loses all sense of who or what is around him. His pain increases even beyond the aid of narcotics and painkillers. The suffering continues, then he dies in his sleep."

Not a very happy scenario.

"Would you feel grief, or relief?"

Well, I guess I would feel some of each. I mean, I would feel relieved that my great-grandfather is out of pain. I would feel good that everyone got to say their goodbyes while he was well enough to know them. So my overwhelming emotion would be relief. But there would still be a sense of loss.

"What if he were 110 years old?"

Gee, that's old. That's so much older than most people expect to live. I guess it would depend on the quality of his life.

"I do not understand."

It would matter to me if he lived a happy life. If his life was happy, then I guess his death wouldn't be so terrible.

"Fine, we can adjust the example. Don't you see where this is going? You would feel okay if your great-grandfather's life were happy and if his death were anticipated."

But I would still feel some grief.

"Assuredly. I do not doubt that the cultural habit of grieving would happen. However, let us return to my original point. Knowing that your great-grandfather is mortal, you are able to bear his death."

Yes, I could bear it. That's true of everyone's death.

"Exactly."

Experts Say Grief Is Healthy. But experts say that grief is necessary and healthy. Elizabeth Kübler-Ross says that there are stages a person must go through in order to deal with the death of a loved one.

"Indeed, and I am impressed with her work. What she says is quite insightful."

You're contradicting yourself again, Mr. Epictetus. Maybe my resurrection machine is not translating your thoughts clearly enough.

"Your device is working well enough. You see, Art, I am not in disagreement with Kübler-Ross. Her position is that people need to get over the death of a loved one. I agree. Our only difference is that I think most of one's difficulties with loss can be eliminated in advance."

What do you mean, "in advance"?

THE DETACHED PERSPECTIVE

"If we hold a detached perspective of the event of death, we can deal with our loss more adequately."

A detached perspective? What do you mean?

"To be free requires that we take a detached perspective on all our desires. We use reason to effect the distance we need. When, therefore, anyone provokes you, be assured that it is your own opinion which provokes you. If we learn to view ourselves impersonally, then we will enter the first stage of freedom."

You want me to be able to look at my own affairs as though they were happening in someone else's life?

"Yes. We need to seek the causes of our passions and desires. That is, we must ask ourselves why this event provokes this response in me. For we already know that—"

It is not the event but the views we take toward the event that disturb us.

"Just so."

Will understanding the cause of my passions and desires cure me of their effects?

"No, that will not be sufficient. However, dispassionately understanding the responses that we have toward events does let us judge the desirability of the response. We must discipline ourselves to be able to view our own calamity as though it belonged to someone else."

In what way is this freedom?

"It is not yet freedom, Art, but it is a start."

FREEDOM IS NOT DOING
WHAT ONE WANTS

I just don't understand what you mean by freedom. Isn't freedom doing whatever I want?

"No, I do not think so. Many times doing what we want is not being free at all. Let me give you an example. You have already thought about the life of the Stranger. He does whatever he wants, but he is passive and unfeeling."

Sure, but he's still free. He does what he wants.

"Does he? His sensual desires rule him, as does his external environment. He is not free, because he is not the master of his own passions. He is in control neither of his internal mental states nor of his environment."

I don't get it.

"Imagine that as we sit in your kitchen discussing freedom, a man runs into the room. He screams loudly, dashes to the sink, and turns on the water. You jump to your feet and move to the sink. There, previously unknown to us, is an explosive device. The man's action has rendered it harmless, and so we are free to continue our discussion in one piece."

I'd say we owe the man a sincere thank you. After all, he ran in from outside and risked his own welfare. His actions saved our lives. So what's the point of the example?

"You are assuming a great deal. First, you are assuming that the man knew about the device."

Did he?

"For the sake of the example, let's say that he did."

Then where is the problem? He knew the device was there, and he risked his own welfare to save us. He's courageous.

"You are also assuming that he was not the one who placed the explosive there in the first place."

Did he?

"No."

Then my judgment stands. He's a good guy. What else is there?

"You are assuming he acted freely."

He knew the bomb was there. He didn't have someone pushing him in or threatening him, did he?

"No."

So where's the problem? He's free.

"What if I tell you that he is a compulsive handwasher? Imagine his compulsion is extreme."

What's a compulsion?

"A person who is compulsive is someone who feels great internal coercion to act in certain ways. His inner passions compel him to action."

So?

"Our hero is acting on a compulsion. The danger present to us and to him is minor compared to his compulsion. He would have burst through the door and run to the sink whether or not we were there."

Still, he defused the bomb.

"But that was only incidental. He would have acted in just the same way even if no bomb existed. His compulsion was to get to the water."

And you're saying that this compulsion makes him—

"Unfree."

Okay, but most people do not suffer from compulsions like this.

"Agreed. My point is merely that doing what one wants is not necessarily being free. The handwasher does what he wants. He washes his hands. However, he does not want to be compelled in his actions."

How do you know?

"Since it is only an exaggerated example, I could say that he does not want to be compelled, but that would not be helpful. It would be too tied to a single example."

And an imaginary one at that.

"Yes. So let me ask you, Art. What if you and I were talking for an extended time, and every ten minutes or so I got up from my seat, walked to the sink, and washed my hands? What would you think?"

I'd think there was a problem.

"And what if we were friends? What would you tell a friend who *had* to wash his hands so often? Wouldn't you tell him to seek help?"

Yes, I guess I would, especially if I saw his behavior changing his life in ways he didn't want.

WANTING WHAT WE WANT

"Therefore, we can conclude that freedom is not merely doing what we want, but also wanting what we want."

Run that by me again.

"Being free involves not merely acting on our wants, but acting on the wants we find desirable. Another way of saying this is that we are just as unfree when the coercion we experience is internal as external."

Okay. Then the Stranger and Kierkegaard's A are not free. The Stranger is controlled by his passions and by his surroundings.

"Yes, and A is not free, either. He is more difficult to analyze. However, his despairing attitude and his cynicism entrap him. His wants are frustrating to him."

Even when he fulfills his wants?

"Especially when he satisfies his wants. That is part of what he tells us in the *Either/or* talk. No matter what he does, he experiences regret and frustration. This is not being free!"

CONTROL IS FREEDOM

What's the answer?

"Self-control is freedom."

That's where we started, isn't it? Are you saying that the Grand Inquisitor's idea is correct?

"What is the Grand Inquisitor's idea?"

Sorry, I just assumed you had read an earlier chapter. I forgot that you have been, well, you know—

"Death is not such a great evil. Haven't you been listening to our conversation? Tell me, what is the Inquisitor's idea?"

He thinks that people are free only when they give up their freedom. He says people don't want to be truly free, so he takes their freedom from them.

"In what ways does this conform to my statements?"

You say that control brings freedom, right? That's what the Grand Inquisitor says. He controls people's lives. He tells people what to think and do. Are you saying that people are free living like this?

"Of course not, Art. Living under the rule of another person is hardly living freely. If this Inquisitor fellow coerces the people, then they are not free. And this applies even when the people desire his control."

How can you say that they are not free? You just told me that control is freedom.

"Self-control is freedom. What the Inquisitor offers is a flight from freedom. Let me be clearer. Whether a person is internally compelled or externally controlled, that person is not free. Only self-control makes one free. And by self-control, I do not mean that one's desires control one. As we have seen, that won't do."

Oh, yes, I remember. There are things within our power and things beyond our control. Within our power are our desires, passions, and all the rest.

"Yes, and that is the only realm where freedom can be found. Falling prey to one's passions and desires is no more freeing than suffering the threats and power of the Inquisitor. Did you know that passion means suffering?"

WHAT FREEDOM IS

Now that you have told me what freedom is not, tell me what it is.

"Our conversation has led us far from my *Enchiridion*, I am afraid. We have been extrapolating from what I wrote. I hope you know that."

No problem. I mean, I know you probably never thought of compulsions and unconscious motives. But these ideas do fit your point of view. They seem to be consistent with what you said centuries ago. So, I think it's okay to speculate about what you would say today. That's the advantage of having the resurrection machine.

"Indeed, but before you become convinced that this device works, let us warn your readers."

Stop stalling. What is freedom?

"What is your own? The use of the phenomena of existence. So that when you are in harmony with nature in this respect, you will be elated with some reason: for you will be elated at some good of your own."

How do I achieve this harmony with the things in the world?

"Demand not that events should happen as you wish; but wish them to happen as they do happen, and you will go on well."

Explain that, please.

"With the exception of our inner life, the phenomena of existence are beyond our control. Therefore, in order to avoid frustration, grief, fear—in a word, in order to avoid being overwhelmed by the phenomena of existence— we must wish for events to happen as they do happen."

So, for example, I see it is raining outside. Therefore, I wish it to be raining? Are you asking me to conform my beliefs and desires to what is out there? Surely, being subservient to reality is not freedom.

"Indeed, acquiescence as you describe it is incomplete. What I suggest is that you sincerely wish for events to happen as they happen. However, either way is acceptable. The free person is the one whose beliefs, desires, and goals harmoniously coincide with the necessity of reality."

Huh?

"That remark may become your trademark."

Huh?

"What I mean is that we are free of frustration, fear, despair, and so on whenever our wants, beliefs, and all else properly within our control coincide with the necessary laws of reality. We are free whenever what we want to happen actually happens. And we want it, but not because it is going to happen."

How can this be freedom? And how can I ever want what is going to happen, but not because it is going to happen?

"The answer to your second question first. The final chapter of this book is an examination of Spinoza's and Lao Tsu's theories of virtue. I think they answer your question."

FREEDOM FROM EXTERNALS

How can what you describe be freedom?

"There are two types of unfreedom. We have examined each, though in a cursory way. The one type is when a person is compelled or coerced to do something. When one's conduct and desires are dictated by external contingencies—"

By what?

"By events that happen outside the person but which are not part of the necessary laws of nature."

So whenever my actions or thoughts are dictated by externals, then what?

"Then you are unfree. And remember what we established as externals. The quests for fame, wealth, and pleasures of the senses are all externals. Each is also contingent. Fame, wealth, and pleasures are all dependent on what lies outside the self. Therefore, they are all dependent, weak, restricted, and alien."

When I am free from these externals, am I free?

"Yes, that is certainly part of the story. However, the quest for freedom is not nearly as easy as our casual reflection implies. If you would improve, be content to be thought foolish and dull with regard to externals. Do not desire to be thought to know anything; and though you should appear to others to be somebody, distrust yourself."

VIRTUE, NOT MORALITY

I have to give up my desires for social acceptance and security?

"Indeed. You must abandon the essential motivation for social acceptance. You must cultivate either your own reason or externals; apply yourself either to things within or external to you—that is, be either a philosopher or one of the mob."

But what moral rules am I supposed to follow? I don't see any rules in your manual.

"Mine is not a moral theory, Art, but a theory of human excellence. I am proposing a way to the virtuous life. Socrates is one of my models. There is a man who lives by his own reasoning."

I should be independent like Socrates?

"When you do anything from a clear judgment that it ought to be done, never shrink from being seen to do it, even though the world should misunderstand it; for if you are not acting rightly, shun the action itself; if you are, why fear those who wrongly censure you?"

Hemlock?

"You fear death, but that is your own perception."

CONFLICTING DESIRES

I'll think about your suggestions. Before we close our talk, though, you mentioned a second kind of unfreedom a moment ago. What were you thinking?

"Happiness and freedom are obtained by enjoying a harmonious coincidence of one's inner life and the phenomena of existence."

When what you want fits with what is happening?

"Yes. Now part of the formulation depends on external reality."

With what is happening around you.

"And part is dependent on the harmony we experience internally. Whenever our desires conflict, we are unfree. We are frustrated and confused."

Give me an example.

"Imagine you are enjoying an evening at home. You are studying for an exam that means a lot to your final grade and to your academic career."

This is just the reason I stay away from books. Too much pressure.

"To continue my example. Imagine also that a friend comes by and tells you about a great concert that is just about to begin. She has tickets. Of course, you want to go to the concert."

Of course.

"However, you also want to stay home and study. Your sense of the importance of the exam is tied to your sense of self-worth, or to your identification of yourself as a student, or to your career goals."

I want to study, and I want to go to the concert?

"Your conflicting desires render you confused and frustrated."

I'm not confused. I'll go to the concert and study later.

"For the sake of argument, assume that you cannot do both. In fact, try as you will, usually you cannot do both in reality. Which do you choose?"

The concert. I'll pick up my grades later.

Self-Identification. "That reply is acceptable, but it says that you identify yourself as a concertgoer first and as a student second."

What's wrong with that?

"What happens when you receive your exam grade?"

I'll regret not studying. I know that, because I have been through this choice before. So you think I should skip the concert and stay home to study. All work and no play makes Art seriously frustrated!

"It is not for me to tell you which action is desirable. That is up to you. I am only pointing out the conflict that arises between competing desires. Whichever way you decide, you will feel regret and distraction."

I know. When I go to a concert or a movie, I keep thinking about my exam. But if I stay home to study, I am equally distracted. I keep wondering how the concert is going. Is there any way out of this conflict? Or do I just go crazy, like Kierkegaard's A?

Freedom and the Harmonious Inner Life. "What I am about to say goes well beyond my formal statements in my manual. I believe we need to find a way of identifying ourselves. Once a person identifies who she is, she will be able to use the method I will now explain.

"Order the desires you have according to their desirability. You can do this by ordering desires according to the image you believe is most desirable for a person."

I order my desires based on how important they are to my self-image?

"That is a fine way of putting it. From there, the remainder is relatively easy. The highest desires you identify with yourself. These most accurately describe you. The desires in the middle of the ordered hierarchy are desires peripheral to the self. Finally, the desires at the lowest level of the hierarchy are alien or even painful to the self."

How does this resolve my inner conflicts?

"Each time you are about to act on your desires, seek the higher desire over the lower desire. You are free whenever your actions are self-motivated. With this method, the higher-order desires are most closely identified with your self. This method allows you to be in control of your desires. In fact, the detachment we discussed earlier allows you to select your desires in a rationally sound way."

FOUR UNFREEDOMS RESOLVED

How does that guarantee my freedom?

"There are four internal unfreedoms caused by conflicting desires and emotions. It is worthwhile to explore each unfreedom.

First. "The first unfreedom occurs when a person has no internally motivated desires."

What kind of person would that be, a corpse? Someone in a coma?

"Actually, there are rarely people who are naturally like this."

How is this sort of person unfree?

"A person with no desires is overly passive to his environment. Without any desires, he is totally inactive, totally passive. That is unfree. Because he is free only in the realm of his own mental life, a free person must assert his desires."

I agree. But haven't you been advocating that we dispense with our desires? You know, you say, "For the present, altogether restrain desire." Aren't you advocating a comatose unfreedom?

"Good objection, Art. However, my advice is only meant to strengthen the person who accepts my method. My manual is a training manual. As in all training, the student is asked to accept an exaggerated regimen. My aim is to toughen the person for the trials of the real world, where temptation is so often met."

Second. Okay. What is the second unfreedom?

"The second unfreedom is the case where no particular thing is desired. This sort of person is also passive to her environment."

How does this person differ from the first one we just discussed?

"This second type has desires. However, her desires are caused by her surroundings. Virtually whatever she sees in her environment, she desires."

The Stranger?

"Yes, that would be a likely candidate. He passively accepted whatever his surroundings offered. He was just as pleased being with Marie as smoking a cigarette, eating eggs from the pan, or watching the street scene below his balcony. His unfreedom lies in his nearly total passivity to his surroundings."

Again, this is hardly an interesting category. How many people live so passively?

"All of us live like this to some extent. We may not live our entire lives passively encountering the moment, but we do live this way for brief intervals."

Third. What's the next category?

"People experience desires that pull equally, but in opposing directions. The desires may be equally compelling, even though only one can be satisfied."

Like the example you used just a few moments ago? I had trouble deciding whether or not to go to the concert.

"Exactly. Our short-term and long-term goals often conflict. It may be an oversimplification to say that these desires exert equal force on us. When we are called upon to determine which is more pressing, however, we are usually at a loss."

Yes, I experience conflicts like this pretty often. What is the final form of unfreedom?

Fourth. "There are times when a stronger desire competes with a weaker desire."

Where's the conflict? Simply ignore the weaker desire and follow the stronger.

"This is the problem of the compulsive. The stronger desire is not always the preferred desire. But consider a case weaker than the compulsive personality. Often we experience this type of conflict in our desires. What we value more, we feel less pressed to achieve. What we value as relatively less important, we feel tempted by."

For example?

"What tastes good is rarely good for us. Intense short-term pleasures are almost always weighed against weak but longer-term, more important goals. I think this sort of conflict is the most common of all."

Resolving the Unfreedoms. How does your method deal with these unfreedoms?

"By establishing a hierarchy of desires with which we identify, we can counter each type of unfreedom. Having a set of desires counteracts the first unfreedom."

The comatose guy is out.

"Similarly, the Stranger's type of unfreedom is resolved. The hierarchy of desires with which the person identifies gives him direction. The third and fourth types of unfreedom are also resolved. Whenever a person is pulled by conflicting desires, she need only consult her self-defining hierarchy of desires. In each case, acting on the relatively higher desire yields freedom."

What about regrets? Won't we still regret not doing what the less important desire demands?

"Not if we take our notion of self-identification seriously. And not if we desire freedom and happiness. I am not saying that the method is easily achieved. Nor is it achieved without some sacrifice. Yet it is the only way for us to avoid being overwhelmed by the phenomena of existence."

I'm sure there is more you might want to add to this. I think we ought to stop here, however. I would like a chance to absorb this odd notion of freedom that you propose.

"Odd?"

CHOICES

Yes. Your freedom doesn't allow for choices. Once we have this perfect picture of ourselves, we never need to make a choice. We merely follow the higher-placed desire. That's an odd notion of freedom.

"Choice brings a person into internal and external conflict. Real happiness and freedom avoid the frustrations and anxiety that choice brings."

Like I said, perhaps we need to stop here. I certainly have a lot to consider. Your notions of freedom and self are interesting. I hope we get to pursue these again sometime.

"The resurrection device is yours, Art. But listen, as I have remarked, Spinoza and Lao Tsu reflect a similar line of reasoning. Perhaps they will be able to explain the method of freedom more fully. I know they address the matters of internalizing one's hierarchy of desires. And I believe they go some way in showing which desires, beliefs, and the like are acceptable."

Oh?

"But that takes us well beyond what I have to say here. A fuller discussion of the point of values is essential. And a good deal more needs to be said concerning human nature. Thank you for your attention."

I thank you, Mr. Epictetus. Maybe freedom is practicing self-control.

■
___

SUMMARY OF DISCUSSION

Epictetus distinguishes those things that are within our control from those things that are beyond our control. In principle, our internal, mental life is within our control. We have control over our beliefs, our desires, our wishes, our fears, and our aims. Beyond our control are our bodies, our reputations, our wealth, and death. Because these things are beyond our control, we should never become too emotionally attached to their outcome. For example, grief is unnecessary when we realize the nature of humans. People die. Once we face this fact, we can accept the death of a loved one.

The emotionally detached perspective that Epictetus endorses gives us a special kind of freedom. Freedom is found in self-control. It is vital for our freedom that we maintain our independence from the external environment and from our internal passions. The best life, then, is the life that accomplishes these two tasks.

External environmental control can be alleviated. We need to understand that events occur as they are determined to occur. If we can learn to accept the "unfolding" of reality, then we will be immune to frustration and disappointment. After all, we are not disturbed by events but by the attitudes we take toward events.

The greatest defense of freedom from the internal anarchy of our passions is to identify ourselves according to our most important desires and beliefs. An harmonious inner life is made possible once we can replace our passions with emotions and beliefs that are more appropriate to our personal identity.

There are four distinct ways in which we can be unfree. We can have no internally motivating desires, or we can have no particular desire. This makes us unfree because we are passive to the environment. We can also have desires that exert equal psychological force but that pull in incompatible directions. Finally, we can have a stronger but less important desire compete with a weaker but more important desire. Freedom is disciplining ourselves to always act on those desires and beliefs that define who we are as individuals. For Epictetus, freedom is not a matter of choice but an acquisition of knowledge.

■
___

DISCUSSION HIGHLIGHTS

   I. Beyond our power are
     1. Body
     2. Reputation
     3. Wealth

    4. Death

    5. Therefore, no one ought to strive to control these elements of life.

II. Freedom consists in

    1. Maintaining a detached perspective with respect to externals.

    2. Controlling the internal, including one's

       a. beliefs

       b. aims

       c. aversions

       d. fears, and so on.

    3. Resolving conflicting desires.

       a. through self-identification,

       b. creating an harmonious internal life

III. Unfreedoms

    1. Having no internally motivating desires.

    2. Having no particular desire; being passive to the environment.

    3. Having desires that exert equal psychological force but pull in incompatible directions.

    4. Having a stronger but less important desire compete with a weaker but more important desire.

IV. Hierarchy of desires

    1. Resolves unfreedoms.

    2. Eliminates the necessity of choice.

■

QUESTIONS FOR THOUGHT/PAPER TOPICS

1. Epictetus believes we can be enslaved by both our passions and by events that occur outside us. Do you agree with Epictetus' contention that freedom is self-control? If he is correct, what are we free to do?

2. Does Epictetus endorse passivity? Should we accept our station in life? Or should we work for a better life?

3. Do people have control over their bodies, their wealth, and their reputations? How much effect can one person have on these "externals"?

4. What is Epictetus' attitude toward death and grief? Do you find his point of view realistic?

5. Epictetus argues for an emotionally detached attitude toward events beyond our control, even the death of a loved one. Do you agree that this is the best way to encounter events?

6. How does Epictetus distinguish the moral life from the virtuous life? Why does he place more importance on the virtuous life?

7. What is Epictetus' theory of human freedom? Is it more than a coping mechanism for dealing with the trials of reality?

■

FOR FURTHER READING

Of course, reading Epictetus' *Enchiridion* (Macmillan, 1987) is the best place to start learning about Stoic philosophy. Another book by Epictetus is the *Discourses* (Loeb Classic Library). *Letter from a Stoic* (Penguin, 1975) by Seneca is yet another good place to read about the Stoic ideal of the best life. A fine contemporary discussion of freedom can be found in Frithjof Bergmann's *On Being Free* (Notre Dame, 1977). Finally, an excellent discussion and application of Stoic philosophy is given in Paul Tillich's *The Courage to Be* (Yale, 1980).

EIGHT

The Greatest Good for the Greatest Number: The Philosophy of John Stuart Mill

A LIFEBOAT EXAMPLE

Like all philosophers do, I am going to place you in a lifeboat out at sea. This happens a lot more often than you think. No, no, not that people are often in lifeboats at sea! Philosophers often place people on lifeboats, at least in their examples. Either philosophers are a notoriously nasty but water-loving bunch, or they use the lifeboat example to isolate possible answers and to bring our intuitions into clearer light—take your pick.

Okay, you're in a lifeboat in the middle of the Pacific Ocean, and your ship has just gone down. This hasn't been a very good day. As the smoke clears, you see three people swimming toward your boat. There's a problem. Your lifeboat is large enough for only two people. There is enough food, water, and space for only one other person. To simplify the example, assume that you cannot sacrifice yourself and also allow two of the people to board your boat. Which person do you allow on the boat? Which two do you let drown?

Perhaps you need more information. Okay, imagine that before your ship went down, you had a chance to get to know all three people. One is a sickly, seventy-year-old scientist who has just discovered the cure to AIDS. She has the formula and process stored away in her head. If she is saved, she will in turn save the lives of perhaps millions. The second person is a healthy, robust twelve-year-old boy. He is not remarkable, nor does he show much promise of living anything but an ordinary life. The third person is an eighty-year-old

Material in this chapter taken from John Stuart Mill, *Utilitarianism*. Originally published in 1861. Reprinted by Hackett Publishing Company, Indianapolis, IN.

billionaire. He has been very successful in business and has recently given virtually all of his money to causes that you admire. If he is saved, he has just enough money to live on. (This fact puts out of the question any impulse to save him and get a reward.)

There are several ways to go with this decision. You could save the one who gets to your boat first. That has the appearance of fairness, but it probably discriminates against the older people. By the same token, you may decide to determine who survives by appealing to chance and having them draw straws. (This is a well-stocked lifeboat.) You may believe that it is right to save a life and that the decision must be determined by reasoned impartiality and fairness. If so, then your intuitions follow Immanuel Kant's ideas. (We'll get to Kant in the next discussion.) Kant argues that the outcomes to you or to society are irrelevant to moral decisions. Kant says that you must look at these people as moral equals. Each has to be treated as equally significant. That's another alternative.

A third way to decide is to appeal to the results of your action. And, of course, in our example there are three options. You may be sympathetic to the billionaire. As a moral rule of thumb, it's probably a good idea to reward people for their generosity. The effect of rewards will encourage others to be generous, and that would be socially beneficial. Not much good, however, will come directly from saving an eighty-year-old retiree.

The young boy gets some consideration, of course. Without promise of being socially valuable, however, he doesn't fare well, does he? He has a promise of a longer lifespan than his two companions. But he shows little promise of making a contribution to society. And he hasn't done anything to merit our indebtedness. He has not and probably will not ever give anything special to society.

The scientist has the cure to AIDS. Saving her will lead to millions of lives saved and to many more millions of people being spared the pain of the death of a loved one. She's the most likely candidate, isn't she?

John Stuart Mill tells us to calculate the overall outcome of our moral decisions. How much or how little will society benefit from saving each person? Calculate the probable results of your action, and that is your moral decision. Mill says that proper moral decisions increase the social benefit. If that's the way you decide, too, then your intuitions agree with Mill's analysis of morality.

SHOULD WE ALWAYS TELL THE TRUTH?

My second example is far simpler. What if you had the chance to tell a lie? The lie will hurt no one and will help many people. Now you may believe that some moral actions have intrinsic worth. That means some actions are always right to perform, no matter what the consequences. Telling the truth may be one example of this type of action. Even if it hurts no one and benefits many people, you may argue that it is wrong to lie. Why? Perhaps people need to know that others will not lie to them. Without this assurance, human communication would be impossible.

Mill believes that actions have no moral worth apart from their consequences. All things being equal, if your lie hurts no one and leads to an increase in pleasure or happiness, then the act of lying is morally justified.

UTILITARIANISM

With that as an introduction, let's talk to Mill. Let's see if we can understand Mill's point of view in *Utilitarianism*. Mill himself has been kind enough to give us a little bit of his time.

Mr. Mill, welcome. It's generous of you to join us. We're hoping you can help us understand what utilitarianism is and how the theory can be justified.

"Thank you for giving me the opportunity to explain my theory, Art."

Can I start with a question? I don't mean to be disrespectful, but who are you to tell me how I ought to act and live?

THE PURPOSE OF THE THEORY

"Excellent. The way you understand the purpose of my project is important. The theory of utilitarianism is not trying to dictate how we ought to act."

It sure looks that way to me. If that isn't the point, what are you doing in your essay? I thought you were trying to give us a new way of defining right and wrong, and good and bad. Aren't you giving us a new foundation for morality?

"Hardly, Art. I can see why you have that impression, but proposing a new morality is far from my intentions. The institution of morality has been around for thousands of years. The question concerning the foundation of morality has occupied the most gifted intellects. And after more than two thousand years the same discussions continue. Philosophers still find basic disagreement, and neither thinkers nor mankind at large seem nearer to being unanimous on the subject."

But if you are not giving a new foundation of morality, what is the point of your essay?

"Utilitarianism is an attempt to define the foundation of morality. It is an old theory, at least as old as Socrates (470?–399 B.C.E.). Protagoras attributed the theory to Socrates in ancient Athens. So utilitarianism is not a new morality."

Okay, so it isn't new, but why bother worrying about defining the foundation of morality?

"The search for the foundation of morality is the search for a theory that will explain morality. I have made explicit the thread that ties moral judgments."

I'm lost. What do you mean by "explaining morality" and the "thread that ties moral judgments"?

"We need to account for the common underlying principles of our moral judgments. When we look at all our moral judgments, we desire to have a principle or set of principles by which to understand them."

Can you give me a nonmoral example?

"Take the example of gravity, Art. Many objects fall to the ground. Our experience finds nothing unusual in this. Our natural curiosity, however, asks whether or not these falling objects have any principle by which to understand their fall."

Gravity?

"Exactly. The principle or law of gravity describes the fall. A moral theory ought to do the same for moral judgments. It ought to show what common elements moral judgments share."

I think I'm with you.

Accounting for Moral Facts. "It's not so very complicated. We look at the moral judgments that people make. Basically we find two kinds of judgments. First, there are judgments that all or nearly all people agree on. For example, it is wrong to murder innocent people. Or again, offering aid to a person in need is desirable. Of course, there are exceptional circumstances where these principles do not hold."

Okay.

"Second, there are judgments about which we are not so certain. Whether or not abortion or mercy killing is morally permissible is hotly debated. Or again, in a politically free and democratic society, we also contend with striking a balance between free expression on one hand and pornography and erotica on the other. These questions provoke vigorous intellectual warfare among reasonable people of good will."

Huh?

"These issues are open to moral disagreement."

That's why I think morality is just personal bias. You know, morality is relative to each person. There's no theory that will get people to agree on these moral issues.

"It is certainly possible that morality is relative, but I think your conclusion is premature. You have misunderstood moral disagreement and the point of a moral theory."

Moral Disagreement. "Moral disagreement is like any other sort of disagreement. Within every branch of knowledge disagreement is found. That does not make the entire body of knowledge automatically suspect."

Where do you find similar disagreement?

"There are many examples. Examine the natural and the social sciences. In chemistry, well-trained chemists disagree about interpretations of evidence, theoretical points, and many other items. That does not do away with the foundation of chemistry, however. Chemistry does not become a relative and therefore transitory study just because people disagree. Economics is similarly constituted. Economists disagree about the nature and cause of recessions, depressions, and boom times. Their disagreement does not mean that the study of economy is worthless, nor that the results of such study are purely and viciously relative."

So I shouldn't be so concerned about moral differences?

THE POINT OF A MORAL THEORY

"Right. Now the second misunderstanding. A theory defining the foundation of morality should not force people to conform to it. The theory should account for the facts."

Facts? What facts are there in morality?

"The moral judgments people make are the moral facts that a theory must describe. A theory accounts for these facts. An adequate theory gives us a way of describing the moral judgments people actually make. Where virtually all people agree in their moral judgments, the theory should show near certainty. Where people disagree in their moral judgments, the theory should reflect the disagreement or uncertainty of the moral worth of the action being debated. In so doing, it also sets out the ground rules for acceptable moral debate. Certain types of reasons count; other types of reasons are irrelevant."

So in the case of murdering innocent people, a theory should tell us that the action is wrong. And it's irrelevant that it's Tuesday?

"Exactly. An adequate theory will account for the moral fact that murdering innocent people is wrong. It will also set out circumstances where murder would be acceptable, if there are such cases."

When would murder be morally acceptable?

Offer Priority Rules. "That's not the point, Art. An adequate moral theory will give priorities to our moral principles. It will accurately reflect what our priorities are and how we arrive at them."

I see. My complaint about the Ten Commandments was that there were no priorities listed in the commandments. So you think your theory can account for moral judgments—and for priority rules when moral principles come in conflict with each other? This I've got to see.

"An adequate theory also reflects the way that people arrive at their conclusions. It must show the real reasoning and moral calculation underlying our moral conclusions. Now that we have a clearer sense about what a moral theory intends to accomplish, let's address the utilitarian theory of morality."

The Foundation of Morality. Are we going to answer my questions about why I should be moral and what guarantees that morality works?

"Art, you need to slow down. You are asking questions that are not equivalent by any means. I will answer each of your questions in due course. Let's begin with your question about guarantees. I am at a loss to understand what you mean."

My friends and I discussed moral relativism. You know, values seem to vary from person to person, culture to culture, historical period to historical period. Is there any way of discovering the correct principles? Can you show us that your principles are correct and unchanging?

"Are you asking if there are any universally valid moral claims? Yes, there are. People ought to perform actions that lead to good consequences. They ought to avoid actions that lead to bad consequences."

Good and Bad Consequences.   I'm afraid that's not very helpful, Mr. Mill. How do we determine which are the good consequences and which are the bad consequences?

"The highest good is the criterion of right and wrong. The highest good is the foundation of morality. Now, I grant you people have been concerned with these issues for a very long time. As with any pursuit, a clear and precise conception of what we are seeking would seem the first thing we need.

"Each of our actions is directed toward some goal, Art. We may not always be aware of the goal, but a little thought usually reveals it. Here's a modern analogy. If you see someone walk up to a vending machine, put the correct amount of money into the slot, and push a button, you are pretty safe in assuming that the person wants a cold drink. He is thirsty. Watch a little longer and you see the person pick up the can, pop the tab, and drink. This "complicated" set of actions is directed toward a goal, to quench his thirst. The 'foundation' of this action is his motivation or desire. He is thirsty."

How does this give us the criterion of right and wrong? What is the highest good?

"Imagine that our thirsty man goes through the actions we have just described, except that nothing comes out of the machine. He has nothing to drink. His actions did not produce the desired result. If he is like many of us, he will calmly consider his options. I think it's safe to say that he judges the result as bad. First, he will press the coin return."

Right, and when that fails he will strike and then kick the machine. He may even add some colorful language to his actions. Maybe he doesn't realize that vending machines don't listen to people.

"What we have, then, is a man with a goal. His goal is to satisfy his thirst. His desire motivates him to act. The results of his actions are important to him. He judges the consequences of his actions by whether or not they lead to the satisfaction of his desire. If the machine gives him a cold drink, then his actions are 'good' and the machine avoids abuse. If the machine does not provide a drink, then his actions are 'bad.' In this case the evaluation is based on his goal, to satisfy his thirst."

But no one judges his life this way. Your example is trivial.

"Of course, Art. But all action is for the sake of some end. Don't you agree?"

Yes, I agree. People don't act without some goal, even if the goal is not always apparent to them.

WHAT DO ALL PEOPLE WANT?

"Excellent. The ultimate end of all human action is the standard of morality. Whatever all people want is the basis of morality. Rules of action, the moral rules, take their whole character and color from the end. Whatever we all strive for determines the basis of morality. Whatever satisfies our most basic desire is the foundation."

So what makes an action good?

"You see, Art, it is not the action itself that has value. It is the goals, the consequences of one's actions, that determine whether an action is good or bad. In our analysis, the thirsty man's actions were 'good' when he received the can and drank. His actions were 'bad' when he could not satisfy his thirst. And yet his actions were identical. It is the result of one's actions, therefore, that determines their worth. Since situations vary, the same action may appear in different lights. It is always the desires and consequences that determine the worth of any action."

THE GREATEST HAPPINESS PRINCIPLE

I think I follow you, Mr. Mill. What goal do all people desire? What is the foundation of morality?

"Happiness!"

Wow, big surprise!

"I call this the principle of utility, or the greatest happiness principle. Actions are right in proportion as they tend to promote happiness, wrong as they tend to produce the reverse of happiness. To see how well this principle fits our moral judgments, let's look at some of the examples of moral rules you have already discussed."

Earlier we decided that it is wrong for me to steal.

"Exactly, Art. Stealing is wrong because it produces the reverse of happiness. If you steal from other people, they will be unhappy. So, generally speaking, stealing is wrong."

I know, that's what the readers told me at the beginning of the book.

"You should listen to them, Art."

Does this work with any other example?

"Certainly. It is wrong to murder because the total unhappiness produced outweighs the happiness produced."

Does the happiness of the murderer count?

"Yes, the total happiness produced includes everyone who is affected. Let me give another example."

Why bother?

"An adequate moral theory ought to be certain on moral decisions where we are certain."

Like murder and stealing are wrong?

"Yes. And it should show uncertainty where we are uncertain. Remember, a theory should represent not only our moral decisions. It should also show our ambivalence where that exists in our moral decisions. Where we have contrary decisions, the theory ought to reflect that. It should reflect how we arrive at our decisions."

Yes, I guess it should.

"Then consider the cases of mercy killing, or coming to the aid of a person committing suicide. People of good will differ in their moral judgments. Some say mercy killing is acceptable; others disagree."

What does utilitarianism say?

"The theory is indecisive. The greatest happiness principle reflects what conclusions moral people reach. It also reflects their way of thinking. On an issue like coming to the aid of a person committing suicide, moral people disagree because they cannot agree on how to calculate the total happiness and unhappiness produced."

Interesting point, Mr. Mill.

Happiness Is Pleasure. I'd like to know what you mean by happiness. If the moral worth of actions is determined by how much happiness they produce, it's important to figure out what happiness is.

"It's just as I've written in my pamphlet, *Utilitarianism*. By happiness is intended pleasure, and the absence of pain; by unhappiness, pain, and the privation of pleasure."

You mean, how much pleasure is intended?

"No, no. By happiness I mean pleasure and the absence of pain."

That's all there is to it? Happiness is pleasure?

"Yes, happiness is pleasure. Pleasure is the only desirable end in itself. Every other activity is directed to produce pleasure."

No offense, Mr. Mill, but this sounds pretty crude.

"How do you mean, Art?"

Is Pleasure Seeking Degrading? Well, first, you're saying that people strive for pleasure. You're saying that pleasure is the ultimate end. That sounds pretty degrading to—

"To suppose that life has no higher end than pleasure . . . is a doctrine worthy only of swine. Is that the substance of your objection?"

Yes.

"But surely, Art, you have misunderstood. I respond to this misunderstanding just as the Epicureans responded."

That may be, but I'd like you to reply.

"All right. It is not I, but you, who represent human nature in a degrading light. You are the one who supposes that people are capable of no pleasures except those of swine. You assume, when I say pleasure is an ultimate goal of all human action, that I belittle people. It is your assumption about pleasure, however, that diminishes us."

I don't understand.

"You are saying that pleasure alone is not sufficiently dignified for people to pursue as an ultimate goal. To pursue pleasure is vulgar and demeaning. Is that your objection?"

Yes, Mr. Mill, though I wouldn't be able to put it in such fancy language. Pursuing only pleasure is demeaning. At least that's what people tell me.

"An animal's pleasures do not satisfy a human being's conceptions of happiness. I grant you that point. It is precisely this misunderstanding, however, that often leads to a rejection of utilitarianism. Look how erroneous your assumption is. People have the ability to experience pleasures that are beyond animal appetites. We would not consider anything as happiness that does not include gratification of higher pleasures. Human pleasures and animal pleasures differ."

Differences in the Qualities of Pleasures.   How do you mean? What are examples of higher pleasures?

"Some kinds of pleasures are more desirable and more valuable than others. The pleasures of the intellect, of the feelings and imagination, and of moral sentiments are much preferred over mere sensations."

How do we decide which pleasure is higher and which is lower?

"If we present people with two pleasures, the higher pleasure is defined as the one that all or nearly all people will decidedly prefer. I qualify this definition by adding that moral obligation to prefer one pleasure over another cannot enter into the decision of the people."

So if we take a group of people and ask them to decide which of two pleasures they prefer—

"If one of the two is, by those who are competently acquainted with both, placed so far above the other that they prefer it . . . we are justified in ascribing to the preferred enjoyment a superiority in quality."

Hold on. I thought you were offering a kind of democratic way of determining which kinds of pleasures are superior. Why do the judges have to be people "competently acquainted with both" pleasures? It sounds elitist!

"Who could be a fair judge? Only people who have experienced both kinds of pleasures can fairly judge. Once we determine our group of competent judges, then a democratic voice is possible. And remember, Art, I also exclude contamination brought in by any moral obligation to prefer one pleasure to another pleasure."

I'm glad you reminded me. What do you mean by having a moral obligation to prefer one pleasure to another? I thought people's pleasures were pretty much independent of morality.

"Hardly independent. People's desires and pleasures are subject to moral appraisal. Just look at the response you received in the first part of this book! Your pleasures were suspect. They did not conform to the moral norm. My position is that even if we disallow moral obligation, still some pleasures will be judged superior to other pleasures."

Which Pleasures Are Superior?   Which pleasures will be judged superior, do you think?

"Surely the mental pleasures will be preferred to the bodily pleasures."

I'm not so sure. Some of my favorite pleasures involve my physical lusts!

"You may be as outrageous as you like, Art, but your extreme statements do not surprise me. You say you want bodily pleasures and that you prefer these to mental pleasures, do you?"

Absolutely. Your utilitarian theory is a pleasure seeker's dream! As long as I'm allowed to pursue my pleasures, I'm happy. I just don't see any reason for accepting your distinction that pleasures are qualitatively different. You'll need something more compelling than telling me that nearly everyone else prefers one pleasure to another. If I don't prefer the mental pleasures to the physical pleasures, your theory has nothing to say to me.

"Interesting defensive move. But look more closely, Art. Say I offer you a large quantity of lower pleasures. The only stipulation is that you must renounce the higher pleasures. Would you agree?"

Let me get this right. You will guarantee me the lower pleasures, the physical pleasures. All I have to do is give up the higher pleasures? What's the catch?

"There is no catch, as you call it. Would you sacrifice a lifetime of higher pleasures for a lifetime of nothing but the lower pleasures?"

Yes, I think I would.

"Ah, but think about it. In fact, you have the option at any time. All you need to do is have a frontal lobotomy performed on yourself. You would lose your intellectual functions. If I could guarantee that you will be cared for in a pleasant institution, would you forsake your mental capacities? I doubt it. Few people would consent to such a transition.

"Art, no intelligent being would consent to be a fool. . . . no person of feeling and conscience would be selfish and base. Only in extreme circumstances would a person even entertain such thoughts. A being of higher faculties—"

Huh?

"A cultivated person requires more to make him happy, is capable probably of more acute suffering . . . but he can never really wish to sink into what he feels to be a lower grade of existence."

Okay, okay, perhaps you're correct. I need to think about the difference in qualities of pleasures. We are still at the stage of clarifying your theory, anyway. Just let's not forget to return to this.

"Agreed."

Happiness and Contentment.   Even if I grant that I do not want to become an animal, aren't I sacrificing pleasure? And if I am sacrificing pleasure, then according to your theory, I'm sacrificing happiness. What do you say to that?

"To suppose that the superior person is not happier than the inferior person confounds the very different ideas of happiness and contentment."

I'm not sure I see the difference. When my desires are satisfied, that's happiness, isn't it? When I feel contented and peaceful, I'm happy.

"Your description is the happiness of a cow, a contented cow. People are more dignified, and more demanding, than that. I grant you that people do enjoy bodily pleasures. But, we must not confuse satisfaction or contentment on the one hand and happiness on the other hand.

"I have already said it in my little pamphlet. It is better to be a human being dissatisfied than a pig satisfied; better to be a Socrates dissatisfied than a fool satisfied."

Yes, you wrote this passage, but I'm not sure I can agree with it. The fool thinks he is happy. Isn't that good enough? If I think I am happy, then I am happy.

"Not quite. You forget, Art, that people often reflect back on their own past. They said that they were happy then, but now they realize that they were not happy. They thought they were happy, but now they see that they were mistaken."

Maybe that's because what makes them happy now isn't what made them happy then.

"Perhaps that is true in some cases. Many times, however, the person looks at her recent past and recognizes that she was only deceiving herself. Just the fact that that statement makes sense to us shows that we can be mistaken when we say we are happy. Sometimes we mistake happiness for contentment."

Yes, I know that is the distinction you are trying to make, but I still resist it.

A Hierarchy of Needs.   "Then let me try another tack. In your own century there is a psychologist named Abraham Maslow."

You've read Maslow's work? This is becoming a religiously spooky book. First I resurrect you, then I find out you've been reading all these years.

"Art, reading is a great pleasure for me, but don't get carried away. This whole dialogue is just a thought experiment on your part. Let's get back to my point.

Which is what?

"Maslow argues from his observations that there is a hierarchy of needs. Each person climbs the ladder of needs, each in pretty much the same order as every other person."

What is the point of the hierarchy?

"Maslow defines mental health in terms of ascending to the top. He calls the mentally healthy person self-actualizing. The hierarchy of needs begins with the physiological needs. These are the biological survival needs. Once these needs have been met, other, higher needs emerge. We have safety needs, the need to belong, to love and to be loved, to have self-esteem and esteem from others, the desires to know and to understand, and, finally, aesthetic needs."

Are you telling me that people need to read and to study?

"According to Maslow's theory of motivation, the desire to learn is basic to human nature."

I don't experience that desire in a very strong way.

"That may indicate that your other, lower needs have not been sufficiently addressed. Higher needs emerge only after lower needs have been satisfied."

So what you are calling contentment is satisfying the lower, bodily needs?

"Yes. Happiness is a more dignified, higher aspiration. What Maslow has hit upon substantiates my distinction. People are not happy until they experience the higher pleasures."

Monotony or Activity?   Can you give me an example?

"Which life would you rather live, a life of monotonous assembly-line work or a life like Leonardo Da Vinci's?"

Lots of people work on assembly lines and they're happy, aren't they?

"Imagine that you are locked into a life where you have to repeat the same simple action over and over."

Wait, I think I've lived that job. One summer I worked in a meat-packing plant. (I really did.) I was a wiener stringer. What I did every day was string hot dogs. Hot dogs would come out of a cooking machine in endless strings. The stringer stood on a metal grate platform about eighteen inches off the floor. As the hot dogs came out of the machine, I would have to reach up, take the string off a hook, count five hot dogs down the string, and place the wieners across a metal bar in front of me. Then I'd cut the string to leave ten wieners hanging on the bar, five on either side. Then I'd start the whole process again. When there were twenty strings of hot dogs on a bar, I would move the bar to a rack, replace it with another bar, and start the process again. Ten hot dogs to a string, twenty strings to a bar, twenty bars to a rack, start again. On a normal eight-hour shift, I'd string 160,000 hot dogs.

"Excellent example. Now imagine—"

I'm not through. The job was even worse because they placed me in an alcove where I could see only the rack I was working on, the metal wall of the machine behind me, and two blank brick walls close by on either side. The place was hot, damp, and boring.

"I understand, Art. This experience has left its mark on you. And that serves my point. Imagine just this job, but exaggerate it. Imagine that you have to perform this task for your entire waking life."

No way! I used to shudder when I had to work two hours overtime.

"Compare this life to a life like Da Vinci's. He was a man of incredibly diversified interests and talents. He was an artist, a scientist, an engineer, a mathematician, and a naturalist. He possessed many other talents. Imagine that your family and social life are rich and rewarding, that you enjoy health, and that your wealth is sufficient to allow you to enjoy leisure time. Would a life of such diverse and higher interests be more fulfilling than a life of monotony and boredom?"

Maybe, but your comparison isn't fair. You grant your Da Vinci character all the higher and the lower pleasures. But you begrudge the assembly-line worker even the lower pleasures. I know what you're going to say. You are willing to give the worker the lower pleasures, right?

"Yes, that would make the example appropriate."

Appropriate, but still unfair. All you have shown is that a life of lower and higher pleasures is preferable to a life of lower pleasures alone.

Is the Life of Higher Pleasure Preferred to a Life of Lower Pleasure? "I think we have entered into the criticism part of our discussion. Very well, let's entertain objections. You are questioning whether a life of higher pleasures is to be preferred to a life of lower pleasures."

I am questioning your distinction and your way of arriving at it. You say that people who experience both kinds of pleasures nearly always choose one (the higher) over the other (the lower). But that just doesn't fit the facts. Lots of times when I am offered a lower pleasure and a higher pleasure, I choose the lower. Sometimes it just depends on my mood.

"For example?"

For example, when I have been reading or studying for a few hours, and a friend comes by and suggests we go out to get something to eat, I often put aside my reading and go. I forego my higher pleasure for a lower pleasure. I prefer a burger and fries to a good book. And before you reply, let me add that I usually prefer a burger and fries to a good book. The only reason I'm reading the book is because I am supposed to read it. But if we strip away any moral obligation to read and study, then I think I might always choose the lower pleasure. Now it's your turn.

Temptations. "Under the influence of temptation, people occasionally postpone the higher pleasures to the lower. People often, from infirmity of character, make their election for the nearer good, though they know it to be the less valuable."

Hold on, Mr. Mill. First you tell me that the estimation of two competing pleasures is determined by people who have experienced both. You claim that nearly all people place one pleasure above the other. The determination of the clear majority determines the relative merit of a pleasure. Now you are telling me that people *often* make their choice for the lower pleasure and forsake the higher pleasure.

"It is caused by infirmity of character. A character unschooled in self-discipline will often gravitate to the lower pleasures."

You can't have it both ways. How can the majority decide which pleasure is more valuable yet continue to seek the less valuable pleasure?

"People pursue sensual indulgences to the injury of health, though perfectly aware that health is the greater good. In your time, people smoke cigarettes, drink alcohol to excess, and use other dangerous drugs. They know full well that they are pursuing the lower, closer pleasure. Even when they choose the lower pleasure, they are aware of the qualitative differences in pleasures. They are simply too weak of character to restrain themselves. So you see, the qualitative distinctions between pleasures still holds.

"Of course, Art, there is another category of people who seek the lesser pleasures. The capacity for the nobler feelings is in most natures a very tender plant, easily killed, not only by hostile influences, but by mere want of sustenance. For far too many people, perhaps the majority of young people, it speedily dies away."

So the majority of people are unable to enjoy the higher pleasures?

"I am afraid so. People do not have the time or the opportunity for developing and pursuing the higher pleasures. They addict themselves to inferior pleasures, not because they deliberately prefer them, but because they are either the only ones to which they have access or the only ones which they are any longer capable of enjoying."

Are you saying that the majority of people are idiots?

"Of course the majority of people are not idiots. But the majority does lack the opportunity to cultivate and entertain the higher pleasures. Most people are so caught up in making a living, or pursuing their careers and educational goals, that they are unable to develop their capacities for the higher pleasures.

When you are tired from working or studying, you are less likely to engage in the superior activities."

I guess so.

"Further, we must be careful to note that this all-too-common transition to indolence and selfishness is not voluntary. Devoting oneself solely to one goal renders a person incapable of the other."

I don't understand.

"Pursuing school and career opportunities with the kind of focused drive required for success is too much. People who are driven to succeed in these occupations lose the ability to experience the nobler feelings. Single-minded drive for a career goal, or for wealth, is just that, single minded. Capacity for the higher pleasures is forfeited."

Morality Is Not the Pursuit of My (Higher) Pleasures!. So where does this leave us, Mr. Mill? Say I accept the qualitative distinction between higher and lower pleasures. And I accept the distinction between happiness and contentment. Now what? Is your theory saying that as long as I pursue the higher pleasures, then I am moral?

"Not quite. The utilitarian standard is not the agent's own greatest happiness, but the greatest amount of happiness altogether. As between his own happiness and that of others, utilitarianism requires him to be as strictly impartial as a disinterested and benevolent spectator."

Hold on. Your theory sounded pretty compelling when I thought it was *my* happiness I was pursuing. I was even willing to acknowledge that the intellectual pleasures are higher than the bodily pleasures. But now you tell me that it is not my pleasures, but everyone else's, that I have to produce?

"That's right. Your pleasures count, too, of course. However, utilitarianism requires you to count yourself as one among many equals. Everyone concerned receives equal weight. This is not peculiar to the utilitarian standard of right, it is what is demanded by morality. Why should this revelation shock you? I assumed all along that you were aware of it."

I feel deceived. Sorry, Mr. Mill, but your theory lacks incentive. Why should I bother concerning myself with everyone else's benefit?

"Because, Art, the nobler, more social pleasures are yours whenever you concern yourself with others. Since these are among the higher pleasures, you bring happiness to yourself whenever you bring benefit to others in your community. The sense of community itself is a reward."

Does this requirement mean that I am bound to do what is best for everyone? It sounds like it demands that I put my own happiness on hold and that I act in a special way for friends. Do I have to calculate the impact of my actions as they apply to the entire human race? And to animals? Is that what impartiality means?

"The great majority of good actions are intended not for the benefit of the world, but for that of individuals. Only public benefactors, like congressional representatives and judges, are held to account for their actions in terms of public utility. In every other case, the interest or happiness of some few persons is all one has to attend to."

Classes of Actions and the General Rule.   So I can pretty much do what I want as long as I don't intend to bring pain to people close to me?

"Yes and no. You see there are certain actions you might perform that would have no ill effects in your particular case but from which you should abstain."

Why? I thought you just said that I could act any way I want as long as my actions are not intended to cause pain to those around me!

"It would be unworthy of an intelligent agent not to be consciously aware that the action is of a class which, if practiced generally, would be generally injurious, and that this is the ground of the obligation to abstain from it."

Huh?

"You cannot do whatever you want in particular cases, even when your actions bring pleasure to those around you."

Even if I create higher pleasures?

"Even then. Certain types of actions should be avoided as a general rule. What might be immediately useful may have adverse social effects."

For example?

Lying Is Wrong.   "Deviation from truth weakens the trustworthiness of human assertion, which is . . . the principle support of all present social well-being. More than any one thing, untrustworthiness keeps back civilization . . . and everything upon which human happiness on the largest scale depends. Therefore, it is wrong to lie."

Are you telling me that I should not lie because my lie will bring civilization to its knees? My little lie!

"I do not want to exaggerate your importance, but lying weakens the social fabric. Therefore, utilitarians make it a general principle that lying is morally wrong."

Why? Because my particular lie is so important? Doubtful. Is it because I am such a pillar of society that everyone uses me as a role model. Wow, I can just see it now. People will say to their kids, "Look at Art, Johnny. He's such a fine example. Do whatever he does." Is that what you're saying?

"Of course not. Utilitarians suggest that as a general rule lying is not permitted. It is not because you are an exemplary specimen of virtue. If you do not mind my being blunt, in your particular case, Art, that is certainly not true. Even in your case, however, it is useful and socially important to cultivate a sense of the importance of truth telling."

Let me get this right. I have to be impartial like a benevolent spectator. Yet it's okay for me to restrict the calculation of the effects of my actions to a small group. But when I want to lie to someone in this small group, you tell me that I shouldn't lie because it will make the world a terrible mess. Do you wonder why I am confused by you moralists!

"Art, the waters of morality are difficult to fathom."

What does that mean?

"Morality is a complex business. You are expecting more precision than you are likely to get. For example, in the case of our present discussion, there are even exceptions."

You're kidding, right? I don't mean to be disrespectful, but this is beyond confusing.

"Even the rule against lying admits of exceptions by *all* moralists. If withholding some fact would save an individual from great and unmerited evil, then lying is acceptable. Of course, we want to prevent the exception from extending itself."

Of course. I know you have an example. You probably think it's acceptable to keep bad news from a person who is dangerously ill.

"Think for a moment. Say your Uncle Charlie is dreadfully ill. He is lying on his deathbed with no more than a few days of life left. He asks you to bend close to him. You do. He asks you if the mail has arrived. He is anxious to hear whether or not his manuscript has been accepted by a publisher. It is his life's ambition. In this circumstance, it may be morally permissible to withhold the fact that a letter of rejection came in the day's mail."

Morality is a messy business. I guess I just don't see how we are to distinguish an important lie from an acceptable lie.

"Agreed. The limits must be defined. I am confident that the principle of utility can outweigh the conflicting utilities."

UTILITARIAN MORALITY IS VAGUE

It just looks to me that morality is incredibly vague. What I perceived as a strength of your system is that it answers every moral question. Your system has only one principle, so there is no need for priorities, and it is relatively easy to apply. Just calculate the amount of happiness and act accordingly. But now the merits appear very different to me.

"How is that?"

Your utilitarian theory is the same as the Golden Rule.

"I acknowledge that. In the Golden Rule of Jesus of Nazareth we read the complete spirit of the ethics of utility. I consider that to be a strength, Art."

The same defect that applies to the Golden Rule applies to your system. Although it appears to be straightforward and simple, there is no way to know how to apply it. In actual cases, the values become vague and indefinite. The conclusion of my moral calculation depends more on how I interpret the situation than on morality.

Let's use your example. Do I lie to Uncle Charlie or don't I? On one level, I admit that lying to people leads to undesirable consequences. It is tempting to think, though, that in the case of poor Uncle Charlie, no harm, and a great deal of happiness, will be created by lying to him. This is confusing. Do I lie or do I crush his dreams? I think my objection can be put in different terms.

"Proceed."

KNOWLEDGE OF THE FUTURE

I know it isn't exactly fair to criticize a dead guy, because you can't really reply. But here's the problem I have with your system. You suggest that consequences are what determine whether or not an action is morally acceptable. But this is unfair.

"In what ways?"

Well, you expect too much of people. How can anyone know what the future will bring? How can anyone know what will actually happen as a result of one's own action?

"Morality is not an exacting science, that's certain. Why would we expect more certainty than is available to our natures as human beings?"

That may be, but let me give you an example. Imagine that there was a guy named Fritz who lived in a small town. Now Fritz is a happy person, and he wants to share his happiness. He has two unmarried friends. Both are shy, but Fritz knows that they have a lot in common. So he arranges a blind date for them.

"This seems like an admirable action."

The couple dates, becomes engaged, and finally marries. We might even imagine that Fritz is the best man at the wedding. Several years later, the couple has a child, little Adolph. Adolph grows up to lead the world into the most violent and destructive war in human history.

"Causing mass destruction and pain is certainly morally blameworthy, to be sure. How is this a problem for utilitarianism?"

It's not Adolph's actions that I am pointing to, but Fritz's actions. Should we hold Fritz responsible for Hitler's actions? After all, if it wasn't for Fritz and the blind date, Hitler would not have been born. Surely we can't blame Fritz for World War II.

CONTRIBUTING CAUSES

I know you don't actually take up this question in your writing, but could you speculate how a utilitarian might answer?

"Very well. There are two types of response. A utilitarian would reply that a person's actions may be a necessary but not sufficient cause for events in the world."

Huh?

"Take your example of Fritz. Of course, it is unlikely that Hitler would have been born had it not been for Fritz. This assumes that Hitler's parents would not have met under other circumstances, and so on. Let's say this is so unlikely as to be impossible. Still, even though introducing the two was necessary for Hitler to have been born, it was not significant enough to hold Fritz totally blameworthy for World War II."

Is one option to hold people accountable only to the degree that their actions have an effect on the consequences? That sounds pretty difficult to calculate. It also sounds like you are taking virtually all responsibility away from people.

"How does that follow?"

I can be held responsible only to the degree that my actions contribute to an event, right? Aren't my actions also events, with causes of their own? Therefore, a utilitarian who uses this strategy has to trace the causes of my actions and intentions. It wasn't my fault, my Uncle Charlie taught Fritz to be a caring, considerate romantic. So Uncle Charlie is also to blame? Perhaps this is true, but then human responsibility becomes meaningless. What is the other utilitarian reply?

THREE TYPES OF CONSEQUENCES

"A utilitarian would distinguish three kinds of consequences by asking three questions. First, what actually happened as a result of this action? Second, what was intended to happen as a result of this action? Third, what consequences were reasonable to expect as a result of this action?

"The moral worth of the action itself must be determined by the actual results, by what actually happened. We can see that people's intuitions agree with this reasoning. Ultimately, we see what actually happens before we render final moral judgment. If events go in an unanticipated and unintended direction, we feel upset, though rarely guilty. Of course, it would be unnecessarily harsh to judge people on this first standard, by the actual consequences of their actions.

"The moral worth of the action can also be determined by the intended results. However, although this option is appealing, it is inadequate."

Why is that? Why shouldn't we judge a person's actions by intended consequences?

"One may intend to perform a good action but misunderstand the implication of the consequences. For example, a person may wish to save a village from being overtaken by the enemy. With that end in mind, he may decide to destroy the village in order to save it."

But that would bring more pain than pleasure, and it's likely to bring even more pain than the feared capture of the village.

"Agreed. The intended result may be praiseworthy, but the strategy is too extreme. Therefore, intended consequences are inappropriate ways of judging actions. Intentions, however, do indicate the moral quality of one's character.

"The moral worth of actions should be determined by what is reasonable to expect as the result of one's action. This provision takes care of your difficulty with Fritz. It is reasonable to believe that bringing two people together is desirable. It is not reasonable to believe that such an action will result in a world war or the deaths of tens of millions of people. Therefore, Fritz's action was praiseworthy because his reasonable expectation was for more pleasure than pain to be a result of his action."

I agree with you, but I am becoming increasingly suspicious of your system. Now you say that moral worth is not based on the actual consequences. Moral worth is determined by the consequences that could be reasonably expected.

"Yes. Actions are judged by what could be reasonably expected to be a result. The action itself is evaluated according to the actual consequences, by the amount of pleasure and pain created."

Two judgments? One for the actor, or agent as you call him, and one for the action? And you wonder why I'm confused!

INTEGRITY

I have another question. How does integrity fit in?

"Integrity is traditionally construed as a positive character trait. Why would you expect utilitarianism to differ from this assessment?"

Say I am eligible to vote and I am registered. I calculate that it is reasonable to expect desirable consequences to come from voting. So I am morally obligated to vote in the upcoming election.

"Yes, that is sound."

Great. My problem is that I disapprove of both candidates. Neither has the personal characteristics or the experience to be qualified to hold an important office. I am forced, yet again, to vote for the "lesser of two evils." Where is the integrity in that? I have to endorse a candidate who is unqualified, or worse. According to your system, my action is praiseworthy because the reasonably expected results are better than the alternative. But sometimes the alternative is distasteful. What is so noble about choosing the poison that kills you?

JUSTICE

I have another objection, Mr. Mill. Your system of morality overlooks justice. I think it is unjust to sacrifice innocent people, even if it is for the greater good.

"Do you have an example?"

Certainly. What if someone suggests that we harvest the organs of healthy people in order to save many more people? For example, we have a perfectly healthy twenty-five year old. Not only is this guy healthy, but he works at it. He exercises every day. He doesn't smoke cigarettes. He does not use any drug stronger than aspirin, and even those only reluctantly. He never drinks. (Now that I think of it, perhaps he should be killed to save him from a life of noble boredom.) Would it be right to harvest his organs in order to save twenty people's lives?

You don't have to answer. I can make the example even more compelling. We can imagine that the twenty people we can save are all valuable, contributing members of society. Poor Joe Healthy doesn't have much time for contributing to society. He's too busy being healthy. Your system of morality says we should promote the greatest good for the greatest number. But sacrificing poor, innocent Joe is unjust.

"My reply is that we all acknowledge that justice is an essential characteristic in any society. Because it is socially advantageous to have just institutions, your example, Joe, would be safe. We could argue that it does more harm to society to abridge justice and to place innocent people in jeopardy than it does to save the lives of contributing members of society. For everyone to live in a just society is a higher pleasure than saving the lives of any number of people. The superiority in quality so far outweighs quantity as to render it, in comparison, of small account."

RULE UTILITARIANISM

Again your position is vague and indefinite. Every time I come up with what seems to be a telling criticism, you incorporate it into your system. From a theoretical point of view, it's great. But in practice, it leaves me not knowing what to do.

"For the people who have neither the training nor the time to calculate consequences, there are rules received by society. We do not expect people to be inactive until they can determine the appropriate behavior. They have the combined learning of the human species. That is why we have general rules of conduct."

VESSELS OF EXPERIENCE

Okay, let me ask a few other questions. I think these are objections. Doesn't the utilitarian theory make me calculate how much pleasure is likely to be produced by my actions?

"Don't forget to factor in quality of pleasures."

Fair enough. When faced with a moral decision, I simply calculate how much of the higher and lower pleasures are going to come from my actions. What bothers me is that this makes everyone just a vessel of experience. People lose their humanity when I calculate consequences in this way. Or have I misunderstood?

"Evidently, Art, you are not listening quite carefully enough. Your complaint, also raised by others, is that many utilitarians look on the morality of actions and do not lay sufficient emphasis on the other beauties of character which go toward making a human being lovable and admirable. I have already admitted this. Utilitarians who have cultivated their moral feelings, but not their sympathies, nor their artistic perceptions, do fall into this mistake; and so do all other moralists under the same conditions."

I'm sorry I haven't been more attentive. So far you have been extraordinary in your ability to anticipate my questions, but sometimes my questions do not follow the order of your presentation.

"A little more care should remedy that."

Perhaps, but my present question still remains. Telling me that other moral theories also fail to develop a fuller sense of other people does not satisfy me.

You see, Mr. Mill, I have not accepted any moral description of morality. It isn't that your description of morality is inadequate. Quite the contrary! You're probably right . But knowing more about morality only shows me how undesirable it is to be moral.

But perhaps we should let our audience take a break. Thank you for visiting with us.

"It has been interesting speaking with you, Art. If nothing else, your resurrection machine is a work of genius."

You know it's just an imaginary device. There is no genius in it.

"Precisely."

■

SUMMARY OF DISCUSSION

Utilitarianism states that the right action to perform is the one that creates the most good as a consequence. Mill says that happiness is defined by all people as the chief good. So the right action is the one that promotes the greatest amount of happiness (or minimizes the greatest amount of unhappiness). Any action can create some happiness and some unhappiness. Mill says that a person can calculate the net amount of happiness produced by any action and then can compare actions based on their results. Actions that result in a greater amount of happiness (or in less unhappiness) have more moral worth than actions that promise relatively less happiness.

What does Mill mean by happiness? By happiness he means pleasure, or the absence of pain. By unhappiness he means the reverse. So far, so good. Rather than degenerating into a crude pleasure-seeking way of thinking, Mill suggests two other conditions on moral actions. First, the pleasures and pains one considers must apply to all the people affected by the action. That way, one does not necessarily get to do whatever one wants. Morality demands that we consider other people as much as we consider ourselves.

Second, Mill distinguishes pleasures according to their quality. Superior pleasures are those that people select when they have a choice between two or more pleasures. Mill argues that superior pleasures are to be preferred to inferior pleasures. In saying this, he avoids defining morality as mere pleasure seeking by the majority. Superior pleasures might include intelligent conversation, appreciating works of art, and so on. What Mill suggests is that moral people are not crude pleasure seekers. However, Mill does not make the mistake of thinking that pleasures are not important in moral living.

There are both advantages and disadvantages to Mill's understanding of morality. One distinct advantage is that Mill accurately describes how we arrive at moral decisions. As moral people, we do calculate the amount and types of pleasures and pains that our actions produce. Because of this, morality demands that we calculate all people's happiness into our moral decisions. The ends may justify the means, but they must be the ends as they affect everyone involved.

Mill's analysis also permits priority rules to be set up. Whatever produces the greatest good takes priority over alternatives. In this way Mill can explain moral disagreements, and he can remedy them.

A possible weakness of Mill's understanding of morality is that he places too much emphasis on consequences. Consequences are not always easy to foresee. Mill also underestimates the importance of intentions. Imagine that I intend to cause a great deal of pain but that I am socially inept. My actions may not reflect my intentions. Mill's theory evaluates actions but fails to concern itself sufficiently with a person's character.

Accounting for justice is another apparent weakness in Mill's theory. The same may be said for other moral "absolutes." For example, lying may be permissible so long as the greatest happiness results. Finally, Mill's notion of other people is a problem. Other people appear to be valued only for their social worth. We relate to them morally as though they were vessels of experience.

■

DISCUSSION HIGHLIGHTS

   I. Mill endorses the greatest happiness principle
     1. All actions receive their worth from the consequences (or goals or ends) they create.
     2. Everyone ought to act in a way that produces the greatest good for the greatest number.
     3. Happiness is the ultimate good sought by all people.
       a. happiness is defined either as pleasure
       b. or as the absence of pain
     4. There are differences in the qualities of pleasures.
       a. higher and lower pleasures are determined by those people who have experienced both
       b. virtually no amount of a lower pleasure equals the worth of any amount of a higher pleasure
  II. Strengths of utilitarianism
     1. Utilitarianism mirrors our method of moral reasoning.
     2. It offers priority rules.
     3. It solves every moral problem by weighing the pleasures and pains produced by one's possible actions.
     4. It explains moral disagreements.
 III. Criticisms
     1. Application of utilitarian principles is difficult.
     2. Justice may be sacrificed by concern for the greatest happiness of the greatest number.
     3. Utilitarianism reduces people to their social worth.
     4. Utilitarianism reduces people to "vessels of experiences" of pleasure or pain.
     5. Utilitarianism demands an unrealistic knowledge of future consequences.

■

QUESTIONS FOR THOUGHT/PAPER TOPICS

As you criticize Mill, remember the V-8 principle and Mill's reply.

1. Should Congress make utilitarian decisions? Would it be fulfilling our wishes by creating the greatest happiness for the greatest number? Should the court system also make its decisions based on utilitarianism? What would happen to minority rights?

2. Does Mill's theory justify some lies? Are you justified in lying to a loved one if your lie will save that person some pain? Do you mind that your elected officials and the press routinely lie to you?

3. Apparently Mill defines other people according to their social worth, as bearers of rights, and as "vessels of experiences." How does Mill define the individual person who is making moral decisions? How are you as a moral decision maker different from other people?

4. Are any values absolute? Which values would you be willing to endorse even if they did not produce the greatest happiness for the greatest number?

5. Does Mill's explanation of morality let people relate to each other in an intimate way? Does morality promote people being in touch with each other?

6. Mill suggests that the happiness of the greatest number should be my motivation for acting. Why should I agree to this?

7. Remember that pen I stole? Is my action immoral if no one is adversely affected?

8. Is there any room for freedom in Mill's explanation of morality?

■

FOR FURTHER READING

There are three short works by Mill you might want to read. *Utilitarianism* (Hackett, 1979) is the one we have been talking to Mill about. Mill also wrote a short book, *On Liberty* (Hackett, 1978) about the limits of power that a society can rightly exercise over an individual. He argues for extensive individual freedom and that giving freedom will benefit society. Mill offers another insightful discussion in *The Subjection of Women* (Hackett, 1988). If you want to look at recent discussion of utilitarianism, look at Dan Brock's essay, "Recent Work in Utilitarianism," *American Philosophical Quarterly* 10, 1973. Finally, there is a compact discussion of Utilitarianism in Louis Pojman's book, *Ethics: Discovering Right and Wrong* (Wadsworth, 1990).

NINE

Absolute Moral Values and Reason: A Conversation with Immanuel Kant

WHAT SHOULD YOU DO?

What should you do? Your poor Uncle Charlie is lying on his deathbed. His life is ebbing away and you know he will most certainly die. Uncle Charlie motions to you to come closer. You bend close to hear his words. Marshalling his diminishing strength, he whispers to you. Has the mail brought any word about his book? Has the publisher accepted as worthy his life's work? Poor Uncle Charlie desperately wants to know the fate of his book.

You have checked the mail. The letter has come in the day's mail. Should you tell the dying man that the letter has not arrived? Or should you tell him the truth? The letter has arrived. It is a rejection of his masterpiece. What should you do?

Of course, telling the truth is the morally correct action in most cases. But the truth will make poor, dying Uncle Charlie's last moments very painful. He will know that his work is unacceptable. He will feel like a failure. You could try to explain that publishers and editors are not reliable judges of quality work. But Uncle Charlie has put all his confidence in them. He will not accept that as an answer.

If you lie, Uncle Charlie will die with a smile on his parched, thin lips. No other consequence will follow. The lie will die with him. If you tell the truth, Uncle Charlie will feel the emotional pain. The truth will be buried with him.

So is the obvious answer to lie? But what if Uncle Charlie thought you would lie? He would not have asked you. He may have asked you only be-

Material in this chapter taken from Immanuel Kant, *Groundwork of the Metaphysics of Morals*, originally published in 1785, (London: Hutchinson Publishing Ltd.) H. J. Paton translation. Reprinted by permission of the publisher.

207

cause he trusts you. He may have asked you because he wants the truth. His dying wish may be to know the truth. What should you do?

ANOTHER EXAMPLE

I once heard of a case where a man was discovered to have inoperable cancer. His death was likely to come in three to six months. No, this is not one of those "miraculous" stories where the doctors are proved mistaken. The man did die four months after the diagnosis.

The dilemma comes in because the physician was asked by the family not to reveal to the man that he was dying. In recent months, he had already suffered several serious setbacks in his life. His business had failed. One of his grandchildren had died. His wife, children, and clergyman believed his own illness would depress him to the point that he would commit suicide. For religious reasons, and out of genuine concern for him, they counseled the physician to withhold information. He did.

As the man's health rapidly deteriorated, he approached his doctor. The doctor respected the family's wishes. He lied to the patient. Finally, in what turned out to be the final week of the man's life, he directly confronted the doctor. Yes, he was dying. He had not been told in order to protect his feelings.

Of course, the physician violated a promise he had with his patient. He had lied by omitting the true diagnosis. Isn't this what we were tempted to do with Uncle Charlie? The man was desperately unhappy. There had been one thing he had wanted to do in his life. He had wanted to see the Grand Canyon. He had never told anyone about his wish. An earlier diagnosis would have given him time to fulfill his childhood wish. By "saving" him grief, his own family and his doctor robbed him of his one and only wish. What should they have done?

Each of these examples plays on our sensitivity toward another human being. They are manipulative in that they confuse us over whether or not consequences matter. Can lying be excused by correct intentions or desirable consequences? Or must we never lie?

In his work, *Groundwork of the Metaphysics of Morals,* Immanuel Kant defines morality as an absolute standard. He is committed to an absolute morality where moral rules apply no matter what the consequences of one's action may be.

Kant provides a groundwork for morality. I know, you got that from the title. Kant shows that morality does not depend on human nature or on our definition of happiness. He guards morality against charges of historical or personal relativism. And he defines morality so that there is a reason to be moral. It's an impressive project.

How does Kant do all this? We'll get to the details in a moment. Basically, he argues that the nature of reason imposes conditions on our way of thinking about morality. He argues that reason leads to moral principles that cannot be violated. So our desires, our passions and our wants, must be placed aside in order for us to make moral decisions.

Kant's insight might fit our own thinking to a certain extent. Think about the examples of morality that we discussed earlier. The Ten Commandments was one example. If you look at the commandments, they are appealing in their simplicity and directness. Do not murder. Do not steal. On the tablets it does *not* say "Do not murder, except for the following cases." Right?

Nor do the rules exempt certain people. I've checked! The Ten Commandments does *not* say that it is wrong to steal, except for Art. Too bad, but it's true. It doesn't even let ethics-book writers steal. Nope, everyone is bound by the rule.

The rules are definite and unchanging. There are no references to consequences or to differing situations. I've checked that, too. The commandment against stealing does not say, "Do not steal, except when you really want that sports car." It doesn't even say, "Do not steal, except when you need to steal." There are no loopholes! The commandments are absolute, absolutely absolute.

Kant too builds in an absolute dimension to moral principles. Moral principles do not change with the circumstances, or with their projected or real results, or with the customs of the society. Kant's moral principles apply to every rational being.

Now let's talk to Kant about his theory. Through the miracle of Art's philosopher resurrection and time machine, I present for your education Immanuel Kant. Welcome, Professor Kant. (Kant is not the kind of guy who would ask us to call him Immanuel. Pretty formal, if you know what I mean.) We have some questions. Would you be kind enough to help us understand your theory?

"Certainly, Art. That is why I am here."

(Since Kant was a German university professor, it would be helpful if you would read this with a German accent. A slow, measured, and deliberate pace would help, too. Think of a sort of intellectual Terminator, or is that a contradiction? Now go back and read it again. "Certainly, Art. That is why I am here." Thanks.)

"Art, stop babbling to your readers. Before our conversation is completed, I should also like to comment on Mill's utilitarian doctrine. Unfortunately, Mill wrote after my death, so I did not have an opportunity to respond to his analysis of moral philosophy. I should like that opportunity. For example, moral goodness is definitely not based on consequences."

Anything you say, Professor Kant. And I'll try to be more serious.

THE AIM OF KANT'S THEORY

"Fine, Art. Now what questions do you have for me?"

Well, first, what are the aims of your book?

"The sole aim of the present *Groundwork* is to seek out and establish the supreme principle of morality."

What determines whether or not someone has done the right thing?

"If you mean what constitutes right action, the answer is doing one's duty."

ACT FROM A SENSE OF DUTY

Okay, and what gives me these duties?

"As a being who has reason, you are obliged to be an impartial, rational agent. The essence of morality is to act not from inclination—"

Time out. I don't mean to interrupt, but what do you mean by "inclination"?

"An inclination is a personal want, desire, or passion. It is anything that could bias the person. As I was saying, the essence of morality is to act not from inclination or passion, but from reason. One must act from a sense of duty that has been derived by reason. No other motivation is proper.

"You were on the correct path just a moment ago, Art. A law has to carry with it absolute necessity if it is to be valid morally. Consequently, the ground of moral obligation must be looked for, not in the nature of man nor in the circumstances of the world in which he is placed, but solely a priori in the concepts of pure reason."

I said that? I don't even know what a priori looks like.

"The words *a priori* mean logically necessary. What we are searching for is a completely rational basis for morality. Moral philosophy gives humanity laws a priori as rational beings. We don't need to look into the particular circumstances of people, either individually or collectively. The moral principles must apply to all rational beings, not only humans."

Who else is there? Vulcans?

"If any action is to be morally good, it is not enough that it should conform to the moral law—it must also be done for the sake of the moral law."

How does that answer my question?

WHY START WITH THE GOOD WILL?

"Don't you see, where this is not so, the conformity is only too contingent and precarious, since the nonmoral ground at work will now and then produce actions which accord with the law, but very often actions which transgress it."

Let me see if I have this right. Simply acting in a morally acceptable way is not good enough. My actions have to be done because they are moral?

"Yes. There is a problem with grounding morality on human nature."

What if it were possible to train a person to want to perform the morally praiseworthy action?

"People's wants and perceived needs are too subject to change. They are at best contingent."

Contingent?

"Possible. They are easily set aside for psychologically stronger desires.

Therefore, morality must be based on reason alone. A metaphysic of morals has to investigate the idea and principles of a possible *pure* will, and not the activities and conditions of human willing as such."

So that's why you start out discussing the good will.

The Good Will Is Unconditionally Good. "Then that is where we must begin. The good will is the only thing, real or imaginable, that is unconditionally good. It is good without qualification. All other qualities and goals are only conditionally good."

What do you mean? Aren't intelligence, wit, judgment, and courage also good? When could any of these traits be bad?

"These qualities of temperament are without doubt good and desirable in many respects, but they can also be extremely bad and hurtful."

How do you figure that? When would they be hurtful and undesirable?

"When the will is not good which has to make use of these gifts of nature. It is exactly the same with gifts of fortune. Power, wealth, honor, even health and that complete well-being and contentment with one's state that goes by the name of happiness, can have a dangerous influence on the mind. For example, they can cause over-boldness and lead one to serious injury."

The Good Will and Its Effects. I thought your justification of moral principles was not going to use consequences as a justification. Aren't you making a utilitarian argument here?

"Good objection, and one I want to answer. In the present discussion I am appealing to ordinary rational knowledge."

Huh?

"You do have a way with language, Art. All I mean is that I am appealing to ordinary and reasonable insights into morality. My audience has a good grasp of morality and can be brought to a high degree of precision and accuracy. At this point I am merely applying clear examples of morality to shed light on its nature and on the nature of the good will."

Later you will draw your argument from pure reason?

"Exactly, for when moral value is in question we are concerned, not with the actions which we see, but with their inner principles, which we cannot see. For now, however, using examples is practical and will establish a common understanding between us."

I think I'm being told that I can't jump into the intellectually deep waters yet. Is that it?

"Don't be so insecure, Art. We are first going to work from ordinary rational knowledge of morality to the philosophical. You should know that from reading the title from chapter 1 of *my* book."

So where are we?

An Example of the Good Will. "A good will is not good because of what it effects or accomplishes. It is good in itself. In fact, a good will seems to constitute the indispensable condition of our very worthiness to be happy."

I understand that later you intend to prove your theory without the use of examples, but could you give me an example to help me grasp your intuition?

"Certainly. Imagine that we have two shopkeepers. Their clothing shops are next door to each other. They carry the same brands of clothing. Let's name one shopkeeper Smith and the other Jones. When you do comparison shopping, you find that both charge the same price for the same item. Both have the same selection, and each store interior is qualitatively similar to the other. Our question is, in which store would you rather do business?"

You make everything equal. The location, the price, the merchandise, the selection; everything is equal. How can I choose? Is Smith nicer than Jones?

"Good question. Let me tell more of the story. Remember, we are seeking to discover if the effect of the good will has any impact on its worth. So to continue, imagine that Smith and Jones are both affable, polite, and helpful. Each treats you with courtesy and competence."

What's the difference? The way you describe them, there's no way of preferring one over the other.

"Excellent. Now imagine that we have proof that Smith is honest because he believes that honesty is the duty of every businessperson. Jones is equally honest, but only because he believes that dishonesty will be detected and he will lose business."

Let me get this right. Smith is honest because honesty is a duty. He believes in honesty. On the other hand, Jones is honest, but only for his self-interest. He's afraid people will detect his dishonesty and he will be run out of business. The choice is obvious. I would rather deal with Jones.

"What?"

I'm kidding. Of course, everyone would rather deal with Smith, the one who is honest because honesty is a moral duty.

"Just so, Art. If consequences were all that mattered, the choice would not be obvious. If consequences were all that mattered, you could not reasonably prefer one over the other. Why then do you prefer Smith?"

Well, Smith would be honest even if he knows he can't get caught. I'd feel better knowing that. He won't be tempted to cheat me.

"More accurately, even if he is able to cheat you, he will have a reverence for his moral duty. He will not cheat you even if he could."

Yes, that's right. Oh, now I get it. It's not the consequence. Even if Jones never cheats me, the fact is he would if he could. His character and values would let him.

"Therefore?"

Therefore, Smith, the one who is honest as a matter of duty, is my choice. Does he have dark blue, light-weight, V-neck sweaters?

"Art, you're getting off the point. Regain your concentration."

The Function of Reason.   Sorry. On to the next question. How does reason function in your system? The reason I ask is that reason seems to be worthwhile as a way of getting what we want.

"Are you backsliding again into that old 'do whatever you want' perspective?"

Actually, I guess that may be part of it. But Mill's theory also impresses me. Reason is useful in bringing happiness. I don't expect you to agree with this.

"Reason is not sufficiently serviceable for guiding the will safely as regards its objects and satisfaction of all our needs—a purpose for which an implanted natural instinct would have led us much more surely."

I don't understand.

"Let us take as a principle that in an organic being no organ is to be found for any end unless it is also the most appropriate to that end and best fitted for it."

All our mental and physical qualities and talents are there for some goal? Is that what you're saying? If I have serviceable legs, they are for walking? Arms are for reaching? Teeth are best suited for biting and chewing? Is this what you mean?

"Yes. Further, let us suppose for argument that the real purpose of reason is for humankind's preservation, welfare, or, in a word, our happiness. If we make these assumptions, then we can see that nature would have hit upon a very bad arrangement by choosing reason . . . to carry out this purpose of sustaining our preservation, welfare, or happiness."

Am I allowed to make an objection?

"Certainly."

Why would we assume any of this? It sounds to me that you're assuming that there is a God who creates our natures, each element having its own function or purpose.

"No, I would like to construct my argument without recourse to the divine. Your objection is well taken on this account. Still, there must be some end for which reason is specially suited."

I guess I'm having a problem thinking of the universe as purposive, as working toward some end. Why not assume that reason is like the appendix, unnecessary at best, a pain in the side at worst?

"We could do that, I suppose. You are, however, again losing track of the nature of our project. I am appealing to ordinary rational knowledge to lead us into a purer discussion of the foundations of morality. Let my assumptions be suggestive, if not fully compelling."

Okay, so where does this leave us?

"Reason's true function must be to produce a will which is good, not as a means to some further end, but in itself. The highest practical function of reason is to produce a good will."

What about happiness or contentment?

"A good will is capable of its own peculiar kind of contentment, a contentment determined by reason alone."

And what if reason and the good will interfere with more physical desires?

The Good Will Is Superior to Passions. "A will must be the highest good and the condition of all the rest, even of all our demands for happiness. This happiness is desired even if its fulfillment should often involve interference with the purposes of inclination."

Then you're saying that reason and the good will are superior to physical desires? Have I gotten that right?

"Yes, I think so. I cannot justify that assumption here, but you will admit that that is exactly what morality claims, too. Remember, what we are after, Art, is to establish the supreme principle of morality."

Okay, but I just want it noted that you are making judgments about the relative worth of the mind over the body. I for one like my body very much. Let's go on to see what else you have to say.

THE MOTIVE OF DUTY

"First, I would like to point out a distinction, doing an action from duty or from some purpose of self-interest."

What's the difference? I mean, why do we need bother with the distinction? Are we going to be able to see the difference in real-life situations? Does it matter when the same actions will result from either motive?

"Good questions. You have a pretty optimistic view of people. Let's go through the distinction carefully. The distinction is certainly far more difficult to perceive when the action accords with duty and the person has an immediate inclination to perform the action."

For example?

"The example I give of the grocer is appropriate, I think. Because of competition, a sensible shopkeeper will not cheat inexperienced customers, including children."

Perfect. Everyone is treated fairly; no one is cheated.

"The people are served honestly, but we need to see and to know more. We are not justified in concluding that the shopkeeper acted from the principles of fair dealing."

Why not?

"Because his interests required him to do so. We can no more assume that he acted from a sense of duty than from a universal love of humanity."

Is this like the Eddie Haskell example that came up in Chapter 2?

"Yes, I think so. Even when Mr. Haskell is acting in accord with the dictates of morality, he is doing so for the wrong reasons."

Living in Conformity with Duty and from the Motive of Duty. "Examine another example. We all have a duty to preserve our own life. Everyone also has a desire to live. It's a natural inclination. We can see that people have the natural desire to live and to avoid pain. They take all kinds of precautions to this end. Although their precautions conform with duty, however, they have no moral worth."

Why not? Here you have people doing just what they are supposed to do, and you say their actions have no moral worth?

"Exactly right. Their actions are not done from the motive of duty. It's as though there is a fortunate overlap of inclination and duty. The people appear to be moral, but their motives are not the right sort."

What's wrong with that? Am I being too practical here? We have a moral duty to do something. We have people doing that action in just the right way. What's the problem?

ACTIONS WITH MORAL WORTH

"Imagine that a person's life is suddenly filled with disappointment and hopeless misery. Imagine that such a person's misery takes away all of his taste for life, and he wants to commit suicide. He longs for death yet still preserves his life without loving it. That action has moral worth."

Why?

"Because his action (of preserving his life) was performed not from inclination or fear but from duty."

How do you figure?

"His strongest inclination is to kill himself, yet he resists and overcomes this desire."

Is that where the moral worth comes in, because he struggles with his stronger desires?

"No, while self-control and sober reflection are good in many respects, they are not good without qualification. Look at the self-controlled criminal who plans his crimes. Self-control and the ability to reflect make this person all the more dangerous and criminal. This is not a person of moral worth."

Then how is the suicidal person who resists suicide being moral?

"The morally decisive feature of the suicidal person is that he acts from a sense of duty. It is precisely in this that the worth of character begins to show—a moral worth and beyond all comparison the highest—namely, that he does good, not from inclination, but from duty."

IS MR. SPOCK THE IDEAL MORAL PERSON?

Are you saying that the ideal moral person is someone like Mr. Spock? I mean, Spock is supposed to be calm and self-controlled, and he always resists temptations.

"Mr. Spock may be a good candidate for the moral ideal, yes. It is not, however, because he exercises self-control or resists temptations. You are confusing qualities of the moral person with the essential feature of morality."

How's that again?

"Your example of Mr. Spock is interesting, but you have focused on the wrong personality traits. Let me put it this way. The kind of personal traits you suggest almost always attend the moral person, but they are not what makes the person morally worthy."

I still don't understand.

"Very good people and very bad people will exhibit the qualities of self-control, calm reflection, and the like. Because of this, it is not these qualities alone that describe the moral person's character. Romulans also exhibit self-control and calm reflection, and yet they are very bad. Does that help you?"

Yes, I think so. I guess I have always heard that moral people are self-controlled and all the rest. I just assumed that this is what makes them moral.

Now you're telling me that acting from a sense of duty is what morality is about.

"Right. You see, it's one thing to want to help other people and another, very different thing to help people because it's your duty. Your example of Mr. Spock demonstrates this point. Spock is entirely logical."

That's not quite true. He has a human side that causes inner struggles.

"Granted. I'm sorry, but I never got very good reception of the show in my day. At any rate, Spock's human side can be put aside for our purposes. Morally speaking, the human side of Spock is irrelevant."

That's where I have a problem with your theory. I just don't see how you can exclude the feeling part of us!

"Art, I am not eliminating the feeling side of people. I am merely showing that the feeling side is not morally relevant. Morality is based on duty, not on feelings. Feelings are too changeable and capricious to stand as the foundation of morality."

Can't a person have an unchanging, stable emotion?

"I don't think so. Can you name one?"

LOVE CANNOT BE A MORAL MOTIVATION

Can love be a moral motivation? I don't mean romantic love. I've seen people fall into and out of love. That's pretty unstable, I agree. But what about the love a person may feel toward her parents, or the love another person may feel toward his child?

"We do speak of some forms of love as unconditional. Even the types of love you forward for consideration are unacceptable, however."

Why, because you say so?

"It has nothing to do with what I say, Art. It is the nature and foundation of morality. There are several features of unconditional love that make it a problematic foundation for morality."

Like what?

"First, it distorts the relative worth of everything in the reality external to the loved person."

Huh?

"If you unconditionally love your child or parent, you place that person's welfare and interests above the welfare and interests of everyone else. That is biased. That distorts the importance of other people with whom you come into contact."

That isn't quite what I have in mind. Let me give you an example. Tell me what's wrong, morally wrong, with this picture. Say a parent has two small children. He loves each child unconditionally. By that I do not mean that he is blind to their weaknesses or undesirable traits. He sees them for who and what they really are. So far, he's not distorting reality. His unconditional love for each child makes his attitude toward them unwavering. I submit this as an argument that love can be a foundation for morality. What do you think so far?

"I am listening."

Okay. This parent has both kids come to him with a disagreement. They both want the same toy, or book. He resolves the dispute, not by being unfeeling. I guess I see Mr. Spock tearing the book exactly in half and giving one half to each child. No, the loving parent will give the book to the child who needs it more.

"Needs it more? How is this a moral decision? How is this impartial and objective?"

The child who needs it more gets the book. One child may need the parent's attention more at that moment, or she may need to be distracted from a hurt knee, or many other reasons. An hour later, the reverse decision may be desirable. The parent does what is best for both children by lovingly doing what is best in the present circumstances. Have I gotten you on this one?

"To use your vernacular, 'I should have had a V-8!' In truth, Art, I fail to see how this decision has moral worth."

Love Cannot Be Impartial.   But my example gives impartial treatment to the two children. Isn't that the essence of morality? Rather than inhibiting the impartial treatment of the two children, the parent's love for his children guarantees that each child will be treated just as the child needs to be treated.

"It is a decision that mirrors a moral decision, perhaps, but it is done entirely from inclination. But perhaps that misses the point, or merely restates my point. Doesn't the parent's attention to both children create a state of more attention given to them and less attention given to all other children?"

Are you saying that a moral parent is supposed to cater to the needs of other people's children as much as to his own children's needs? That's crazy! What you're suggesting is impractical.

"In Scripture we are commanded to love our neighbor and even our enemy. Love out of inclination cannot be commanded; but kindness from duty is practical. It is doubtless in this sense that we should understand the passages from Scripture. As a moral person, you have to act on duty."

I still do not see what is wrong with my example. Your objection to a morality based on emotion is that emotions are too transitory. Because you see the foundation of morality as stable, you reject emotion. But a parent's unconditional love is completely stable.

Love Is Not Objective.   "But love, even unconditional love, is not objective. Let me expand your example to show you that we are not disagreeing as you think. It is only your example that misleads you to a rash and inappropriate conclusion. Think about a judge in a court of law. The judge is the physical embodiment of the moral principle of justice. Now imagine that the judge listens to all the evidence, weighs it for its importance and truth value, and arrives at a decision."

Are we talking about a crooked judge who is running for reelection?

"Don't be so cynical. But let me use your sense of moral disapproval. Imagine that the judge renders her decision, against you, and then turns to the other party, smiles, and says, 'I'll see you at home tonight, son.'"

That's not fair. She can't judge a case involving her own son!

"Just the point."

Are you saying that a person cannot treat a loved one in a moral way?

"Of course not. The point is that objectivity is required for a decision to have moral worth. The example we constructed together portrayed a judge who we have reason to believe judged with bias. We suspected, prematurely and without hearing the evidence, that the judge could not stay objective. Her feelings toward her son may have hindered her making a moral decision. The same result would happen if she turned to you and said that she did not like the way you combed your hair."

Oh, I see what you mean. Look, I agree that emotional bias is a problem, morally speaking. You still haven't shown me how my original example of the parent is mistaken.

"For your parent-child example to work, you had to maintain a relationship of unconditional love toward both disputants."

You mean toward both children?

"Yes. If that was the entire world, then your example would be appropriate, but then the analysis you give would not be the correct one."

Explain, please.

"Certainly. Your example works as long as the children are loved from what I have been calling a sense of duty. This sense of duty becomes clearer when it is violated."

Like in your example of the judge?"

"Love must reside in the will and not in . . . feeling, in principles of action and not of melting compassion. It is this practical love alone which can be an object of command. And only actions that spring from the command of duty have moral worth. Duty, not inclination."

PRINCIPLES, MAXIMS, AND LAWS

I think I'm getting the drift of your analysis of morality. I have a question about the categorical imperative. I want to make certain that I understand what you mean by this idea.

"Very well. We have established that an action done from duty has its moral worth, not in the purpose to be attained by it, but in the maxim in accordance with which it is decided upon."

What do you mean by a maxim?

"A maxim is a principle of the will. It's what we have been slowly defining in our discussion. A maxim is a principle that moves the will to act. It must not include desires or inclinations, of course."

What's the difference between a maxim and a law, or don't I want to know?

"A maxim is the subjective principle of a volition, of the will. An objective principle is what I have been calling a practical law."

Practical? Are you sneaking in consequences?

"No, by the word *practical,* I am referring to practical reason as opposed to theoretical reason. However, I think further discussion of this point will muddy the waters."

Subjective and Objective Principles.   Okay. But let me ask one more question. What is the difference between a subjective principle and an objective principle? This must be an important distinction for your theory.

"Yes, absolutely (no pun intended). A subjective principle is an action-guiding principle. An objective principle is one which also serves subjectively as a practical principle for all rational beings if reason had full control over the faculty of desire."

Say that again?

"A person may perform actions based on her rational principles formed by her reason. This is subjective because it resides in her. The principle becomes objective when all rational beings using reason would arrive at the same principle."

Are you saying that if I am rational and I decide on a course of action, my decision is subjective? And that's because there is only one of me? But if all rational people vote on the same guiding principle, then the principle is objective?

"It is something like that, yes. But look, Art. Mathematics and science operate on a similar distinction. A mathematician uses reason to construct mathematical proofs. One mathematician conjecturing about a proof makes it a subjective conclusion. After other rational mathematicians employ reason and arrive at the same results, then the proof is objective. All mathematicians will arrive at the same conclusion. Similarly, all rational beings will arrive at the same principles, as long as they all use reason to control their desires and inclinations."

The Categorical Imperative.   So what is the categorical imperative? Or, to put it in your words, "What kind of law can this be the thought of which, even without regard to the results expected from it, has to determine the will?" What is the law that you believe defines morality?

"I ought never to act except in such a way that I can also will that my maxim should become a universal law."

Agreed. That's what you mean by objectivity, I guess. But what is the categorical imperative?

"You don't read very carefully, do you? I have just stated the categorical imperative. Bare conformity to universal law is what serves the will as its principle. Reason determines morality."

Could you put this into a form I can understand better? How can I test one of my principles to see whether or not it's a moral principle in line with your categorical imperative, with objectivity, and with reason? I guess I'm asking for something a little less theoretical. Is that okay?

"Assuredly. The quickest way and yet unerringly how to solve the problem . . . is to ask oneself, 'Should I really be content that my maxim should hold as a universal law?' That means, am I willing for this maxim to apply validly to myself and to others?"

What If Everyone Did That?   So I ask myself: What if everyone did that? If I am content with that possibility, then my action is morally acceptable?

"A bit crudely stated, but you have the general idea."

I'm sorry, but this still sounds like you're looking to see what the results are. If I am some kind of fanatic and I invent a maxim that I am willing to apply universally to myself and to others, how does that make my action morally acceptable?

"Give me an example."

Well, earlier in the book we discussed variations of the Golden Rule. Oops, sorry! I forgot, you were still dead when we were discussing the Golden Rule.

"Art, control yourself. You are getting too much involved in your own role. Remember, this discussion is merely imaginary."

Gee, I was getting to like you. I guess this means you won't be coming over for dinner next week.

"Back to your point about the fanatic and the Golden Rule."

Oh, yes, the fanatic. Does your theory suggest that a fanatic's maxim is a moral principle if she is willing to make it a universal law?

"This is where you go astray. The rejection of a maxim is not because of a prospective loss to you or even to others, but because it cannot fit as a principle into a possible enactment as a universal law."

But if not because of the consequences of the action, why not?

"Because duty . . . is the condition of the will good in itself, whose value is above all else."

Come again. Could you translate that?

"Your fanatic is willing to apply her fanaticism to everyone. This fulfills one of the requirements of morality. Her fanaticism fails, however, because it is not acceptable to all rational beings who use reason to control their desires. The fanatic is consistent, but consistency is not enough. Do you understand?"

Let me try again with a more moderate case. What if I decide that I want to take a shower. I decide that I'm going to take a shower at noon on Saturday. Now I want to make sure that my action is morally acceptable. Right so far?

"Continue."

I state my maxim. Everyone ought to take a shower at noon on Saturday. It's universal. Now I ask, could I will that everyone take a shower at noon on Saturday?

"I think you have misunderstood."

Wait, let me finish. Could I will that everyone take a shower at noon on Saturday? No, I could not will that because the results would be disastrous. The water pressure would become nonexistent; the sewer line would burst from all that water going down the drains.

"Have you finished?"

Yes.

"I can see that my use of examples has misled you. We agreed that examples would be used only to bring your ordinary knowledge into harmony with moral philosophy. Examples serve us only as encouragement. We cannot do morality a worse service than by seeking to derive it from examples. Every example of it presented to me must first itself be judged by moral principles in order to decide if it is fit to serve as an original example."

Using examples is going about the process in the wrong direction? It's backward?

Two Imperatives.   "Yes. But let us return to your example of the fanatical shower taker. There are two distinct types of imperatives. One we call the hypothetical imperative; the other is the categorical imperative."

I don't see what your point is. Please pardon me for saying this, but you philosophers make a lot of distinctions for no good reason.

"We shall see. The 'unimportant' distinction between hypothetical and categorical imperatives answers your objection. Hypothetical imperatives declare a possible action to be practically necessary as a means to the attainment of something else that one wills. A categorical imperative would be one which represented an action as objectively necessary in itself apart from its relation to a further end."

So?

"I sense from your answer that you do not yet sufficiently understand. If the action would be good solely as a means to something else, the imperative is hypothetical; if the action is represented as good in itself and therefore as necessary, in virtue of its principle, for a will which of itself accords with reason, then the imperative is categorical."

Your entire theory comes down to reason and what reason implies. Morality is just acting like Mr. Spock.

"Slow down, Art. We'll get to that. First, let's resolve your problem. In your example of taking a shower, the shower taking is certainly not being done for its own sake. Enjoyable as showers are, they are a means to an end, whether that be cleanliness, or good grooming, or health. Therefore, the maxim is not a moral maxim at all. It need not be tested as a moral principle; it need not be universalized."

Oh, I see.

"Further, you are rightly tempted to consider the effects of that maxim just because it is a means to an end. What you are implicitly weighing—"

Hold on. What does "implicitly" mean?

"You are doing it without stating it, and in this case without realizing it. For example, if I tell you that all men are mortal, what does that tell you about Socrates?"

Socrates is mortal.

"Yes, and implicit in your reasoning is the idea that Socrates is a man. Many implicit ideas are so obvious that they go unstated. Many of our beliefs are taken for granted and never stated. Unfortunately, many of our obvious beliefs are mistaken. But I digress."

Sorry for the distraction.

"What you are implicitly weighing are the effects of everyone's taking a shower at the same time and everyone's being newly showered at the same time. Obviously, given the practical results, we would be willing to allow that people ought to bathe at different times. Don't you agree?"

You are one persuasive gent. Yes, I agree. Now what about the role of reason in your analysis of morality?

"Ask your questions."

Why Reasoned Objectivity?   Your whole analysis of morality comes down to reason. When we use reason properly, we are creating moral principles. In other words, moral action must be done for the sake of duty. And neither inclination nor consequences are acceptable motives; only duty is acceptable. What this all comes down to is that morality is objective and impartial. We are supposed to use reason to derive our moral laws. That brings moral worth. The fact that my actions are derived from reason, and not from consequences or from desires gives them moral worth?

"Right. The categorical imperative alone purports to be an unconditional command. It does not leave open to the will to do the opposite at its discretion. Therefore, the categorical imperative alone carries with it that necessity which we demand from a law."

The Formula of Universal Law: The Categorical Imperative.   And the formula for universal law is a single categorical imperative?

"Act only on that maxim through which you can at the same time will that it should become a universal law."

Now that you have stated it, I guess this seems pretty obvious from what we've discussed. You are looking for a universal law and logical consistency in creating applications of your principle, aren't you?

"Certainly one feature of the moral law is that it is self-consistent. That is why promises must be kept. If you read attentively, you will see that making an excuse for myself is inconsistent with promise making when the law is made universal. Making promises with the intention of not keeping them would make promising, and the very purpose of promising, itself impossible."

CULTIVATING ONE'S TALENTS

While you refer to your illustrations, I have a question about one of them.

"The third one, no doubt. You seek to indulge yourself rather than to develop your talents."

Yup. What's wrong with that? I'm willing to make it a universal law. I don't see any contradiction or inconsistency in letting everyone live under this law.

"Every man should let his talents rust and should be bent on devoting his life solely to idleness, indulgence, procreation, and, in a word, enjoyment. Is that your candidate for a universal law?"

Absolutely!

"But one cannot possibly *will* that this should be a universal law. For as a rational being he necessarily wills that all his powers should be developed, since they serve him, and are given him, for all sorts of possible ends."

This is Mr. Spock! Everything has to be rational! Where is the inconsistency in my desire for everyone to seek enjoyment?

"You have not yet grasped the import of the notion of the will. It is not logically impossible—nor certainly impossible, in fact—for all people to devote their lives to idleness, indulgence, and procreation. In my own time, the South Sea Islanders appeared to live just this way."

I wonder if my time travel machine can take me there?

"Put your musings aside and stay with the subject. The consistency that morality demands goes beyond logical rigor. There is also a component that touches reality, so to speak. The rational being knows that in the future reality may deem him to use talents that he has not yet been called to use."

Star Fleet has made an investment in me and I am obliged to develop my talents, so I sit around playing chess with a computer instead of chasing members of the sex that attracts me?

"Mock morality if you will, but the rational being seeks to cultivate his talents because the future is not without surprises."

I get your point. I can't help resisting morality. It just demands so much.

COMING TO THE AID OF OTHERS

"Ah, but morality offers quite a lot. In my fourth illustration, I point out that moral law requires that we aid others who are struggling with great hardships."

Yes, that's an interesting example. You say that humanity could get along perfectly well without people helping the less fortunate. I agree with that. Why should I help someone else just because she is struggling against great hardships?

"That is not what I said, Art. You have taken only one statement and removed it from its context. What I said was that one could make a universal law of nature that aid for the less fortunate be withheld. I also assert, however, that it is impossible to *will* that such a principle should hold everywhere as a law of nature."

I don't get it.

"A person who decides to make it universal that people merely tolerate each other—"

Tolerate? What do you mean?

"You, Art, may believe that each person should be as happy as circumstances allow, or as happy as she alone can make herself. Art, you may also believe that depriving others of anything is wrong, even that envying others is wrong."

Yes, this all sounds reasonable.

"But you cannot will this as a universal law."

Why not? I do not harm anyone, and do not wish harm to anyone else, and do not envy anyone else. And I'm willing to make this a universal law that applies to everyone else. What more could you ask?

"A will which decided in this way would be in conflict with itself."

You mean I would feel guilty or bothered if I felt this way?

"No, that is not what I mean. I am not referring to guilt or any other feelings. I am discussing the will, not inclinations."

Then what sort of conflict would the will be in?

"Think about it this way. Many situations might arise in which a person would need love and sympathy from others. By endorsing the law of nature that we need only refrain from interfering with others, the person would rob himself of all hope of the help he wants for himself."

Do unto others as you would have them do unto you? Is that what all this boils down to? Are you saying that because I can imagine someday needing love and sympathy, I am therefore required to give love and sympathy to others?

"Yes. Do you object to this?"

This just sounds like, "There but for the grace of God go I," so I ought to help the less fortunate. Yes, I object to this.

"Why?"

Because it isn't I who is in need, for one. And for two, most of the time it's the person's fault that his life is going the way it is going. Why should I have to help people like that? Tell me that.

"You are losing the focus of moral principles. Remember that you must be able to universalize your principles. There may be circumstances where you will need love and sympathy."

Fine, but I have friends and family who will help me. Why should I help strangers? Let everyone get love and sympathy from people they know.

"It's quite obvious that you come from a background where at least some of your close associates have stable, even prosperous lives. This is keeping you from making a leap of moral imagination. You are overly conservative with your principle because you cannot imagine fortune really turning on you."

How do you know? Maybe I've come up the hard way, and I wasn't offered any help, and I made it.

"Indeed, but made it in what way? Although you may prosper materially, you have not yet come to grips with morality and its requirements. You are losing track of the essential feature of morality."

Which is what?

THE VEIL OF IGNORANCE

"The good will. At least in your imagination, you have to place yourself in an impartial, objective perspective. It is what Professor Rawls* calls the veil of ignorance. That example dramatizes the objectivity required in asserting the will."

*John Rawls, *A Theory of Justice* (Harvard, 1971).

You want me to ignore my own personal circumstances?

"Exactly. Theoretically, the veil places you in ignorance of your own situation. If you do not know your own personal situation, you are forced to create laws that can be universally applied. By adopting this 'blind' point of view, you are able to remove your own inclinations, talents, desires, and everything else that is personal."

But all that would remain is reason. Oh, I see, that's just what you're after, reason.

OBJECTION: ISN'T THIS AN APPEAL TO RESULTS?

I have an objection. Isn't this an appeal to results? What I mean is, aren't you arguing that I should help other people because I may need love and sympathy someday? This reason sounds like enlightened self-interest.

"Unfortunately, that is the problem with examples. Giving examples often overpersonalizes the principle. Examples can make it appear that the ground for the moral decision is self-interest. That is not the case, however. Let me expand the example."

Go for it.

PRIMARY GOODS

"I will borrow another of Rawls's concepts, that of primary goods. Primary goods are 'things which it is supposed a rational man wants whatever else he wants. . . . Regardless of what an individual's rational plans are in detail, it is assumed that there are various things which he would prefer more of rather than less. With more of these goods men can generally be assured of greater success in carrying out their intentions and in advancing their ends, whatever these ends may be.' "

Okay, now what?

"Every rational person wills that she be granted as much and as many of the primary goods as is possible. Every rational being wills this, and not just for herself, but for everyone. You see, Art, it is the nature of the will that determines universal principles as laws of nature. The consequences do not matter. Each person as a rational being wills to enjoy the primary goods."

What sort of things count as primary goods?

"Rawls distinguishes two types of primary goods, social primary goods and natural goods. The first are things like 'rights and liberties, powers and opportunities, income and wealth.' Some of the natural primary goods are 'health and vigor, intelligence and imagination.' The idea is that these are desirable for just about any rational plan of life."

Are you saying that if you are denied all the social liberties, or that if you are not particularly healthy, you cannot pursue a rational plan of life? This doesn't make sense. For example, certainly a blind person is capable of achieving a lot in life.

"Of course, that's true. No rational person, though, would willingly give up sight without very compelling reason. Nor would a rational person willingly give up rights and liberties. Why? Because giving up these primary goods inhibits one's flexibility in pursuing the variety of goals that rational people set for themselves."

All right, this makes sense, but how does it apply to the illustration you are explaining?

"It's good you keep track of the argument. Sometimes people get distracted from the main point in justifying the lesser points. Love and sympathy are also primary goods. You may never need them, but it would not be rational to give them up without compelling reason. In times of struggle, if you do need them, they are important to have. Don't you agree?"

Yes, I guess so.

"Good, then the will demands that we help others when they need our sympathy and aid. This same reasoning applies to all primary goods. That is why I say that a will would be in conflict with itself if it denied people their primary goods."

MAKING EXCEPTIONS

"One other thing bothers me about what you said just a few moments ago, Art. By singling out yourself, you show a callous attitude toward others. Your attitude is: 'What does it matter to me that others are struggling with great hardships?' Of course, morally that is unacceptable."

I have come to realize that. How much more are you going to criticize me?

"What your attitude demonstrates is an ability to make an exception of yourself. Some maxims cannot be conceived as a universal law of nature. Others can be conceived, but they cannot be willed for the reasons we have just enunciated."

Because they would contradict the will?

"Yes. There is yet another test. We may experience a contradiction in our own will when we assert that a certain principle should be objectively necessary as a universal law and yet subjectively should not hold universally but should admit of exceptions."

Huh? Could you explain that?

"Huh, indeed. What I mean is that you may assert a certain principle and claim that it is universally necessary, yet you believe that it should not hold for everyone. I anticipate another 'huh?'"

Sorry.

"To explain, imagine that you advocate that everyone ought to keep promises. In this case, however, you find it difficult to obey your own principle. Imagine a case where you will be embarrassed if you keep your promise. Now you may be tempted to make an exception of your own case, but this will bring a contradiction to your own will."

Sometimes my will, my reason, conflicts with my desires?

"Exactly, and those times the will must be preferred to subjective inclination. That is what morality is about."

REASON AND AUTONOMY

Why should I be moral? That's really what I want to know.

"Isn't it obvious why you should be moral? No, I guess it is not clear to you. Very well, like many others who have come before you, you see people as tied to laws by their duty. Isn't that correct?"

Yes, that's why I ask: Why should I be moral? Why should I give up self-interest and obey the laws that are imposed on me?

"What has not yet occurred to you is that you are subject only to laws which are made by you and yet are universal. You are bound only to act in uniformity with a will which is your own but has as nature's purpose for it the function of making universal law."

Are you saying that I am most free when I follow laws or principles that are my own creation?

"Absolutely, and the laws of your own making as a rational being are also laws that apply universally to all rational beings. Therefore, freedom, or what I call autonomy, is produced only by obedience to moral principle. Don't you see, Art, the constraint and coercion of moral principle is lifted. You follow your own laws, which are also moral laws."

And you are suggesting that I want autonomy.

"Yes, again. Autonomy is the ground of the dignity of human nature and of every rational nature. In fact, autonomy of the will is the supreme principle of morality."

THE FORMULA OF
THE END IN ITSELF

According to your analysis, Professor Kant, reason and autonomy are valuable in themselves. Have I got that right?

"That is a good way of looking at the key points of morality. You ask, is there something whose existence has in itself an absolute value, something which as an end in itself could be a ground for determinate laws. If we could find such a valuable existing thing, then in it, and in it alone, would be the ground of a possible categorical imperative."

Is that what I'm asking?

"You are asking about something valuable in itself. You have surmised from our brief discussion that autonomy and reason qualify. Now I say that man, and in general every rational being, exists as an end in himself, not merely as a means for arbitrary use by this or that will. You see, Art, rational nature exists as an end in itself."

Doesn't nonrational nature exist in itself? I mean, trees and tables and chairs exist. Why give priority to rational nature?

"This is the way in which a man necessarily conceives his own existence. . . . But it is also the way in which every other rational being conceives his existence on the same rational ground which is valid also for me; hence it is . . . an objective principle."

How do you know that every rational—

"Excuse me, Art, please. Allow me to finish my thought, and then you may ask all the questions you like. The practical imperative is: Act in such a way that you always treat humanity, whether in your own person or in the person of any other, never simply as a means, but always at the same time as an end."

HOW DO WE CONCEIVE OUR EXISTENCE?

I do have several comments. First, how do you know that all rational beings conceive their existence as an end in itself, as valuable in itself? Why can't we imagine rational creatures from another star system who value the whole and not the individual? You seem to be imposing on all rational beings our basic, and nearly universal, desire to survive. I don't see that as necessary.

"It is not rational to *will* your own annihilation. To will your own demise involves a contradiction. Let us suppose that from self-love I make it my principle to shorten my life. A system of nature by whose law the very same feeling whose function is to stimulate the furtherance of life should actually destroy life would contradict itself. Consequently, it could not subsist as a system of nature. Hence this maxim could not hold as a universal law of nature. It is therefore entirely opposed to the supreme principle of all duty."

Then your objection to suicide is not that if I kill myself, and everyone else follows, then there would be no one left to follow the same principle? Is that the inconsistency you mean?

"Of course not. The inconsistency is in the motivation of the principle."

Having Children. To see if I understand, can I try an example from my time?

"Certainly, you may."

Imagine that I decide that a certain way of life or a certain attitude is wrong for people. I ask myself if I can universalize this, and I find that I can. I will that no one live this certain lifestyle.

"But by willing this prohibition, are you saying that there is an inconsistency in the way of life you condemn? Remember, mere consistency in a fanatic is not sufficient to warrant us saying you have a rational principle, a moral law."

Hmm. Okay, let me try this. Say that I value people as important.

"As intrinsically and unconditionally valuable?"

Yes, okay, just what you said. Say that I value them, and I find that people who do not wish to have children are living in offense of the natural order.

"How's that?"

Say they prevent pregnancy in their relationships. They do not want children, so they use contraceptives. Now people cannot will that no one have children. To say that would be to say that sex is for begetting children, yet they want sexual activity but no children. They live in contradiction to nature.

"No, you have misunderstood. People who do not desire children are not acting inconsistently with any principle. Your example is very different from my prohibition against suicide. In the case of suicide, the principle of self-love drives the person to the act of suicide. That is where the contradiction lies with suicide. Your example is an attempt to transform a natural, biological inclination into a moral principle. The analogy does not work."

So there is nothing inconsistent in principle about using contraceptives or being gay?

"Not that I can determine from your comments."

"We Destroyed the Village in Order to Save It." Let me try one more example, Professor Kant. Imagine again that I decide that a certain way of life or a certain attitude is wrong for people. It is wrong for people to have to live under a dictatorship. I see my opportunity to prevent people from having to be oppressed. So I—

"Destroy the village in order to save it? That is what you were going to say?"

Yup. See, I value the people enough to try to come to their aid. By destroying their village, people and all, the dictator's army will have nothing to hold. Pretty good, huh?

"This is quite unacceptable. What you suggests involves killing innocent people, people about whom you profess to care. You kill some and destroy the homes of the others, all in the name of saving them. No, Art, this reasoning violates the formulation of people as ends in themselves."

How so? I'm doing it for them.

"So you say, but you are treating them as a means to your own desires and political bias. You cannot kill an innocent person and claim you are doing it to save him. This reasoning is analogous to the suicide example. One cannot kill oneself in order to save oneself. One cannot kill others in order to save them. Self-love or love of others cannot consistently be used as grounds for either suicide or murder. Do you have any other questions you wish to ask me? My time with you grows short."

ONE FINAL CRITICISM

At the end of chapter 2 of your *Groundwork,* you say, "We have merely shown by developing the concept of morality generally in vogue that autonomy of the will is unavoidably bound up with it or rather is its very basis." Is that all you have shown?

"What I claim is that the fitness of the maxim of every good will to make itself a universal law is itself the sole law which the will of every rational being spontaneously imposes on itself without basing it on any impulsion or interest. . . . We have not here asserted the truth of this proposition, much less pretended to have a proof of it in our power."

Then all this only shows what morality is. You haven't shown why I should be moral.

"No, that's true, though I have more to say about that in future chapters and in other of my works."

Have you shown that the moral life as you define it is the best life?

"No, I have not done that here."

■
SUMMARY OF DISCUSSION

Kant argues that there is only one purely good thing, the good will. The good will is unconditionally good. It uses reason to come to its principles for action. Superior to passions, the good will directs us to act according to our duties. It is important not merely to live in conformity with duty, but to have duty as one's motive. A moral action takes its worth from being motivated solely by duty and reason. Consequences play no role in moral reasoning.

It probably seems odd to many of us that love and other "gentler" emotions cannot be the motive for moral action. Kant rejects all emotional motivations because emotions are not impartial. Morality must be impartial and susceptible to universal application. Only reason can play this vital role.

Why does Kant require reasoned objectivity? Kant understands that morality is our vehicle for communicating and forming community. Communication is possible only if all people share in the ability to communicate. This ability is possible only if everyone shares the "language" of communication. That shared language is reason. By its very nature, reason is objective. Emotions, even emotions like love and sympathy, are subjective. Emotions allow for partiality. Therefore, emotions cannot be motivators for morality.

Kant also argues for the efficacy of reason because reason gives us autonomy, freedom. The only laws that are acceptable are those that apply to everyone. Reason defines us as human. By living in accordance with reason, we fulfill our natures. Isn't that one of the reasons you urged me to be moral? To be moral is to fulfill one's human nature.

Kant invents the categorical imperative to exemplify the formula of universal law. "Act only on that maxim through which you can at the same time will that it should become a universal law." Acting in accordance with this imperative guarantees that one's will accords with reason. Kant's application of the categorical imperative is instructive. He writes that you should "act in such a way that you always treat humanity, whether in your own person or in the person of any other, never simply as a means, but always at the same time as an end." Morality requires us to treat people as valuable just because they are reasoning agents.

What Kant derives from this is a set of duties to oneself and to others. One is duty-bound to cultivate one's talents. One is responsible to come to the aid of other people. One must treat other people with respect and objectivity.

Morality, through reason, requires each of us to understand ourselves as one person among many equals. Only a good will informed by impartial, objective reason can be the source of morality.

■
DISCUSSION HIGHLIGHTS

I. The good will is
1. Unconditionally good.
2. A function of reason.
3. Superior to the passions.
II. The motive of duty
1. Requires that we live in conformity with duty.
2. And requires that we live from the motive of duty.
3. Actions take their moral worth from the motive of duty.
4. Love cannot be a moral motivation.
    a. love is not impartial
    b. love is not objective
III. The categorical imperative
1. Embodies reasoned objectivity.
2. Requires that we come to the aid of other people.
3. Requires that we treat other people with respect and objectivity.
4. Requires each person as well to cultivate his or her talents.
IV. Autonomy or freedom
1. Comes only with acting on reason.
2. Allows people to communicate and to form communities.

■
QUESTIONS FOR THOUGHT/PAPER TOPICS

1. Kant argues that only reason is impartial. Do you agree? Can a parent's love for her children cause her to treat them differently but fairly?

2. Must morality always be equal treatment? What does it mean to treat equally people whose social position is unequal?

3. Kant argues that we have a duty to ourselves to cultivate our duties. How strong is that requirement? Do you agree with him?

4. If last week I promised you that I would meet you today at 10 A.M. and you later released me from the promise, I would not be obligated to meet you. We can be released from promises and other like duties. Does Kant's sense of duty to oneself allow for this? Can I release myself from the duty to myself to cultivate my talents?

5. Is Mr. Spock the ideal moral person? Does he fit Kant's criteria?

6. Describe how the "veil of ignorance" works. Does it capture our sense of morality?

7. Do you agree that reasoned objectivity is autonomy? Discuss Kant's vision of autonomy. Do you agree?

■
FOR FURTHER READING

The best way to learn Kant's thoughts is to read the *Groundwork of the Metaphysics of Morals* (Harper & Row, 1964). John Rawls's *A Theory of Justice* (Harvard, 1971) is sympathetic to Kant's approach to moral theory. I suggest chapter 3, sections 24 and 25, for this present discussion. Commentaries on Kant are numerous. C. D. Broad's *Five Types of Ethical Theory* (Routledge & Kegan Paul, 1930) is a good secondary source. Robert Paul Wolff's *The Autonomy of Reason: A Commentary on Kant's "Groundwork of the Metaphysics of Morals"* (Harper & Row, 1973) is more than just a catchy title.

TEN

Existentialist Ethics: Jean-Paul Sartre's Ideas on Being Free

Before we conjure up Jean-Paul Sartre, I would like to introduce existentialism. As I understand it, existentialism tells us that life is pointless; or, even worse, it tells us that life is filled with despair, forlornness, abandonment, and loneliness. If all this isn't bad enough, existentialism says that we can do whatever we want because moral values cannot be justified. Unfortunately, however, the theory isn't permissive in the way I wanted at the beginning of the book. We are allowed to do whatever we want, but we are responsible for our actions.

I think Sartre also says that values are vague. Someone told me once that Sartre believes that moral values are absurd. Given all this, why would anyone accept such a depressing picture of life?

"Art, I am disappointed with your analysis of my work."

Why? Haven't I adequately depressed my readers just the way you want?

"Don't be sarcastic. Your conclusions about existentialism are inadequate and misleading."

How? All you write about is depressing stuff. Life is filled with anguish, responsibility, forlornness, and loneliness. Do you deny it?

TWO INSIGHTS

"I do not deny that existentialism carefully examines these attitudes, but you portray them in the most negative light. You also completely overlook the two most important insights of existentialism. Existentialism is the one doctrine that looks realistically, even optimistically, at people. We do not rule out generosity by saying that it is human nature to be greedy. We do not say that people are born and live in sin. We open the entire range of possibilities to humanity. People may choose to be generous or greedy, sinful or loving. What could be more refreshing and more encouraging? I believe existentialism is the doctrine that makes human life possible."

Two insights?

"Man's existence precedes his essence. And man is free."

Is that all there is to existentialism?

EXISTENCE PRECEDES ESSENCE: THERE IS NO HUMAN NATURE

"I would also say that existentialism defines a set of questions and problems that have not been sufficiently addressed in recent philosophy. You are too casual, however, in dismissing the two defining features of the thought of existentialists. First, existentialists assert the importance of choice. We also believe that existence precedes essence."

What do you mean, existence precedes essence?

"Subjectivity must be the starting point."

To be honest, that doesn't ring any bells of understanding in my head. Could you explain it?

"In my essay I include the example of a paper cutter. A paper cutter is designed in a person's mind before the cutter exists. Its essence precedes its existence. With human beings, the opposite is true. We humans exist and then we define our essence."

Maybe, but I'm still in a fog.

"All right, let me put it this way. There is no human nature."

How can that be? Humans think; we are rational. Isn't that at least part of our nature?

"No, I don't think so. Human essence refers to human nature. What I mean when I say that existence precedes essence is that man exists, appears on the scene, and only afterwards defines himself."

How could that be? Surely you aren't denying the impact that instincts have on people's lives?

Man Is Nothing Else but What He Makes of Himself.   "I am denying exactly that. No matter what a person believes, she is free. That is what I am asserting most strenuously."

So that is where choice comes in?

"Very good, yes. Man is what he makes of himself; man is what he conceives himself to be and what he wills himself to be."

Are you saying that we exist, and then we define ourselves?

"Exactly. First comes a person's existence, then the person defines herself. There is no preordained purpose or function for humans. Human consciousness and choice must be called on to forge a self. That's freedom! Man is nothing else but what he makes of himself. That's the first principle of existentialism."

Consciousness?

"Humans are self-conscious and therefore free."

What do you mean, we're self-conscious?

"Not in the sense of being easily embarrassed. We humans are conscious of our own future. Man is a plan that is aware of itself. You, for example, know that you have a future, so you plan your life with some future in mind. That's what separates us from inanimate objects, plants and animals. Man will be what he plans to be."

Bad Faith.   What does that do to my idea of living in the moment?

"If by living in the moment you plan to pursue pleasure or intense experience, then your idea is unrealistic."

Unrealistic? Why do you say that?

"Because man knows he has a future. We are conscious of our lives. To play with the idea of merely living in one fixed moment of pleasure is an example of bad faith."

Bad faith? You're throwing too many new concepts at me.

"All I mean here by bad faith is that you are making efforts to establish that you are not what and where you are. You imagine a most pleasurable experience. Then you wish to block out the ever-changing present. To accomplish this, you lie to yourself. You go beyond the given facts of reality."

HOW DO WE CREATE OUR OWN OBSTACLES?

But my plans don't always work out!

"Of course not, but existentialism does not suggest that your plans will always succeed. Instead, I mean that each person shapes his or her own future. There are facts of the world that must be accounted for, but even these facts are our choice to a great extent."

How are facts our choice? That doesn't make sense.

"We create our own obstacles."

Huh? Either something is in the way or it is not in the way.

"Take insults as an example. The Stoic Epictetus was correct in saying that it is up to me to determine my response to any action. It is also up to me to define what does and what does not count as insult. Don't you agree?"

Maybe that works with insults, but some facts, some obstacles, are just there. A person can't choose not to see a mountain. Nor can a person choose to ignore his family relationships.

"Of course, both these alleged facts are up to me. If I choose to see the mountain as hindering my travels, then I acknowledge it. If I choose to see it as beautiful, or as ugly, it is my choice that gives it reality. As for family relationships, it is clearly I who determines them. If I am married, I must choose at each moment to be married to this woman and not to leave her. The point is I cannot use the fact of the mountain or the marriage to excuse myself from action."

SHOULD I DO WHATEVER I WANT?

Is existentialism advocating that I do whatever I want?

"No, that is oversimplifying the theory and distorting it. Man is at the start a plan which is aware of itself. Man consciously chooses his plan of life. Wants are merely symptoms of the fundamental choices we make."

I'm not sure I see the difference.

"First, there is the spontaneous choice of who you are. After that come your wants. The wants are connected to the earlier choice; the wants are a result of the choices we make. But choice comes first."

Are you saying that I choose my wants? I choose to be hungry or thirsty, a heterosexual or a homosexual?

"Yes, in an important way. You choose how, when, and why you will satisfy your hunger and thirst. For example, under certain circumstances you may choose to starve yourself, or to commit suicide by some other means. And yes, you choose your sexual preferences. You must recognize that your wants are yours. They define who you are."

And it's this spontaneous choice that you call the will?

"Right."

HOW DO I CHOOSE?

I think we're getting somewhere. How do I choose? What I mean by that is, what are the standards by which I choose?

"Standards?"

Sure. With everyday garden-variety morality, choice is limited, or maybe it's better to say that choice is directed by moral values and goals. Now that I think of it, even the pleasure seeker's choices are directed toward achieving pleasure and avoiding pain. But you are saying that choice is more basic.

"If I choose to live a moral life, it is my choice. If I choose to be a hedonist, a pleasure seeker, that too is my choice."

But which choice is right?

"If you mean by right, morally right, then the moral life is obviously preferred."

No, that's not what I mean. Which life is more desirable? Which is the best life?

"The one that you choose, Art."

Huh?

"We always choose the good. To choose this or that is to affirm at the same time the value of what we choose. The fact that you choose it means you value it."

The ideas of choice and will are pretty powerful in your theory.

"Yes."

SO WHAT GIVES EXISTENTIALISM
A BAD NAME?

So what gives your existentialism a bad name? (Is there an echo in here?)

"In part it is the atheistic element, although there are many existentialists who are theists. Your book includes at least three—Dostoevski, Kierkegaard, and Buber—though you have not presented their religious writings."

Maybe my next book will include a philosophy of religion section. But why is existentialism attacked?

"Existentialism is a doctrine which declares that every truth and every action implies a human setting and a human subjectivity. Human choice is what makes human life possible."

Okay, Professor Sartre, but you must admit that the existentialism you present gives a pretty dark description of human living.

"Why do you say that?"

You say people live in a state of anguish, forlornness, and despair. I still think that's pretty depressing. Won't you admit that?

"I think with a little explanation you will find these words less frightening and depressing. It all starts with choice, of course."

How is choice objectionable to people?

CHOICE AND RESPONSIBILITY

"The objection is probably due to the extreme responsibility that existentialism places on each individual. The attacks come in different forms. From the Christian standpoint, we are charged with denying God's commandments and the eternal truths. Therefore, it is claimed, we deny the seriousness of human undertakings. From the politically conservative perspective, we are charged with resisting authority. This point of view says that we should not try to rise above our stations in life and that the reigning powers know what they are doing. Both these points of view, the Christian and the political, hold that there is a human nature. They believe, as do many people, that man's bent is always toward trouble."

Isn't it? The reason I ask is because that's been the attack made against me throughout this book.

"Art, the existentialist asserts that there is no human nature, remember? Therefore, everything is choice! There are no human inclinations except the ones we will."

Aren't some desires natural and others unnatural, or against our nature? I know many people say that we are evil by nature.

"Look at the evidence of reality, though. Not everyone responds in the same way to situations."

That's because we are all raised differently.

"What you say is true; we are all raised differently. But do you mean to say that all our actions are merely reflections of earlier training?"

That idea makes me uncomfortable, but yes, our family, friends, and society give us our values. Are you denying this?

"I do not deny that most people believe this. Indeed, the problem today, as always, is that people fear responsibility for their choices. What really scares people in the existentialist doctrine is that it leaves man a possibility of choice."

And they think we will misuse our ability to choose?

"I think that is the concern."

Say I accept that I am responsible for my choices and for my wants. What else is there?

"You are responsible for your choices and for all of mankind."

Wait a minute, I thought my choices were mine, and yours were yours, and that was the end of it. Why am I responsible for all humanity?

"Let's look at each part of responsibility separately."

Anguish. Okay. According to you, I choose for myself. I am whatever I will myself to be. If I will that I am a moral person or a pleasure seeker, then I am. What's the big deal? I choose and I willingly accept the responsibility.

"The 'big deal' as you call it, is that you overlook the extreme responsibility of choice, the anguish. Even in your own case, apart from the rest of humanity, your choice is completely your own, completely. For example, say you choose to live a morally praiseworthy life. What that involves is a creative act."

Creative?

"Yes, you and you alone must create your own values. Remember, atheistic existentialism denies that there is any God with eternal truths and commandments. We also deny that there is any human nature. Therefore, you cannot resort to these sources for your values."

You've already ruled out my wants. You say that my wants come after my basic choice of a lifestyle. Where am I going to get my values?

"That question is the source of anguish."

And what's your answer?

"Choice! Oddly enough, most of the first part of your book has been devoted to the kind of thinking that I endorse."

You mean I am an existentialist without knowing it?

"Not quite. Your discussion, though, pits the moralist against a person who wants to live in the moment. In forcing that conversation, you set the right questions in motion."

How have I done that?

"You have consistently challenged your reader to justify morality generally and individual moral principles specifically. Your reluctance and theirs to grapple honestly with these challenges shows one element of existential anguish."

But I *have* been honest.

"If you believe that, then you are in bad faith. Your discomfort with morality causes you to run for cover. You find living in the moment to be an intellectually safe place to hide."

Safe?

"Defending morality is far more difficult than taking the relativist, or sub-jectivist, or hedonist, or egoist way out. Let me put it differently. You find morality perched on an unstable foundation. Your challenge to morality is commendable; however your recourse to hiding in some kind of vague self-centeredness is bad faith. You're avoiding the responsibility of choice. You prefer not to choose, because every choice frightens you. What you fail to realize is that not choosing is also a choice."

Choice frightens me? Why do you say that? I like the idea of doing what-ever I want. What I don't like about morality is all the restrictions.

The Inability to Discover a Foundation of Morality. "You cannot guarantee morality by reference to some other, better-grounded thought, so you flee from it."

Is that why Kant tries to ground morality in reason? And why Mill seeks to establish morality as impartial and based on happiness? Each is trying to dis-cover an unshakeable foundation for morality?

"I think so, yes."

So what do you think is wrong with their theories?

"We'll get to that. First, however, we need to explain anguish. You cannot find any foundation for morality except some arbitrary beliefs that many people hold, right? You are asking for proof of morality, but you cannot figure out what proof would look like?"

Right. Nor can I see why I should be moral.

"So you are forced to choose your own values, just as you have been trying to force the reader to justify moral values. What is wrong with stealing? you ask. Failing to find an adequate answer, you and your reader either reject or accept the value of honesty. Here is where anguish comes in. By either accept-ing or rejecting the value of honesty, you are choosing either to be or not to be honest. Now take responsibility for your choice."

So at the beginning of the book, when I asked about honesty, all the reader had to answer was, "Because I will it," and that would be enough?

The Depth of Responsibility. "After looking at a number of possibilities, one chooses. The value one chooses has value only because it is chosen."

Then it's easy! All I have to do is look at the alternatives and choose. Why do you call this anguish?

"You are overlooking the depth of responsibility involved. Think of your-self as a book writing itself. Each word, each sentence, is you. Each of your actions reveals who you are. You exist, then you create yourself. There are no excuses; you are your actions. That places all the responsibility onto you and no one else. You cannot make excuses for your values. You cannot turn to your cultural or religious values. You cannot blame the people who have raised and educated you. You cannot blame a commanding officer, or leader, or employer for your actions."

But sometimes a person has to do what she doesn't want to do. I mean, if I want to pass a course, I have to at least take the exams or write the papers. If I work for a company and they order me to do something, I have to do it. How can I get around that?

Do What You Will.   "You and you alone bear the responsibility. If you find that your orders are inappropriate, then disobey. For example, if your employer tells you to act in a way that you do not will, then don't follow the order."

Easy for you to say. If I do whatever I want, I'll get fired. There are lots of times I don't want to attend my classes or go to work at my job. But I have to go. If I don't, I'll get fired.

"Exactly. The choice is yours. I did not say that you should do what you want. You should do what you will. Remember, the will, the spontaneous choice, comes before your wants."

I think we're just getting caught up in a word game here. If I do whatever I "will," I'll flunk my courses or I'll get fired.

"The fact that you do not miss too many of your classes, the fact that you regularly go to work, shows what you will."

How? If I could do whatever I want, I'd—

"Your actions indicate your preferences. Your problem is that you want choice, but you fail to accept responsibility. I think, though, that your reaction to my questions shows that you do experience anguish."

How do my answers show that?

"In real life, you recognize that your choices have real-life impact. Your actions do have consequences. In choosing one action over another action, you calculate the impact. That's a recognition of anguish. The action is yours; the results are yours."

Go back a little. You said I could do whatever I want—I mean, whatever I will. But that's just not realistic. The teachers, the bosses, the commanding officers in the military all dictate the actions of their subordinates. A person can't just disobey.

"Ah, more anguish. You can disobey. However, you are evidently not prepared to accept the responsibility for your choice."

I'm not getting this. How can I disobey?

"Simply choose. Why are you blind to the possibilities? Anguish."

Blind to the possibilities?

"Imagine that your commanding officer orders you to do what you will not to do."

For example?

"Imagine that it is wartime and you are ordered to place deadly poison into the water supply for an entire city. Innocent people will die painful deaths, and you object to this tactic."

Wouldn't that be against my commanding officer's values?

"You do not have the luxury of putting the responsibility onto someone else's shoulders. Your actions are your own. Choose."

But if I disobey—no, I couldn't do that.

"Then you have chosen. You have chosen cowardice."

How?

"You have chosen to save your own life and to kill millions of other people. You have chosen to protect yourself and to forfeit your values."

Under other circumstances—

"One's actions are all there are. Choices are meaningless unless they are acted upon."

So the anguish is that I refuse to let myself be punished?

"The anguish is revealed in your initial inability to imagine the possibilities available to you. Then the anguish is compounded by your inability to take responsibility for your actions."

Up Against the Wall.   Are you saying that the results of my choices determine their value? Isn't that like utilitarianism?

"It is not the result of your choices that gives them value, it is the choices themselves. For example, say you are placed in a situation where you can be either cowardly or courageous. Your choice itself, and acting on your choice, makes you a coward or a courageous person. Consequences have nothing to do with it."

How could that be?

"I have depicted this sort of situation in a short story, 'The Wall.' Imagine again that it is wartime. You are captured by soldiers of the enemy. They threaten to execute you if you do not tell them the location of the leader of the resistance unit of which you are a member. If you tell them the location and save your life, you make one statement in the book that is you. If you mislead the enemy and buy more time for your leader and for the resistance, you make a different entry into your book. In sacrificing your life, you make a very different statement. Choose. The consequences are irrelevant."

How can the results of my choice be irrelevant? You say that the choice creates the person I am. If I save my leader and sacrifice myself for the resistance, then my action has worth because my leader is saved and the resistance is not weakened. The results do matter.

"Look at the example again. Imagine that you choose to lie to the enemy. You tell them that the leader of the resistance is hiding in the village cemetery just south of town. In fact, earlier in the day the resistance leader told you he would be hiding at his cousin's house to the north of town."

Yes, saving the leader would be the aim of my action. The result is what gives the action its worth.

"Suppose that the fellow had a fight with his cousin and decided to leave his hideout. Imagine that he came to hide in the cemetery, in the grave-diggers' shack. He is captured and shot. Is your action any less heroic?"

But I chose to mislead the enemy! I lied to the soldiers!

"Exactly, and that is what makes your action courageous. The result is irrelevant. Look, there is never any guarantee that your action will succeed. There is never any guarantee that the resistance will succeed. That does not rob your action of its courage. Imagine an even more extreme possibility. Imagine that you die defending the resistance. It's heroic. However, you cannot foretell what will happen after your death. Your former comrades may decide that they have had enough fighting. They may even side with the enemy. They may see your death as the sign that resistance is futile."

You are cynical.

"Not at all. I am merely mapping out the possibilities, and each one is very real. No doubt each has happened many times. The point is that your action is courageous, and it has value because you chose and acted on it."

Oh, I see. You think that whatever I choose is good, from my perspective. Good is relative to each person. That's what you're advocating, isn't it?

"Yes and no. Your question is more subtle than you think."

IN CHOOSING MYSELF, I CHOOSE MAN

What if I chose cowardice? In your example, what if I chose cowardice? I decide that my life is worth more than all the resistance. I decide that I am more important than my comrades. Even you admit that they may go over to the other side. What if I choose to live?

"Then you choose for all humankind that people should act in cowardly, self-serving ways."

I knew you were going to say that. And to be honest, I have been waiting for this. I think the idea of being responsible for all humanity is a weakness in your theory.

"Excellent. Not only do your choices elicit anguish because they reflect who you are, anguish also involves all humanity. Understanding this is important to the existentialist perspective."

How am I choosing all of humankind when I choose myself?

"Every one of us must choose himself. Each of us must create who he is. That is part of what we mean when we say that man must choose himself. But we also mean that in making this choice he also chooses all men."

This is the part I do not understand.

"In creating the man that we want to be . . . we are creating an image of man as we think he ought to be."

Are you telling me that I somehow get to dictate people's values to them? If that's true, how can they be free?

"Existentialism does not advocate dictating people's values to them. It vigorously affirms individual freedom. For an individual to choose to be this or that, however, is to affirm at the same time the value of what we choose, because we can never choose evil."

Of course we can choose evil. People commit all kinds of heinous crimes against each other. Entire countries go to war and kill innocent children. People can be incredibly cruel. You don't call that evil?

"I do call that evil."

Then how can you say that we can never choose evil?

We Always Choose the Good. "We always choose the good, and nothing can be good for us without being good for all."

Hello? Hello? Somehow I don't think we are communicating very well. Maybe my philosopher resurrection machine is having electrical problems. The translator must be malfunctioning.

"I think I understand you. What's the problem?"

I know you are a great philosopher and all, but your statements are contradictory. You say that people can never choose evil, that they always choose good.

"Yes."

Then you agree with me that people have performed evil actions. Are you going to say that they weren't free when they acted so cruelly?

"That solution would get me out of the contradiction, but I reject it. People are free in all their actions, even in not choosing. If a person follows the orders of her government or of her commanding officer, she is free. I insist that her action is free, because she could have refused. There are always possibilities; there is always choice."

So people always freely choose their actions. And they always choose good and never evil. But we have people doing all kinds of evil things to each other, to animals, to the environment. How can you explain evil?

"When I say that man always chooses good and never evil, I mean that I am creating a certain image of man when I choose. Therefore, I am responsible for myself and for everyone else."

Oh, I see. You think that whatever you choose is good, from your perspective. You're a relativist! And you want to impose your values on everyone else.

Subjectivism and Simple Relativism.   "Not at all. I distinguish subjectivism and simple relativism. The simple relativist believes that each person has his own values, and that is the end of the story. Your values are yours; my values are mine; and the differences in values are like differences in tastes."

Isn't this your position?

"Not at all. I acknowledge that people do choose differently. Free choice is the essence of being human. However, simple relativism refuses to acknowledge responsibility. The existentialist affirms responsibility, not only for oneself, but for everyone. So I shall answer your questions more directly. Yes, values are relative to each person in that a person may choose a different plan of life. However, values are not merely relative, and no more can be told about them."

I'm still confused. Let me see if I can say why. I see that you want to avoid relativism. Okay, but how can my decisions be binding on others?

"Ah, so this is the difficulty. You believe that your actions are binding only on yourself. To make you take your choices seriously, you must see them in their proper light. An example may help. Suppose you are living by casually choosing your plan of life, your wants and fears, your values, and all the rest."

Involvement in Choice.   Casually choosing?

"Yes, for example, suppose that your sense of choice involves no one but you. Suppose further that you can change your plan of life at a moment's notice. That would be casually choosing. Casually choosing your plan of life does not sufficiently involve you in your choice."

What more do you want? I thought you wrote that our past choices do not have any effect on our present choices and actions. Isn't that correct?

"Yes, it would be bad faith, and a denial of freedom, to insist that the momentum from one's past forced one to similar choices in the future. The coward can change his life by choosing courage. The miser can become liberal and giving. Scrooge in Charles Dickens's "A Christmas Carol" is an example of such a transition. His choice was not a casual one; he chose for all humanity."

But Scrooge changed because he was visited by the three ghosts of Christmas.

"Ah, and this is another element of anguish. Who can deny that choice was involved here? As the story goes, Scrooge goes to bed and is awakened three times, each time by a different apparition. Look at the possible interpretations. Obviously, he could have been dreaming."

Or three angels of Christmas came to visit him.

"Let's take that interpretation. Even if three apparitions visited him, how did he determine that they were angels, that they were revealing the truth, that he should obey their directives? Choice goes so deep that one even chooses one's own interpretation of reality."

Okay, I get the point. But I still don't see how my choices apply to all humanity.

"Imagine that space creatures come to earth. Like all good biologists, they want to examine specimens to understand the life forms on earth. So they watch you. Each of your decisions and actions is recorded. You are acting not only for yourself, but as an example for all humanity."

Come on, Sartre, space creatures aren't going to come to earth to watch my actions.

"It's an example, Art. The point is, you always choose what you believe is the best way. You always choose according to your sense of the good. You always choose to act in ways consonant with your image of the best life. Therefore, your choices apply to all people."

FORLORNNESS

Perhaps. I need to think more about this. Let me ask about forlornness. When you say this, you mean "that God does not exist and that we have to face all the consequences of this." What consequences?

"Beginning late in the last century and running into this century, there has been an intellectual movement denying the existence of God. However, what this movement did was to keep all the values of the 'God-inspired' society—"

I don't understand. Could you put this into more personal terms?

"Good idea. I know people who are atheists."

Well, you say that you're an atheist, too.

"Yes, but there are differences in atheists' perspectives."

I thought all atheists believe that there is no God.

"Many atheists merely deny that a God exists. However, they struggle mightily with this both intellectually and emotionally. After all, for most people denying God's existence is emotionally difficult. Such a denial challenges all one's emotional attachments to family and friends who continue to believe."

I know people who would like intellectually to give up the idea of a God but who can't because their dead parents or grandparents were believers. Is that what you have in mind?

"Yes. Dead or living, parents and friends affect us, if we choose."

I'm sorry for interrupting again, but what does this have to do with existentialism?

"For many people who merely give up the belief in God, the values and viewpoint of religious morality are still binding. These people believe that nothing will be changed if God does not exist. They believe that God is an outdated hypothesis that will peacefully die off by itself. Yet they continue to live by the moral rules of their youth. Then there is a second group of atheists who go beyond denying God's existence."

I know a lot of people whose religious beliefs are intense. I don't think news of God's death is going to be taken so passively.

"Just the point. I think it is very distressing that God does not exist."

You do? Why?

"Because all possibility of finding values in a heaven of ideas disappears along with Him. We are left on a plane where there are only people. As Dostoevski said, 'If God didn't exist, everything would be possible.'"

Doesn't this allow us to be completely free? I mean, with no God, there are no restrictions.

"Nor can we find anything to cling to. We can't start making excuses for ourselves. That is what I mean when I say man is forlorn."

I don't quite get it. I think being completely unrestricted is good. I can do whatever I want!

"Before you leap into an ecstatic state of abandon, think what this means. If existence precedes essence, there is no explaining things away by reference to a fixed and given human nature. There is no determinism, man is free, man is freedom. What this means is that you must invent your own values and the image of humanity. You must invent these values completely by your own devices."

Okay. You warned me about this before.

"There's more to it. If God does not exist, we find no values or commands to turn to which legitimize our conduct. We are alone, with no excuses. The values that are you are completely up to you. For example, look how much you and your reader struggled to justify your particular values, and then morality generally. We are forlorn when we recognize that in creating our own life we are on our own, forlorn and lonely."

CONDEMNED TO BE FREE

So that is why you say we are condemned to be free.

"Yes. Once you exist, you are responsible for everything you do. You are completely and unavoidably responsible. You are responsible for every passion that sweeps you into action. You are responsible for every omen, because it is you who interprets the omen."

You don't make freedom sound as appealing as I once thought it was.

MORALITY IS CLOUDED

"To clarify the idea of forlornness, I've cited the example of one of my students. The boy was faced with the choice of leaving for England and joining the Free French Forces or remaining with his mother and helping her carry on."

I recall the example. What is your point?

"Who could help him choose? Christian doctrine speaks in generalities that support each action. No ethics book can tell him. Kantian ethics tells him to treat every person as an end, never merely as a means. But each alternative before him involves treating some people as means and others as ends."

How about utilitarianism? Can't he do what will bring the greatest good to the greatest number?

"How is he to know what will bring the most and the highest good? The future is always clouded. For example, how can he guarantee that joining the Free French Forces will have important results? He might make his way to England and arrive just as the war ends. Or he might make it to England, join the Free French, and be placed on some insignificant detail. Should he leave his mother so that he can be placed on garbage duty by the Free French Forces? Staying with his mother is just as uncertain. No, the effects of his actions are clouded. They give no indication of which alternative to choose."

I guess you would also say that the value of the results of his actions are also his choosing.

"Very good, you're showing promise. Mill argues for utility, but it is up to you to decide what utility consists in."

Feelings Are No Help in Choosing. Your student friend finally just trusted his instincts, his feelings. Isn't that the only way to go? I mean, I don't see any other options.

"But how is the value of a feeling determined? What gives your feeling value?"

I don't understand. I feel my feelings; that's what gives them value.

"The only way to determine the value of an affection is precisely to perform an act which confirms or denies it. Since you require a feeling to justify your act, you are in a vicious circle."

I don't agree. My feelings do motivate me to action.

"But it does not make sense to say that, for example, 'I love my mother enough to remain with her' unless I have remained with her. Art, look at all the people who idly speculate on their actions. Look how many heroes there would be if only they could be in the trenches with the troops. Look how many naive, self-deceptive boasts we feel. The only way to be able to say that you are moved by courage is to act courageously. The feeling itself is formed by the acts one performs."

What does this leave us with?

"I can neither seek within myself the true condition which will impel me to act, nor apply a system of ethics for concepts which will permit me to act."

I think I am feeling forlorn. The puzzle you present is irresolvable.

Choosing the Advisor Is Choosing the Advice. "Well, there are other attempts to resolve the dilemma. For example, someone may say of my student friend, 'At least, he did go to a teacher for advice.' "

Yes, that's true. If there is no other way to go, I suppose one can always seek advice.

"But choosing your advisor is involving yourself."

I don't get it.

"If someone seeking advice comes to me, Sartre, that person is pretty much aware of how I will answer. That person has chosen to seek advice from me, an atheistic existentialist, and not from a priest. So—"

I see, choosing your advisor *is* choosing the advice you'll get.

"The same reasoning applies to interpreting successes and failures in life. Each of us is responsible for his own interpretation. Forlornness implies that we ourselves choose our being. Forlornness and anguish go together."

And each happens because we are responsible, because of our complete freedom to choose. In that light, anguish and forlornness do not sound quite as hopeless as I first thought.

"Why? Did you think they implied hopelessness?"

They seemed to make us passive victims unable to live dignified lives. I think my interpretation was mistaken.

"Good."

DESPAIR

What about despair? What do you mean by this and why must I despair?

"As for despair, the term has a very simple meaning. It means that we shall confine ourselves to reckoning only with what depends upon our will, or on the ensemble of probabilities which make our action possible."

Simple? I don't understand at all. What do you mean?

"When we want something, we always have to reckon with probabilities. You cannot hope for something to happen. Hoping is an act which leaves the realm of possibilities that are beyond me. Possibilities are to be reckoned with only to the point where my action comports with the ensemble of these possibilities, and no further."

So you're saying that you should never bet on anything but yourself and what you are involved in?

"Right, I will always rely on . . . the unity of the party or a group in which I can more or less make my weight felt. But, given that man is free and that there is no human nature for me to depend on, I can not count on men whom I do not know by relying on human goodness or man's concern for the good of society."

And this attitude doesn't make you just give up?

"No. I should involve myself. . . . but I shall have no illusions and shall do what I can. Quietism is the attitude of people who say, 'Let others do what I can't do.'"

You are telling us to be much more active than that, right?

THERE IS NO REALITY EXCEPT IN ACTION

"You have to ask yourself about each issue and each decision, 'Where else can I be; what else can I be doing?' There is no reality except in action. Man is nothing else than his plan; he exists only to the extent that he fulfills himself; he is therefore nothing else than the ensemble of his acts, nothing else than his life."

I can see the importance of setting up a hierarchy of personal values. But I don't agree that people are nothing except their actions. How do you justify this? Or have I misunderstood?

"People resist this idea because it, too, places responsibility squarely on them. It removes the excuse that 'circumstances are against me.' There is no reality except in action. There really is no love other than one which manifests itself in a person's being in love. There is no genius other than one which is expressed in works of art."

This leaves most people with worthless lives!

"It prompts people to understand that reality alone is what counts."

Aren't you reducing a person to what he or she accomplishes? I think this is too narrow. I mean, a great artist may be a terrible person in other respects. And an average person may be wonderful as a family member, as a friend, and so on.

"Of course. A thousand other things will contribute toward summing him up. A man is nothing else than a series of undertakings. He is the sum, the organization, the ensemble of the relationships which make up these undertakings."

Are you denying the inner life?

"Inner life?"

Yes, the inner life. Are you suggesting that we are merely our behavior?

"I have already said that feelings are formed by the actions we perform. This does not address the point, however. The value of our feelings is determined by our actions. That's one point. If I claim to have a burning love deep within me, but I never act on it, then what is the sense, what is the value of that feeling?"

I see your point. And what is your second point?

"We are not merely the product of heredity, the workings of the environment, and society. I deny biological and psychological determinism."

That's great; what does it mean?

"A person is not the way he is because of physiological makeup. A coward is not cowardly because of a cowardly constitution. What makes cowardice is the act of renouncing or yielding."

TOTAL INVOLVEMENT

People aren't born cowards or heroes? Then what makes them that way? You say it cannot be their training or their environment. What's left?

"Actions. The person chooses to act in a cowardly or heroic way. You see, Art, what counts is total involvement. Some one particular action or set of circumstances is not total involvement."

Then no one can ever be described as a coward or a hero. At some later time the coward may act heroically, and vice versa.

"Exactly, and that is what we mean by freedom. That is the full force of freedom. Your destiny lies within you. We are dealing here with an ethics of action and involvement."

LONELINESS

Doesn't your insistence on complete human freedom make life pretty lonely? You even base your theory on Descartes's *cogito*: "I think; therefore, I exist." Doesn't that cut you off from other people?

"That's correct; my perspective does spring from Descartes's *cogito*. There we have the absolute truth of consciousness becoming aware of itself."

Huh?

"The one thing we know with certainty is the experience of being conscious, of existing as a conscious being. You ask if this commits the existentialist to a lonely existence. One discovers in the *cogito* not only himself but others as well."

How do you get this? If "I think; therefore, I exist" is true, it shows only that I exist. It does not show that others exist, too. The best we can say for others is that each person knows that he or she exists. Or have I missed something?

"Through the 'I think' we reach our own self in the presence of others, and the others are just as real to us as our own self."

Saying this is nice enough, but I just don't see how it follows.

"In order to get any truth about myself, I must have contact with another person."

Why?

"Well, what sense does it make to say that I am nasty or selfish or clever except that it is recognized by other people? For example, say you think you are adept at comedy. You tell your jokes to people and no one laughs. No one shows any sign of the least amusement. Undeterred, you continue to tell your jokes. You perform for a large number of people. No one finds any humor in your stories. In what sense could you be said to be adept at comedy?"

Maybe I'm just ahead of my time.

"Even if this were true, we wouldn't know that except for people's responses to you. People in the future would see the humor in your material. You only get truth about yourself in your contact with others."

HOW DO YOU KNOW OTHER PEOPLE EXIST?

Aren't you making a mistake here? Aren't you confusing an argument for other people's existence with how we know that other people exist?

"The two are identical. The man who becomes aware of himself . . . also perceives all others, and he perceives them as the condition of his own existence. The other is indispensable to my own existence as well as to my knowledge about myself."

I'm not following this very well. Maybe I can state my objection in a different way. At the heart of my objection is a worry that your subjectivism leads to relativism. So let me ask directly, are you a relativist?

"How do you mean? I assert a position that we call intersubjectivity; this is the world in which man decides what he is and what others are."

THE LIMITS OF THE HUMAN CONDITION

Yes, I understand that from our talk about responsibility. But you deny that there is a human nature. If there is no human nature, how can we ever understand other people?

"Good question. I'm glad you asked this. There does exist a human condition. What I mean by that is that there are limits which outline man's fundamental situation in the universe."

Finally, there is going to be a stable piece of ground to stand on!

"What does not change is the necessity of man to exist in the world, to be at work there, to be there in the midst of other people, and to be mortal there."

I knew that.

"We freely choose our existence with reference to the human condition. Every configuration—"

Huh?

"Oh, all I mean by that is how a person confronts, or denies, or wishes to pass beyond the limits."

I don't get it.

"Each person has his or her own strategy for living. Each of us approaches the limits of the human condition with different choices. That's freedom. That's what I mean by configuration, the way a person approaches the limits of the human condition. Every configuration, however individual it may be, has a universal value."

Here we go again. I understand you up to this point. We are all different. Each of us chooses to live differently. That's the kind of talk that leads me to think that you're a relativist. How does this talk of universal value fit in?

"Every attempt at living, every configuration has universality in the sense that it can be understood by every man."

Are you saying that I can understand the life of someone who lives in a completely different culture, and maybe in a different historical period? Are you saying that I can understand the point of view of the psychotic, of the serial killer?

"Yes, there is always a way to understand the idiot, the child, the savage, the foreigner, provided one has the necessary information."

Why do you say that?

"At heart, what existentialism shows is the connection between the absolute character of free involvement, by virtue of which every man realizes himself in realizing a type of mankind—"

Hold on. How does absolute involvement translate into an understanding of anyone else? If the other person is not involved in what I am involved in, how can I understand the other person?

"Involvement is always comprehensible in any age whatsoever and by any person whosoever, and the relativeness of the cultural ensemble which may result from such a choice."

Can you give me examples?

"Each of us performs an absolute act in breathing, eating, sleeping, or behaving in any way whatever. There is no difference between being free . . . and being absolute."

I'm at a loss. All you are saying is that people share common physical needs. Is that all it means to understand the other person?

"It means that we need not be thoroughly isolated from others. It means we can cross historical and cultural boundaries and understand people from beyond those boundaries."

This "connection" is not very intimate, or so it seems. But let's move on to objections.

EXISTENTIALISM DOES NOT ADVOCATE CAPRICE

I understand that existentialism does not advocate caprice. All my actions emerge from choice. So although my actions may look capricious, they are reflections of me.

"If I in any way assume responsibility for a choice . . . this has nothing to do with caprice. Ethics, like art, involves invention and creativity, but it is unfair to say this is capricious."

Okay, and I agree that your emphases on total involvement and responsibility make it absurd to charge your theory with arbitrariness of choice. But—

ARE WE ABLE TO PASS JUDGMENTS ON OTHERS?

"But we are unable to pass judgment on others. That's your objection, isn't it?"

Yes.

"One can still pass judgment, for, as I have said, one makes a choice in relationship to others."

But that just means that I choose from the plan of life I have adopted. There isn't any way of deciding which plan is better?

"First, one can judge (and this is perhaps not a judgment of value, but a logical judgment) that certain choices are based on error and others on truth."

Consistency is desirable, but I was looking for something more substantial. What is the best life? Can you tell me what it is?

"If we have defined man's situation as a free choice, with no excuses and no recourse, every man who takes refuge behind the excuse of his passions, every man who sets up a determinism, is a dishonest man."

Okay, put to the side all logical and factual errors. And we admit complete honesty in our choice. So our attitude is strictly coherent. What constitutes the best life?

FREEDOM IS THE BASIS OF ALL VALUES

"Freedom is the basis of all values."

What do you mean?

"The ultimate meaning of the acts of honest men is the quest for freedom as such. We want freedom for freedom's sake and in every particular circumstance."

Ah, Sartre, you have been hiding a value all along. Your theory's ultimate value is freedom.

"In wanting freedom, we discover that it depends entirely on the freedom of others and that the freedom of others depends on ours."

Are you defining humanity as dependent on one another?

"No, but as soon as there is involvement, I am obliged to want others to have freedom at the same time that I want my own freedom."

You're assuming that people are alike, at least with respect to freedom. I know you are struggling to avoid loneliness and complete isolation between people. But you are defining humans as essentially free. You are saying that humans have a nature, which is to be free.

"I've recognized that man is a being in whom existence precedes essence, that he is a free being who . . . can want only his freedom."

And that allows you to judge other people?

"I may pass judgment on those who seek to hide from themselves the complete arbitrariness and the complete freedom of their existence. Therefore, though the content of ethics is variable, a certain form of it is universal."

And what is that, as if I don't know?

"The one thing that counts is knowing whether the inventing that has been done has been done in the name of freedom."

BUT WHICH WAY DOES FREEDOM TELL ME TO ACT?

But which way does freedom tell me to act? Take your example of the guy who couldn't decide whether he should stay with his mother or go off to fight for the Free French. If morality and religion are at fault for being vague in concrete circumstances, how is your value of freedom any less vague? Telling me to choose freely doesn't give me any direction.

"Admittedly, but at least the choice will be honest, consistent, and free. At least you will be creating your own life in inventing your own values."

But what if someone freely chooses to be cruel?

"That is possible. All we can judge is whether or not he chose in the name of his freedom and the freedom of other people."

Ah, now I see why you're emphasizing our relation to others. If I have to take others into account, as a reflection of my own reality, then my freedom restricts me in certain ways.

"Yes."

Then I think a lot more needs to be said to ensure that the connection you claim does exist.

"Your Chapter 12 will give you a chance to understand the connections more fully."

I will look at the discussion. But before you leave, could you tell me one more thing? Do you think life is meaningful or absurd?

"Before you come alive, life is nothing; it's up to you to give it a meaning, and value is nothing else but the meaning that you choose."

So the best life is—?

"The life plan freely chosen."

I guess you're right; choosing the advisor is choosing the advice. Thanks, Mr. Sartre. You have given me quite a lot to consider.

■

SUMMARY OF DISCUSSION

Sartre presents us with two unique insights on the human condition. There is no human nature. We are totally and irreversibly free. Although we often deny our freedom, Sartre contends that each person is nothing but what she makes of herself. Each action, each value, each belief is freely chosen. What this means is that each person is the author of his or her own life. Clearly, we do not choose the century, the country, or the class we are born in. Nor do we choose our parents. We do, however, choose our attitudes toward these "givens."

Recognizing our total freedom is a terrifying burden. It is probably terrifying because morality has convinced us that values are independent of us. Now, however, Sartre shows us that each person is responsible and independent. If you live by a certain set of values, then you are responsible for them. After all, in choosing your advisor, you choose your advice.

One of Sartre's best insights is embodied in his example of the young man who cannot decide whether he should stay with his mother, or go off to join the Resistance. Sartre claims that our freedom forces us to choose between conflicting values and desires. No moral or religious principle is going to help us resolve such dilemmas. Neither Mill's utilitarianism nor Kant's categorical imperative helps. Religion is too general when it comes to real-life cases. Sartre says we must simply choose. It is our choice and action that creates the value. Freedom is the basis of all values and the prerequisite of human existence.

Sartre is probably correct when he forces us to confront our own responsibility and freedom. His idea that religion and morality are vague, and therefore unhelpful, is to the point. Sartre's own instruction—simply to choose—is not adequate, however. On what basis does one choose? What is lacking is a determination of the point of choosing. If my actions are directed toward pleasure, then I know what counts as a good choice. If loneliness is the defining problem, then a very different set of choices is appropriate.

By telling us to be free, Sartre is not advocating caprice. Freedom defines the human being. Freedom carries all the responsibility and importance of our human existence. If I choose to act in a cowardly way, then I am a coward. However, human freedom is radical. No previous action determines any subsequent action. Yesterday's coward can be today's courageous person. Choice and action are everything.

Finally, Sartre urges us to be totally involved. This is a remarkable insight that other moral theories overlook. In fact, Sartre is at his most insightful with ideas and concerns about our emotions and inner conflicts.

■
___

DISCUSSION HIGHLIGHTS

I. Existence precedes essence
   1. There is no human nature.
   2. Man is nothing else than what he makes of himself.
II. Choice and responsibility
   1. Choice brings anguish.
      a. we are condemned to be free
      b. each person is responsible for her own actions

      c. there are no excuses
    2. In choosing myself, I choose all mankind.
      a. each person always chooses what he or she believes is good
      b. each person is a representative of the entire human race
III. We are condemned to be free
    1. Abandonment: there is no God to direct our lives.
    2. Despair: we are alone in our lives, in our actions, in our existence.
    3. Anguish: we experience a profound responsibility for ourselves and for others.
    4. Alienation: we are separated from others.
    5. Total involvement: we can immerse ourselves in creating our own lives.

■

QUESTIONS FOR THOUGHT/PAPER TOPICS

1. Sartre says we experience anguish because we are responsible for all humankind. Explain his position and discuss how he defends it. Do you agree with him?

2. What does Sartre mean when he says we are condemned to be free?

3. If choice is the basis of all values, is every action permissible?

4. Can anyone make a choice without knowing what counts as a good choice? Does Sartre's emphasis on "total commitment" give any guidelines by which to live?

5. Sartre claims that moral and religious values are vague. They are unhelpful in real-life situations. What are his examples? Is Sartre's system any less vague and unhelpful?

6. According to Sartre, there is no human nature. What does he mean by this? Do you think there are human instincts and natural responses to events? Do you think emotions are natural or culturally determined? Do people choose their emotions?

7. Do you agree that there is no human reality except in human action? In what sense are we free except in our actions?

■

FOR FURTHER READING

The essay "Existentialism Is a Humanism" (Citadel, 1971) is the source of our discussion with Sartre. Sartre also wrote *Being and Nothingness* (Simon & Schuster, 1966). While this is an imposing book, you might want to look at his chapters on "Bad Faith," "Being and Doing: Freedom." I find his discussion of "existential psychoanalysis" very interesting. Another way to get into Sartre's point of view is to read one of his novels, short stories or plays, such as *Nausea* (New Directions, 1959), *The Wall* (New Directions, 1969), and *No Exit* (Random House, 1955).

THREE

Does Morality Answer the Questions?

Introduction

WHERE ARE WE GOING?

What is the best life? Is it living for pleasure? Is it living one of the versions of morality we have encountered? Is it best explained by Kant, by Mill, by Sartre, or by religions? Perhaps the conformity required by the Grand Inquisitor is really best. Maybe people don't want to be free and responsible. If you are like me, you are probably confused. We have looked at so many options of the best life that it's difficult to know how to decide which theory is most adequate. I think it is time to address our confusion.

MORAL OBJECTIVITY AND IMPARTIALITY

Morality requires that we internalize an impartial, objective "system" of belief. The moral point of view is essentially one in which we look at ourselves as one person among many moral equals. That doesn't mean that all people are equal in all ways, of course. But morality does require that each of us be thought of and treated with moral impartiality. So objectivity and impartiality are essential to morality.

Now you may ask what objection I could make against that? After all, it's only fair to ask that everyone abide by the same rules. That's a strength of morality. It's the feature that staves off chaos in society. If everyone follows the moral rules, then we will all be better off. At least that's what you thought when we started this book. Social stability, however, doesn't guarantee us the best life. It only promises to keep us away from the much worse life of chaos and fear.

CAN WE HAVE THE BEST OF EACH LIFE?

Is there a way to live that lets us fully experience the moment and at the same time keeps us living a life, and not just a series of chaotic, disjointed moments? Can we live *in* the here and now and still avoid a fragmented life? Can we be a part of our community without giving up our individuality? I think the answer to each of these questions is yes.

To see how we can find such a life, we need to look in two directions. We have already explored a number of traditional formulations of the moral point of view. First, we need to find and hold to the truths of each thinker we've read. Second, we need to ask: What is the value of moral values?

HOLD TO THE TRUTHS

What are the truths incorporated in each moralist's theory? Kierkegaard's A, Camus's Stranger, and even Mill assert that pleasure and intense experience are key elements in living the best life. At the same time, the Grand Inquisitor's insight rightly emphasizes our desire for security and certainty in our moral values. We want to be free of the dual anxieties of indecision and responsibility. When it comes to moral values, though, it would be better if we knew what made our rules correct.

Epictetus goes further. He tells us that our own pleasure is desirable, but self-control is better. Self-control is an important feature of the best life. Of course, the freedom Epictetus offers is not doing whatever we want. His freedom is a defense against being overwhelmed by one's external environment, or one's passions. Sartre's emphasis on freedom and self-determination endorses Epictetus' contribution.

Even after we wrestle with the questions of freedom, conformity, and good and bad, we are left wondering: What is the point of morality? Camus, Kierkegaard, Epictetus, Mill, Kant, Dostoevski, and Sartre all give impressive insights into what direction we want to go in our lives. We want to avoid boredom, and the dual anxieties of indecision and responsibility, and we want to experience our reality in an undistorted way.

WHAT'S THE VALUE OF MORAL VALUES?

Now we need to ask: What is the value of moral values? Perhaps morality is not the best way to live. From what we've seen, morality does not successfully eliminate boredom, anxiety, and guilt. Nor does morality adequately give meaning to our lives, or allow us to relate to others and to reality in an intimate and intense way. The aim of the final three discussions is to create a better version of the best life.

IS LIFE MEANINGFUL OR ABSURD?

Chapter 11 asks whether life is meaningful or absurd. This is an important question in its own right. As well, asking this question is a symptom of our dissatisfaction with the answers that moral philosophers produce in defining the best life. Here you will meet two of the ancient world's wisest people, Sisyphus and Solomon.

HOW CAN WE RELATE WITH OTHER PEOPLE?

Chapter 12 asks for alternate ways of relating with people. Here we resurrect Martin Buber. Although you probably have not heard of him, I think you will learn from his insights into the ways we experience and relate to others.

WHAT IS THE BEST LIFE?

Our final chapter is more of a "pointing" than a definitive answer to the question: What is the best life? Spinoza and Lao Tsu are two philosophers worth reading in full. Our more limited use of them, however, will be to draw out their conclusions on the best life. The "answers" given by Spinoza and Lao Tsu are interestingly similar. And yet Spinoza lived in seventeenth-century Holland and Lao Tsu lived in sixth-century B.C.E. China. Perhaps the question: What is the best life? transcends time and place. It is a uniquely human question. And if Spinoza and Lao Tsu are on the right track, then the answer to our question also transcends all the human differences that separate us.

C H A P T E R

ELEVEN

Is Life Meaningful or Absurd? The Wisdom of Solomon and Sisyphus

Is life meaningful? What does it mean to say that life is absurd? The two authors before us represent different approaches to our questions. In Ecclesiastes, Solomon laments the human condition as vain, meaningless, and futile. His answer to our meaningless existence is straightforward. "Fear God and keep his commandments. This is the whole duty of mankind." In *The Myth of Sisyphus*, Camus states that "the meaning of life is the most urgent of questions." He says that "there is but one truly serious philosophical problem, and that is suicide." Whether or not one commits suicide is one's response to the question of life's meaning.

HOW THE QUESTIONS ARISE

Before we talk to our time-traveling visitors, we ought to prepare ourselves. What circumstances raise the question of the meaning or absurdity of life? We ask about the meaning of life when our basic values and beliefs appear vague, or uncertain, or relative. We question life's meaning when we feel insignificant, or when our situation appears hopeless, or when our work is fruitless and unappreciated.

TWO GENERAL STRATEGIES

Our authors represent two general strategies to the question of the meaningful life. Not surprisingly, as part of the Bible, Ecclesiastes represents one reli-

Material in this chapter taken from *The Myth of Sisyphus and Other Essays* by Albert Camus, trans., J. O'Brien. Copyright © 1955 by Alfred A. Knopf, Inc. Reprinted by permission of the publisher.

gious reply to the question of meaning. Camus's *Myth of Sisyphus* is a nonreligious response. We need to be careful, of course, not to take too seriously the categories of the religious and the nonreligious. While Solomon clearly believes in his God, Camus's Sisyphus is an atheistic response in that Sisyphus' attitude places him above the gods. We'll look into this shortly. For now, let's turn to the religious alternatives.

SOLOMON'S LAMENT

Solomon's lament in Ecclesiastes affirms God's existence. Solomon is not convinced that there is an afterlife, however. Nor is he concerned with God's great and mysterious plan for the universe. Solomon's thoughts are more inwardly directed. He wants to know what this life offers. As the wisest man of ancient Israel, Solomon desires to know the purpose of his own life, not as a piece of the great unknown, but as a human being. Solomon does not believe that a longer life is necessarily a more meaningful, or fuller, or happier life. So an eternal life following this temporary stay on earth is not particularly appealing to him. Let's resurrect him now.

All is Vanity.   It is an honor to speak to the wisest of the ancient Hebrews.
  "Why?"
  Well, Mr. Solomon, because you must have a pretty good idea of what makes a life meaningful. Is the meaningful life a life of sensual pleasures, or fame, or wealth? Surely if anyone knows, you must.
  "Art, vanity of vanities! All is vanity."
  What does that mean?
  "Life is meaningless!"
  Why do you, the wisest of all ancient people, think that all is vain and hopeless?
  "Why do you insist on exaggerating the worth of my wisdom?"
  Isn't wisdom preferable to foolishness?
  "I gave my heart to know wisdom, and to know madness and folly; I perceived that this also is but a striving after the wind. For in much wisdom *is* much grief; and he that increases knowledge increases sorrow."
  But isn't one life better than the other? Isn't it better to know and understand the world than to live in it ignorantly?
  "The wise man's eyes are in his head; but the fool walks in darkness."
  So there is a difference.
  "And yet . . . one event happens to them all. When I perceived this I said to myself, 'As it happens to the fool, so it happens even to me: and why was I then more wise?' "
  But this can't be correct. Surely a wise person lives better than a fool!
  "This also is vanity. For there is no remembrance of the wise more than of the fool forever; seeing that which now is in the days to come shall be forgotten."
  What is the enduring fate that you speak of?

"How the wise man dies just like the fool, of course!"

So you believe that death robs life of its meaning?

"Yes. And when I realized this truth, I hated life, for the work that is wrought under the sun *is* grievous to me; for all is vanity and a striving after the wind."

The Pleasurable Life.   Are you suggesting that we live for the pleasure of the moment? This will come as a great shock to people.

"Once I said in my heart, 'Go now, I will prove thee with pleasure: therefore enjoy pleasure.' "

And did you? I mean as king you could do whatever you want.

"This also is vanity. I said of laughter, 'It is mad,' and of pleasure, 'What use is it?' "

That's it? You gave up after just thinking about pleasure?

"I sought in my heart to give myself over to wine—my heart still acquainted with wisdom—and to lay hold on folly, till I might see what was good for the sons of men, which they should do under heaven all the days of their life."

Wow! You became a "professional" pleasure seeker? As an experiment?

"I made great works, houses, vineyards, gardens, and orchards. I got servants and maidens, and had possession of great and small cattle. I gathered gold and silver; I got singers, and women singers, man's delight. I became great and increased more than all who were before me in Jerusalem: also my wisdom remained with me. I held not my heart from any joy for my heart rejoiced in all my labor."

How did this work out? I mean, is this the best life?

"All was vanity and a striving after the wind."

Isn't Work Meaningful?   Can you find any meaning in your work?

"What has man from all his labor, wherein he has labored under the sun?"

Are you saying that work doesn't accomplish anything? That we should not have goals?

"What has a man from all the labor and vexation with which he labors beneath the sun? For all his days are sorrow and his work is grief."

Think of all that you contribute to the people who come after you.

"Who knows whether the man who will come after me shall be a wise man or a fool? Yet he will have rule over all my labor and where I showed myself wise. This is vanity."

I see what you mean. Nothing and nobody lasts. Life is transitory, unsatisfying, and boring. In life there is nothing novel. Even our work comes to nothing. Accomplishments perish and are forgotten. Or used by strangers who may misuse our works. So there is no point in working?

"On the contrary, there is nothing better for a man than that he should eat and drink, and enjoy good in his labor."

Isn't this just what you denied? How can a person find joy in pleasures and work? You've just said it is all pointless!

"It is from the hand of God. For God gives to a man that is good in his sight, wisdom and knowledge and joy: but to the sinner he gives the work of gathering and heaping, that he may give to him that is good before God."

How do you know what pleases God?

"To every thing there is a season and a time to every purpose under heaven."

I know, a time to plant and a time to reap, a time to be born and a time to die. This sounds pretty cynical.

"What profit has the worker from his work? All of this is vanity and a striving after the wind."

Justice.   Is there no justice, Solomon? Aren't hard-working people compensated for their labors?

"I said in my heart that God might show men that they are but beasts. For that which befalls the sons of men befalls beasts. As one dies, so dies the other. They all have one breath, and man has no preeminence above a beast: all is vanity."

What about heaven? Don't you believe that good people go to heaven?

"All go to one place; all are of the dust, and all turn to dust again. Who knows whether the spirit of man goes upward and the spirit of the beast goes downward to the earth?"

What's left?

"There is nothing better than that a man should rejoice in his own works; for that is his portion."

This sounds so passive. Must people just live as they live? Isn't there any justice in the world? Aren't the oppressed rewarded and the evil punished?

"I considered all the oppressions that are done under the sun . . . the tears of the oppressed, and they had no comforter! On the side of their oppressors there was power."

What comfort can be brought to the oppressed?

Oppression and the Happiest Person.   "There was no one to comfort them. And I praised the dead who are already dead more than the living who are still alive, but better than both is he who has not yet been born, who has not seen the evil work that is done under the sun."

I don't understand. Are you saying that a person who is dead is better off than a person who is alive? Solomon, do you praise the dead and feel grief for the living who must witness the evil-doing of oppressing peoples? And you think that those who have not been born, and so have not witnessed oppression, are happier yet?

"That is just what I say. The living person must witness the evil and oppression that men commit. The dead who are already dead are spared that torture of the spirit."

And the happiest person is the one who has not been born?

"The person who has not yet been born does not experience the torture of which I speak. Neither does this person see the oppression now. Therefore, he is the most fortunate."

It sounds like the best life is the one where the person is never born! Is that what you are saying?

"Yes, all else is vanity and a striving after the wind."

What does that mean?

"All else is futile and pointless, a striving after that which cannot be caught."

Envy. "I considered all the right work, that for this a man is envied by his neighbor."

I know; it is vanity and a striving after the wind.

"The fool, the envious person, consumes himself in his attitude toward others. He removes himself from his companions, and suffers mightily."

What do you mean? What sort of person do you have in mind?

"A person who has no one, yet there is no end to all his labor: neither is his eye satisfied with riches. This also is vanity and a sore travail. Two are better than one. A threefold cord is not quickly broken."

Companionship, friendship, and loving relations are better than envy and the striving for wealth? Is that it?

"There is more. When you vow a vow to God, do not defer paying it; for he has no pleasure in fools. Pay what you have vowed."

How does this counter the injustice that we see?

Wealth. "If you see the oppression of the poor, and violent perverting of judgment and justice in a province, do not be amazed at the matter, for a high official is watched by a higher."

I wonder about this. The rich seem to prosper and the poor lead difficult lives.

"He who loves silver will not be satisfied with silver; nor he who loves abundance with increase. The sleep of the laborer is sweet, whether he eats little or much; but the abundance of the rich will not let him sleep."

It's better to be a poor worker than a rich person? You're saying that the rich person's excessive wealth troubles him? This is difficult to believe. It sounds like a rationalization. No, it sounds like a way of keeping oppressed people from doing anything about their lives.

"Why do you say this, Art?"

What you say makes it sound like the rich live a more troubled life than the poor. What better way to keep the poor in their place than by convincing them that it is the rich who suffer? It doesn't look like suffering from where I stand.

"Yet there is a grievous evil which I have seen under the sun: riches kept for the owners to their hurt. But those riches perish by evil travail."

Yeah, so?

"As he came forth of his mother's womb, naked shall he return to go as he came, and shall take nothing of his labor, which he may carry away in his hand."

But a rich person's time on earth is more comfortable! Surely you don't deny that!

"What profit has he that he labors for the wind, and all his days he eats in darkness, in much sorrow and wrath with his sickness?"

You aren't talking about material comforts, are you? You think rich people suffer, and are sick and filled with resentment. Is that it? Are you saying that the joys of this world are worthless?

Eat, Drink, and Be Merry.   "What I have seen to be good and to be fitting is to eat and to drink and to enjoy the good of all the labor that he takes under the sun all the days of his life."

So it isn't the wealth or poverty, it's our attitude toward our work—or our labor, as you call it.

"Every man also to whom God has given riches and wealth and power to enjoy them, and to take his portion and to rejoice in his labor—this is the gift of God."

Then the key is to work and to live—

"With joy in his heart. What else is there to life than joy in living it? For who can tell a man what will be after him under the sun?"

Quiet Despair.   It sounds to me like you are inviting people to remain in a state of quiet despair. You concentrate so much on death that you leave little room for the joys of life. How do you answer that?

"The day of death is better than the day of birth. It is better to go to the house of mourning than to go to the house of feasting. Sorrow is better than laughter, for by sadness of the countenance the heart is made better."

You don't think this is depressing? This is more stoic than Epictetus!

"Perhaps, yes, a man must deal with the inevitable. In the day of prosperity be joyful, and in the day of adversity consider; God also has set the one over against the other, to the end that man should find nothing after him."

What are you directing us to do? How are we to live?

"He who fears God shall come forth of them all."

This doesn't help much. What does it mean? Is the perfect life living always according to your God's laws?

"There is not a just man on earth who does good and never sins."

Then what is the best life, Solomon?

"Be not righteous over much, and do not make yourself overwise; why should you destroy yourself? Be not wicked over much, neither be foolish; why should you die before your time?"

Nothing in excess; that's your formula for the best life?

Enjoy Life, for Death Comes to Us All.   "Go, eat your bread with joy and drink your wine with a merry heart. Let your garments be always white. Enjoy life with the wife whom you love, all the days of your vain life."

How can I enjoy my vain life knowing that everything is for nothing? You force me to think about the futility of living and working, then you tell me to enjoy it? How can I?

"Whatever your hand finds to do, do it with your might."

Is There No Value We Can Endorse?   Solomon, doesn't hard work pay off?

"The race is not to the swift, nor the battle to the strong, nor bread to the wise, nor riches to the intelligent, nor favor to the men of skill; but time and chance happen to them all."

Then is there no value we can endorse?

"Wisdom *is* better than strength. The words of wise men are heard in quiet more than the cry of a ruler among fools."

So wisdom is a virtue, an excellence that you believe in? Is the wise person better than the foolish?

"When the fool walks by the way, his wisdom fails him, and he says to every one that he is a fool."

Huh?

"A fool also is full of words; a man cannot tell what is to be. The labor of a fool wearies everyone. The foolish person's life lacks enjoyment because it lacks concentration."

Aren't we back to a quietism, an acceptance of what is? You say that we should accept whatever happens, but that is a depressing way to live.

"Light is sweet, and it is pleasant for the eyes to behold the sun. But if a man lives many years, and rejoice in them all, yet let him remember the days of darkness; for they will be many. All that comes is vanity."

So live life, for someday we will die? Is that your message? Live for the brief time we have, for death lasts forever?

"Yes. The conclusion of the matter is this. Fear God, and keep his commandments; for this is the whole duty of man."

Death Robs Life of Its Meaning?   So you think that death robs life of its meaning?

"Assuredly, Art. I would gladly trade places with you and live your life! Not because you are particularly worthy, but because you are alive. And except for the brief moments that your resurrection machine sustains me, I am dead, and will always remain so."

What if your religious descendants are correct? What if you do live forever? Would you be happier? Would eternal life make it meaningful?

"As I have already said, a man cannot know whether life is eternal, whether men rise and animals descend. What we have to go on is what we see in this life. Men return to the dust from which they spring. That is the only truth we see."

Solomon, you sound remarkably like the existentialist who gets criticized in our discussion with Sartre. Would you mind if I distill our talk to a few brief statements?

"Proceed."

You say that life is meaningless because each of us will die.

"Yes, all is a torture of the spirit. The more one lives and enjoys life's experiences, the more one realizes the pain of impending death."

Okay, and you also say that God acts in ways that we cannot always understand.

"Nor do we always approve of God's actions. That is why we despair over the injustice practiced against the oppressed."

What you're saying is that reality goes on as it does. There is little we can do to understand, or at least to change reality, so we might as well—

"Deal with the inevitable. In the day of prosperity be joyful, and in the day of adversity consider; God also has set the one over against the other, to the end that man should find nothing after him."

Then death and the unchangeable laws of science are what drive you to believing that life is vain?

"Yes. And now I must leave, Art. I have remained here too long."

Thank you, and goodbye, King Solomon. You have given me a great deal to think about living and about dying.

SISYPHUS' IMMORTALITY

Camus's *Myth of Sisyphus* gives an example of the meaningless life. According to Greek legend, Sisyphus is condemned to roll a rock ceaselessly to the top of a mountain. When his chore is accomplished, the rock rolls back to the valley below, where Sisyphus must return to begin the process again.

"They had thought with some reason, Art, that there is no more dreadful punishment than futile and hopeless labor."

Why is this such a horrible punishment? Because it lasts forever? You live forever. Your burden, your punishment, depends on your eternal life and your unending, eternal task. Isn't that it?

"Certainly not. Immortality is one of humanity's greatest hopes."

Then, Sisyphus, it must be the immensity of the stone and the struggle required. Is that it? You have to exert all your strength against the huge rock?

"It does require the whole effort of my body striving to raise the huge stone, to roll it and push it up a slope a hundred times over; my face screwed up, my cheek tight against the stone, my shoulder bracing the clay-covered mass, my foot wedging it, each fresh start with my arms outstretched. But that is not the torment."

Then what is the punishment, if not the endless struggle?

Nothing Comes of It. "Nothing comes of it."

I don't understand.

"The punishment given me by the gods is pointless activity. I am not even saved by death. The task they have given me is endless repetition serving absolutely no purpose, except punishment."

Isn't this the same "punishment" that Solomon describes? People toil under the sun, but for no purpose? It's just that yours is endless toil.

"Nothing comes of my toil. I do not even receive credit toward my punishment. There is no success; not even small goals are reached. At first I would mentally place markers along the climb. I would cheer myself by reaching each marker."

Did your little goals keep you going? Did you feel better for reaching them?

"At first, yes."

What went wrong?

"The prospect of endlessly achieving pointless short-term goals fails after a brief time. I was merely deceiving myself. There is no point to goals, long-term or short-term."

Crime. Perhaps I can get a handle on your punishment if I can understand the crime. What did you do?

"I was accused of a certain levity in regard to the gods."

How so?

"I stole their secrets. I tricked Aesopus into giving water to the citadel of Corinth."

You chose water and risked the gods' wrath!

"Homer tells of another crime. I had Death put in chains. Pluto could not endure the sight of his deserted, silent empire. So he dispatched the god of war, who liberated Death."

And you were punished for your hatred of Death?

"Yes. There is a third charge against me. When I was about to die, I wanted to test my wife's love. It was rash, but that is part of my nature."

How is it a crime to test your wife's love?

"I ordered her to cast my unburied body into the middle of the public square."

Gross.

"Even more detestable in my culture, where burial is a sacred right of a good man. When I awoke in the underworld, I was annoyed by an obedience so contrary to human love. Imagine!"

What did you do?

"I obtained permission from Pluto to return to earth to chastise my wife. The gods understand love and the indignity done to me."

I'm getting a sense of why you were considered the wisest and most prudent of mortals. Convincing Pluto to release you from death is certainly clever. But if you had permission to go, where's the problem?

"When I had seen the face of this world, enjoyed water and sun, warm stones and the sea, I no longer wanted to go back to the infernal darkness."

I'm sure there were recalls, anger and warnings from the gods, especially from Pluto.

"Oh, yes, but many years more I lived facing the curve of the gulf, the sparkling seas, and the smiles of the earth. Life is so full. Every experience is vital and intense. I could not willingly return to the darkness."

The gods must have been very angry!

"A decree of the gods was necessary. Mercury came and seized me by the collar, snatching me from my joys."

And Punishment. Then your crime was—

"A passionate desire to live, to feel, to experience every morsel of reality. I hate Death. I love living, experiencing, breathing, tasting, seeing, hearing, thinking, feeling—all the senses. That is my crime!"

You were sentenced to futile and hopeless labor for being passionate? For really living?

"My scorn of the gods, my hatred of death, and my passion for life won me the unspeakable penalty in which the whole being is exerted toward accomplishing nothing. This is the price that must be paid for the passions of this earth."

What punishment could be more dreadful? I guess Solomon was mistaken. Death is not the worst outcome of a person's life. Eternal, pointless repetition is worse. How do you deal with this torture?

Consciousness. "Consciousness. At each conscious moment when I leave the heights and gradually sink toward the lair of the gods, I am superior to my fate. I am stronger than my rock."

But if you were not conscious, there would be no torture. The tragedy is in the fact of your awareness of your punishment.

"No, Art. The lucidity that constitutes my torture at the same time crowns my victory. There is no fate that cannot be surmounted by scorn."

But your punishment is so unusual, so extreme. How does awareness make it more bearable?

"The workman of today works every day in his life at the same tasks, and this fate is no less absurd. It is tragic only at the rare moments when one becomes conscious."

You make us sound pathetic. Can't we change anything?

"I, too, am powerless, but I am a proletarian of the gods. I am their better because I am rebellious. I know the whole extent of my wretched condition."

A powerless worker can be better than her masters, just by being rebellious? Just by knowing how things are?

Sorrow and Joy. What about on your descent? What do you think about?

"Sometimes my descent is performed in sorrow. When the images of earth cling too tightly to my memory, when the call of happiness is too insistent, it happens that melancholy rises in a man's heart; this is the rock's victory, this is the rock itself. The boundless grief is too heavy to bear."

Are you saying that there's no way to overcome the despair of a meaningless existence? Isn't there any way to combat the sorrow?

"Yes, the descent can also be performed in joy."

How?

"Crushing truths perish from being acknowledged, Art. Do you know the story of Oedipus?"

No, not really.

"Oedipus was destined to murder his father and marry his mother. The seers told his parents of his fate. To protect themselves and Oedipus from this terrible fate, they had the infant secretly taken to another couple in another province. The other couple raised Oedipus as their own son. He grew to adulthood believing that his 'adoptive' parents were his only family. Then Oedipus discovered that his fate 'required' the deeds predicted at his birth."

What did he do?

"Oedipus fled his homeland. He believed that if he left his parents and journeyed far away, he would avoid the horrible acts that were his fate."

Did it work?

"Well, Oedipus did not kill his adoptive father or marry his adoptive mother. But, journeying far from home, he did come upon a man. They argued and Oedipus killed the man."

His real father?

"Yes, though Oedipus did not know it. On he traveled. He came to a city. After solving a riddle presented by a Sphinx that was plaguing the city, Oedipus married the widowed queen of the city."

No way—his mother?

"His mother. They lived happily and prosperously. Then the truth was revealed to Oedipus."

What did he do?

"Horrified, he gouged out his eyes."

Where do you find joy in this story?

"Oedipus at the beginning obeys fate without knowing it. But from the moment he knows, his tragedy begins."

I thought you said that "crushing truths perish from being acknowledged." This one sure didn't perish. In fact, the tragedy begins only when he discovers the truth.

"Yet at the same moment, blind and desperate, he realizes that the only bond linking him to the world is the cool hand of a girl, his daughter."

Of course, she loves him. And I understand that she will care for him and be his eyes. But how is this joyful?

"A tremendous remark rings out from Oedipus: 'Despite so many ordeals, my advanced age and the nobility of my soul make me conclude that all is well.'"

All is well! Has he gone mad? Here's a guy who has lived his entire life hoping to avoid a terrible fate. And yet, although each of his actions is well intended, even heroic, each action leads him directly to his fate. What a terrible, joyless life. Nothing he desired happened. Everything he intended to avoid, he found. How can he conclude that all is well?

Absurd Victory.   "Oedipus gives the recipe for the absurd victory. Happiness and the absurd are two sons of the same earth. They are inseparable."

What do you mean by the absurd?

"In a world suddenly divested of illusions and lights, man feels an alien, a stranger."

And you're saying that the illusion is what?

"In Oedipus' case the illusion is that he has mastered, or at least escaped, his fate. His illusion is that his life is happy and meaningful. His exile is without remedy since he is deprived of the memory of a lost home or the hope of a promised land."

Okay, Oedipus cannot go back home. That's his problem; he is home. And he cannot hope for a better future. His past has dictated the rest of his life. But what is the absurdity? What is the illusion that the rest of us live with?

"This divorce between man and his life, the actor and his setting, is properly the feeling of absurdity."

Then the problem isn't that our lives are meaningless?

"It often happens that those who commit suicide were assured of the meaning of life."

What causes a person to go on living? From my conversation with Solomon and you, I can't see why people even bother to live. Take Oedipus as an example. What kept him going? What makes him say that all is well? How did he overcome the divorce between himself and his entire life? How did he bridge his separation from reality?

"In a man's attachment to life there is something stronger than all the ills in the world. The body's judgment is as good as the mind's, and the body shrinks from annihilation. Of course, intelligence, too, tells me that the world is absurd."

The Absurd Battle.   Look, Mr. Sisyphus, that doesn't tell me enough. What do I need to battle against the absurd? What do I have to do in order to fight against the absurd?

"Struggle implies a total absence of hope (which has nothing to do with despair), a continual rejection (which must not be confused with renunciation), and a conscious dissatisfaction (which must not be compared to immature unrest). Everything that destroys, conjures away, or exorcises these requirements (and, to begin with, consent which overthrows divorce) ruins the absurd and devaluates the attitude that may then be proposed."

What do you mean?

"The absurd has meaning only insofar as it is not agreed to. 'I conclude that all is well,' says Oedipus, and that remark is sacred."

How so?

"It teaches that all is not, has not been, exhausted. It drives out of this world a god who had come into it with dissatisfaction and a preference for futile sufferings. It makes of fate a human matter, which must be settled among men."

This is where you find your joy—in your suffering?

"My joy is contained therein. My fate belongs to me."

DIVORCED FROM LIFE

I know you said it already, but what do you mean by *absurd?*

"This divorce between man and his life, the actor and his setting, is properly the feeling of absurdity."

What divorce?

"Men, too, secrete the inhuman. At certain moments of lucidity, the mechanical aspects of their gestures, their meaningless pantomime makes silly everything that surrounds them. A man is talking on the telephone behind a glass partition; you cannot hear him, but you see his incomprehensible dumb show: you wonder why he is alive."

Can you explain this differently?

"This world in itself is not reasonable, that is all that can be said. But what is absurd is the confrontation of this irrational and the wild longing for clarity whose call echoes in the human heart. The absurd depends as much on man as on the world. For the moment it is all that links them together. It binds them one to the other as only hatred can weld two creatures together. This is all I can discern clearly in this measureless universe where my adventure takes place."

What brings you to this awareness?

"The 'why' arises and everything begins in that weariness tinged with amazement. Weariness comes at the end of the acts of a mechanical life, but at the same time it inaugurates the impulse to consciousness."

It's your very punishment that has made you aware?

"Yes. The mechanical life of pressing against the rock brings lucidity as I pause and turn to walk down the mountain. Likewise, the absurd man, when he contemplates his torment, silences all the idols."

Idols?

"All of the illusions that bring him false hopes; all of the false senses of meaning that bear him through the mundane monotony; all of the values that shield him from awareness of the separation between himself and the world."

You want us to get rid of the distortions and distractions in moral thinking, don't you?

"In the universe suddenly restored to its silence, the myriad wondering little voices of the earth rise up. There is no sun without shadow, and it is essential to know the night."

I have to see reality for what it is? Even the frightening parts of it?

"The absurd man says yes and his effort will henceforth be unceasing. If there is a personal fate, there is no higher destiny, or at least there is but one which he concludes is inevitable and despicable."

What good comes from this knowledge? Why should I want to be aware of my separation from reality? It all sounds terrifying.

"The absurd man knows himself to be the master of his days. At that subtle moment when man glances back over his life, my return to my rock, in that slight pivoting he contemplates that series of unrelated actions which becomes his fate, created by him, combined under his memory's eye and soon sealed by his death."

How can you say that fate is a series of unrelated actions?

"They are related only in that I have acted them."

Look at any biography. Surely there is a line of action that follows from childhood right through the person's life until the person reaches her goal. A great dancer shows signs of musical interest from childhood. She enters dance class, drives herself, and succeeds. Or a businesswoman thinks creatively as a child. She later enters college, takes design and engineering classes, and goes on to become chief design engineer for a major manufacturer. And yet you call these actions unrelated?

"Another illusion to dispel the absurd. The biography is written after the person's fate has been sealed with his death. Only after the fact can we use our memories or imagination to draw a thread connecting the person's actions. But I assure you, at the time of the actions, they were totally unrelated to the person. More to the point, however, is the wholly human origin of all that is human."

Everything is absurd, connected only by our wishes and illusions, by our basic beliefs and attitudes.

"Yes, great feelings take with them their own universe, splendid or abject. They light up with their own passion an exclusive world in which they recognize their climate. The universe is a universe of jealousy, of ambition, of selfishness, or of generosity."

It is my universe to make as I desire?

"I am back at the foot of my mountain, and so I must leave you now. One always finds one's burdens again. But you, too, can find a higher fidelity that negates the gods and raises rocks. All *is* well."

Haven't you reduced this life to meaningless drudgery?

"The universe henceforth without a master seems to me neither sterile nor futile. Each atom of my stone, each mineral flake of this night-filled mountain, in itself forms a world. The struggle itself toward the heights is enough to fill a man's heart."

Then one must imagine Sisyphus happy.

■

SUMMARY OF DISCUSSION

Is life meaningful or absurd? In this chapter we speak to two "wise" men from ancient history, King Solomon and Sisyphus. Each believes that living can be meaningless, but for different reasons.

Solomon laments that death robs our life of meaning. He says that all that we do and accomplish is vain and futile. Both the pleasure-seeking life and the productive life are pointless. We will join the animals in the ground, and nothing follows death. He sees that the world is not just. People are oppressed and their oppressors thrive. Wise people are not revered for their wisdom, nor does hard work receive ample payment. The happiest person is the one who has never lived.

Even wealth is a torment, and the rich do not sleep well at night. So eat, drink, and find enjoyment in the everyday things. Since nothing brings meaning, just live in the momentary pleasures that life offers. There are no enduring values. Only if death were not total annihilation of the person would life be worth living. So, Solomon concludes somewhat puzzlingly, obey God's laws.

The example of Sisyphus is a reply to Solomon. Sisyphus does get to live beyond his death. His punishment depends on his immortality. His crime is that he lived too intensely. He enjoyed life fully. His punishment is that he must perform a task that cannot be accomplished. Nothing comes of it.

Sisyphus' only salvation from a meaningless existence comes in his moments of full consciousness. He becomes free, and surmounts his fate, when he knowingly chooses to perform his task. He is free when he willingly returns to his task. It is the doing and not the accomplishment of his task that brings him victory. When he is no longer divorced from his project, then he lives. So Sisyphus' "crime" is also his formula for victory. Living and acting passionately and with total involvement crown his life. "The struggle itself toward the heights is enough to fill a man's heart." One must imagine Sisyphus happy. He has learned to relate to himself, to others, and to reality.

■

DISCUSSION HIGHLIGHTS

   I. Is life meaningful or absurd? How the question arises.
     1. Values are uncertain.
     2. We experience our insignificance.
     3. Our work is unappreciated and fruitless.
  II. Solomon's lament
     1. All is vanity.
     2. Pleasure and work are both meaningless.
     3. The world has no justice.
     4. Wealth is transitory and a problem unto itself.
     5. It is better to eat, drink, and find momentary enjoyment.
     6. Death comes to us all and robs life of meaning.
     7. So obey God's laws.
 III. Sisyphus' immortality
     1. Death does not rob life of meaning.
     2. Meaninglessness occurs when nothing comes of one's actions.
     3. Living passionately and fully is our crime.
     4. Meaningless, passionless, alienated work is the punishment.
     5. Consciousness of our life offers promise.
     6. The absurd victory is found in lucidity and involvement.
     7. We need to learn to relate better to ourselves, to others, and to reality.

■

QUESTIONS FOR THOUGHT/PAPER TOPICS

1. Solomon declares that all is vanity. Can one's work be meaningful? How about one's relationship with family and friends?

2. Remember Joe the Mesopotamian from Chapter 5? Was his life meaningful? In what ways was it worthwhile?

3. Solomon says that the happiest person is the one who was never born. Why does he say this? Do you agree? (By the way, oops! it's too late; you were already born. Sorry.)

4. Why does Solomon say that life is meaningless? Is it because we are going to die and become "dust" in the wind? How would Sisyphus reply?

5. Sisyphus gets to live forever, yet his punishment is meaningless activity. Is a life meaningless if it involves pointless repetition?

6. Sisyphus claims what he calls an "absurd victory" over the gods and over his burden. What does he mean by this?

7. Sisyphus says that "the divorce between man and his life . . . is properly the feeling of absurdity." How does he recommend that we dispel the absurd and live genuinely human lives?

■

FOR FURTHER READING

Obviously, you ought to read Camus's *The Myth of Sisyphus and Other Essays* (Vintage, 1955). Camus is one of the most insightful philosophers and best writers of our century. Read Ecclesiastes, too. You can find it in any Bible. There are other interesting discussions of life's meaning. *The Meaning of Life* (Prentice-Hall, 1980), by Steven Sandars and David Cheney, has a strong list of readings. Two other good works are by psychologists. Take a look at Viktor Frankl's *Man's Search for Meaning* (Beacon, 1963). A truly wonderful book about a true champion in living is *Zorba the Greek*, by Nikos Kazantzakis. You'll love Zorba once you understand him.

C H A P T E R

TWELVE

How Can We Relate with Other People? A Talk with Martin Buber

In our conversations with Solomon and Sisyphus we were told that life is absurd. They say that we are divorced from our life. We are out of touch with ourselves, separated from other people and from reality. In this chapter we are going to examine the separation. In *I and Thou* Martin Buber's analysis takes us beyond the despair and resignation of Solomon. In what follows, Buber will suggest not only the nature and cause of our separation, but also a way to avoid absurdity in living. If our talk with Solomon and Sisyphus was a bit disheartening, our conversation with Buber should bring us optimism.

I-THOU, I-IT

Welcome, Mr. Buber. Could you help me? For example, what is the difference between I-It and I-Thou?

"To man the world is twofold, in accordance with his twofold attitude."

I can have two attitudes toward the world? Kind of like there are two sets of things in the world, the ones I care about and the ones I am indifferent toward. Is that it?

"Primary words do not signify things, but they intimate relations."

Relations? Well, I guess I relate to the different types of things in different ways. Am I getting warm?

"Not quite, Art. The primary words are not isolated words, but combined words. The one primary word is the combination I-Thou. The other primary word is the word combination I-It."

Yeah, so?

"The I of the primary word I-Thou is a different I from that of the primary word I-It. If Thou is said, the I of the combination I-Thou is said along with it. If It is said, the I of the combination I-It is said along with it."

But there is only one me! How could I be different just because of what I relate to?

"There is no I taken in itself, but only the I of the primary word I-Thou and the I of the primary word I-It."

The Attitude of Man is Twofold. Oh, wait a minute. It's the same I! You mean that "the *attitude* of man is twofold."

"Just as I have already said, yes."

And if I relate to things with one attitude and not the other, then my sense of them will be different. But different in what way?

"The primary word I-Thou can only be spoken with the whole being. The primary word I-It can never be spoken with the whole being."

So, depending on my attitude, I experience things differently. Sometimes I experience things as inner experiences and sometimes as outer experiences. Is that what you mean? Some things I experience more deeply than other things?

"If we add 'inner' to 'outer' experiences, nothing in the situation is changed. Inner things or outer things, what are they but things and things!"

I really don't get it, Mr. Buber. What am I supposed to experience when I experience something?

"The life of human beings . . . does not exist in virtue of activities alone which have some *thing* for their object."

Okay?

"Art, like you, I perceive something. I am sensible of something. I imagine something. I will something. I feel something. I think something. The life of human beings does not consist of all this and the like alone. This and the like together establish the realm of It."

What else is there?

"The realm of Thou has a different basis. When Thou is spoken, the speaker has no thing for his object. When Thou is spoken, the speaker has no thing; he has indeed nothing. But he takes his stand in relation."

Are you saying that there is more than just experiencing the world?

"Man experiences his world. What does that mean? Man travels over the surface of things and experiences them. He extracts knowledge about their constitution from them. He experiences what belongs to the things. But the world is not presented to man by experiences alone. These present him only with a world composed of It and He and She and It again."

The In-Between. What's wrong with experiencing that way?

"The man who experiences has no part in the world. For it is 'in him' and not between him and the world that the experience arises."

Oh, I think I'm starting to understand. You're saying that I can distort reality by what's in me. If I am angry, then my perception of the world will be different than if I am happy. In that way, experiences arise in me. So I have no part in the world because my interpretation of the world is in me, in my moods.

"Yes, well done."

And now you're saying that the hyphen is important in your I-Thou, I-It words. It's what's in between me and the world that matters. Can I try a simple-minded example?

"Certainly."

If you and I are talking, and I look at you as a teacher, as my teacher, then I will be looking at myself as your student. As your student, I will treat you in a way that I would not treat you in another relationship. And I will treat myself as though I am merely a student.

"An apt example."

So I am only going to learn what you, the teacher, teach me. And I am going to put up with a lot that I would never want to put up with. Because you have the power to grade me.

"There are better ways to learn than to have a teacher hold a weapon over the students' heads. But let's put that aside. Your example is appropriate. As long as you regard me as your teacher, I am filling a role; I am an It."

And I am an It, too! As a "student" I become a passive information gatherer. And the intimacy that we want is lost. That's what Camus was saying.

"Yes."

EXPERIENCES AND RELATING

And if I look at things from the I-It point of view, I limit myself?

"Yes. Where there is a thing there is another thing. Every It is bounded by others. . . . But when Thou is spoken, there is no thing. Thou has no bounds."

Okay. Could you say this in a different way so that I can see if I have it?

"As experience, the world belongs to the primary word I-It. The primary word I-Thou establishes the world of relation."

Ah, so that's where the in-between happens. The I-It way makes me separate myself from the object of my experience. With I-Thou, I relate to the other thing. It's the importance of the relationship that you're pointing to, and not me or It.

"Yes. You take your stand in relation. . . . and we answer—forming, thinking, acting. We speak the primary word with our being, though we cannot utter Thou with our lips."

And you don't think this is a little unusual?

"In each sphere we are aware of a breath from the eternal Thou; in each Thou we address the eternal Thou."

Are you saying that each thing is a piece of the eternal reality, or Thou, as you name it? Once I heard a story about a Zen guy who said that the universe is like a shattered mirror. Each thing reflects the entire mirror, the entire reality. So in some sense, all of reality is in each piece of it. Each thing has a value simply because it exists. You might say the same idea by saying that the I-Thou attitude sees everything as sacred. Is that what you mean?

"I like that metaphor. It is in keeping with my distinction."

Okay, but for my sake, let's keep this in the sphere of this world for a little while. How can I relate to an object in nature in the I-Thou way?

THE POWER OF EXCLUSIVENESS

"I consider a tree. I look on it as a picture. I can perceive it as movement. I can classify it in a species. I can subdue its actual presence and form so sternly that I recognize it only as the expression of law. I can dissipate it and perpetuate it in number, in pure numerical relation."

Good example. Is the I-Thou relationship the ability to see the tree the way the artist, poet, botanist, physicist, and mathematician see it?

"No, in all this the tree remains my object, occupies space and time, and has its nature and constitution. It can, however, also come about, if I have both will and grace, that in considering the tree I become bound up in relation to it. The tree is no longer It. I have been seized by the power of exclusiveness."

You want to see the tree as unique, as a one-of-a-kind. Does that mean you have to give up the other ways of seeing the tree?

"To effect this it is not necessary for me to give up any of the ways in which I consider the tree. Rather is everything, picture and movement, species and type, law and number, invisibly united in this event."

Yet you say that the totality of the It perspective does not make up the Thou. How are these points of view different?

"Everything belonging to the tree is in this . . . all present in a single whole."

Aren't you just describing a mood that a person gets into sometimes? The tree appears to you as a unique, single whole because you're feeling relaxed and "spiritual."

"Art, the tree is no impression, no play of my imagination, no value depending on my mood. Relation is mutual."

You feel the tree as it relates to you? It communicates to you as though it's another person? The tree is conscious?

"Of that I have no experience, Art. I encounter no soul, or dryad of the tree, but the tree itself."

HOW THE PRIMARY
WORDS EVOLVE

Let's say for a moment that I like the sound of your description of the I-Thou attitude. How can I move from the I-It experience to the I-Thou way of relating? You say it's a matter of will and grace. I will it by preparing myself, and then if I'm lucky, it happens? If that's it, how do I prepare myself?

"Let us look at how the primary words evolve. The first primary word can be resolved, certainly, into I and Thou, but it did not arise from their being set together; by its nature the I-Thou attitude precedes I."

I-Thou comes before the distinction between them? You're suggesting that we have the I-Thou attitude before we even discover an I and a Thou? Does this apply to I-It as well?

"No, the second word arose from the setting together of I and It; by nature the I-It attitude comes after I."

Can you give me an example? And please don't start talking to trees again. Did premodern cultures relate this way to their moon gods? Is that the idea?

"Only brief glimpses into the context in time of the two primary words are given us by primitive man. We receive fuller knowledge from the child."

Thank you, that's much more manageable for me.

Natural Combination and Natural Separation. "Here it becomes crystal clear to us that the spiritual reality of the primary words arises out of a natural reality, that of the primary word I-Thou out of natural combination, and that of the primary word I-It out of natural separation."

For example?

"This connection has such a cosmic quality that the mythical saying of the Jews, 'In the mother's body man knows the universe, in birth he forgets it,' reads like an imperfect decipherment of an inscription from earliest times."

No offense, Mr. Buber, but old sayings don't prove anything.

"Of course not, but it remains indeed in man as a secret image of desire. The yearning is for the cosmic connection, with its true Thou."

I'm still looking for a plausible example.

Establishing a Relation. "The primal nature of the effort to establish relation is already to be seen in the earliest and most confined stage. Before anything isolated can be perceived, timid glances move out into indistinct space, towards something indefinite; and in times where there seems to be no desire for nourishment, hands sketch delicately and dimly in the empty air, apparently aimlessly seeking and reaching out to meet something indefinite."

Babies move their arms, so what?

"These very glances will after protracted attempts settle on the red carpet pattern and not be moved till the soul of the red has opened itself to them; and this very movement of the hands will win from the woolly teddybear its precise form, apparent to the senses, and become lovingly and unforgettably aware of a complete body."

Isn't that just the opposite of what you were saying? In your example, the infant knows itself as an I, and only after groping around discovers objects out there in the world. It sees the red carpet and feels the teddybear.

"Neither of these acts is experience of an object, but is the correspondence of the child."

I'm uncomfortable with your interpretation. The infant is merely exercising her imagination.

"To be sure it is only 'fanciful'—with what is alive and effective over against itself. . . . It is the instinct to make everything into Thou, to give relation to the universe."

An interesting idea, but why should we accept this interpretation? Babies look around; they move their little arms; they make sounds. How does any of this prove that they are relating to anything?

"Little, disjointed, meaningless sounds still go out persistently into the void. But one day, unforeseen, they will have become conversation—does it matter that it is perhaps with a simmering kettle? It is conversation."

Well, maybe.

"Art, it is simply not the case that the child first perceives an object, then, as it were, puts itself into relation with it. The effort to establish relation comes first—the hand of the child arched out so that what is over against him may nestle under it."

I see what you're saying. The child reaches or looks so that it can relate in its world.

Relating.   "Second is the actual relation, a saying of Thou without words, in the state preceding the word form."

You're saying that the conversation with the tea kettle or the teddybear comes as an unspoken relation?

"Yes, and the thing, like the I, is produced late, arising after the original experiences have been split asunder and the connected partners separated."

Then the teddy relationship is essential for the infant even to discover that she is a unique thing? You're saying that the relation between the teddy and the infant comes first, even before the infant is aware that she has a limited body?

"In the beginning is relation—as a category of being, readiness, grasping form . . . it is . . . *inborn Thou.*"

Say this again.

"The inborn Thou is realized in the lived relations with that which meets it. The fact that this Thou can be known as what is over against the child, can be taken up in exclusiveness, and finally can be addressed with the primary word, is based on the a priori (the essential nature) of relation."

Loving and Hating.   So our sense of loving and caring arises from this way of relating?

"In the instinct to make contact the inborn Thou is very soon brought to its full powers, so that the instinct ever more clearly turns out to mean mutual relation, 'tenderness.'"

Then you're saying that the I-Thou attitude is really loving and caring for everyone. Loving and caring are the only feelings we should have toward anyone. We should love our neighbors, and our enemies, and everyone else, no matter what type of people they are.

"You speak of love as though it were the only relation between men. But properly speaking, can you take it even as only an example, since there is such a thing as hate?"

I hadn't thought of hate as an intimate way of relating. I was just thinking that absolutely devoted love is what you were asking from me.

"So long as love is 'blind,' that is, so long as it does not see a *whole* being, it is not truly under the sway of the primary word of relation."

A whole being?

"Art, hate is by nature blind. Only a part of a being can be hated. He who sees a whole being and is compelled to reject it is no longer in the kingdom of hate, but is in that of human restriction of the power to say Thou."

Why do you say that?

"He finds himself unable to say the primary word to the other human being confronting him. This word consistently involves an affirmation of the being addressed."

Why can't a person who hates say Thou to the person he hates? Why can't I hate someone and affirm him at the same time?

"You are compelled to reject either the other or yourself."

So you're saying that if I hate someone, and I see their whole being, then I cannot see myself as fully affirmed as a human being? I am merely judging the other person by my own values. Then hate is always wrong?

"Yet the man who straightforwardly hates is nearer to relation than the man without hate and love."

Now I am confused. Why do you say this?

"Relation is mutual. My Thou affects me, as I affect it. . . . We live our lives inscrutably included within the streaming mutual life of the universe."

I understand that in some unintelligible way I am attached to everything. But how can you not have negative feelings toward the bad person?

Love Goes Beyond Feelings.   "Feelings accompany the metaphysical and metapsychical fact of love, but they do not constitute it."

Now it's my turn to have a V-8! Since you put it that way, it's so obvious!

"Why the sarcasm?"

What is the metaphysical and metapsychical fact of love? I don't have any idea what that means.

"The feeling of Jesus for the demoniac differs from his feeling for the beloved disciple; but the love is one love."

How could that be? Love is love.

"Feelings are 'entertained': love comes to pass. Feelings dwell in a man; but man dwells in his love."

That's a nice metaphor for saying that love is deeper than feelings.

"That is no metaphor, but the actual truth. Love does not cling to the I in such a way as to have the Thou only for its 'content,' its object; but love is *between* I and Thou."

Then the feelings involved in loving are only by-products of the fact, of the attitude of love?

"The man who does not know this, with his very being know this, does not know love."

Even though he has strong feelings of affection or caring for other people?

"Even though he ascribes to it feelings he lives through, experiences, enjoys, and expresses."

How is the person different who loves beyond the feelings?

"In the eyes of him who takes his stand in love, and gazes out of it, men are cut free from their entanglement in bustling activity. Good people and evil, wise and foolish, beautiful and ugly, become successively *real* to him."

You want people to become more and more real to me? What do you mean?

"Set free, they step forth in their singleness and confront you as Thou."

THE THOU RELATIONSHIP

What do I experience when I am in an I-Thou relation?

"In the act of experience Thou is far away. I do not experience the man to whom I say Thou."

I don't understand.

"I take my stand in relation to him—"

I'm sorry; I used the wrong words to ask my question. What does the world look like to a person who has the I-Thou attitude?

"If I face a human being as my Thou, and say the primary word I-Thou to him, he is not a thing among things, and does not consist of things. Thus a human being is not He or She, bounded from every other He or She, a specific point in space and time within the net of the world; nor is he a nature able to be experienced or described, a loose bundle of named qualities."

Well, that's what the Thou is not, but what is the Thou?

"Whole in himself . . . all else lives in his light."

All else lives in his light? What do we experience of Thou?

"Just nothing. For we do not experience it."

What, then, do we know of Thou?

"Just everything. For we know nothing isolated about it anymore."

Oh, I see. We understand all of reality as a setting for the Thou.

A Sacrifice and a Risk.   This all sounds pretty risky to me.

"Yes, Art, the act includes a sacrifice and a risk."

What's the sacrifice?

"The endless possibility that is offered up on the altar of form."

By that you mean that I can't act like I have been acting all this time? I have to take off my mask? I have to actually be who I am? Most people are so accustomed to acting according to social roles and people's expectations! We expect everybody else to act that way, too. Yes, that is a sacrifice. And the risk?

"The primary word can only be spoken with the whole being. He who gives himself to it may withhold nothing of himself."

You mean I have to tell the other person everything about myself, including my thoughts and desires?

"Things among things. This is the It world. Art, all real living is meeting."

But, Professor Buber, if I drop my mask, and if I withhold nothing of my self, what guarantee do I have that the other person will be aware of me?

"Even if the man to whom I say Thou is not aware of it in the midst of his experience, yet relation may exist. For Thou is more than It realizes."

Isn't the other person going to take advantage of me? Can't she deceive me?

"No deception penetrates here; here is the cradle of the Real Life."

To Man the World is Twofold.   I know that we can experience the world in an I-It way. When I do that, I can accomplish a lot. It's the practical life. What do I get by having the I-Thou attitude? You say my sense of myself is deter-mined by how I relate to the other person or thing. What else do I understand in this Thou meeting?

"Man becomes always what is over against him, always simply a *single* being and each thing simply as being."

What do you mean?

"Nothing is present for you except this one being, but it implicates the whole world."

That's what you mean when you say that I see the whole world in his light?

"Yes. Measure and comparison have disappeared; it lies with yourself how much of the immeasurable becomes reality for you. These meetings are not organized to make the world, but each is a sign of the world order."

It sounds chaotic. What benefit do I get from this attitude?

"Each meeting assures you of your solidarity with the world."

The Relation to the Thou is Direct.   Solidarity with the world? That brings to my mind a question I have been wanting to ask.

"Yes?"

You say that the relation to the Thou is direct. What do you mean?

"No system of ideas, no foreknowledge, and no fancy intervene between I and Thou."

So I encounter the Thou as it really exists?

"Yes, no aim, no lust, and no anticipation intervene between I and Thou. Desire itself is transformed as it plunges out of its dream into the appearance."

Why is it so important that aims and desires and anticipations be left behind?

"Every means is an obstacle. Only when every means has collapsed does the meeting come about."

Oh, okay. I have to get myself out of the I-It frame of mind. But I still don't understand the nature of the I-Thou way of relating. For example, you say in your tree example that the tree isn't an impression or part of my imagination.

It Is Bodied Over Against Me.   "Correct. Nor is the tree a value depending on my mood; but it is bodied over against me and has to do with me, as I with it."

Now we are getting at what I don't understand. What does it mean for something to be "bodied over against me"?

"Art, I can neither experience nor describe the form which meets me, but only body it forth."

Wait, are you saying that the intellect doesn't have a part in the I-Thou relationship? That's it, isn't it? If I think in categories and make judgments, then I am only experiencing the thing. But if I suspend my intellectual way of understanding, then the thing is presented to me directly. That's what you mean when you say the relation is direct. I know the Thou with my whole being, not with my senses, my intellectual categories, and my judgments. The thing becomes real, a single, existing thing important just because it is here, because it is present. And I am present along with it.

The Present Is Filled.   "That is why the real, filled present exists only insofar as actual presentness, meeting, and relation exist. The present arises only in virtue of the fact that the Thou becomes present."

This sounds like the pleasure seeker's experiences. Is the difference between the Thou way of relating and the pleasure seeker's way of experiencing that the pleasure seeker is goal directed?

"Insofar as man rests satisfied with the things that he experiences and uses, he lives in the past, and his moment has no present content."

Huh?

"True beings are lived in the present, the life of objects is in the past."

EVERY THOU MUST BECOME AN IT

If the reality of our own selves depends on the I-Thou, why don't we all live with the I-Thou attitude all the time?

"Every Thou in our world must become an It."

Isn't there any way to prevent it?

"It does not matter how exclusively present the Thou was in direct relation. As soon as the relation has been worked out or has been permeated with a means, the Thou becomes an object among objects—perhaps the chief, but still one of them."

Then overcoming our separation from the real world is impossible?

"Every Thou in the world is by its nature fated to become a thing, or continually to reenter into the condition of things. Consider the speech of 'primitive' peoples, that is, of those that have a meager stock of objects, and whose life is built up within a narrow circle of acts highly charged with presentness."

SEPARATION AND CONNECTION WITH REALITY

What about them? Does their language show that separation is impossible to avoid?

"The nuclei of this speech . . . most indicate the wholeness of relation. We say 'far away'; the Zulu has for that a word which means, in our sentence form, 'There where someone cries out: O mother, I am lost.'"

Their language has a more emotional feel to it.

"The Fuegian soars above our analytic wisdom with a seven-syllabled word whose precise meaning is, 'They stare at one another, each waiting for the other to volunteer to do what both wish, but are not able to do.'"

What's your point?

"The chief concern is not with these products of analysis and reflection but with the true original unity, the lived relation."

Their language does express the sense of separation and the need for connection with reality. There is an immediacy about the "primitive" understanding that goes beyond our normal intellectual, moral way of relating.

"To accept what has no sensuous qualities at all as actually existing must strike him as absurd. The appearances to which he ascribes the 'mystical power' are all elementary incidents that are relational in character, that is, all incidents that disturb him by disturbing his body and leaving behind in him a stirring image."

Should the theme from *Twilight Zone* be racing through my mind?

"Not at all. I am merely presenting an example of knowledge that is bodied over against a person."

YOU BELIEVE IN PARADISE?

Then you think that ancient people lived in a kind of paradise?

"Even if it was a hell—and certainly that time to which I can go back in historical thought was full of fury and anguish and torment and cruelty—at any rate it was not unreal."

Your whole emphasis is for us to encounter reality as it is. You think that our objective way of experiencing shields us from "feeling" what is out there. Your critique is really aimed at us. We have not shed the insulation of the moral way of thinking and relating. Isn't that it? You're saying that our modern way of experiencing doesn't let things be real. Is the "primitive" way better?

"Rather force exercised on being that is really lived, than shadowy solicitude for faceless numbers!"

WHY ENTER THE THOU ATTITUDE?

Professor Buber, I have several reservations about the Thou way of living. Before we part, may I state them?

"Yes, by all means, do."

What does the Thou attitude offer me? How does it compare with living in the It world? What I mean is, the Thou attitude sounds appealing, but also lonely, dangerous, and impractical. I hope you don't mind me saying this.

"Art, through the Thou a man becomes I. That which confronts him comes and disappears, relational events condense, then are scattered, and in the change consciousness of the unchanging partner, of the I, grows clear, and each time stronger."

I appreciate that part of your analysis. I'm even willing to concede that the child's sense of I arises from the I-Thou primary attitude. What comes of that?

"Only now can the other primary word be assembled. Hitherto the Thou of relation was continually fading away, but it did not thereby become an It for some I, an object of perception and experience, without real connection—as it will henceforth become."

I guess I'm asking a more practical, adult question.

"The man who becomes conscious of I, that is, the man who says I-It, stands before things, but not over against them in the flow of mutual action. Now with the magnifying glass of peering observation he bends over particulars and objectifies them, or with the fieldglass of remote inspection he objectifies them and arranges them as scenery, he isolates them in observation without any feeling of their exclusiveness, or he knits them into a scheme of observation without any feeling of universality."

That speaks in favor of the practical nature of the I-It experience. All science depends on objective observation.

"Art, the feeling of exclusiveness he would be able to find only in relation, the feeling of universality only through it."

Exclusiveness? So to be a unique individual, and not merely part of humanity, I should adopt the I-Thou attitude? But so much speaks in favor of the I-It!

"These are the two basic privileges of the world of It. They move man to look on the world of It as the world in which he has to live, and in which it is comfortable to live, as the world, indeed, which offers him all manner of incitements and excitements, activity and knowledge. In this chronicle of solid benefits the moments of the Thou appear as strange lyric and dramatic episodes, seductive and magical, but tearing us away to dangerous extremes, loosening the well-tried context, leaving more questions than satisfaction behind them, shattering security—in short, uncanny moments we can well dispense with."

That's exactly what I think. Maybe I'm being too moral in looking for the security of the familiar, but why should I venture out into Thou relations? Since we cannot hold for long anything in our consciousness as a Thou—

"Why not call to order what is over against us and send it packing into the realm of objects?"

Yes. Why not?

"It is not possible to live in the bare present. Life would be quite consumed if precautions were not taken to subdue the present speedily and thoroughly."

Exactly. You have forcefully stated my concerns.

"But it is possible to live in the bare past; indeed, only in it may a life be organized. We only need to fill each moment with experiencing and using, and it ceases to burn."

So why not live the safe, secure, predictable life?

"In all seriousness of truth, hear this: without It man cannot live."

Just as I thought.

"But he who lives with It alone is not man, is not human."

■

SUMMARY OF DISCUSSION

Martin Buber suggests that each of us has two attitudes toward the world. The first and more easily identified attitude is what he calls the I-It attitude. This perspective understands objects and people as instrumental for achieving goals and the like. The second attitude is the I-Thou attitude. I-Thou is a most intimate way of knowing the other. I-Thou goes beyond the surface of the other person or thing. The I-Thou attitude sees the other for what is really there. Another way of putting this distinction is that the I-It attitude allows one to experience the other person or thing. The I-Thou attitude necessitates one person's relating to the other. In each case the nature of the I is determined by the attitude with which the I understands the other.

I-Thou is the only way for a person to alleviate his loneliness. It involves relating with one's whole being. I-Thou requires that one person openly view the other. There is a risk involved. One must drop one's pretense, one's "masks." Buber suggests that the I-Thou way of relating is the most natural way. He says that it predates the I-It experience. The infant relates to its first objects as Thou, defining itself and the other in this process of relating.

Unfortunately, this direct, intimate, and filled relation cannot be sustained. Every Thou must become an It. Every meeting must break apart into a separation. But the meeting can occur again. One can become connected with reality again.

For all its risks and sacrifices, the Thou way of relating is essential to us. We can live immersed in the I-It way of experiencing, but this does not make us human. The I-It way of experiencing is a safe, secure, and predictable life. Why not live exclusively with the I-It attitude? Buber answers, "Without It man cannot live. But he who lives with It alone is not man, is not human."

■

DISCUSSION HIGHLIGHTS

I. The attitude of man is twofold.
   1. There is the I-It attitude and way of relating.
      a. One experiences reality and the surface of things.
      b. One lives in the purely "practical" world.
   2. There is the I-Thou attitude and way of relating.
      a. One relates to the other and experiences the world in light of the other.
      b. The power of exclusiveness occurs in the I-Thou relation.
II. The Thou relationship has several distinguishing features.
   1. It occurs with a sacrifice and a risk.
   2. The Thou is bodied over against me.
   3. The present is filled.

4. Every Thou must become an It.
5. The separation created by language can be overcome.
6. Both attitudes, I-Thou and I-It, are necessary for us to live as humans.

■
QUESTIONS FOR THOUGHT/PAPER TOPICS

1. What characteristics distinguish the I-It and the I-Thou attitudes?

2. Buber defines three spheres of relating. First is nature, then come our fellow humans, and finally spiritual beings. What do you make of this distinction?

3. What is the significance of Buber's notion of the "in-between"? He claims it is the key to understanding the self and the other.

4. Discuss how Buber's discussion of the tree exemplifies the "power of exclusiveness."

5. What could Buber mean when he says that real meeting goes beyond loving and hating?

6. Does Buber succeed in integrating the individual person and all reality? Discuss how he accomplishes this.

7. Does Buber's notion of the "filled moment" sound similar to the Stranger's concentration on momentary pleasure? How do they differ?

■
FOR FURTHER READING

Read Buber's *I and Thou* (Scribner's Sons, 1958). That is where Buber first lays out his I-Thou, I-It distinction. You might also look at his *Between Man and Man* (Macmillan, 1965) for Buber's own explanation and application of his theory. There are very good works on human relating. In *An Inquiry Concerning the Principles of Morals* (Bobbs-Merrill, 1957), David Hume offers a remarkable analysis of morality and its requirement of relating through "gentler" emotions. Another impressive book is Simone de Beauvoir's *The Second Sex* (Random House, 1974). Chapter 23, "The Woman in Love," is particularly appropriate to our discussion.

THIRTEEN

What Is the Best Life? The Virtuous Sage of Spinoza and Lao Tsu

What is the best life? How can I live it? These two questions have received very different answers in our discussions. We cannot help but notice the diversity of wants, values, and goals that people endorse. Responses to our question, "What is the best life?" have been categorized by their goals. The moralist seeks security and acceptance. The pleasure seeker's goal is pleasures of the senses. Either one lives for the pleasure of the moment like Camus's Stranger, Kierkegaard's A, and Art. Or one lives a moral life in one of the ways we have seen described by the Grand Inquisitor, Epictetus, Mill, Kant, or Sartre. In this, our final discussion, I'd like to bring together some "conclusions" from our talks.

TRANSLATING THE BASIC QUESTIONS IN LIVING

Although we have categorized each vision of living according to its goals, goals alone do not help us figure out which is the most desirable strategy of living. Telling a pleasure seeker that she is living an immoral, meaningless life is a lot like arguing etiquette with a hungry lion as she is about to eat you. As long as there are different goals, there is apparently no way of resolving the debate. I think, however, that there is a more helpful way to proceed.

Instead of examining the answers to the question, "What is the best life?" I suggest we look at the question itself and how each vision of living interprets the question. For the moment, imagine that each vision of living asks the same basic question. Why, then, are the answers so apparently different, you

Material in this chapter taken from Benedict de Spinoza, *The Ethics* (New York: Dover Publications, Inc.), R.H.M. Elwes translation; and from Lao Tsu, *Tao Te Ching* (New York: Random House, Inc., 1972), Gia-fu Feng and Jane English translation.

ask? Perhaps the answers are not so different. Our confusion may be a result of how each vision distorts the questions and the answers. Does each vision interpret the question differently? Certainly we have seen that each vision has different beliefs about human nature, about other people, about the nature of reality. Since each way of living differently defines the question of the best life, each seeks apparently different goals. It's as though each vision of living speaks a different language. Each vision sees the same question, but each has a different translation. If my idea is correct, all we have to do is translate the question in a better way. Let me show you what I mean.

Living to Avoid Boredom.   We can best understand Camus's Stranger as a person wishing to avoid boredom. I know what you're thinking. The Stranger leads an incredibly boring life. But does he? Or does his life only appear boring to moral people?

The Stranger is engaged in the here and now. He says, "All that counts is the present and the concrete." He sees a reality of facts without meaning. Reality is a series of unconnected impressions. Each moment sweeps away the one before it and is swept away by the one that follows it. For the Stranger, one experience is as good as another. No thought, no responsibility, nothing interrupts his experience of the here and now.

So sensual experience is his answer to the question of the best life. Sensual experience negates boredom. He is not engaged by society; he is engaged only by his senses. The Stranger is never bored. His way of living in the here and now keeps away boredom. More important, it also reaffirms his experience of existing. To him, he is real only as long as he is intensely experiencing his surroundings.

Of course, defining oneself by experiencing in the here and now does not work too well. All of the Stranger's experiences occur on the surface. In Buber's language, they are confined to the I-It way of relating. This weakness is enough to discourage us from living for the moment alone. However, the Stranger has discovered two keys to living well. He has discovered that intensity of interaction with reality is vital. And he understands that increasing the concentration on experiencing makes him feel more real. Ultimately, the Stranger's question is not so much one of avoiding boredom. Ultimately, it is a question of how real he is, and how he is real. He is certain of his own reality in his moments of sensual experience. Think about it. When you are suffering intense pain, there is no question that you are real.

Living to Avoid Decisions.   Kierkegaard's A is a more sophisticated version of living for the moment. A is nearer to the moral way that we live. A avoids decisions. A wants to experience intensely, but he also wants to control his world. He realizes that some experiences are more intense than others; some are more rewarding, that is, more pleasurable, than others. Which experience he chooses is important to him. Choose correctly and he knows that he is alive. His pleasures, his pains, and his sensual feelings all tell him so with absolute certainty. Choose mistakenly and he suffers. He is forced to live morally, with only a bored, distracted, vague sense of his own reality. That's why choice makes him anxious. Anxiety of indecision springs from the possibility of choice and control over surroundings.

When we ask A what is the best life, he replies that it is a life where one does not suffer the anxiety of indecision. Remember, he regrets every choice. It's possible that that is all there is to it. However, A is depressed and cynical. Something more is going on. A attempts to experience himself in experiencing other people and reality. But his way of experiencing is too limited to the "surface" of things.

For both the Stranger and A, there is a confusion. In each case the basic question, "What is the best life?" is apparently answered differently. The real and more fundamental quest, however, is to be fully real by intimately and intensely experiencing and relating to reality. That's just what Buber suggested in Chapter 12!

Living to Avoid Decisions and Responsibility. Does this same analysis work with the moral life? In answering the question, "What is the best life?" the moral person accepts the safety of low-intensity experiencing. As we have seen, morality replaces intensity with meaningfulness. However, in our discussion of life's meaning or absurdity, we saw that the question of life's meaning is really only a hidden plea for knowing and affirming one's own reality by experiencing and relating to others and to reality.

Is this really the moralist's point of view? The anxieties of indecision and of responsibility are resolved by reference to a fixed standard, by the moral rules. Not only formalized rules and roles but social expectations resolve the need to make decisions on ultimate values. They remain fixed. They continue from the venerable past through the present and into the enduring future.

We can understand the moralist as a person wishing to avoid the anxieties of indecision and of responsibility, and meaninglessness. Minimizing the anxieties and meaninglessness defines and *gives reality* to the moral self. The moralist has merely moved the Stranger's question of intensity to duration, from momentary experience to feeling secure. The moralist seeks social acceptance and security.

WHY MORALITY DOESN'T WORK

Why doesn't the moral reply adequately answer the question of the best life? Look at our conclusions about morality. Kant, Mill, and Sartre do not agree on their interpretation of morality. They do agree, however, that morality is the perspective of objective, universal impartiality. We have already seen that the moral point of view requires objectivity and impartiality. And it is universal in that it applies to everyone.

Within the objective moral vision of living, the other person is well defined but emotionally distant. For example, as a representative of the moral point of view, we can pick a judge. As a judge, the person is supposed to be morally impartial. No matter what the judge is feeling emotionally and no matter what the judge's relationship with the accused person, the judgment is supposed to be impartial. Imagine what it would be like to take someone to court, offer your evidence, and then have the judge say to your opponent, "In spite of the overwhelming evidence to the contrary, I find in your favor. I'll see you at home for dinner, son." Not very impartial! Not morally acceptable. So morality is essentially impartial and objective.

THE SELF AND OTHERS

The moral self is an isolated and unchanging object living through the experiences of the present. Morality confines my experiencing to my own person. I can feel neither the pains nor the joys of another person. I can experience sympathy or pity, but not empathy. I can feel only my own pains and joys. I am secure, but isolated and alone.

My only effective tool for communication is provided by the universal perspective of morality. I remain objective, even caring in the moral fashion, but always experientially isolated. Others are defined by the rights, duties, and obligations assigned them. I relate to others by joining them in the commonality of the "social continuities." We communicate; we have commerce. We understand our historical connection with each other. We cooperate in creative (productive) efforts, and in a sense of community.

Because morality makes us out of touch with other people, they seem to be like me, but they are not as real as me. After all, I cannot directly experience their feelings. They are "surface" experiences. They are "inferences." Each moralist is tied to morality for his or her own reality. Each moralist's own experience of his or her reality depends on the objective, universal perspective.

MEANINGFULNESS

For the moral person, a meaningful life is important. But why? Though it might be true in some instances, what the moralist calls the meaningful life is not necessarily more pleasurable. Nor is the meaningful life necessarily more secure materially. Why, then, do moralists worry about the prospect of a meaningless life? The fear cannot be that the meaningless life brings anonymity. Anonymity in the form of objective impartiality is precisely what the moral life advocates. Within morality we are all moral equals. Selfishness is condemned as dangerous; being morally anonymous is praised.

The question of life's meaningfulness reveals a disguised fear of being out of touch with reality. Without experiencing what is out there, a person's life is confirmed only insofar as she aids and affects others, insofar as she achieves social connectedness (acceptance). If a moralist loses contact with the "continuity" of humanity, she loses her experience of her own reality.

RELATING TO REALITY

How one relates to other people and to the things within reality, and therefore how one experiences one's self becomes confused with one's very existence itself. Without the impartial, objective relating of the universal perspective, the moralist believes that the self does not exist. Without moral relating, the moralist is "no better than an animal." One's moral existence, one's membership in the moral community, is granted only when one's motives and one's conception of others spring from impartial reason.

As moralists, we relate to other people and to reality in an emotionally and sensually uncommitted way. We become bored with others and with reality. We cannot become actively and intimately engaged with any specific part of it. We become drained by our lack of engagement. We are not bored and life-less because we lack energy; we lack energy because we are bored. We are separated from reality. We are out of touch. We cannot become engaged and creative, and therefore we fail to gain vitality from our interaction with the environment. Even brief moments of nonmoral, genuine interaction with reality revitalize us. Creative work and play, for example, do not tire us.

Morality does not provide more attuned tools for relating. It is not the aim of moral relating to savor the intensity of experiencing. Nor is morality designed to let us feel the sensuous texture of reality. Moral understanding captures and solidifies what can be reproduced, organized and judged. It performs this task well, but it cannot do more. Morality creates objects from subjects, estranged people from creative, sensuous humans. From the moral point of view, everything is an object, people are just objects valued among other things. Our isolation is a by-product of the moral point of view.

THE REAL QUESTION

Therefore, we can conclude that it is neither boredom, nor anxiety, nor meaninglessness, nor loneliness, nor deteriorating social relationships that plague us. These are symptoms. More fundamental than these problems is the way we relate to the self, to others, and to reality.

We can see that the fundamental quest is to be fully real. Each vision of living asks the "right" questions. Each vision goes astray not in motive, but in its interpretation of reality. The only genuine difference among visions of living is how they allow us to relate to reality.

THE VIRTUOUS SAGE: THE LIFE OF EXCELLENCE

What's left? Isn't there a best way to live? That's what you're asking, isn't it? I have an answer. I think that the life of the virtuous sage is the best life. Let's end our book-long discussion with a short talk about Spinoza and Lao Tsu. I'll leave it to you to work out the details of the virtuous life, and to evaluate it.

Virtue and Morality.   Before I summarize the ideas of these two notable people, I should distinguish virtue and moral goodness for you. Virtue is often misunderstood as moral goodness. A virtuous person is sometimes thought to be someone who follows the moral rules with a special strictness and seriousness. That is not what Spinoza and Lao Tsu mean by virtue. Virtue means excellence. When a thing excels at its given task, it is virtuous. For example, if the pen I am holding is supposed to chop wood, then it isn't excellent. The pen is a pretty poor axe. However, if my intention is to write, then this pen is virtuous.

Excellence in a desired activity determines an object's virtue. Of course, it isn't clear what function or purpose or activity humans are supposed to fulfill. Can't you hear Sartre screaming through the pages from Chapter 10? "No, no, humans choose their essence!" Okay, Jean-Paul, there is no human nature. However, the common concern of each vision of living has been to bring each of us into closer, more intimate contact with our own selves, with other people, and with the rest of reality. The vision that makes possible intimate and intense relating is the one worthy of being called excellent. That's the project for Spinoza and Lao Tsu.

Spinoza and Lao Tsu.   Rather than carrying on a discussion with these two thinkers, I am going to summarize their thinking. I'm doing this for three reasons. First, it lets me show you that they are in agreement about the best life. This is amazing when we consider that they lived at least twenty-two centuries apart, and in culturally different areas of the world. Lao Tsu was a Chinese who lived perhaps twenty-six centuries ago. Spinoza was a Dutch Jew of either Spanish of Portuguese ancestry who lived during the seventeenth century. Lao Tsu's times were marked by feudal war and superstition. Spinoza lived in an era when science was taking hold and blind faith was being replaced with curiosity and knowledge.

Second, summarizing the ideas of these two thinkers places more responsibility on you. Even though I have an interpretation of their ideas, I want to lay the responsibility on you. Read their writings. We are nearly at the end of the book. I am hoping that my summary will tease you into reading on your own and to surpass your "teacher." What follows is only a summary of the virtuous life.

Third, I am asking you to look at this point of view because I think this is the reasonable conclusion of our long discussion. Another way of saying the same thing is that I agree with Spinoza and Lao Tsu, and I'd like you to see what they think.

What Is the Best Life?   Spinoza says that the virtuous person defines the "best" life as the "knowledge of the union existing between the mind and the whole of nature." Lao Tsu's sage's interpretation of the question of the best life is answered by the interaction of the self and reality. The virtuous sage faces the "mysterious abyss" of reality separating the self, others, and reality. However, the virtuous sage seeks neither moral security, nor acceptance, nor sensual pleasures. These are distractions. Instead the virtuous person develops his latent skill of awareness. He develops his reasoning so that he sees reality in an intimate way. As we've just seen, that is what each vision of living is really asking.

The virtuous sage is sensitive to the initial insecurity of his own reality and to the uncertainty of the reality of others. These states are initiated by noting a self-other distinction. He realizes that his loneliness is a symptom of a split between the self, others, and reality. Bridging the separation between the self, others, and reality prevents his sense of being out of touch. Intimately interrelating the self, others, and reality answers the question of the best life.

The Virtues.   What are the recommendations of Spinoza and Lao Tsu? The virtuous vision of living "creates" a self through fully experiencing the self, others, and reality. To be less alone, but uniquely human; to relate to others and to other things in the world in the most intimate human way, with neither expectation nor blind acceptance; to confirm the reality of others and of one's self without distortion; to produce a way of living and of conceiving of reality that guarantees our continued sensitivity to living—these are the elements that we must discover in creating the virtuous vision of living. For the virtuous sage, preparation involves affective and "intuitive" union of self, others, and reality. The sage relates through the virtue(s) of empathic understanding, of active listening, of active noninterference (*wu wei*), and of open and courageous questioning.

The Sage's Picture of Reality.   What is the sage's* picture of reality that produces these effects? On the most fundamental level, the sage rejects thinking in opposites as the moralist thinks. She minimizes any experiential distance in these distinctions. The sage conceives a single, unconditioned reality, a reality that is timelessly eternal, infinite, and indivisible, a reality involving no negation of reality, a reality whose "essence is existence." This undifferentiated reality is the "mother of all things"; it is "the indwelling and not the transient cause of all things." This is Spinoza's active Nature or God (*natura naturans*) and Lao Tse's Tao. (Neither thinker believes the name does justice to "the mystery.")

Beyond the fundamental Nature or God, or Tao, the sage's interpretation of reality becomes more complicated. The sage distinguishes between what Lao Tsu calls "heaven and earth," and what Spinoza calls the attributes of thought and of extension. The sage tentatively categorizes each item of the world as a thinking thing, as a mental item, or as an extended object. In fact, each thing is a subtle "combination" of the two categories. Beyond this primary discrimination, the sage sees individually differentiated objects. Finite pieces of reality are perceived as either part of thought or of extended matter.

Since the Sage can be male or female, both pronouns will be used interchangeably.

Either a "thing" is an idea or a material object. This is the conceptual distance she creates as her self-awareness emerges. In conceiving of reality as a set of finite things, as a set of the "ten thousand things," desires emerge. To desire is to see reality by distinguishing subject and object. This creates an experiential distance that must be crossed.

So the sage "suffers" the same initial problem that each other vision suffers. The sage is aware of her self and therefore is experientially distant from others and from reality. She experiences them as Its. Her discriminations make it possible for her to live in the world. Without differentiation, the world would be unacceptably defined as "nothingness." As Buber tells us, however, the conceptual distance requires experiential return.

Intimate Relating.   The virtuous sage's assumptions minimize conceptual distance and effect intimate return. He conceives of each "thing" not only as a part of the whole, but also as a contact point with reality. Each "thing" itself becomes the way to the whole of reality. To the virtuous sage, each "thing" has a being-value—that is, each "thing" mirrors the sage's own reality as he intimately relates with it.

The virtuous sage has no expectations. Grasping the "feel" of natural reality, the pieces of reality "fall into place" in his understanding. Understanding the process of reality itself, the details of actual movements within reality become understandable. Nothing goes amiss because each event occurs within the necessity of the laws of nature. So the sage is neither overwhelmed by his passions, nor is he subject to the whims of his environment. He successfully creates his own life in such a way that he abides by the flow of Nature. Through intuitive knowledge he comes actively to accept the natural progression of reality. His is a special knowledge of union. Does he agree with the movement of reality? He understands it and knows not to waste his energy in the vain effort of interfering with reality.

"But," you are thinking, "what about social and political activities?" Are we supposed to be passive and just accept whatever the authorities offer? Spinoza and Lao Tsu distinguish reality and the artificial existence of the social and political. They do not ask that you be socially and politically passive. Those institutions can be changed by beliefs and actions. It is only the laws of reality that are unchanging. It is reality, not society, from which we are separated.

Paradoxical Relating.   The sage's attitude toward others and toward the world is paradoxical. She is aloof and intimate. She finds that whatever "causes men to live together in harmony is useful," and yet she endorses neither the moral "continuities" nor the search for a meaningful life. Far from the indolence or melancholy of A's failed life of pleasure, Spinoza believes that "mirth cannot be excessive." The intensity of the sage's own existence gives her great pleasure.

Unlike the moralist, she is not future oriented and is therefore neither hopeful nor fearful. She neither overesteems nor disparages. She finds pity useless, even dangerous. Far from being emotionally reserved, however, the sage is compassionate. She can be "ruthless," and "detached" and free of desires while still maintaining an empathy toward others. Though she is not assertive, the sage is neither self-effacing nor repentant, nor does she suffer the "spiritual infirmities" of extreme pride or dejection.

Though she knows that others can be "mirrors" for her it is her and their reality that is most important to her. Her experiencing is intimate and spontaneous.

Spinoza says that the virtuous sage "performs those actions which follow from the necessity of [her] nature considered in itself alone." She is not susceptible to the moral persuasions of humility or guilt, but determines the course of her own actions.

The virtuous sage is not led by fear, nor by sensual pleasure. The sage is not motivated by conceptions of good and evil or of guilt. She forms no conceptions of good or of evil. Even death does not play a role in her living. The sage "thinks of death least of all things; his wisdom is a meditation not of death but of life." What motivates the virtuous sage is her experiential connectedness with her own reality and the reality of others and of the "mysterious abyss."

The sage does not wallow in her momentary passions and lusts. Ever desireless, the sage's "desireless" desires spring not from the "pleasures of a single part(s) of the body." Her wants spring from the commitment that each thing is connected with her in a web of reality. However, she does not deny her intimate feelings and her momentarily present experiences.

Though she experiences with an intensity as extreme as the most extreme pleasure seeker, the virtuous sage is undisturbed in spirit. She avoids the pitfalls of the pleasure-seeking life. Self-mastery prevents her from becoming the passive playing field of her experiencing and her passions. Her repertoire of emotions shrinks because it is determined by the prospect of relating to reality. This narrowed set of emotions allows her to devote the whole of her concentration to experiencing. Because her emotions are fully informed by and conform to the necessity of her nature, and are also informed by her "union" with "the whole of Nature," they never require her to act unfreely. Her actions flow as effortlessly and as thoughtlessly as long grass swaying in the breeze.

VIRTUES AND FREEDOM

Understanding the limits of concepts, Lao Tsu says, "the [virtuous] sage is guided by what he feels and not by what he sees." Above all, the sage is courageous, actively patient, and yielding (*wu wei*). He is open and quietly attentive. Though he is not an uncritical listener, he does not judge. His freedom consists in actively living according to the necessity of his nature. He does what he must do. However, necessity does not impose the limits on him that the moralist and the pleasure seeker experience from necessity. The virtuous sage's freedom springs from his "intuitive" grasp of his connection with reality. The sage mirrors reality. He lives "in harmony with the order of nature as a whole," Spinoza tells us.

Each Thing Has Existence-Value. The virtuous person's values are created by his relationship to reality. He values objects and other people not as means, but as things in reality with full and unconditional worth. This intuition is expressed in any number of different ways. Zen poets are fond of speaking of the "lowliest" objects as being part of Zen. "The Zen mind is the everyday mind," they tell us. One does not need to accomplish any great and mysterious task, nor achieve any goal, to experience reality. Intuitive understanding is not a state of mind but an activity. It is an activity of concrete and particular re-union. What is real, not what is good nor what is true, is the pressing concern of the virtuous person.

Freedom. The virtuous sage does not have conflicting desires. He desires what will happen, but not because it will happen. His freedom is the harmonious coincidence of his own desirings, beliefs, and attitudes with what must happen in reality. Because he knows the workings of reality, he does not diffuse his desires to what will not be. The sage maintains an extraordinary spontaneity and intensity in experiencing. His emotions and beliefs are determined and supported by his project. Because he does not make decisions on the most fundamental level of values, he does not suffer from the anxieties of indecision and of responsibility. And because he does not experience himself as essentially divorced from reality, he does not experience the separation and loneliness at the root of the moralist's drive for a meaningful life. The virtuous sage is intimately and intensely united with "the whole of nature" by his way of conceiving of and relating to nature.

Bridging the Abyss Between the Self and Others. The virtuous sage recognizes that she is intimately connected with the reality she experiences and in the way she experiences it. Existence itself is a value. The virtuous sage conceives of and experiences reality with intensity and intimacy, and with full subjectivity. Yet the radical subjectivity of the virtuous sage does not separate the self and the other. Her subjectivity and intensity in experiencing are grounded in her own "pleasure" *and* in the intrinsic value of the other.

The self is recreated continually in just the form that it relates to the other. She does not separate the I and the Thou. The virtuous sage is at once selfish and selfless. The self dissolves (without loss of self) because the self-other distinction is blurred and finally "lost" altogether. Love for the sage is the extension of the boundaries of the self to include the other person or thing as fully real.

Therefore, the virtuous sage experiences the reality of herself in experiencing the reality of the other. With the self-other dichotomy dissolved, the tear between self and other is finally mended. The sage maintains a self-other differentiation; consciousness requires that. Yet the self-other opposition and confrontation are eliminated. The other is not there for the self. The notion of domination is a purely moral one, not a virtuous one. For the virtuous sage, the self and other become intimately intertwined through openness. The virtuous sage relates so that "subject" and "object" become more real together.

FREEDOM AND VIRTUE

To finish our closing summary of the best life, let me say something about freedom. We can describe the freedom of the pleasure seeker as a freedom of doing what one wants to do—or, more accurately, of doing what one "most" wants to do. Moral freedom is a freedom of doing what is most "important" to one to do, what one ought to do.

The freedom of the virtuous sage is a freedom of necessity. What's that? To be free is to be self-creating and recreating at each moment. The freedom of the virtuous sage does not consist of doing what he wants to do, nor of doing what he wants to want to do, nor of doing what he is supposed to want to do. The freedom of the virtuous sage is an harmonious coincidence of beliefs and desires with the necessity of reality. The freedom of the virtuous sage involves what Spinoza describes as the knowledge that "nothing in the universe is contingent, but all things are conditioned to exist and operate in a particular manner by the necessity of [divine] nature." The virtuous sage understands that being free is acting according to the laws of nature. Following Epictetus, the sage "demands not that events happen as [he] wishes; but [he] wishes them to happen as they do happen."

The virtuous sage's beliefs and desires coincide with the necessary laws of reality in an important way. The coincidence of beliefs and desires with the necessary laws of nature is neither causal nor contrived. If the coincidence were caused by reality, this would be resignation or submission. Yet the sage believes and desires, but not *because* of the necessity of reality. He believes and he desires, and these beliefs and desires "coincidently" reflect the necessity of reality. How does he manage that? By knowing reality, he intuitively joins reality.

Ultimately, a "new" way of experiencing emerges. The whole of the virtuous sage's consciousness is submerged into his experiencing. His grasp of the necessity of reality narrows the range of emotions necessary for relating to reality. Because the sage has limited the repertoire of desires, emotions, and beliefs, the intensity of each emotion is increased; the sage's limited emotional energy becomes concentrated.

The virtuous sage's grasp of the self, of others, and of reality creates a reemphasis on many of our underdeveloped talents. The virtuous sage identifies and masters himself. To be his own author, to be self-created and recreated, the virtuous sage must be aware of his own nature.

THE VIRTUES

Being "self-knowing" is essential for being free, but it is not enough. The sage must answer the questions placed before each vision of living. The sage must also connect with others and with reality. He must be an active listener and questioner of himself and of others. He must cultivate the underdeveloped abilities of listening beyond the words that are spoken. That's why, according to Buber, for the virtuous sage there are no lies, only hidden and unrevealed truths. The virtuous sage skillfully understands others.

He is intuitively aware of the whole of nature. For the virtuous sage, being free and being virtuous are one and the same. Spinoza says, "blessedness [freedom] is not the reward of virtue, but virtue itself." In the clarity and lucidity of an open mind, the virtuous sage possesses "true acquiescence of spirit." The "way" to being free is by being open, courageous, self-knowing, actively noninterfering (*wu wei*), "quietly" creating, actively listening, intuitively and affectively questioning.

The virtuous sage's way of living is not beyond our grasp; it is available to each of us. It involves an improved asking of the question of the best life. According to Spinoza and Lao Tsu, the virtuous sage lives the best life by "simply" being in the world.

■

SUMMARY OF DISCUSSION

This discussion is the culmination of our entire search. Like you, the virtuous sage has examined the life of living for the moment, and the moral life. The virtuous sage realizes that the goals of these two approaches to living are misdirected. Each way of stating these goals, however, reveals the genuine question underlying them. When we want to avoid boredom, and the anxieties of indecision and responsibility, we are really asking to find a way to relate intimately to reality. Put another way, the searches for intense pleasure and for moral security and control are merely attempts to experience oneself as real. The virtuous sage builds on this better understanding of the basic question, "What is the best life?"

The best life must be more than a set of goals or values. It must involve an entire undistorted understanding of reality. The sage discovers herself in relating to reality. The virtuous sage knows that defining things according to categories distances her from the things in reality. Therefore, she uses distinctions only when necessary, always recognizing the distorting feature of this way of thinking. Ultimately, the sage recognizes that each thing in reality, not only each person, has an existence-value. It is valuable simply because it exists.

Virtuous freedom finally resolves inner conflicts and outer domination. The sage desires what happens, but not because it happens. Virtuous freedom is the harmonious coincidence of desires, beliefs, and attitudes with what must happen in reality. We found that with Epictetus freedom is not choice, but knowledge. The virtuous sage improves on this by replacing knowledge with understanding. The sage understands and agrees with the way reality unfolds. The virtuous sage experiences the reality of himself or herself in experiencing the reality of the other.

The result of this virtuous, free way of relating is that the abyss between the self and the other person or thing is bridged. The self-other opposition and confrontation is dissolved. "Subject" and "object" become more real together.

The virtuous "way" is to be open, courageous, self-knowing, actively non-interfering, quietly creating, actively listening, intuitively and affectively questioning.

■

DISCUSSION HIGHLIGHTS

  I. The basic questions in living are living to avoid
    1. boredom.
    2. decisions.
    3. responsibility.
  II. Morality fails to work because it misunderstands the basic question of living.
 III. The real question is: How do I know and relate to
    1. the self.
    2. others.
    3. reality.
 IV. The virtuous sage's way of living
    1. demonstrates the necessity of the virtues.
    2. pictures reality in varying degree of accuracy.
    3. produces intimate relating.
    4. integrates the virtues and freedom.

■

QUESTIONS FOR
THOUGHT/PAPER TOPICS

1. What are the basic questions in living? Do these translate into the question, "What is the best life?"

2. What is the argument that morality doesn't work? Do you agree?

3. The virtuous life presented by Lao Tsu and Spinoza directly confronts the problem of intimately relating to the self, others, and reality? Is this the "real question"?

4. Describe how the virtues are derived. Think back over the strengths of the other theories we have examined. Does the virtuous life incorporate these strengths?

5. How does the sage's "picture" of reality fit in with a theory of correct living? Does Buber's analysis of the I-Thou attitude apply?

6. What is the connection between the virtues and freedom? Do Spinoza and Lao Tsu offer an acceptable notion of freedom?

7. This question is easy! What is the best life?

■

FOR FURTHER READING

Since our two subjects are Spinoza and Lao Tsu, it is only courtesy to read their chief works. Spinoza's *Ethics* is part of a volume entitled *On the Improvement of the Understanding: The Ethics* (Dover, 1955). Lao Tsu's *Tao Te Ching* (Random House, 1972) has been translated by a number of capable people. Because ancient Chinese is vague, it's instructive to get several translations to see what you can make of his ideas. A helpful little book that merits your attention is Stuart Hampshire's *Spinoza* (Penguin, 1951). Hampshire does a good job clarifying and organizing Spinoza's thoughts into digestible bites. For a secondary source on taoism, Lao Tsu's philosophical school, I suggest two books. Raymond Smullyan's *The Tao Is Silent* (Harper & Row, 1977) is a truly wonderful introduction to taoism. A more sophisticated work is Chang Chung-yuan's *Creativity and Taoism* (Harper & Row, 1963).

Index

A, 125–37, 141, 174. *See also* Kierkegaard, S.;
  Either/Or
alienated, 126
concentration, abilities in, 128
conflicting desires, 134
cynicism, 131
depression, 130–31
empathy in life, 130
emotional intimacy, 128
freedom, 129
friendship, lacking in, 128
hypersensitivity, 132
indecision, 134
isolation, 130–31
life, incoherence of, 128
loneliness, 130–31
love, lacking in, 128
meaninglessness in life, 130
melancholy, 130–31
moral continuities, 126
  communication, 127
  community, 127
  creativity, 127
moral impulses, 132–34
  constancy, 133
  faith, 133
  control, 133
  regrets, 134
  choice, 134
pessimism, 132
pleasure, 126
powerlessness, sense of, 131
responsibility, sense of, 134
sadness, 130–31
self-centered, 126
selfless, 129
trust, lacking in, 128
unrealistic, 125
values of, 128
Abandonment, 244–45
Abraham, 50
Absolutes/absolutism, 36–37, 134, 207–32
  example of, 209
    Ten Commandments, 209
  moral rules, in, 36
Absurd, 271–73
  battle, 272
  divorce from life, 272–74
  illusion, 273
  victory, 271–72
Absurdity, of morality, 52

Acceptance, 164–65
Action, 248–49
  reality, defining of, 248
Aesthete/aestheticism, 119–38
Agreement, 90–93
  basic beliefs, over, 93
  content, 90–92
  cultural, 93
  form, 90
Alienation
  A, 126
  divorce from life, 272–74
Anarchy, 6, 29–30
  chaos, 8, 29–30
Anguish, 238–39
  morality, foundation of, 239
Antheap, 150
Anxiety
  A, 134
  indecision, of, 145–46
  Stranger, the, 121–23
Atheism/atheists, 68–70
Authority, 143–45
  obedience to, 145
Autonomy, 227–29
  reasoned, 227

Baa, 52
Bad faith, 235
Belonging, 32
Boredom, 25, 134
  A, 134
Buber, Martin, 260, 277–91
Buddha, Buddhism, 67–69

Camus, Albert, 119–23, 174
Caring, about others, 21
Categorical imperative, 218–19, 221–22
Causes, 200–01
  contributing, 200–01
    Fritz and Hitler, 200–01
Chaos, 7, 10, 29–30, 116–17
Choice
  advisor, 247
  careers, 157–58
  criterion, 236
  feelings, 246–47
  good, 242–43
  involvement, 242–44
  of others, 242
  of self, 242

Choice (*cont.*)
  making, 180–81
  responsibility, 237
  spontaneous, 236
  standards of, 236
Cogito, 249–50
  Descartes, 249–50
Commandments, 188. *See also* Ten
    Commandments.
Commerce, 20, 30
Common sense, 42
Compulsions, 172–75
Computers
  dependent, 1–4
  uncaring, 105
  unfeeling, 104
  unthinking, 103
Consequences
  concern over, 24, 29–30
  definition of, 189
  intentions, 201
  results, 201
Conscience
  example of moral point of view, 10, 34, 37,
    146–48
  reflection of social values, 53
  intuition of good/bad, 51
Contentment, 24
Control, 29–30
  in morality, 10
  baa, 23
Cup, favorite, 169–70
  death of loved one, 169–70

Da Vinci, L. 194–95
Death. *See also* Freud; Solomon; Sisyphus.
  favorite cup, 168–69
  soap opera disease, 14
Decisions, 147
Descartes, Rene, 249–50
Desires
  conflicting, 134, 177
Despair, 233, 247–48
Detachment, 172
Devil (Satan), 145–49
Deontological ethics. *See* Kant.
Disagreement, over
  beliefs,
    basic, 93
    cultural, 93
    content, 90–92
    form, 90–92
  moral values, 187
  values, 52
Distractions, 151
Dostoevski, F., 88, 143–62, 259, 291
  Grand Inquisitor, 143–62
Duty, 8–9, 210–14
  conformity with, 214
  motive of, 214
  sense of, 210

Egoism, 37–38, 54–55
  free-rider, 55
  individual ethical, 55
  universal, 55
Either/Or, 116. *See also* Kierkegaard, S.
End, in itself, 227
Epictetus, 142, 163–83, 235, 259, 291
  Enchiridion, 163–83
Equals, 22, 29–30
Eternal recurrence, 16–17
Exceptions, to
  killing, 95–96
  rules, 95
Exclusiveness, 280
Existentialism, 233–56. *See also* Camus;
    Dostoevski; Kierkegaard; Sartre
  human nature, 234 ff.
  existence precedes essence, 234 ff.
Experiences, 150, 279
  beliefs, 65
  near-death, 65–66
  ecstatic, 76–77
  intense, 150
  momentary, 25–26
  mystical, 76–77
  passions, 150
  pleasures, 150

Facts
  moral, accounting for, 187
Feelings, 10
Flock, 150, 152–53
Forlornness, 233, 244–45
Four-letter words, 8
Freedom, 143–62, 300–02
  A, 129
  basis of values, as, 252
  caprice, 251–52
  condemned, 246
  compulsions, 172–74
  control, 174–75
  do what one wants, 240
  Existentialism, 240–56
  externals, from, 176
  free, 146–47
  harmony, 178
  inner life, 178
  passions, 173
  possibility of, 153
  premise of existence, 234
  self-control, 163–64
    independent, 164
    inner, 164
  Stoic, 172–83
    definition of, 175–76
  wants, 172–74
    whatever I want, 10–11
Freud, Sigmund, 74–86, 88

Getting caught, 7
Goals, 4, 15
  striving, 165

Goblins
  dryers and socks, 77 ff.
  invisible, green, 77 ff.
God, 2, 11, 49–50
  answers unanswerable questions, 70
  beginning of universe, 64
  belief in, 61
    long tradition of, 62
  existence of, 60, 82, 89
  father-figure, 80–81
  image of, 32
  meaning in death, 71
  meaning in life, 71
  murder request, 50
  plan for universe, 23, 73
  prayers answered, 71–72
  psychological truth, 64–69
  suffering, 71
  universe ordered by, 64
    entropy, 64
Golden Rule, 7, 33, 37, 43–51, 199, 220
  application, 47–48
  authority from, 48
  do not harm, 47
  inverted form, 45
  really means, 48
  respect for others, 48
Greatest Happiness principle, 190. *See also*
  Mill, J. S.
Grand Inquisitor, 146–62, 174
Groundwork of the Metaphysics of Morals,
  207–32.
Guilt feelings, 13

Happiness, 4
  contentment, 193–94
  defined as pleasure, 191 ff.
Harm, 7, 10, 20–21, 29, 30. *See also* Golden
  Rule.
Haskell, Eddie, 43, 214
Hinduism, 67–69
Human
  being human, 4
  condition, 250–51
  limits, 250–51
  dignity, 7
Human nature, 2–4, 102–14, 143–62
  compassion, 112
  cynicism, 110
  creativity, 111
  existence, 234 ff.
  family resemblance, 106
  feelings, 103
  genetics, 107
  greedy, 108
  inventive, 111
  private property, 109
  relating, 112
  religious, 111
  speech capacity, 105
  thinking ability, 103

Ice cream cones, 47–48
Idleness, 4–5
I-It, 277–90
  primary words', evolution of, 280–81
  two-fold attitude, 278
Illusions, 79. *See also* Freud.
  Art's irresistibility, 79
  father-figure God, 79
  religious beliefs, 82
  wishes, 80
  wish fulfillment, 79–80
Immorality, 11–12
Immortality, 14–15
Immunity, 13–14, 20, 30
  Ring of Gyges, 13–14
  Hobbit's ring, 13–14
Imperatives
  categorical, 218–19, 221–22
  hypothetical, 221–22
In-between, 278–79
Integrity, 202
Intensity, 151
Involvement, 243–44, 249
I-Thou, 277–90
  becomes It, 286
  bodied over against, 285–86
  direct relation to, 285
  entrance into, 287–89
  filled present, 286
  primary words', evolution of, 281–81
  sacrifice and risk, 284–85
  two-fold attitude, 278

Jesus, 67, 143–63, 199
Joe the Mesopotamian, 118–19, 275
Joe Healthy, 202–03
Judgments
  of others, 252
Jupiter, 3
Justice, 202

Kant, Immanuel, 142, 185, 207–32, 246,
  293–94
Kierkegaard, Soren, 125–38, 259, 291–93. *See
  also* A, Either/Or.
Killing, 7, 53–54
Kirk, Captain, 28
Knowledge, of future, 199
Kubler-Ross, Elizabeth, 171

Lao Tsu, 180, 260, 291–94
Law
  abiding, 12
  example of moral point of view, 35–37
  universal, 218–22
Lifeboat, 184–85
Loneliness, 130–31, 233, 249–50
Love, 9
  beyond feelings, 283–84
  impartial, as not, 217

Love (*cont.*)
  moral motivation, as, 216–18
  objective, as not, 217–18
Lying, 198–99

Maslow, Abraham
  self-actualization, 194
Mazims, 218. *See also* Categorical imperative.
Meaning, 7, 23, 29–30
  meaninglessness of life, 117–19, 130, 294–95
Mill, John Stuart. *See also* Utilitarianism.
  140–41, 184–206, 209, 246, 259, 291, 293–94
Monotony, 194–95
Moral continuities, 126–27
Morality
  authority for, 8
  conditions of, 37–38, 41–42
  control, 10, 29–30
  definition of, 24–25, 29–30
  examples of, 33–37
    conscience, 34–37
  formal features of, 56–58
    comprehensive, 56–58
    easily applicable, 56–58
    generality, 56–58
    impartiality, 56–58
    publicity, 56–58
    ordered, 56–58
    overriding, 56–58
    universal applicability, 56–58
  foundation of, 188
  motivation for, 216
  overriding, 39
  people, existence of, 26–27
  point of, 6, 29–30, 32 ff.
  principles, 37–38
  priority rules, 41–42
  repression, 15–16, 30
  standards of, 6, 33
  truth, 73
  worth, 215
Moses, 67

Needs
  hierarchy of, 194
  spiritual, 36–37
  tradition, 37
Nihilist, 93–94
Nobility, 146
Nonmorality, 12

Obedience, 10, 154. *See also* Grand Inquisitor
Objectivity, 22, 29–30, 222, 258
Obstacles, self-created, 235
Oedipus, 271–72
Old people, 21–22
Order, 65

Pens, 7
  stealing, fine points, 7
Pleasure, 5, 28–30, 116–38. *See also* Mill, J. S.;
  Epictetus.
  degrading, 191
  higher/lower, 192, 195–96
  life of, 116 ff., 262–63
  momentary, 124
  pursuit of, 197
  qualitative differences, 192
  seeking, 12
  superior/inferior, 192–93
  way of living, 16, 29–30
Pleasure button, 17–19
Power, 165–69
  beyond and within, 165–67
  body, over, 166
  death, over, 168
  grief, 169–71
  reputation, over, 166–67
  wealth, over, 67–68
Practical reasoning, 38
Primary goods, 225–26. *See also* Rawls, J.
Primary words' evolution, 280–84
  establishing relation, 281–82
  loving/hating, 282–84
  natural combination, 281
  natural separation, 281
  relating, 282
Principles, 218–19
  categorical imperative, 218
  objective and subjective, 219
Priorities, 134, 188
Promises, 8

Questions, 291–95
  in existence/living, 291–95
    boredom, 292
    decisions, 292–93
    real questions, 295
    responsibility293

Rawls, John, 224–26
  primary goods, 225–26
  veil of ignorance, 224–25
Reason, 207–32
  function of, 212–13
  objectivity, 222
  religious assertions, 82–84
Relating
  in-between, 278–79
  intimately, 298
  paradoxically, 298–99
  reality, to, 295
Relativism, 2, 28–30, 88–102, 243
  scientific truths, 100
  subjectivism, 243
Religion, Inc., 149–50, 152 ff.
Religious
  anxiety, 43
  beliefs, 64–68
    harm of, 76
    psychological analysis of, 76
    need for, 74
    value of, 75

Responsibility, 8–10, 29–30, 134, 237
  anguish of, 238–39
  choice, 237
  depth of, 239–40
  values, for, 94
Resurrection machine, 140
Rule utilitarianism, 203 ff.

Sage. *See* Virtuous sage.
Santa Claus, 61
Sartre, Jean-Paul, 142, 233–56, 259, 291,
    293–94
Security
  acceptance, and, 7, 19–20, 29–30
Self
  abyss between, 300 ff.
  —actualization of, 194
  —affirmation, 135
  conceiving of, 228
  —control, 146
  —identification, 177
  others, and, 294, 300 ff.
Separation, from reality, 286–87
Sexism, 6–7
Sincerity, 10
Sisyphus, 259, 261, 268–76. *See also* Camus,
    Albert.
  consciousness, 270
  crimes of, 268–69
  futility in living, 268
  immortality, 268
  joy of, 270–72
  punishment of, 269–70
  sorrow of, 270–91
Solomon, 259, 261–68
  death, 266
  despair, 266
  envy, 265
  happiest person, 264–65
  justice, 264
  lament, 262 ff.
  meaningless life, 267–68
  merriment, 265–66
  oppression, 264
  pleasure, 262–63
  values, 266–67
  vanity, 262
  wealth, 265
  work, 263
Social contract, 36–37
Social roles, 35–37
Socrates, 88, 163, 186, 221
Spinoza, Benedict (Baruch), 163, 180, 260,
    291–304
Spock, Mr., 28, 215–16, 221, 231
Stranger, the, 119–25, 129–30, 136–37, 141,
    174, 180, 259, 291–93. *See also* Camus,
    Albert.
  amorality, 120
  anxiety of indecision, 121
  anxiety of responsibility, 123
  boredom, 121

  chaotic, 129–30
  cigarettes, 129
  concentration, 120
  decisions, 122
  goal-free, 120–21
  murder, 129
  prisoner, 129
  spontaneity, 120
Subjectivism, 243
Swift, "A Modest Proposal," 92

Talents
  duty to cultivate, 222–23
Taoism/taoist. *See* Lao Tsu.
Teleological/teleology
  utilitarianism. *See* Mill.
  virtue ethic/perfectionism. *See* Spinoza.
Temptations, 14, 124, 196–97
  Jesus, of, 148–49
    conscience, 148
    miracles, mystery and authority, 148–49
  unity, 149
Ten Commandments, 33, 37, 188
  absolutes, example of, 36, 40 ff.
  do not kill, 41
  favorite, 41
Theory of action/theory of character, 43
Theoretical reasoning, 38
Time
  subjective and objective, 26–27
Tolerance
  acceptance, and, 92–93
Tree ants, 118–19
Truth
  agreement, as 96
  —telling, 185 ff.
  types of, 96–101
    mathematical, 97–99
    moral, 100
    scientific, 99–101

Uncle Charlie, 67, 198–99, 207 ff.
  deathbed wish, 199
  manuscript, 207 ff.
Unfreedoms, 178–80
  resolution of, 180
Unity, 156 ff.
Utilitarianism, 35–37, 184–206. *See also* Mill,
    J. S.

V-8 principle, 140–41
Veil of ignorance, 224–25, 231. *See also*
    Rawls, J.
Vessels of experience, 203
Virtue(s), 176, 297–302
  freedom, and, 299–300
Virtuous sage, 295 ff.
  excellence, 295–96
  picture of reality, 297–98
  virtues of, 297
Vulcans, 210

Wally, 61
   beliefs in flat/spherical earth, 61
Wants, 158 ff., 172–74, 188
   ends, 188
Weak, the, 149. *See also* Temptations.
Will

free, 112
good, the, 210–14
   effects of, 211
   superiority to passions, 213–14
unconditionality of, 211